The Hedgerows Heaped
With May

The Hedgerows Heaped With May

The Telegraph

Book of

THE COUNTRYSIDE

Edited by

Stephen Moss

First published 2012 by
Aurum Press Limited
7 Greenland Street
London NW1 0ND
www.aurumpress.co.uk

ISBN 978 1 84513 843 1

10 9 8 7 6 5 4 3 2 1
2016 2015 2014 2013 2012

Typeset in Fournier MT and Priori by
SX Composing DTP, Rayleigh, Essex SS6 7XF

Printed by MPG Books, Bodmin, Cornwall

Contents

The Wonders of Nature

Disappearing Worlds

Town and Country

Conflict

Hunting, Shooting and Fishing

Down on the Farm

Acknowledgements

I would like to thank Caroline Buckland, Kylie O'Brien and Gavin Fuller at the *Telegraph* for all their help with this project – Gavin in particular for all his assistance finding all these pieces in the paper's archive; and Graham Coster, Melissa Smith, Lucy Warburton and Anandi Vara at Aurum.

S.M.

The quotation by Max Hastings on p. xi is from *Editor* (Macmillan, 2002).

Introduction

'God made the country, and man made the town'
William Cowper, 1785

'One area in which we are achieving real success,' wrote Max Hastings in 1987, not long after assuming the editorship of *The Daily Telegraph*, 'is coverage of the countryside.' This, he went on, was a welcome corrective to most British newspapers, 'overwhelmingly written by and for an urban and suburban constituency. Yet even many of those who don't live in the country wish they did, and we do well to show we can identify with them.'

For *Telegraph* readers, who might reasonably be described as tending towards the traditional and conservative, the word 'country' has a very special resonance. It means not only 'the non-urban landscape' but also, quite simply, 'the nation'. And, to them, the one stands emblematically and literally for the other. The Americans may have the wilderness, the Australians the bush, and the French *la campagne* or *le paysage*; but none of these has quite the mystical, the mythical, the political resonance even, of the simple English word 'countryside'.

Until quite recently, in the pages of the *Telegraph*, 'the countryside' essentially meant one man: J.H.B. Peel. From the early 1960s until his death in 1983, John Hugh Brignal Peel contributed a fortnightly essay, 'Country Talk', from his home on Exmoor.

Born in 1913, Peel was the archetypal countryman. Born into an old North Devon family, he spent his whole life – apart from education and War service – in the area along the border of Devon and Somerset made famous by R.D. Blackmore's novel *Lorna Doone*.

Indeed, the poet John Masefield wrote of his friend that Peel 'knows more than any other living man about the life of the English countryside'. This is an interesting claim because it suggests that there was a settled and finite amount of knowledge about the English countryside, and that one man was capable of possessing it, even if it is a notion we would consider absurd today.

Peel, though, wrote about a countryside that was timeless and unchanging. His job was both to celebrate it and to explain it to his readers; he did so delightfully, for example, in a whimsical yet erudite survey of the ancient origin of field names.

How very different Peel's approach is to today's *Telegraph*, and how different his background to the list of more recent contributors in this volume. These include the presenter of a hugely popular TV motoring programme, an Australian TV critic, the man who founded the Glastonbury rock festival, and even the mayor of London. And just look at some of the subjects covered here, each of them reflecting an aspect of today's countryside: from property prices to bus shelters; from camel breeding to swingers' parties.

What this remarkable diversity of contributors and subjects reveals is that nowadays not only does the countryside mean something different to everyone – indeed, every square foot of it is fought over by competing interests – but also that, as with every other facet of British society, constant change has become its defining characteristic. Indeed, already since Malcolm Smith wrote his piece about rare birds in Britain in 1999, the little egret has become a common sight and the spoonbill has bred several times, while the otters whose survival prospects seemed so pessimistic to Brian Jackman in 1993 are now present on most rivers in Britain, with road traffic the newest risk to their numbers.

So the landlord of a country pub can be a refugee from the City of London, downsizing to avoid stress. Conversely, as *Top Gear* presenter James May suggests, he may have brought the stress with him because, in May's words, 'the countryside belongs to the car'. The subject of rural crime rears its ugly head within these pages, but the perpetrators are now more likely to be from the local community rather than the big city.

Opinions differ radically, too: Joanna Trollope passionately defends the Countryside Marchers; Ross Clark mounts an equally heartfelt diatribe against them. And among several pieces on the joys of moving from town to country is a contrary view, by Sinclair McKay, about how he found the countryside a rather disagreeable and forbidding place.

As with James May's contribution, a consistent pleasure of the pieces collected in this book is reading about traditional, apparently timeless rural institutions examined from very modern, worldly perspectives.

So, as you might expect, we examine *The Archers*, but via the stethoscope of the *Telegraph*'s medical editor Rebecca Smith. She ponders the longevity of the soap opera's characters, noting that they are rather more likely to die in a nasty accident than the average Briton. Then there is the country vicar. However, instead of the clichéd figure of the elderly male cleric from a Thomas Hardy novel, the Church of England is represented here by the formidable (and unquestionably female) figure of the Vicar of Dibley.

Just as intriguing is reading about how some of our most distinguished naturalists unearthed wildlife in the least rural of surroundings. Who could have imagined that Canvey Island – home of oil refineries and the pub-rock band Dr Feelgood – could also be, as Peter Marren reveals, a bug-hunter's paradise?

In recent years Britain has seen a resurgence of what is usually called 'nature-writing', a tradition that stretches back through Kenneth Allsop, Gavin Maxwell and Richard Jefferies all the way to Gilbert White. Peter Marren is joined here by Richard Mabey, with a learned dissertation on birds and their folklore, and John Lister-Kaye, observing how Scotland's wildlife copes with harsh winters.

Above all, as you would expect from the *Telegraph*, this book contains a great deal of robust common sense and strongly held opinions. Bernard Ingham fulminates against the 'giant lavatory brushes' marching across our hills in the guise of wind turbines. W.F. Deedes brings his magnanimity and experience to the question of multiculturalism in a countryside context. And Geoffrey Wheatcroft makes an elegant defence of Nimbyism.

We may not always agree with the forthright views of one of J.H.B. Peel's successors, Robin Page, but no one can doubt his depth of knowledge and passion for his beloved countryside. His account of a major incident alert mounted by a primary school when one of its pupils picked 'a deadly fungus' – which later turned out to be an edible mushroom – is all too credible.

Certain things about the countryside will always appeal to *Telegraph* readers, and I hope they will be reassured to learn that there are pieces about birdsong and butterflies, green country buses and village shops, grouse shooting and fly-fishing, willow trees and the WI, as well as poignant elegies to the cuckoo, the skylark and the English elm.

Every reader will have his or her favourites. I particularly enjoyed Mia Davis's witty, self-deprecating and ultimately futile search for love as a single woman in rural England, and David Walton's delightful ramble through the Somerset countryside, fuelled by copious draughts of cider.

But top of my list is Byron Rogers, a long-time resident of a small Northamptonshire village, but who brought the worldliness of a Fleet Street journalist and previous domicile in the capital to his new surroundings. Why should writing about the countryside always be reverent or earnest? Byron's pieces can be hilarious, surreal and poignant all at once. He manages simultaneously to be both an insider, guiding the reader through the intricate details of a story, and an outsider, observing rural eccentricities with a forensic objectivity.

Rogers's style and approach reflect the changes we have witnessed during the past few decades, from a homogenous, standardised 'countryside' to the multi-layered complexity that is rural Britain today. While every spring the hedgerows will always be 'heaped with may', in the words of A.E. Housman's poem, in years to come as the British countryside changes in ways we cannot even begin to imagine, Byron Rogers's successors at the *Telegraph* will continue to cover the subject with the same wit, intelligence and insight to be found in the pages of this volume.

Stephen Moss
Mark, Somerset
August 2012

Country Life

A River Running with Cider
David Walton

There is something about rivers. Last winter, as we sweated up a Niger sandbank, my friend Roger (a geography man) waxed lyrical about the strong brown god before us. 'Y'know this goes to the Sahara, then 2,000 miles on to the sea – three months from source to mouth. Wouldn't you just love to follow it?'

A flock of screaming parrots landed at the water's edge. 'Know of anything shorter?' I mopped my brow. Roger (also a West Country-man) nodded. 'There's one back home we could walk in four days.'

So it was, some months later, we stood with our backs to Chedington village, listening to the music in the hill. Somerset lay below, pretty as a watercolour, and all around tiny springs chuckled underground. I heard the River Parrett before ever I saw it.

We'd decided to follow the Parrett Trail, which links arms with the river for 50 miles, from top to toe. Picturesque villages, ancient drove roads, sacred burrows and cider orchards lay before us.

We stumbled down the tussocky grass of the escarpment, two bootleg Laurie Lees, chewing grass stalks and arguing over a battered sun hat and tatty umbrella – our twin insurances against English weather. It was liberating to have all we needed in backpacks (change of clothes, shoes, blister repair kit) and no bigger decision to make than the midday cider stop (bed and breakfasts had been booked along the way). Among frisky lambs and droning insects, we got our first glimpse of the Parrett – a trickle between tufts of grass.

Our first village, South Perrott, was carved from warm local hamstone and had cats sleeping on doorsteps and wisteria climbing porches on to thatch. Wallflowers, honeysuckle and stocks perfumed the air. We stopped for a cider at the Coach and Horses.

The afternoon, in a pattern to be repeated, saw us negotiate plough-land, hay meadows, barley fields and much else besides, as the trail crossed and recrossed the Parrett. Kingcup, water violet, bladderwort and flags had almost turned several stretches into ponds. A kingfisher dazzled between some bulrushes and a fox stared at us before turning contemptuously into the long grass.

Shortly after, we found ourselves in a scene from a child's story book. A stile, fashioned from a massive tree fork, led to an idyllic water meadow. The stream babbled gently under willows. Marsh bedstraw, pepper saxifrage and ragged robin covered the lower part, while meadowsweet, sorrel and buttercups carpeted higher ground. Goldfinches plucked thistledown and a family of long-tailed tits tumbled among the cow parsley.

If Red Riding Hood or Bo Peep had appeared, we wouldn't have blinked. As it was, two young girls, carrying what looked like curved shrimp nets, skipped across our meadow and disappeared downstream, chattering like magpies.

A mile farther and we crossed the A30 between careering caravans and screaming lorries. As the mayhem died away, we continued past Tail Mill where the linen sails for Nelson's ship, the *Victory*, were made. Flax, once a staple of the area, now survives in occasional patches of blue, and a cheerful group of the mill's workforce (now making machine parts) waved their tea mugs in greeting as we walked past.

That night, in a cosy South Petherton pub, we mentioned the shrimp nets to a pair of whiskery old characters. 'They bin elverin,' said one.

'Elverin', we learnt, was a local passion. Every spring, the waterways teem with 3-inch-long baby eels (elvers), which journey thousands of miles from the Sargasso Sea. In due course they will return, enjoy a spasm of ecstasy, then die exhausted, leaving their eggs to hatch amid the Atlantic seaweed.

When the first elvers are spotted, often wriggling across grass like worms, people grab nets or plastic containers. 'They fetch a couple of bob each. You can turn pounds – 1,000 a night if you've a mind.'

Next morning a cuckoo chimed us into the hamlet of East Lambrook. The Parrett was wider now, with huge umbrella weeds clouding below the surface. Herons staked stretches of river, like anglers, and buzzards lazily circled the upper air. The tang of young cider apples, rejoicing in such names as Brown Snout, Chisel Jersey and Porter's Perfection, filled our nostrils.

The land flattened and Kingsbury Episcopi church tower beckoned above the trees. Kingsbury Episcopi boasted a fine octagonal lock-up and startling willow figures in front gardens – a reminder that we were in the Somerset Levels, where, for centuries, 'withies' (willow wands) have been grown for local basket-makers. The landscape was slashed by drainage channels and lines of mature willows. A pumping station ('Sixties' office block-style) in the middle of nowhere heralded a wealth of birdlife as swans, geese, duck and other waterfowl fished the aerated streams.

It was also a sign to turn for Muchelney (Anglo-Saxon for 'large island'), which is still isolated in floods. The wisteria-clad pottery, suggestive of a pleasantly run-down garage in a Will Hay movie, was bustling inside. We'd hit a 'firing day' (one happens every month or so), when glazed pots are fired in a traditional Oriental kiln.

Muchelney Ham Farm, a stroll away, was calm contrast – golden stone smothered with honeysuckle outside, thick Afghan carpets and plump pillows inside. 'Lord, I remember flood waters coming up to the doors in 1990,' Ann Woodbridge reminisced at breakfast next morning. 'It was beautiful, though, just trees and fences above water and swans gliding in the garden.'

Her husband, Jim, joined us. 'My grandfather made coffins in this house,' he said, 'and he had to live upstairs for days at a time before they got the pumping stations.'

We rejoined a wider, muddier Parrett below Langport, scene of Royalist defeat in the Civil War. Thick embankments presided over the flood plain. At Oath Lock the river became tidal and red-brick chimneys of 'withy' boilers (for stripping willow) stood on the bank. At Burrow Mump, where we stopped for a pint at the King Alfred Inn, the green mound and ruined church looked like a mini-Glastonbury.

The Parrett eddied thickly now, like melted chocolate, and carried the smell of the sea. Narrow, vegetation-choked lanes led us away towards the Bridgwater canal at Fordgate. Passing under the M5, we reached Bridgwater via sunken towpaths.

Woodlands, our third stop, was secluded Strawberry Hill-gothic at the edge of town. Diane Palmer runs a stylish establishment and has a fascinating video of a previous owner, Donald Crowhurst, the 'round-the-world-yachtsman' who didn't make it. After a generous evening meal, we watched Crowhurst, on film, strolling eerily round the very gardens we overlooked.

Equally unexpected was a late-evening knock on our bedroom door. 'The badgers are here,' whispered Diane. 'Come down to the dining-room.' Two minutes later we watched through French windows as half a dozen cuddly brocks played on the terrace, illuminated by garden lights. They demolished kitchen leftovers and the young ones obligingly wrestled. 'I've waited 30 years for this,' said a fellow guest.

We caught sight of the Parrett next morning, just beyond the remains of Bridgwater docks. They, like the town, had seen better days. Fresh winds from the Bristol Channel greeted us as we cut across clay flats, while the Parrett meandered away in a huge curve.

By the time we rejoined the river, the air was full of screaming gulls. The Parrett looked a major waterway now. Exposed mud banks had cracked and fissured into crocodile shapes. The Old Ship Inn at Combwich did us proud with tangy cider. Patrick, the barman, who was having his head and beard shaved for charity that night, pointed us along the headland for our final lap.

Farmhouses at Steart have their backs to the sea. A cutting onshore wind explained why, but we puzzled over pairs of lampshades dangling from poles. Later, at Steart bird hide, an imaginative folly near the edge of the point, we got an explanation from a man in a Barbour.

'Radiation dust checks . . . because of that,' he waved towards Hinkley Point power station in the distance. Through binoculars we saw seabirds wheeling above it. 'They say fish love the warm water and that brings the birds. So, perhaps it's an ill wind.'

The Parrett merged into the Bristol Channel amid endless mudflats. Hard to believe the elvers can detect its characteristic 'flavour' a thousand miles out in the Atlantic. Hard to believe we'd reached journey's end. Four days, rambling some of the West Country's least trodden paths, had taken us along one of its least known rivers, through a quintessentially English countryside warmed by friendliness, if not the sun.

11 October 2003

At Home on the Range

Tamasin Day-Lewis

'I'm quite bossy,' says Amy Willcock. 'Agas are designed to cook in, not on. The rule is to cook 80 per cent of your food inside and 20 per cent on top. Once you know that, you know everything.'

The Aga guru has a day to teach me, a vestal Aga virgin, how to cook. Willcock had watched the first of my *Tamasin's Weekends* series where I confessed to never having cooked on my new Aga until the cameras rolled. Horrified, she offered to demystify me.

Why do people love Agas more than their children, husbands and dogs when they can't even control the cooking temperature? Do Aga owners secretly rise at dawn to put in their Sunday roast, offering up prayers to the gods of fire and the hearth?

Amy has a full fry in the roasting oven before I can even ask, and is whisking batter for Yorkshire pudding. She is intent on proving that it can be made in advance.

'Cook it completely because of the heat loss and lack of space later,' she says. 'Melt the dripping on the floor of the roasting oven – the hottest place – then cook it on number four. The next hottest is number one, at the top, for grilling.'

I didn't know this great cast iron beast of burden could grill. But it can. The full fry, which has been merrily grilling for 15 minutes (as well as locking in moisture, Agas lock the food in tighter than Wormwood Scrubs so you can't smell anything cooking), is set down on the worktop. Amy extols the virtues of the sheet of Bake-O-Glide that has been laid on the bottom of the roasting tin (no need to decrust), with a rack above it from which the sausage and bacon fat can dribble into the juicy depths of the tomatoes and mushrooms.

A full fry with no greasy worktops, no hissing cook, no spitting fat, no malodorous smells and the kitchen still a smokeless zone? Heaven or what? But what about the eggs? A circle of the greased sheet is laid on the hotplate. Amy cracks an egg on to it and it fries in seconds. 'If you want it easy over, just put the lid down when you cook it,' she says. 'You can toast sandwiches like this too.'

In an instant she has unwrapped the loaf she gets sliced lengthways ('the slices fit perfectly into the tennis-racket toaster'), filled it with Cheddar and plonked it on the Bake-O-Glide. The hotplate lid is down and in seconds she's made a perfectly crisped and oozing toasted sandwich. But is she really going to reheat a Yorkshire pudding? Not only is Amy Willcock going to perform this unlikely trick, she is about to show me that the potatoes she part-roasted the evening before are as delicious crisped-up and finished today as those made on the day. She is clearly certifiable.

'Always under-time things with an Aga and move things around,' she says. 'Agas create intuitive cooks because you get to poke and prod with your fingers and listen to your food.' Amy illustrates this point later with her cider vinegar cake, removing it from the oven so that we can hear the moisture crackling, which means it is not quite ready.

I learn that pastry doesn't have to be baked blind, but can be put directly on to the roasting-oven floor – even from frozen – and that if it browns too quickly it can be covered with the 'cold plain shelf'. I risked it for *Woman's Hour* recently and it worked. You can bring chicken stock to the boil, put it in the simmer oven and abandon it for hours.

The ovens are self-ventilated so that they don't steam, and you don't need to clean them. I learn about hot spots, the best places for baking, bringing root veg to the boil then cooking them, drained, in the simmer oven. Risotto – and I say this as a stir-the-stuff risotto snob – can also be cooked behind closed doors. My son, Harry, and I ate Amy's risotto heated through two days later and he pronounced it the best he'd eaten in ages.

'No one buys an Aga to cook on. It's an emotional buy that transports you back to that time and that place where your mother cooked the roast,' says Amy. And the Yorkshire? Still risen and perfectly cooked. The potatoes? Good, but with my six-oven Aga I'll make them on the day. I suggest Aga updates its image and gives copies of Amy's books to all new Aga drivers. We're paying a lot to buy into the dream and we could do with her thoroughly modern handholding.

5 February 2006
Berkshire
Max Hastings

On a map, Berkshire is shaped like a rough-hewn hour-glass laid upon its side, at its narrowest between Reading and Riseley. We west Berks types would be happy to see the eastern bulge – Windsor and Twyford, Wokingham and Sandhurst – broken off and given to suburban Surrey and Buckinghamshire, their cultural brethren. Down our way, in Hungerford and Lambourn and Newbury and the Sheffords, we think of the east with a shudder, as a land of poncified pubs and Sky dishes, rock star mansions and industrial estates. Go west, young man or woman, if you want to see real rural England, with wild mushrooms in the fields, mayfly on the Kennet, the rolling chalk downs above Streatley, and the Aldworth Bell, one of the best pubs in southern England.

There now, I have given away my age. My vision of west Berkshire was formed when I was christened there 60 years ago, in the Norman church at Aldworth, famous for its knightly effigies. In those days, many villagers had never travelled to London, barely 45 miles away, and some not even the nine miles to Reading.

Today, in truth, west Berkshire possesses almost as many industrial parks as east, likewise commuters. This is a place where huge wealth – no longer earned from the land but from urban businesses – is laid out on gentrifying farmhouses, manicuring cottage gardens, creating home cinemas in Georgian rectories. Where once my mother pressed wild flowers in her own childhood, there are now BMW dealerships. Big, black wooden barns harbour children's games rooms rather than cattle.

Yet in many ways, what is most remarkable is not how much Berkshire has changed, but how much fine countryside survives, within 60 miles of London. So much land remains in the hands of big estate-owners, who preserve it for shooting and the pleasure of the eye. Given that the roar of the M4 cuts through the heart of the area, it is extraordinary that one can walk in relative tranquility through fields and woodlands where I still see the primroses and bluebells I picked in childhood, and as rich a variety of wildlife as anywhere in southern Britain. One can relish the burr of the Berkshire accent in the conversation of older men and women. The views from our house across the Kennet valley to the splendid mountain of Inkpen Beacon, 1,011 feet up, remain unsullied.

I fish on the Kennet, which I was taught to revere as well as to love. The prettiest stretches of this legendary chalk stream remain a summer delight. My father told me, fallaciously, that the river was the setting for Kenneth Grahame's The Wind in the Willows, which in fact had its genesis on a rather prosaic stretch of the Thames near Taplow. But in consequence, I still expect to see Ratty or Mole emerge from the Kennet rushes below Chilton Foliat, as I cast to a rising trout.

My mother bought a cottage at Aldworth, ten miles north-east of Newbury, in 1938. The district became the paradise of my childhood. In the late 1940s most people round us worked on the farms, or maybe in the racing stables of Compton and the Ilsleys. I came home from prep school via a tiny steam train that puffed through Hermitage and Hampstead Norreys, and rowed inexpertly on the Thames below those enchanting twin Victorian waterside havens, Goring and Streatley, four miles down the hill. Punts and heavy clinker-built rowing-boats were hired out with red velvet cushions.

Today, almost every village of my childhood has grown prodigiously, but Aldworth is largely unchanged, save that every cottage is pampered and painted in a fashion the inhabitants of 50 years ago lacked the cash to achieve. There is even an apparently normal vicar at the old church, after a long succession of eccentrics, one of whom liked to toll the bells at midnight. The countryside is duller, now that sanity is deemed a virtue.

Today we live some miles further west, near Hungerford, the perfect small country town. It possesses every amenity anyone could want, without having lost its intimacy. The steep high street, with a delightful bookshop and crowds of antiqueries, might have been created by Hollywood. The old town hall puts me in mind of Hardy's sturdy corn merchants and mayors, even though his Wessex starts some way south of us. My father persisted in calling the A4, which runs through the south end of the town, the Bath Road. That vision of 18th-century romance, too, has lingered in my imagination. A remarkable number of fine houses and inns landmark the old coaching route for miles in both directions, today alas blighted by traffic.

West Berkshire shares with Hampshire and Wiltshire a host of handsome brick-and-flint farmhouses with big, pleasing Georgian windows. Critics would say that the region is too rich and smart for its own good. Of course it is true that modern Berkshire lacks the lyrical decay of the 1940s. Yet a village like Yattendon, still strongly rooted in the huge Iliffe estate amidst which it lies, remains a pleasure, because so much of the surrounding countryside is perfectly tended. Like many old Berkshire pubs, The Royal Oak at Yattendon is nowadays a touch grand for my taste, but still a pretty place for lunch. The racing villages, of which Lambourn is the biggest and most famous, possess that raffish air inseparable from the sport, together with a prevailing sense that any passer-by would give you a hundred-to-eight on something. It is a pleasing curiosity, that today there are more horses in Berkshire than it has known for at least 60 years, though most of these are children's playthings rather than the heavy shires of the old farmers.

Thank goodness for the horses, because otherwise it is a great sadness how much livestock in the fields is diminished. We lament the passing of cattle and sheep, which grazed the downlands for centuries. In a rational world, Berkshire chalk that was ploughed up in the Second World War, and has been growing bad corn ever since, would be returned to grass.

But what would graze it? Even the richest hobby farmer flinches from the cost of keeping beasts for which there is now no economic market.

A relation of mine, a genuine country type, used to say scornfully that my love for west Berkshire reflects essentially suburban instincts. She was probably right. I am hypocrite enough to cherish easy access to cities, the joy of waking up to green fields and hedgerows, while being able to persuade summer guests from London to join us for lunch. Social life in deep, remote English countryside can get just a teeny bit dull. I love where we are, and what we have got. The challenge now – a very tough one – is to preserve these green places for future generations, amid frightening pressures of population and development. West Berkshire is still a wonderful place to walk, shoot, fish, and gaze out upon the best of southern England. Our job is to keep it that way.

23 April 2005

Just Bats About the Art and Craft

Bridget Stott

It's not often that someone is able to combine two strikingly different passions in one job, but Andrew Kember has done just that. A keen cricket player who was once dragged out of an exam by his headmaster to play for his school's First XI, he also loves woodwork. His job? A bat-maker – and one of England's finest.

Growing up on his family's fruit farm in Kent, Kember found plenty of tools at hand and put them to use by making his first bat at the age of 12. He cut down a willow tree, then shaped and sanded the wood into a blade shape. He fashioned a handle by covering a few of his father's draining rods with a rubber grip made from an old gumboot, and gluing everything together.

'I was always curious about how cricket bats were made but could never get the shape nor the finish right. It was much later that I discovered you need machinery to achieve those fine angles and super-smooth finishes,' he says, with a laugh.

Kember now produces about 3,000 hand-crafted bats a year for his firm, the Salix Cricket Bat Company. 'Just before leaving school,

I pestered all the bat manufacturers to give me a job. Luckily, I was offered an apprenticeship with the legendary master bat-maker John Newbery. I left school on Thursday, had the interview on Friday, and started the following Monday.'

Kember learnt not only woodworking skills but also the importance of keeping a traditional British industry alive. 'Some of John's spiritedness definitely rubbed off on me,' he says. Following Newbery's death in 1989, Kember started Salix in 1990 with Hugh Betts. Based at his uncle's pear farm in the village of Langley, near Leeds Castle, the company employs two full-time bat-makers and Kember's affable partner, Vicky Roberts. 'We work together on every aspect of the business, but Vicky stops short of making bats herself.'

'Using the machinery and the other tools to shape each bat requires real skill,' says Roberts. 'If I tried to use a draw blade, I'd probably cut myself in half!'

We pause to watch Kember wind a newly shaped bat into a vice before splicing and then melding the bat and cane handle together by drawing that razor-sharp blade along its face. He pulls the knife towards him in strong, confident strokes, and I start to sense the level of craftsmanship involved as he removes long fat curls of wood to reveal the fine white grain beneath.

Kember's artistry is widely respected and his bats are used by some of the world's top players. He admits that Matthew Fleming, the former Kent captain and England player, once called his bats 'the best'. That's quite an achievement in an industry dominated by international brands.

Kember, who ascribes the high-level success of his small operation to word-of-mouth influence rather than advertising or celebrity endorsements, also likes to demonstrate bat-making to the public. On Saturdays, Salix holds an open workshop. 'People love the atmosphere and are very curious about the manufacturing processes we use,' he says.

A hundred years ago, the Kentish High Weald was world-renowned as the hub of cricket-bat manufacturing, but now, with so much mass production and overseas competition, making bats by hand using traditional skills has become a rare art in Britain.

Kember's bats are made from English willow, as its long fibres can withstand the punishing thwack of a cricket ball. For each willow felled, two saplings will replace it. Kember is interested only in the lower section of the willow trunk. It's the moisture-laden outer layer, or sapwood, that's needed for bat-making. Top-quality willow comes from slow-growing trees that produce a fine, straight, pencil-line grain. Unfortunately this is becoming a rare commodity as farmers are now wise to the value of willow trees, cutting them down to supply to the industry before they are fully matured.

Willow arrives at Salix in raw, 30-inch sections of wood, cleaved along the grain and roughly shaped into cricket-bat blades. Soon after cutting, the ends are dipped in wax to stop the wood drying out. Kember then planes the front face of a cleft 'to find the sapwood and assess its quality'. More expensive, grade-one blades are cut from the whitest sapwood in the trunk. Grade-two blades display a red outside edge of heartwood – the side not used for hitting the ball – and cost less.

The rough bat shapes are pressed to solidify the fibres and provide the necessary outer hardness. This relatively quick stage is followed by the time-consuming hand-shaping, sanding and finishing. The Salix bats then line up smartly in the company's shop: the worthy all-rounder, the Præstantia, along with the Fera, the Zeitgeist and the Satyr. There are bats designed for children too, and as many girls as boys buy them.

'The renewed interest in the game stems from league clubs all over the country encouraging school kids to get involved, resulting in an ever-expanding fan base,' says Kember. 'As a child I always asked for a cricket bat for Christmas and birthdays. Nowadays it's making bats, rather than playing with bats, that fuels my love for the game.'

24 March 2006

The Duchess of Cornwall Joins the WI

Elizabeth Grice

Is it to be best frocks at every meeting now that the Duchess of Cornwall has joined Tetbury Women's Institute or will trousers still suffice? Do they have to put her on the tea rota? Perhaps they should appoint an etiquette secretary? Does she become president automatically, as the Queen is president of Sandringham WI? Can they use By Royal Appointment on their jams?

What exactly, ladies, is the protocol? Have we been told? These are some of the turbulent matters that were engaging a caucus of WI members yesterday as the implications of their most celebrated new recruit began to sink in.

The Tetbury ladies are not easily awed. They intend to treat the Duchess like any other new member – that is, 'lasso her at the door as soon as she walks in and plonk her down with a small group' so she feels instantly at ease.

'We've got to be natural,' says Sallie Dearnley, 61. 'After all, Camilla wears trousers just like we wear trousers.'

There is a warm debate about whether the Duchess will actually turn up to any of their lively monthly meetings in the Dolphin Hall and, if she does, which of the forthcoming speakers' topics are likely to interest her.

What about The Accidental Weaver by Mrs Faye Hankins, on 10 April, the first opportunity Camilla will have to plunge into the oddly unorthodox world of Tetbury WI? Perhaps not.

But The Problems of Intensive Farming later in the year is surely something the wife of a passionate organic farmer ought to hear?

Or perhaps Your House Has History on 12 June? Now there is something, they chuckle, that she really ought not to miss if she is in the country.

'I hope this isn't just a PR exercise,' says Heather Hallett, referring to Camilla's recruitment which has come about after her meeting with some of the WI members who inspired the 2003 box office hit, *Calendar Girls*. The Duchess is a huge fan of the film about the women of Rylstone WI in Yorkshire who bared almost all for a charity calendar and became world famous as a result.

While questions about her commitment to the WI are considered reasonable, the general view is that the suspicion of spin is unfair. Official duties permitting, the Duchess will surely not just be a sleeping member. 'I think she'll get a lot of enjoyment out of our meetings,' says the president, Judi Mason-Smith, 65. 'She's going to be made very welcome.'

'We are all individuals and she is an individual,' affirms Linda Lunn, 63, the treasurer. 'We don't just acquiesce.'

Indeed, no. Tetbury's first demonstration of independence was its decision not to sing 'Jerusalem', as they do at most of the institutes, when the group was founded in 1969.

Why not, I wonder. 'Everyone seemed to be having babies at the time and it seemed we had more important matters than singing 'Jerusalem',' says Heather, 67.

'And we only bake cakes when someone asks us,' Judith Randall, an ex-president, would like to make clear.

'One of our members makes a lot of jam,' she adds, 'and a lot of us buy it – because we don't make jam ourselves.'

Like Women's Institutes up and down the land, Tetbury has come a very long way from the 'Jam and Jerusalem' traditions, though Judith has a justifiable pride in her flower arranging and basket weaving.

The group prides itself on a serious discussion of matters of national importance, such as genetically modified crops (Camilla is bound to have a view), rural doorstep deliveries and the closure of village post offices.

Hot local issues include whether the air ambulance service should remain a charity and the primary care trust's refusal to finance 13 beds, now closed, at the local hospital.

But what difference will Camilla, its 35th member, actually make to Tetbury WI? Heather's husband, Roger, had some thoughts on the subject last night, though not all of them are printable. 'I always said *Calendar Girls* would attract that kind of woman to the WI,' he says, mischievously.

The truth is that Camilla is one of their own, a countrywoman at heart and, after about five minutes, that is how they will treat her. It's not as if the ladies are strangers to royalty.

Sallie, who has been a guest at Highgrove, is a member of the Tetbury Film Society, of which Camilla is patron. Sallie's husband, John, owns Thames and Cotswold, a cycle supplier in Tetbury by Royal Appointment and has the Prince of Wales's feathers above his premises. Prince Charles gives them a wave of recognition as he drives through town. And the women have all, at one time or another, worked as volunteers in the Highgrove House shop.

The Tetbury ladies are not as progressive as the young WI institute in nearby Gloucester, who meet in their lunch hour at work ('unheard of') and communicate on the internet, but they pride themselves on being active, engaged, forward-looking and even – they say it themselves – intellectual.

Members are aged 45 to 80, many of them former professionals with a strong bias towards the medical services. There are poets and artists, too, among them. They are nobody's fools. If a speaker is boring, they will be blacklisted.

'Just because this is a small town,' says Linda, 'don't think it's a dull place. No one is ever at home!'

During the years of her illicit affair with Charles, the ladies say that Camilla could be spotted quite frequently on the streets of this harmonious Cotswold market town, built of stone the colour of ripe cheese and paved with old money. Embedded among the inevitable tea shoppes and antiquities, there is a plumber, a carpet shop and a cheesemonger, advertising their services on painted boards that swing from wrought-iron brackets. At its centre, a fine Market House (1655) stands on fat stone Tuscan pillars. The Snooty Fox has a ballroom for the Beaufort Hunt.

'At the height of the conflict with Diana, Camilla retreated,' says one member. Now, though, she is back at the heart of Tetbury life.

Did anyone raise a dissenting voice when she was so publicly drawn into their circle? Were there any misgivings that having a duchess at the tea urn would skew the middle-aged, middle-class membership profile a bit too far towards privilege? 'We did have one maverick voice,' says Linda. 'Fiona. But, unfortunately, she died. We don't have any maverick voices now.'

Ask what Tetbury WI stands for, and they reply in unison: 'Friendship. That's what we joined for and that's what we've stayed for.'

Fundraising is always a problem for WIs – they have speakers to pay, halls to book and newsletters to write – and Tetbury wonders whether this aspect of their community will be easier now Camilla is in the ranks. Some members believe that her involvement will mean they can attract a better class of speaker. Others wonder if they would ever get to hold a meeting in the Orchard Room at Highgrove. But Heather Hallett reins in these wild imaginings. 'I don't think we can assume anything for the moment,' she says, firmly.

8 October 2011

Real-Life Downtonia

Sophie Campbell

It is Indian summer in Downtonia: pink, chalky fields bulge in the heat, the sky is as blue as a cot blanket and the sun bounces off avenues of

English oak, beech and sycamore, tipping every leaf with a coronet of gold. Then out of the blue a buzzard and a crow wheel into sight, locked in aerial combat, and I nearly crash into an oncoming Porsche Boxster Spyder.

The symbolism! It's like *Downton Abbey* series one (last gasp of Edwardian England, golden light, etc) versus *Downton Abbey* series two (ominous onset of the First World War, dogfights, etc) and here I am, just entering the drive to its epicentre at Highclere Castle, Hants.

Highclere is home to the Carnarvon family and is currently England's most famous stately home. Downtonia – a term coined by *Tatler* magazine, which helpfully produced a map – describes the chunk of north-west Hampshire surrounding the castle. It is just south of Newbury and on the other side of the A4 from Middletonia, which, with its epicentre at Bucklebury, rose to fame during the Royal wedding.

On the map are whopping country houses set in gorgeous grounds and dotted with famous studs – including Highclere's own and Park House Stables at Kingsclere, run by Clare Balding's brother, Andrew.

None of these, sadly, is open to the public, but the Litchfield Downs and wooded valleys with their marvellous walks and excellent, low-key sights and good pubs make the area a pleasure for the rest of us.

Highclere itself does open its doors: filming of *Downton* usually takes place in the spring and is followed by a three-month summer season when you can visit the house and gardens. Next weekend it welcomes the public for four days, with offerings including a fundraising event for Help for Heroes. There is another opening in December.

The mile-long drive winds its way across the folds of parkland, past huge 18th-century cedars of Lebanon and huddles of sheep. The castle sits in a shallow dip, so all I can see of it is the top half of a tower with four pinnacles and a flag, as though the Houses of Parliament have landed too heavily in a Hampshire field. They have, in a sense: Sir Charles Barry built both, starting work after Queen Victoria came to the throne and turning an earlier Georgian mansion into a castle of golden stone.

Step between two boot-scrapers shaped like wyverns – two-legged dragons, the family's armorial symbol – into the hall and you find yourself in a perfect mid-Victorian capsule. Slender columns of red and blue marble soar up to a vaulted roof, designed by George Gilbert Scott, and straight ahead is the saloon, the centre of the house, with gilded leather wall coverings, family portraits and a stone gallery leading to those important scene-stealers, the bedrooms.

As I stare, trying to remember what dramas I have seen in here, a man glides silently from right to left past the door, and seconds later does the same thing in reverse. He is a cameraman; everyone wants a bit of *Downton* at the moment and I am sandwiched in between a local television crew and a local school visit. I feel, in the nicest possible way, like one of the Crawley family's less thrilling guests.

Downstairs, the two big treats are the dining-room, with its mighty Van Dyck portrait of King Charles I on horseback, and the library, running almost the length of the house. This is Bonneville territory, the main haunt of Lord Grantham, with the well-upholstered feel of a gentleman's club.

Among shelves of valuable calf-bound leather books, a door of fake ones leads into the ornate music room, featuring a simple desk that once belonged to Napoleon.

Another hidden door leads to an enfilade of pretty gilded-and-mirrored rooms commissioned by Almina, the wife of the 5th Earl. She was the woman responsible for turning Highclere into an officers' hospital during the First World War and for providing Julian Fellowes with his plotline for series two. The rooms overlook a sweep of lawn; Dame Maggie Smith is said to relax between takes in the morning room.

Upstairs the star attraction is the Stanhope room – let's call it the Scarlet Bedroom – where the lifeless body of the Turkish diplomat Kemal Pamuk had to be removed after a scandalous encounter with Lady Mary. The walls are lined with suitably boudoir-rush red damask, but otherwise it looks fairly normal – almost disappointingly so, though what I was expecting I'm not sure – for despite the spectacular façade one of Highclere's charms is its human scale.

Another is the basement, containing the real housekeeper's and steward's rooms, now converted to a small tea room; a panel of servants' bells for the bedrooms, dressing rooms and bathrooms; and an exhibition focusing on the thing that made the 5th Earl of Carnarvon truly famous: his passion for Egyptology and the discovery of Tutankhamun's tomb in 1922.

The only real artefacts in here are those found during winter excavations in Thebes (today's Luxor) before the Big One – all Tutankhamun artefacts are in the Egyptian Museum in Cairo – but there are excellent replicas of the Boy King's mask, one of his magnificent gilded sarcophagi and his body, complete with golden finger and toe caps.

The best bits are the recreations of the Earl's study, containing models of Lord Carnarvon and the archaeologist Howard Carter that make you leap out of your skin, and a black wall pierced with postbox flaps through which can be seen a replica of Tutankhamun's treasure chamber as they found it: dark, musty and piled high as a castle's attic with treasure, all in solid gold.

When he died, the Earl was buried on Beacon Hill, to the south of Highclere, with views of both the castle and his beloved study. So I walk up to the grave, in the last hurrah of summer, leaving the castle dreaming in its valley and *Downton* quietly turning everything to gold.

9 May 2004
The Grandest Guest
Nigel Farndale

I am sorry to hear that the architectural historian John Cornforth has died at the age of 66. He was a flamboyant character who spent most of his career in the company of aristocrats, ostensibly while writing about their country houses for *Country Life*. There is a story about him, which I suspect is true. The Queen Mother was drawing up a list of guests for a dinner party when someone suggested Cornforth. 'Oh no,' she said, 'he's far too grand for us.'

31 August 2002
Clues for Landscape Detectives
Jack Watkins

Two thousand years ago the Emperor Claudius marched his army, elephants and all, along the old road that passes through Witham, a useful stopping point en route to the Roman capital at Colchester. Today, Witham is a little-known town on the Essex commuter belt, with a medieval core. Dorothy L. Sayers lived here, but there's not much else to make it remarkable. Yet, in its surrounding countryside, the historian Helen Pitchforth has uncovered a subject of endless fascination.

A few years ago she discovered a handwritten notebook in the county records office. It recounted the walk by villagers who undertook the old ritual of beating the parish bounds for the year 1815. So detailed was the account that Pitchforth was able to retrace their footsteps, spotting features intact.

For the past 13 years she has studied the landscape of the area, the pattern of its fields and woodland, and the species that populated them. Now her book, *A Hidden Countryside*, has won the endorsement of the distinguished countryside historian, Dr Oliver Rackham.

The charm of her work is that it is about the sort of country features you pass without thinking about why they are there. It makes you look afresh at your own parish with a new awareness. The idea that our countryside owes its appearance to the enclosure movement of the 18th and 19th centuries is a myth that is taking a long time to die.

In Essex, Suffolk, Kent and Sussex, there was very little enclosure, according to Pitchforth, who thinks the field pattern of Witham dates back to the Iron Age.

She describes the indicators of a pre-enclosure landscape. 'Enclosed fields tend to be larger, with straight lines and hedges primarily planted with hawthorn,' she says. 'Older systems have small fields with sinuous, irregular shapes and mixed hedgerow species.'

She takes me to the north-west corner of the parish. It's only two miles from the town centre but it feels remote and silent, a flat landscape dotted with trees and hedges under a wide Essex sky.

By the side of the lane is a splendid old English oak. There's nothing that evokes the passing of the centuries more powerfully than a gnarled and knotted oak tree. For me, it has a solemnity akin to that of a Gothic cathedral. But this one has been pollarded and has a special meaning.

Pollarding, the craft of cutting back a tree at a level of about 10 feet – out of the reach of foraging deer and cattle – to promote a growth of small wood, prolonged the life of already long-lived oaks, so they made good parish-boundary markers.

But the practice died out long ago. Even the regrowth is huge on this particular oak, and it must have been centuries old even in 1815.

A few yards away from the pollard is the parish boundary bank. 'One of the best ways of discovering the oldest features of your village is to get a 1:2500 scale map with the parish boundaries marked on it and go and look at them on the ground,' says Helen Pitchforth. The great pioneer of landscape studies, W.G. Hoskins, reckoned that boundary banks – with their attendant ditches – were among the oldest features in the countryside. Often created to mark the estates of Roman villas, they were not easily removed before the invention of modern machinery. So the parish system set up around the 9th century invariably reused them as recognisable features in the days before maps. Here, the ditch is 10 feet wide in parts, the bank topped by a hedge winding its way sinuously along the length of the field.

Pitchforth demonstrates 'Hooper's Rule': Dr Max Hooper's theory that, for a 30-yard stretch of hedge, the number of species you can count equates roughly to its age in centuries. There's no question then that this must be an ancient one: it contains dogwood, spindle, hazel and wild rose – all good 'ancient hedge' indicators, since they do not colonise new areas readily – as well as a crab apple and rotting coppice stools of ash and elm.

According to Pitchforth the field that stretches beside us for several acres comprised eight individual fields 20 years ago, but intensification of farming required most of the hedges to be grubbed out. She points to a large ash standing marooned in a crop of beans in the middle of the field, a poignant relic of an old hedgerow. Her keen eyes discern a slight darkening of the colour of the green crop in a declivity either side of it, a sign of where it would have run.

You can spend hours like this, looking for clues to the past like a Sam Spade of landscape detection. But one of the most fruitful areas to examine can be woodland. 'In medieval woods they'd put a large bank round the outside to keep animals out because coppiced woodland was such a valuable resource,' says Pitchforth. She shows me one that was once four times larger.

On its west side the old bank and ditch is substantial – once again sinuous, and with an array of species, from hazel to maple. But on its truncated eastern boundary the ditch is straight and shallow, with a hedge that is ramrod straight, and consisting of a uniform row of hawthorn.

Within the wood are various banks and channels and I suggest that they must have been part of a coppicing rotation system, only for Pitchforth to shake her head. 'You have to be careful,' she says. 'One distinguished historian gave a talk in a wood and pontificated on the medieval origins of the banks, only for an old local to mutter: 'I remember them being dug out for marl.'

But even if your prognostications are inaccurate, there's much to be gained from learning about your locality. It's odd that our maps may be pinpoint accurate, but we're far less familiar with our locale than our mapless predecessors. As Pitchforth says: 'Even the most unprepossessing parish has its history. Once you start looking, there's always far more than you'd expect.'

17 March 1994
Obituary
Jack Hargreaves

Jack Hargreaves, who has died aged 82, was the presenter of the television series *Out of Town*, a miscellany of gentle country anecdotes which ran for more than 20 years.

A Yorkshireman by birth, Hargreaves showed a reassuring familiarity with the timeless affairs of rural life. Sitting at a gnarled workbench in a simulated stable, he would hold forth on such arcana as the art of hurdle-making, a worn briar in his mouth and a battered hat adorned with fishing flies on his head.

At other times he would be shown strolling down a riverbank at twilight, or knee-deep in the wholesome mire of a farmyard.

Out of Town became inordinately popular among those town dwellers prepared to sit out the signature tune, a version of the 1950s hit of the same name rendered by Max Bygraves – later replaced by a Spanish-guitar instrumental.

Hargreaves's ability to talk about most things sagaciously, and without notes, made him an admirable presenter for the ITV children's programme *How?*, in which panellists answered questions on the natural and scientific worlds.

Son of a tenant farmer in Yorkshire's West Riding, Jack Hargreaves was born on 31 December 1911. He learned to shoot and fish, and as a teenager was an avid rider and sailor.

After attending the Royal Veterinary College Hargreaves was employed by Unilever, for whom he wrote technical literature on animal feed; in the 1930s he wrote for the *Daily Express*, and worked on scripts for radio and for Ealing Studios.

During the Second World War he served with the Royal Artillery and the Royal Tanks Corps, and was later on Montgomery's staff.

After the war Hargreaves was commissioned by the BBC to write scripts with an authentic Yorkshire flavour for Wilfred Pickles. He then joined the Hulton Press, and was later editor of *Lilliput* and managing editor of *Picture Post*. But his gifts were to prove more suited to broadcasting, and while working as a consultant to the National Farmers' Union he was discovered by Southern Television.

In 1959 Hargreaves made six short films under the title *Gone Fishing*. These proved popular; 32 films were finally made and the series evolved into *Out of Town*. Hargreaves professed surprise at the programme's success – it often drew larger audiences than *Coronation Street*.

In the late 1960s and early 1970s Hargreaves combined his screen appearances with the job of deputy controller of programmes at Southern Television.

As well as devising *How?* he initiated many programmes with a rural flavour, and presented Southern Television's sea-angling competition. He also produced and presented for Rediffusion, for whom he devised *The Explorers*, a quasi-scientific series.

Hargreaves was appointed OBE, and in 1970 was delighted to be made 'Pipeman of the Year'.

16 December 2011
Life is Long in Ambridge
Rebecca Smith

They have a worrying predisposition for horrible accidents and fatal heart attacks. But the residents of Ambridge are generally a long-living bunch, according to a study that has compared life and death in *The Archers* to that in the real world.

While the desire for audience-grabbing storylines sees most soap operas have death rates more akin to a war zone, the characters in the Radio 4 show live longer than the national average, research has shown.

Rob Stepney, a freelance medical and science writer, found that although deaths through accidents in the fictional farming community were seven times higher than in Britain as a whole, the mortality rate was actually slightly lower than normal.

Over the past 20 years the death rate for Ambridge men has been 7.8 per 1,000 per year, compared with a national average of 8.5. For women it was 5.2 per 1,000 per year compared with 5.8 nationally.

'In the case of overall mortality, *The Archers*, by luck or good editorial judgement, reflected almost exactly the experience of the wider population of England and Wales,' Mr Stepney wrote in the *British Medical Journal Christmas Edition*.

The series has seen several notable deaths since Grace Archer became the first in 1955. She was killed in a stables fire while attempting to rescue her horse.

Mr Stepney wrote: 'Among male *Archers* characters, the three accidental deaths and one suicide (27 per cent of the total mortality) seem to substantially over-represent the risk evident nationally. In 2000, accidents accounted for only four per cent of deaths in men.

'Mark Hebden seems to have been particularly unlucky. In the year of his car crash, the national fatality rate from road traffic accidents was seven per 100,000. That in Ambridge represents an annual incidence of 40 per 100,000.'

The last death in the village was Nigel Pargetter, killed falling from a roof while trying to remove a New Year banner. Although the plotline promised to 'shake Ambridge to the core' listeners appeared to take the death in their stride.

More residents of Ambridge died of heart attacks than nationally, accounting for a third of deaths, when in real life this would be less than one quarter. Mr Stepney concluded: 'In Ambridge, ischemic heart disease seems to have a particularly poor prognosis.'

Ambridge residents are blessed with fewer cases of cancer than would be expected. Mr Stepney wrote: 'If the national pattern prevailed, cancers would account for roughly a quarter of deaths. The two deaths observed (one from melanoma and the other from a malignancy of unspecified site) represent only 13 per cent of the total.'

There has, however, been plenty of ill health in Ambridge, especially from rare conditions. Mr Stepney cited the example of Daniel Hebden who developed juvenile arthritis, which would normally strike only one or two children per 1,000. Despite the condition's poor prognosis, he has made a full recovery.

Dearly departed:

Notable deaths in *The Archers*

1955 Grace Archer died in a fire at stables trying to rescue her horse.
1957 Bob Larkin accidentally shot and killed by Tom Forrest while poaching.
1982 Polly Perks killed after car collided with a milk tanker.
1985 Aunt Laura contracted pneumonia after falling into a ditch.
1986 Dan Archer died of a heart attack while trying to rescue sheep in difficulty.
1994 Mark Hebden died in road accident.
1998 John Archer killed when tractor overturned.
2004 Greg Turner shot himself after Helen Archer left him.
2011 Nigel Pargetter died falling from roof in icy conditions.

21 August 1993

A Crooked Face Behind the Rural Smile

Nigel Burke

'It is my belief that the lowest and vilest alley in London does not present a more dreadful record of sin than the smiling and beautiful countryside.'

So said Sherlock Holmes, long before crime statistics were a regular feature of the news. This week's discovery that the shires suffer a higher rate of car theft per head of population than London has an ominous meaning. It is only the latest signal that urban patterns of crime are spilling out into rural areas, bringing urban anxieties to people who have not budgeted for the human costs of living with the fear of crime.

There are crimes with a distinctly urban flavour, such as the teenage gunfight outside a Brixton wine bar on Monday in which a 13-year-old girl was wounded in crossfire. The country has its own specialities in crime.

Cannabis farms regularly turn up in the smiling countryside, and our coasts and fields are, according to HM Customs, so frequented by smuggler's boats and aircraft that the Revenue men are recruiting country people as watchers and informants, and issuing aircraft recognition guides. A widespread spate of attacks on horses is still causing light sleep among country folk, and vigilance for poachers and badger-diggers can never be relaxed.

To add to these criminal constants of rural England, there now comes theft on an industrial scale, mass delinquency in the form of raves and fake gypsies, violent robbery and even a species of terrorism, thanks to animal rights extremists.

The facts, established by the insurance industry, that Cambridgeshire, Lincolnshire and Gloucestershire are among the least safe places to leave a car cannot quite be explained by a reassuring assumption that country people do not lock doors as diligently as townies. They are catching up. They respond to the level of risk as they see it, and if car theft has dramatically exceeded their expectations based on recent experience it means that change in criminal behaviour is going on. Car crime is in itself the least surprising of all social phenomena. A car is about the only valuable object which people commonly leave outside at night. Everyone is much more concerned about violence, and there has been plenty in rural areas.

A month ago, a retired fruit farmer, Henry Tooze, and his wife Megan, were shot dead at their farm in Mid Glamorgan. No motive has been established.

Tony Evans galvanised public opinion in June when he shot a burglar who had attacked him in his cottage in Pluckley, Kent. It was his eighth burglary, and local supporters agreed that the village was plagued by crime. Similar pressures were held to mitigate the offence of kidnapping when Duncan Bond and Mark Chapman of Harleston in Norfolk abducted and frightened an alleged thief. Farmer Peter Toone from Blaby in Leicestershire shot and blinded a burglar whom he pursued across his land last summer. On reviewing these cases, the words 'following a spate of burglaries' are always buried in the reports, and perhaps they are the real story, rather than the fits of alleged vigilantism that preoccupy the documentary-makers.

The question arises, who is responsible for crime in the country? It would, in a way, be more satisfactory to imagine bands of urban knaves coming out to deprecate, but it is likely that many of the malefactors are country born and bred. A friend who was a social worker, and dealt for years with delinquent city youths, tells me that his boys had a mortal fear of the countryside, based on an apprehension of dogs, shotguns and rural vigilance, which is somewhat borne out by Messrs Toone, Bond and Chapman. Burglary without local knowledge is too risky for most.

Home Office studies indicate that burglars tend strongly to operate within 1.5 miles of home. Local or stranger, the country thieves got away with £12 million from farms alone in 1992, according to insurers, NFU Mutual, taking tractors, machinery, produce, chemicals and fertiliser.

Yet the countryside is being opened up to the town. It was once considered private, but it is coming to be considered as an amenity for the community: a giant pedestrian area. It is not true that criminals are turning to the countryside because of better roads or more cars. There were easily enough 20 years ago. The caravanserais of scruffs known as travellers, and the ravers have psychologically opened the countryside for criminal abuse, even when they intend no harm. Apart from the commuting gangs of commercial townie poachers, who have been with us since towns began, the urban criminal fraternity probably never thought much about the countryside, until ravers and travellers reminded them it was there. The protest-addicts from the animal rights lobby have pushed their own wedge into rural Britain, and have brought a little of London's culture of bomb scares to the shires. A hunt master in Clwyd has received a bomb, and everyone involved in field sports or animal husbandry is as vulnerable to terrorism as a London commuter.

Country people are far from slow to respond. They have an acute and historical sense of property to rely on. Farm Watch schemes have been started in emulation of urban neighbourhood watch schemes, though neighbourhood watching has always been practised in the country. Cheap Russian image intensifiers are selling briskly to estate managers, and the police are making more use of such equipment. A wave of ex-military surveillance technology is on its way to help with rural security.

Villages are as short of police patrols as towns. In a typical beat in the Yorkshire Dales, a motorised policeman will cover eight villages. His presence is somewhat more diluted in the square mileage than a town policeman, but he will command the roads more easily, because they are fewer. Alert locals with mobile phones will increase his effectiveness in intercepting suspects in a way that could not be achieved in a maze of city streets. Mobile phones are the only weapon of the volunteer patrol in the Herefordshire village of Eardisley, where the locals run a well-regulated watch. The Leominster police whom they assist have 104 men to cover 730 square miles.

In essence, Britain has about 160,000 policemen for 94,000 square miles, and most of them are needed in towns, so the traditionally self-reliant countrymen will have to look after themselves once again.

Sherlock Holmes said: 'I look at those scattered houses, and there comes to me a feeling of their isolation, and of the impunity with which crime may be committed there.' As Nick Ross says: 'Violent crime is very rare in Britain.' And every time he says it, it is a little less true.

14 August 2010
The End of the Rural Honesty Box?
Martin Evans

They were once a common sight along rural lanes, but the days of the honesty box could be numbered following a spate of thefts.

In many remote communities, the traditional method of paying for goods such as eggs, milk and honey was to place a box next to the produce asking the customer to leave the correct money.

For decades the system based on trust and common decency worked well, with regular customers never dreaming of taking more than they had paid for.

But recently some producers have found that their goods were being pilfered while others reported the theft of the honesty boxes themselves. Many people who relied on the system are shutting up shop in what has been described as a depressing reflection on contemporary society.

Kate Anstey, who runs Moon Ridge Farm near Exeter in Devon, decided to remove her 'eggs for sale' box from the roadside after her produce and money were stolen twice within days. She said: 'When I went down, all the money and the eggs were gone again and I thought, "Oh, I can't be bothered with this."'

Mrs Anstey has moved the box to a secure area of her property where she can keep an eye on it, but she said it was a sad day for the community.

Her regular customers expressed their dismay at the demise of the popular and traditional system. Ron Lee said: 'It's not very nice, is it, really? People trust you to do it so it's up to you to pay.'

Honesty boxes have been around in some areas for at least 50 years.

The system was revived in recent years as more people began growing fruit and vegetables and keeping livestock. But farmers' representatives warned that such systems were being abused by people who had no respect for the rural way of life.

Ian Johnson, of the National Farmers' Union, said: 'It is tragic but honesty boxes aren't possible in modern society. Theft is happening across all levels.'

Just the Ticket for a Ride in the Country
Graham Coster

Sheep are the major traffic hazard today. Three of them have been reported wandering down the tiny lane to Box Hill. 'Oh well,' muses Peter the bus driver, 'I need a new woolly coat.'

As he revs the engine to pull away from Polesden Lacey, the National Trust's Regency villa in deepest Surrey where the Queen Mother spent part of her honeymoon, a woman pokes her head through the doorway to say how nice it is to see the old Guy out on the road again.

Her husband used to work for Guy Motors in Johannesburg, she explains, and she remembers sadly the day when the cable came through that the firm had become insolvent, and they had to return home. 'Wow!' exclaims a girl on horseback as the bus inches past, wild dog-rose scraping at its windows – 'it's, er, Stephenson's Rocket!'

We are back in the days when a bus was a bus, and not a Hoppa or a Choppa or a Nippa or a Zippa, and when small buses didn't run in busy cities overladen with a double-decker's worth of passengers, but on dreamy bucolic routes out in the country.

The Guy Special was perhaps the quintessential country bus: built in the early fifties for London Transport's far-flung routes in its Country Area, to tootle round villages such as Crockham Hill in Kent and Nup End in Hertfordshire, and painted, of course, green. The Guy that plied the lanes of the Surrey Hills to hamlets such as Coldharbour and Abinger Common used to be parked overnight in the farmyard at Holmbury St Mary, and its local driver, Curly, was not unknown to jump out en route for a quick chat with a friend ploughing the fields.

But with its snouty bonnet, adapted from a Ford Thames lorry, it looked as old-fashioned as the buses it was replacing – Guy Motors was still christening similar models with rustic names like the Otter and the Vixen – and by the time the Special entered service it was already becoming an anachronism. Private cars were appearing in greater numbers, village dwellers and weekend ramblers alike were abandoning the leisurely country bus, and from the mid-fifties onwards services were steadily cut. Guy Motors became part of British Leyland, and the last Guy vehicles – trucks only by now – rolled out of its Wolverhampton works in the early seventies.

But now Graham Seymour, engineering manager at London and Country's Guildford bus garage, is heaving up the big bonnet of Guy Special number 13 and checking everything is in order for the weekend – for this Sunday, as on every subsequent Sunday and public holiday until the end of October, it will be negotiating the Surrey lanes again, on a circular route between Guildford and Dorking that takes in the National Trust houses at Clandon Park and Hatchlands, scenic spots like Newlands Corner and the Silent Pool, and its old haunt of Coldharbour, the highest village in the south-east.

'There's a lot of brass under here,' says Seymour, peering in at the Perkins P6 engine; 'all copper pipes, too. You could polish everything up and have it gleaming.' GS13 cost London and Country £4,000, and apart from a 12-week engine rebuild last year after one driver tried an emergency stop by putting it into reverse, a gentle workload of just 3,000 miles a year (compared to 1,000 a week for the modern fleet) has avoided major trouble.

'There's so much to go wrong on the modern buses,' sighs Seymour as a brand-new Dennis Lance whirrs in: 'That one's got suspension that goes down to let the passengers get on, and if you open up the electrics it's like getting inside a computer. The Guy's electrics box has got wires in it . . .'

The distinctive bonnet looks perfect for tying white wedding ribbons to – a Kent couple have already hired the Guy for their nuptials. Inside, Seymour's mechanics have varnished the wooden floor, and atop the radiator cap sits the stern Guy mascot of an Indian chief picked out in red and white, engraved with Guy Motors' slogan, 'Feathers In Our Cap'.

'The old drivers used to say that if you had to use first gear on one of these to pull away,' says Peter Burchell, nosing the Guy out through the crowds of bikers in Box Hill car park, 'you could roll a cigarette in the time it took to get to second.' Burchell was the last London Country driver to train on Guy Specials; now, with almost 30 years' service, he's one of only two entrusted with this survivor.

The vehicle has vacuum brakes that need pumping in good time, as the disgraced driver who blew the engine discovered; there's a back-to-front 'Chinese gearbox' with third where first should be and no syncro-mesh – 'If you don't get it right she doesn't want to know'; and a traction-engine-size steering wheel with no power-assistance but plenty of shakes. 'You've got to nurse it,' says Burchell fondly, pulling into Denbies's Vineyard. 'Got your duty-frees, dear?' he asks the lady who boards (he dresses up as Santa Claus and brings the Guy here on Christmas specials). 'It's getting old,' he continues. 'You can't rush it.'

As the Guy stops at Dorking Station the first of many cameras goes off: all round the route, bus-spotters lurk everywhere to snap the rare beast. One of the nine passengers who gets on is Stuart Johnson, a bus enthusiast down on business from Peterhead in Scotland, where he's recently ridden on a vintage Bedford around the Trossachs; today, as we creep up through the steep, sun-dappled tunnel of trees towards Coldharbour, he's renewing his acquaintance with the bus he used to catch when a schoolboy in the early sixties for walking trips out to Leith Hill. 'A very attractive little bus,' he nods. Two elderly ladies returning from Polesden Lacey remember catching the Guy out here when they first moved to Surrey – 'that would have been when, Evelyn, 1955?' – and recommend the route in the autumn when all these beech leaves turn golden.

So now the green country bus has brought us out here on a beautiful hot summer Sunday, it's time to stride out into the country; alight at Foxglove Corner, hear Peter Burchell search for first gear and watch the Guy grind away in a blast of black smoke. On the other side of the wood, Coldharbour are playing Mogador Wanderers at the sylvan cricket ground, and the number eleven batsman is just smiting his first ball for a colossal six into the birch trees.

Soon the cricketers are walking off to take tea, and it is time to wander down the hill and wait, as the early-evening swallows skim overhead, for the approaching growl of the old Guy.

30 December 2000
A Real Belter of a Shelter
Rupert Segar

West Milton is a tiny Dorset village made up of about 30 houses and 100 souls and, so they say, the smallest village green in the country. But now it has another claim to fame: the most ornate and stylish bus shelter in the country.

Like many other small rural communities, West Milton has no pub, post office or shop. Two years ago residents realised that the only place where people met was the old bus shelter, a shabby relic from a more utilitarian era.

'It was a cheap and nasty construction made out of synthetic stone, a real eyesore,' says John Laverack, a design draftsman who lives in the village. A more fitting edifice was required.

Laverack drew up some plans. 'I knew we could not afford to knock down the old bus shelter and start again,' he says. 'So I thought we could create a wrap-round disguise by cladding the building with real stone. Of course, we had to use hamstone, because that is the indigenous rock of west Dorset.'

Then he really got carried away. English oak beams would consolidate the vernacular theme. An elaborate porch would give it more character. And, of course, it needed a roof. Inspired by the lych gate to a church in a nearby village, Laverack designed an intricate roof worthy of a French chateau. 'It gives a touch of sophistication to what would otherwise be a very arts-and-crafts construction,' he says.

You may think they take bus shelters very seriously in West Milton. Well, they had to, when they received the builders' estimate. The bill was estimated at more than £3,000.

Was the village prepared to pay? The question was put to the vote, and the erection of a new bus shelter was adopted as the village's Millennium project.

Brian Jackman, a travel writer whose accounts of Africa often appear in the *Daily Telegraph*, took on the task of raising the cash. '£3,000 may not sound much compared with, say, the cost of the Dome,' he says. 'But when you consider there are only about 100 people living in West Milton, it is a gigantic sum.'

As the hat went round, the project began. 'What started as a labour of love almost became a nightmare,' says Nick Poole, a builder who lives in the village.

'The shelter may be modest in size, but it involved a huge amount of work for my stone mason and carpenter.' There were six external corners, which turned the task of stone laying into a three-dimensional brain-twister. The roof was a challenge, too, with an intricate pattern of oak beams.

'Even laying the tiles took for ever,' says Poole. 'In the three weeks it took to transform the shelter, we could have constructed a building 10 times its size.'

Meanwhile, the fundraising continued. Nearly everyone in the village pledged money, but it was not enough. Official sponsors were sought. Brian Jackman had an idea.

'We went to the local electricity company and offered to change our weather-vane, replacing the N for north with a B, so that it spelt out SWEB, their name.' The power company could not resist. A permanent advert on top of a bus shelter was well worth £500. Unfortunately, the company was less permanent and has now changed its name to Western Power. 'So the weather-vane was never altered – but we still got to keep the money.'

The shelter was officially opened this summer by the vicar, Canon Gregory Page-Turner. 'It was the first time anyone had ever asked me to bless a bus shelter,' he says. 'But I felt it right, as it represented an enormous effort by the entire community. Something of which West Milton could be proud.'

'It's more than just a bus shelter,' says John Samways, the parish chairman. 'Though the school children do appreciate the practical aspect of it, particularly on cold winter mornings. But it has also become a real centre for the community.'

Indeed, the bus shelter is West Milton's Piccadilly Circus. Many local residents are forced to make a daily pilgrimage there, as it is where their newspapers are dropped by a speedy delivery man. People pop in at all hours to read village notices. And the shelter has now become an impressive rendezvous point for any outdoor meeting.

And the community spirit has been extended – if in a slightly diluted and liquid form. Having got together to create the new shelter, many of the men also formed a Cider Club. This autumn's harvest of Tom Putts, traditional cider apples still grown in the area, has been pulped and pressed, and now all that remains is to drink it.

This weekend, the Cider Club is expected to meet to wet the bus shelter's head with a commemorative toast.

26 January 2008
In the Sticks with the Wicker Men
Sophie Campbell

In a rare burst of sunshine, after days of January rain, two men are perched on a compact yellow machine as it makes its way busily up and down a field of Somerset clay, slicing down row after row of slender withies and bundling them with twine. All around them is a waterscape: flooded moors stretch off to the south-east, the fields are edged with water-filled ditches known as rhynes ('reens'), and what dry land there is oozes brown water like a wet sponge.

This is the willow harvest on the Somerset Levels. The withies, in hazy brown or pinkish lines according to species, have dropped their leaves with the first frosts and must be cut before the spring. There is an economic imperative too: Morrisons supermarkets are using willow-hurdle panels as signage in its bakery sections this year and P.H. Coate & Son, willow producers on the Levels for 189 years, is working flat out to supply them. As a result, its stock of blackberry-picking baskets, cheese trays, egg holders, traditional nursing chairs, cradles, DVD-holders, shopping baskets and coffins are low, and the willow weavers, racing to catch up for the summer visitor season, are going through the fat bundles of boiled, stripped willow like a dose of salts.

You could easily drive straight past the Levels without noticing them. I did for years, driving down the M5 from Bristol and vaguely registering the rather dull tablelands south of the Mendips, with few hedges and many ruler-straight streams. It's easier now: in the year 2000 a local artist called Serena de la Hey built a 40ft (12 metres) sculpture, *The Willow Man*, standing sentinel between exits 23 and 24 on the motorway near Bridgwater. He strides along the edge of a huge flood plain, once under the sea, through which the Rivers Tone, Parrett and Axe meander incontinently before emptying into the Bristol Channel.

As the sea level dropped over thousands of years, Neolithic man settled on islets – joined by causeways and duck-boarded trackways, some of which still exist under the peat – and on low ridges that splay out like fingers across the wet. One island, to the east of the Levels, is now Glastonbury, with its fine mud pedigree. On one of the ridges sits the village of Stoke St Gregory, home to the Coate family's Willows & Wetlands Centre, as well as to de la Hay and a number of

other artists and craftspeople using willow. All around are villages –
North Curry, Lyng, Westonzoyland, Kingsbury Episcopi – with rich
willow histories, a handful of producers and numerous basket- and
furniture-makers.

Down on West Sedgemoor, as the harvester beetles along, Jonathan
Coate, the 39-year-old great-great-great-grandson of the firm's founder,
is surveying the floods: 'We used to get this sort of thing every 15 years
or so,' he says. 'Now it's every two or three. But back when it was full of
willow that's what it would have looked like. In a way, it has gone back
to how it was.'

Since the days of the Romans, water on the Levels has been controlled.
Monasteries at Glastonbury, Athelney, Muchelney and Wells owned
most of the land in their time, using sluices and ditches. In the 1920s,
steam pumps began to drain the land for grazing. The pumping stations
still work, but are now controlled from Bristol.

Jonathan, a skilled furniture-maker, lives in a house overlooking
Sedgemoor. His garden is willow fenced, his thatch is fastened by willow
spars and his small sons had willow cradles. He has provided props for
operas and films – the latest being *Sweeney Todd*, for which he made 50
chairs – and learnt his craft from an 86-year-old furniture-maker from
Lyng. All his raw materials come from this moor and two others, Curry
Moor and Hay Moor, to the north of the ridge.

His mother, Anne, is in charge of the history side of things, running
the visitor centre, shop and a small café. 'Before the wars, there were
about 3,500 acres of willow down here,' she explains, 'plus 3,000 in
the Norfolk fens and about the same amount up in the Trent–Severn
area. They've all been drained. Somerset is the only area still producing
willow commercially; there are about 150 acres left.' She and her husband
started the artists' charcoal business, which now accounts for 50 per cent
of the willow crop and is exported worldwide.

In terms of tourism, the winter is low season; a good moment to go
because you can see the harvest. After the planting of the 'setts' – new
willow shoots – in spring, the plants are left to grow a mind-boggling
9 feet (2.7 metres) before the frosts. The rest of the processing is visible,
though, carefully spaced out to provide year-round employment for
35 people on site and another 10 working from home, either weaving
willow or packing charcoal into boxes.

John Pipe was born in 1936 in North Curry, where his parents had a
few acres of withy beds, and has worked in willow since he was 15. 'It

was a thriving industry up until the late 1950s,' he says, 'but it collapsed when plastics arrived.' The war years were good, in fact: First World War pilots sat in wicker aircraft seats, and by the Second World War baskets were needed for observation balloons, parachute drops (they could withstand hard landings) and carrier pigeons. Hospitals, laundries and mothers-to-be fuelled the demand for white wicker – cleaner and more hygienic – which was cut and placed in water for six months. Children took three weeks off in May to help strip the whitened willow.

John grades the withies by dropping them into a barrel and holding them against a measure. They are taped into half-bundles known as 'wads', stuffed into open crates, submerged in boiling water for 10 hours and then stripped, steaming, by mechanised rollers, filling the yard with the pungent smell of hot tannin. Now a glowing buff colour, they are dried against wires outside, tied into bundles exactly 3ft 1in (about 94cm) in diameter ('Now there's a strange number,' he says. 'Like a baker's dozen.') and tied with a distinctive 'rose knot' of willow, ready to be supplied to basket-makers or made into charcoal sticks.

'The Levels are very unusual,' says Anne Coate. 'People farm little bits of land, here and there. They're very adaptable, they'll do a bit of ditch-digging or willow or peat.' Similarly, the willow industry has adapted, moving from post office baskets to hanging baskets and from sheep hurdles to living willow sculptures in order to survive. So when you see *Sweeney Todd* in the cinema, forget Johnny Depp – check out the chairs.

28 August 2010
The Perry-Pear Necessities
Jack Watkins

Pear cider is enjoying a surge in popularity but perry is what we should really be drinking, according to expert Jim Chapman. 'A good perry is akin to a fine wine,' he says, reflecting on a drink, once popular but now almost forgotten. 'The tannins in the pears, and the soils on which they're grown, can confer great variety and depth of taste.'

What we think of as perry today is merely pear cider, made from pulped dessert pears, he says. Acceptable enough, but quite different from the real thing.

Perry-making is a precise affair, considerably more complex than that of making apple cider, and the fermentation process has to be closely overseen. But Jim is determined to engineer a perry renaissance at his Orchard Centre in the Gloucestershire village of Hartpury. His week-long perry-making courses are attracting people from as far as Australia and India. Students learn how to use the fermentation equipment and the processes of fruit milling, pressing and the preparation of the juice for fermentation.

The perry pear harvest will take place over the next few weeks and Jim is expecting a bumper crop at his orchards. 'It's important that the pears are pressed as soon as they have fallen from the trees, for many varieties spoil quickly,' he says.

His affection for perry developed relatively recently. For 20 years, with his wife Holly, he ran the Shambles museum in Newent, with its collection of Victorian memorabilia. Then, about a decade ago, he discovered 'Hartpury' means hard pear (the perry pear) and thought it fitting to plant a few trees on his land.

His enthusiasm grew and now his two orchards contain 110 varieties, constituting a National Collection larger even than that at the headquarters of the Three Counties Agricultural Society at Malvern. The purpose-built Orchard Centre opened in May 2009.

'The more I looked into it, the more I found many trees were at risk,' Jim says. 'The National Collection at Malvern holds about 60 varieties, but they have competing demands for limited space. They let me take grafts and then I searched the Three Counties (Gloucestershire, Herefordshire and Worcestershire) for others surviving in neglected orchards or on farms. We found some old trees that had been forgotten about since the fifties.'

Today's perry pears are thought to be a cross between the wild pear and the more culinary types brought over by the Romans. 'It was the cross of the two that retained the "wild" features in the tannins and acids which make it such a delicious drink,' Jim says.

In medieval times the trees were also planted in pleasances for their landscape appeal. 'They can grow to the size of oaks. To see one in spring covered in its white blossom is an amazing sight,' he says.

By 1664, perry making was well enough established in Gloucestershire to be mentioned in John Evelyn's book *Pomona*. 'There's a saying that if the pear trees can't see May Hill, they won't flourish,' says Jim, referring to the distinctive local landmark on the

Gloucestershire–Herefordshire border. 'It's nonsense of course, but it indicates the localised nature.'

Each village near May Hill developed its own variety of perry pear. 'At Hartpury, we've got the Hartpury Green, which thrives on the soils around this village,' Jim says.

But by the middle of last century most orchards had fallen into disuse, largely because of the time-consuming nature of perry production, but also due to heavy frosts. 'The problem with pears is that they flower earlier than apple trees, and if you're prone to frost you can lose the crop,' Jim says.

He estimates there are only about a dozen craft producers left, using traditional, natural fermentation methods. Much of the perry sold today is made via mass-production methods, with pasteurisation killing off natural yeasts and highly controlled fermentation processes. 'It's still a good product and the only way to do it on a really commercial basis,' Jim admits. 'But if you are producing, say, 1,000 litres, you can do it more slowly, using natural fermentation, then sometimes you'll make a really exceptional product.'

It is this rigorous method of production that he is keen to promote. 'I want to encourage people to preserve the old orchards – as well as plant new ones – but they are only likely to do so if they think they'll get a product from them,' he says, adding that long-term global warming could make the trees less vulnerable to frost. 'At the Orchard Centre we show them how to make traditional perry which, perhaps, they will later be able to market as a farm-gate product.'

Providing his students can resist the temptation to sample prematurely, each returns home with a gallon of their own perry, plus the knowledge and ability to use their local fruit in future.

'Learning to make perry properly is essential,' he says. 'If you try to make the drink without the requisite skills, you'll be disappointed. If you make a bit more effort, you'll find out what a fantastic drink it can be.'

15 May 1997
Obituary
Laurie Lee

Laurie Lee, the writer and poet who has died aged 82, made his name and fortune with the publication in 1959 of *Cider With Rosie*, the haunting evocation of his childhood in the village of Slad, near Stroud, in Gloucestershire.

The book showed an intense sensitivity to the natural world, a sensual pleasure in language and an instinctive feeling for the narcissism of youth. It mythologised the landscape of the Slad valley for the English, as Alain-Fournier's *Le Grand Meaulnes* had imprinted the countryside of Solognes on the minds of the French. But for all its romanticism, *Cider With Rosie* never degenerated into charming nostalgia.

Lee retained a memory for the harshness as well as for the joys of the village, and portrayed the yearnings and cruelties of youth alongside the robust pleasures of family life in a place still cut off from the modern world. By the time that Lee wrote *Cider With Rosie*, in the 1950s, it seemed to him that he was writing about a time as remote as the Middle Ages. 'I belonged to a generation,' he remembered, 'which by chance saw the end of a thousand years' life. The change came late to our Cotswold valley, didn't really show until the later 1920s.'

Lee was never prepared to divulge how much in *Cider With Rosie* was poetic licence, and how much an accurate chronicle. But no one else could recall the story of a villager who had emigrated to New Zealand, and was murdered when, on his return, he rashly bragged in the pub of the fortune he had made. Lee gave nothing away: 'It's in the book,' he said, 'so it must be true.'

And who was Rosie Burdock, the girl with whom he drank cider under the wagon during haymaking? 'For a long time we sat very close,' Lee wrote, 'breathing the same hot air. We kissed only once, so shy and dry, it was like two leaves colliding in the air.'

The reader is told that 'Rosie, having baptised me with her cidrous kisses, married a soldier, and I lost her for ever.' But had she in truth ever existed? 'I from Barcelona, I know nutheeng,' Lee would answer such questions, in the style of Manuel from *Fawlty Towers*. 'I am a person of concealment,' he elaborated. 'No one has ever managed to get through.'

To those who met Lee later in life it seemed that, with his floppy handkerchiefs and fizzy-bright jackets, he was rather more Chelsea Arts Club dandy than Gloucestershire yokel. The Garrick Club tie was also often in evidence. Even *Cider With Rosie* had actually been written, with intense labour and over four years, in a London attic.

Jeffrey Bernard had a way of dating events in the 1950s: 'Oh yes, that was three years after the last time Laurie Lee bought a drink.' The book's immediate success – eventually it would become a school text, and sell six million copies – enabled Lee to acquire a house and other property at Slad. But he kept a flat in Chelsea, and was by no means over eager to meet the Gloucestershire locals. He even hit upon the wheeze of recording the sound of a typewriter, so people would keep away from fear of disturbing him.

And of course he was working, albeit with a silent 4B pencil. 'The urge to write', he considered, 'is also the fear of death – the need to leave messages for those who come after, saying "I was here. I saw it too." Also, of course, I wanted to show off to my girlfriends.'

As I Walked Out One Midsummer Morning (1969) described Lee's adventures as a young man in Spain, while his last book *A Moment of War* (1991) continued the story with his experiences in the Spanish Civil War. The three autobiographies, and *A Rose for Winter* (1955), about his travels in Andalusia in 1951, constituted his main prose output.

Laurie Lee was born at Slad on 26 June 1914 into a large family. When he was three his father Reg Lee, a sailor's son, disappeared to London to realise his ambition of becoming a civil servant; years later he would die cranking his car in Morden.

At 20, Reg Lee had married a local merchant's daughter, who bore him eight children (five of whom survived) before dying while still young. Reg Lee then married his housekeeper, Laurie's mother, who had four more children, of whom three survived. Though Laurie Lee had two brothers, he remembered spending his early years among 'a nest of women' – an experience which quite failed to put him off the opposite sex.

After schooling in the village and at Stroud Central, Laurie Lee began work at 14, successively as tea boy, labourer and clerk. These occupations only stimulated his desire to seek a wider world, and in the summer of 1934 he set out, with knapsack on his back and a guitar in his hands.

He headed for London, munching the treacle biscuits his mother had given him, and which 'tasted sweetly of the honeyed squalor of home'. He slept rough and kept the wolf from the door by busking in Southampton. In London he joined the Communist Party, and spent a year wheeling barrows of cement for a builder at Putney, while living over a café in the Upper Richmond Road.

Seeking ever larger horizons, Lee determined to go abroad, choosing Spain because someone had taught him the Spanish for 'May I have a glass of water, please?' During the Second World War, Lee worked for the Crown Film Unit and as an editor at the Ministry of Information, for which he made films in India. In 1950 he acquired a job in the forthcoming Festival of Britain, with the title Caption Writer-in-Chief and Curator of Eccentrics. In general, though, his standing as a poet condemned him to an impoverished existence in literary bohemia, from which *Cider With Rosie* afforded a welcome relief.

In 1995 and 1996 Lee fought hard and successfully to prevent a housing development in the Slad Valley. 'They will clamp the town in these artificial prisons where the young will have nothing to do except lounge and decay,' he complained. 'Perhaps if I were a child today I, too, would be imprisoned by videos and computer games.'

Laurie Lee was appointed MBE in 1952.

He married, in 1950, Catherine Francesca Polge, whom he had first encountered in 1936 at Martigues, near Marseilles, on his way to Spain. They had a daughter.

27 November 1994
Saving the Soul of Souldern
Byron Rogers

I do wonder what will become of these lovely old villages. I drive through them and each name on each immaculate gate is a knell for village life: The Old Rectory, The Old School, The Old Forge. For the blacksmith has gone, and the vicar; schools have closed, the post office and the shop. They should be pulling down the blinds on rural England.

Yet the villages, like Roman Britain on the evening of its last day, have never looked more prosperous. Those who have moved in have been able to afford the new thatch and the restored mullions, tapping out the computer images of the rural dream. So what will become of all these places?

Arthur Goodhart, once Master of University College, Oxford, had the sort of gravelly American voice I had only heard in men who gave misdirections to posses in western films. I can hear it now, for Goodhart, talking about some little town in the midwest, used the bleakest description. This, he said, was 'somewhere on the way to somewhereselse.'

'That is precisely what has saved us,' said Ann Prescott of Souldern, in North Oxfordshire. 'We never were on the way to anywhere else. We have always been a cul-de-sac.'

Just about everything bad that can happen to a village has happened to Souldern. The vicar, the schoolmaster, the shopkeeper, the postmaster – they have all followed each other down the road to oblivion, and the signs of the Old This and the Old That are everywhere. And yet, Mrs Prescott has just published a history of her village.

Souldern, Our Village in Oxfordshire is what can happen when a village hits back, being a history not of the nobs but of almost every house and its occupants. Just as the towns of the Midwest laid claim to some character, putting up signs like Artichoke Capital of the World, so Mrs Prescott attempts to show her neighbours that their village is somewhere.

The irony is that to do this she met part of the cost with compensation money from when the M40 was gouged out of the landscape a mile away. No road from the village leads to the motorway, and if anyone needed reminding that where he lived was nowhere, it would be the sight of the world passing in an unbroken wall of sound. The villagers got between one and five per cent of their house values, depending on proximity, and Mrs Prescott's house was one of the nearest.

What made the motorway so cruel was that Souldern people had in the past appealed for a road out of the village, as they did in 1911 for one to Deddington. They did not get it, so Deddington, like Sidcup to Pinter's Tramp, became a dream. Who knows what might have happened had they only been able to get to Deddington?

Only one lane leads into Souldern from the A41. I have passed it many times, wondering how old the pub might be, or whether there was a pub there. No one stops at a cul-de-sac unless they have some business there. Wordsworth called to stay with the vicar and wrote a sonnet, 'Where Holy ground begins', probably less trouble to him than a thank-you letter. It lacks the depth of feeling of an old farmer whose verse Mrs Prescott quotes: 'I myself am rather fond/Of that corner round the pond.'

But time passes and, every popularly accepted pointer of doom in place, in the winter of 1991 the final birds of ill omen gathered over the village. A BBC2 camera crew came down the lane to film a documentary on 'the sad decline of the English village'.

But Souldern hit back. The post office has opened again, for an hour and a half one morning each week in the village hall, when coffee is served. This has become a community gathering, and once a year there is a village picnic.

Anybody now moving in gets a printed booklet, *Welcome to our Beautiful Village*, with a road map – a heady touch in a place that has so few roads. It introduces them to the parish council and the flower arrangers; they are told when the mobile library calls (twice a month, by the once-loved pond), where the surgery is and the village garage. The need to clean up after their dogs is impressed on all newcomers in heavy type.

Meanwhile, their own Bayeux Tapestry has been unveiled: a collage of the village sewn by residents, which is 20 feet by 5 feet, the length of the village hall. And now they have their own history, which cost £3,183 for 750 copies. Mrs Prescott collected £2,190 from local people and the firm which negotiated their motorway compensation. The shortfall she met herself, but sales have been such that she is now £300 in profit.

It can be done. I would do it myself had I not just experienced a moment of truth in my literary ambitions. Those of you who urge me to get these columns published will be interested to learn that, finding my daughter deluged with homework, I wrote an essay for her on her grandmother. It came back marked B-plus, with the comment 'lively'. One little girl got an A.

10 February 1982

The Hamlet with No Place on the Map

Colin Randall

The Somerset hamlet of Walpole has a population put at 24, a BP oil terminal, three busy wharves, a road haulage training depot, a garage, an hourly bus service, and a problem of identity.

Now one of the 24 is seeking a rates reduction because of the hamlet's isolation.

People living in the small group of cottages and farmhouses forming residential Walpole, three miles from Bridgwater, have Dunball postal addresses, Puriton telephone numbers and are in the parish of Pawlett.

There is no 'Walpole' signpost, and no street sign, and no trace of the name can be found even on fairly detailed regional maps.

During the recent floods firemen reached the general area within minutes but then spent up to half an hour looking for Walpole itself.

In truth, this all seems to be more or less as the majority of residents want it. Only one inhabitant, Mr Satch Kernick, a relative newcomer, has been associated with the demand for a rates reduction.

In fact Harry and June Fleetwood yesterday displayed unqualified contentedness after 25 years in Walpole.

'We used to have fun with people trying to explain where we lived but we are really perfectly happy being left to get on with our lives in peace,' said Mrs Fleetwood.

But if Walpole is not quite the neglected community of Mr Kernick's imagination, there are grounds to indicate that it is largely unknown. At Bleak Bridge, little more than two miles away, two middle-aged locals, when asked the way to Walpole, had never heard of it.

Even in the Henry Fielding Inn, which is in Dunball 200 yards due south, Mrs Karen Sammons, the barmaid, resounded with an incredulous 'Where?' at mention of the mere name.

But then, the Henry Fielding has an identity crisis of its own. A framed sign on the wall records that the cricket-playing novelist, and Whig politician, was born at Sharpham Park, nine miles away in 1707.

'And not a soul seems to know where that is either,' said Mr Ken Butler, the licensee.

2 October 1982

'Mr and Mrs Gorsuch, I presume . . .'

Brian Silk

Dr Paul Gorsuch and his son, Dr Paul Gorsuch Jnr., from Texas, paid a visit to the village of Walkern, in Hertfordshire, yesterday, and kept coming across other people with the same name.

'It's a bit confusing being surrounded by everyone called Gorsuch,' said Paul Snr. 'Back in the States I don't know any other Gorsuch outside the family. In San Antonio, where I come from, I'm the only Gorsuch in the phone book.'

In Walkern, there is nobody with the name Gorsuch to be found in the telephone directory or any other list of the 1,000 inhabitants. But 35 Americans and 45 people from the rest of Britain, who arrived in the village yesterday, were all descendants of the Rev. John Gorsuch, a local rector in the 17th century.

The two doctors from Texas were taking part in a grand reunion of the Gorsuch clan, an event organised by a group of villagers who thought it might bring in some extra money for the £50,000 church restoration fund.

Mr and Mrs Michael Overman have spent two years compiling a list of the Gorsuch family. 'It started when we read about the rector who was here from 1632–1642,' said Mr Overman, breaking off a conversation with someone called Gorsuch. The Rev. John Gorsuch was a Royalist during the civil war who came to an unpleasant end after being chased out of the village by some of Cromwell's men. He hid in a haystack and died from suffocation. Widow Gorsuch was left alone with 11 children. She went off to the New World with six of them and that is how the family grew on both sides of the Atlantic.

The Overmans have managed to trace 863 Gorsuch descendants in America, as well as a couple of hundred in Britain. The 80 who answered the invitation to visit Walkern will spend the weekend enjoying such entertainments as a Son et Lumière and coach tours. Mr and Mrs Overman also have ideas on how the Gorsuch family can help with the restoration fund, but they are keeping that as a surprise item at the end of the visit.

Meanwhile Dr Paul Gorsuch Snr was happy looking around the village where his folks came from. 'It's really wonderful,' he drawled as other visitors nearby were getting to know each other. 'How do you do, Mr Gorsuch. My name is Gorsuch and this is Mrs Gorsuch.'

19 March 2005
Local Shop for Local People
Anthony Gardner

If the word 'empowered' could be used without blushing, it could be applied to the villagers of Tackley in Oxfordshire. Five years ago, following the closure of their only shop, they decided to take matters into their own hands. Today they own and run an emporium that stocks not just lightbulbs and loo paper, but gluten-free muesli, locally raised venison and freshly baked pain au chocolat.

Not satisfied with a delicatessen, they have also incorporated a post office, a café, an internet station and the village hall into their scheme. With a full-time manager and a team of more than 50 unpaid volunteers, the shop offers a model for every rural community. The recent report by the National Audit Office, which recommended the closure of one post office in five, was a sobering reminder of why experiments such as Tackley's are so urgently needed.

With Oxford only 10 minutes away by train, Tackley (population 1,000) could easily have become just another dormitory village. 'It felt as if the whole infrastructure was disintegrating,' says Barbara Vaughan, who took charge of the project with a fellow NHS development consultant, Gill Withers. 'Our post office had closed and so had the shop, and one of the two pubs; even the paper round had gone. So we got an action group together and sent out questionnaires asking what people wanted.' On the villagers' wish list were fresh bread, fresh vegetables, alcohol and dry cleaning – all of which the shop supplies.

The decision was made to build on to and revamp the old village hall, which had all but fallen into disuse. Not only was it perfectly placed – beside the local school, with plenty of parking space – but the idea of a small, multipurpose complex appealed to grant-giving bodies such as Defra and Oxfordshire County Council. (Eighty per cent of the £400,000 bill was met by grants, and the rest from fundraising events.) A year after its reopening, the hall is regularly used for drama, yoga and keep-fit classes, all of which provide income – and customers – for the shop.

Many of the villagers offered free professional advice. One acted as a health-and-safety guru, another did the preliminary architectural drawings, others provided marketing, advertising and training expertise.

The stock on the shelves is a further testament to local resources. The ice cream is made in a neighbouring village; the meat section features free-range chicken and Gloucester Old Spot sausages from the prize-winning Foxbury Farm near Brize Norton; the fish comes from the Coln Valley Smokery. When National Cheese Week comes around, the manager, Samantha de la Querra, makes the short journey to Blenheim Palace to add to her impressive range.

Examine the imaginative cards on sale, and you will find that de la

Querra herself made them; admire the fresh flowers, and you will be told that a villager with a florist's business in Oxford brought them back from New Covent Garden. Should you need a film developed, you can leave it to be done through another villager's photographic company.

'The range is tremendous, but there's much more to it than that,' says Liz Reece, a career-development adviser who – like all the volunteers – does two hours in the shop each week. 'Many people say that they feel a buzz here because it's a central point where everyone talks to you.'

Another team member, Margaret Smith, used to run the village pub, but found herself depressingly isolated in her retirement. 'I was terribly lonely,' she says, 'but since the shop opened, my life has altered completely. I've got to know people again that I hadn't seen or spoken to for years.'

Others point to the healthy mixture of ages among staff and customers. Young parents can collapse in the café while their children rush around the neighbouring playground, teenagers can get work experience to put on their CVs, while pensioners are spared the cut-and-thrust of supermarket aisles.

Although it is still too early to gauge the shop's profitability, Vaughan and her team have created something many of their neighbours considered impossible. The ex-chairman of the parish council was one of the sceptics – 'But now he comes and cleans the windows for us, bless his cotton socks.'

9 January 1982
'Take the *Telegraph*'

An unsolicited testimonial from Dumfriesshire: a reader recently moved to a village there overheard a villager of long standing ask the local bus proprietor: 'Who's living in the cottage now?' The reply: 'I don't know their names but they're nice people. They take the *Daily Telegraph*.'

31 May 1980
No Instant Coffee

Sign in a Berkshire village shop: 'No instant coffee until tomorrow.'

Peterborough

18 April 1992
Another Country
W.F. Deedes

'Can we begin with Stanley Baldwin?' I say to Julian Agyeman, founder member and chairman of Black Environment Network. He is a Yorkshireman, born of an English mother and a Ghanaian father, who works in London as an environmental education adviser.

Foremost among his concerns is what keeps black people away from our countryside.

When English Nature, a government agency, recently announced that it will no longer describe trees or plants as 'native' or 'alien', thus felling our native oak, Agyeman's BEN welcomed the decision as a victory against 'biological racism'.

Armed with a copy of Baldwin's speeches, I invited Agyeman to read one delivered to the annual dinner of the Royal Society of St George in 1924, which established Baldwin in the public's mind as a sort of politicised Lord Emsworth. 'To me,' said Baldwin, 'England is the country, and the country is England'.

'The sounds of England, the tinkle of the hammer on the anvil in the country smithy, the corncrake on a dewy morning, the sound of the scythe against the whetstone, the sight of the plough team coming over the brow of the hill, the sight which has been in England since England was a land, and may be seen in England long after the Empire has perished and every works in England has ceased to function, for centuries the one eternal sight of England. The wild anemones in the woods in April, the last load at night of hay being drawn down a lane as twilight comes on . . .'

No politician would dare to talk like that now. Agyeman reads the speech thoughtfully. Only in the English language, he points out, 'does the word "country" mean both nation and countryside. Which leads to a feeling that the countryside is the place where things are natural, where things are . . .'

'Where the English spirit is buried?' I suggest.

'But it's not. It's alive'

'With the bluebells in the wood . . .'

'Exactly,' says Agyeman. 'When you look at it, 90 per cent of Britain is countryside. Only 10 per cent is urban. And the minority groups . . . they're not exactly trapped – that's not the right word. But they live off 10 per cent – or less – of the landscape, and very rarely venture out into the other 90 per cent. Which I find very interesting.'

Alone of almost all European societies, Agyeman insists, we don't like urban society. Unlike the Belgians, the Dutch, the Germans, the French, we do not have civic pride. He looks at the speech again. 'As Baldwin said, "England is the country, and the country is England."' There is a pause.

'Look at advertising, Bill. Look at what you see on television. They portray archaic landscape, never-changing landscape – where there are still "buxom wenches" milking cows. Whereas in fact they factory farm down there. Advertisers like the small field hedgerow.'

'The English idyll?'

'Idyll. Yes. So the public is sold the image subliminally. They're told, "This is really where your heart is; and when you've made your money in the town, in the city, this is where you come back to – where your spirit belongs."' One of Agyeman's friends at University College has done some research which shows that the most active people in a village action group are the newcomers. They want to keep the place the way it is – or the way they conceive it should be.

There is a concept in geography, Agyeman explains, called 'museumisation', which is often the aim of the newcomers. I confessed that, as president of my county's branch of the Council for the Preservation of Rural England, I had come to much the same conclusion, without the benefit of research.

People, Agyeman goes on, leave the city for different reasons: retirement and so on. 'But I suspect that some of the reasons for leaving are perceived links between rising crime, rising poverty, rising homelessness and – there's always a hint of this in the media – the minorities. These minorities occupy a very weak position in society.'

We branch off into ecology and discuss this debate within the conservation movement about what are called 'native' and 'alien' species. I had talked to George Barker of English Nature about the death of our 'native oak'. He argues that the old jargon is lazy and inexact. Guidance to schools or local authorities is better expressed by phrases such as 'appropriate to particular areas' or 'best suited for the site'. Most blacks, he agrees, do not give a hoot about the words 'native' or 'alien'. 'Those who take umbrage tend to be local minority leaders.'

Native species, Agyeman explains to me, came back of their own free will from the ice ages. Aliens are species introduced by humans. 'Among conservationists there's a great dislike of alien species. They seem less worthy in wildlife terms than the native species – because the natives have had time to equilibrate with local ecology. Conservationists accept aliens in confined areas – like gardens, where a lot are introduced. But they want to keep them behind garden walls. We're talking on the sort of mental plane whereby I feel there is a similar desire to keep black people in the cities.'

I point out that when Hungarians and Poles and others came to this country during and after the war, there was much muttering in the villages. 'You notice,' says Agyeman, 'I haven't used the word racism. It is not racism. It is xenophobic reaction to the outsider.'

We talk about his recent visit to America, to which he carried a mixture of fears and expectations. 'I stood in a crowd at a baseball match and looked around at this melting pot of people; and when the national anthem came on, they all stood up, looking proud. They are Americans, because they want to be Americans. Well, I'm English, but I'll never be accepted, despite my accent.'

He claims that none of the bodies looking after race relations is much interested in his concerns, but he is impressed by the Countryside Commission. 'I've been badgering them. They've turned round.'

But none of their publications or policies showed a positive image to black people. 'How many rangers, how many Commissioners are black? This isn't racism; it's parochialism.' Nonetheless, he is confident that the Commission has 'turned the corner'. They have treated the subject sympathetically in published material.

I point out that the minorities do not show great enthusiasm for a day in the country. Agyeman accepts this and starts to list the reasons. 'Minority groups tend to go for activities they know are safe . . . they have no experience of the countryside.

'There are also cultural reasons for not going to the countryside. When you look at it, most minorities in Britain come from rural areas. The city is associated with progress, with moving forward. To go back to the land is failure.'

'So the countryside is seen as something they have escaped from . . . and do not particularly want to go back to?'

'Exactly. The countryside is associated with backwardness, with farming.

Nigerian students are all doing business classes or law. Business is the big thing. South-East Asian students, they do engineering.' Agyeman adds that in many minds the countryside is associated with spirits – and worse. 'You won't see Asian people or West Indian people walking in long grass, because there is a residual fear of snakes.'

On the other hand, we recalled, back in the 1960s when the dominant ethos in race relations was 'assimilation', local authorities were encouraged to open country homes for foster care and so on. 'The kids loved it,' said Agyeman. 'They helped on the farm. They went out fox-hunting. Later they hankered after this childhood in the countryside.' I said I thought this had happened to some of the children evacuated during the war. Later they looked back on that existence longingly.

'Today,' added Agyeman, 'most children think the countryside is boring. You say, "All right, we'll go for a walk." "Where are we going?" "We're just going for a walk." "But we've got to be going somewhere."' Yet there is evidence of landscape linking. 'They'd see a field, a wheat field. "Look, sir, that's just like home." Some Asian girls, Kashmiri girls, went to the Black Mountains in Wales, and they said, "It's just like back home."'

Julian Agyeman enjoys saying that there were Africans in England before the English. There was, he insists, a black Roman division on Hadrian's Wall in the 1st century AD. It was, he thinks, commanded by a Libyan general. 'Let's tell people that.' There is a plaque on Harewood House outside Leeds, he insists, claiming that it was built on the proceeds of investments in the West Indies. 'What does that mean to you, Bill? Why don't they come up straight and say it was built on the proceeds of slavery? A bit of honesty would go a long way towards getting black people out to see what was there. People like the National Trust could get a lot of sympathy.'

I decide this is a bridge too far. 'If I made my house over to the

National Trust, and they wanted to put up a plaque declaring that my grandfather was a slave driver . . . I would hesitate . . . well, I wouldn't give it to them.'

Agyeman concedes, with a laugh. 'All I'm asking for is some honesty. As a teacher in Carlisle, I'm not aware that the kids up there were told there was a black Roman . . .'

We're back on Hadrian's Wall again, and I am determined to make a point of my own.

'The countryside,' I say, 'it's the last fort, and it's under fire. The British feel a lot has been taken from it in recent years. Our people in the countryside feel that things are going away from them. Now we're to be Europeanised . . . There are two sides to this, nervousness on both sides . . .'

'Exactly.' Agyeman accepts my point, which pleases me. I feel I should say something helpful by way of conclusion.

As we part, I say to him, 'What about Black Environment Network coming out in favour of field sports . . . ? Blacks for Fox-hunting. That would win them a lot of marks in the countryside just now. Come on.' There is no reply. But Julian Agyeman has a thoughtful look as he leaves.

13 November 1976
Finest View in Britain
J.H.B. Peel

Where is the finest view in Britain? Questions of that sort evoke a lively response. Moreover, the liveliness will contain some surprises because 'finest' is often a synonym for 'best-loved', as, for example, the view from Hotley Lane on the edge of Prestwood in the Buckinghamshire Chilterns.

If you descend a few yards from the summit of that lane you will notice a cottage beside a cart track on your left, and if you follow that track you will notice another cottage on your left, and if you then look to your right you will see a meadow which slopes so steeply that it hides the farmhouse in a valley whence the fields climb to a summit of beechwoods stretching left and right, far as the eye can see. Two-thirds of the way up, overlooking a No Through Road, stands one of the smallest churches in Britain, a whitewashed medieval church with a timber Tudor porch. Westward the hills sweep out of sight and are crowned by an even higher hill which creates an impression of distance enhanced by mystery. All in all, the view combines intimacy and spaciousness, height and depth, woods and pastures, solitude and companionship; and the same may be said of thousands of other views in Britain. But I own myself partial because for 35 years I saw the view whenever I glanced up from my desk.

Impatient Scots are waiting for me to praise Ben Nevis, the roof of Britain, more than 4,000 feet above the sea. For perhaps six days in each year the Ben offers maximum visibility, scanning its native land and far beyond, even to the Irish coast. But you do not need to reach the summit in order to gain an impression of height. A few hundred yards short of the top is a narrow ledge, from which you peer down dizzily at a much lower ledge, from which – an hour earlier – you had dizzily peered down at a hostel in the foothills.

'One of the loveliest scenes in England . . .' so says a plaque on the churchyard wall above the River Lune at Kirkby Lonsdale in Westmorland. That testimony, by the way, came from a connoisseur of beauty, John Ruskin. Here, then, is the Prestwood view writ large, with a river to water it, and across the river a surge of green pasture toiling to the brow of Barbon Fell.

And so it goes on, the lucky dip from which your own choice has a million-to-one chance of emerging . . . the view of Lynmouth harbour, deep as the waves, and over it Lynton, high as an eagle, seen from Countisbury in Devon; the view of Stroma, snowcapped under a blue sky, seen from John o'Groats in Caithness; the woods around Battle, site of the Battle of Hastings, seen from Netherfield in Sussex; Bodmin Moor, stony and many-tracked, seen from Brown Willy, Cornwall's apex; Dunkery Beacon, the pinnacle of Exmoor seen from the Brendon Hills in Somerset; Golden Cap and the English Channel, blazoned vert on a field azure, seen from the hills above Shipton Gorge in Dorset; the Eden Valley and the Lakeland peaks, jagged as the ramparts of a ruined city, seen from Cross Fell in Cumberland; Houseman's 'coloured counties' and Quiller-Couch's 'pastoral heart of England', seen at sunrise from Bredon Hill in Worcestershire.

And still it goes on . . . Scotland and the Isle of Man, seen from Slieve Donard, nearly 3,000 feet above the waves that lap the edge of Ulster's Mourne Mountains; the Long Mynd, seen from the Roman Watling Street near Church Stretton in Shropshire; the Quantocks, birthplace of *Lyrical Ballads*, seen from the Beacon at Malvern in Worcestershire;

Tan Hill Inn, England's loftiest, seen from the Pennine Way near Hawes in Yorkshire; the Roman lighthouse, crowning the white cliffs of Dover, seen from a ship in the Channel; The Cheviot, Northumberland's high point, seen from the lane near Ingram; the summit of Snowdon, almost as majestic as the view there from, seen near the precipice at Clogwyn du'r Arddu; the Cotswolds, carved like a blue and static wave, seen from the Ridgeway above Inkpen in Berkshire. There indeed are Marlowe's

Hills and Valleys, dale and field
And all the craggy mountains . . .

The race, however, is not always to the distant nor yet to the lofty. If, for example, you enter the Fens near Spalding, you will find a lane – indeed, you may find a dozen lanes – from which, when you lie down in the sun, nothing is visible except the ears of golden corn swaying beside the verge. When you peer above the corn, still you see only more corn, equally golden and likewise swaying, but when your eyes have adjusted themselves to the glare, you notice a farmhouse marooned in an ocean of corn and if you approach the house you will probably discover that the track leading to it is flanked hip-high by the harvest.

Where, indeed, is Britain's finest view? Rural sentiments must not be allowed to contradict urban facts. When Wordsworth stood on Westminster Bridge he said simply:

Earth has not anything to show more fair . . .

Again, if you venture into one of the alleyways near the summit of Highgate Hill you will look down on a panorama of London . . . secular towers, ecclesiastical steeples, commercial chimneys, residential roofs. Nor is that all, for in clear weather you will sight the Kentish hills and the pageant which impressed Defoe: 'A view over the whole vale, to the city,' he wrote. 'And that so eminently that they see the very ships passing up and down the river for 12 or 15 miles below London.'

If you venture further into bricks and mortar – say, among the back streets of Manchester and Glasgow – you will meet people who, when they return from their holiday at Clacton or Corsica, glance round at the mean houses, the omnipresent gasworks, the derelict canal, and with a sigh of relief murmur: 'Eh, but it's good to be home.'

17 February 2012

What's So 'Great' About Our Countryside Anyway?

Michael Deacon

You know Britain's in a bad way when we're reduced to bragging about our geology. Don't worry about recession or cuts or unemployment – we've got some first-rate granite, and don't let anyone tell you different. This, it seemed, was the message of *The Great British Countryside* (BBC1), a new series that attempts to rouse feelings of chest-thumping patriotism by telling us that our lumps of rock are better than everyone else's lumps of rock.

Britain, we were proudly told, has 'breathtaking landscapes that are world class in their variety' – indeed, it has 'a bigger variety of landscapes crammed into it than anywhere else in the world'. We have 'the moors, fantastic countryside . . . something for everyone'. 'Dramatic', 'incredible' and 'very special', this is 'the great British countryside. Beautiful, glorious. And very, very old'. On the soundtrack, strings soared majestically. It felt like the *Last Night of the Proms*, but with slightly more talk of magma.

Our hosts were *Countryfile*'s Julia Bradbury and the comedian Hugh Dennis. Dennis may not have much documentary experience, but he knows what he likes, and that's Britishness. The bit of the Cornish coast where King Arthur is meant to have been conceived, for example. 'You can't get much more British than this!' he beamed. Another thing that's very British is the British weather. 'It shows how British I am, because I love it,' he cried, above the wind. 'And I'm confident it's going to brighten up later. And that's the most British thing you can say!'

In recent years our landscape has become a favourite topic of TV's. *Coast*, *Britain from Above*, *Martin Clunes: Islands of Britain*, *This Green and Pleasant Land*, *Making Scotland's Landscape* . . . You might say Britain has a bigger variety of landscape documentaries crammed into it than anywhere else in the world. This latest one is very bitty: last night's edition included a copper mine, a lighthouse, ponies, surfing, an ichthyosaur fossil. Nothing was examined in depth. Each subject would arrive, be praised for its stunningness and Britishness, then make way for another subject.

Is Britain's landscape worth the time TV devotes to it? String me up for treason, but I'm not convinced our countryside, much as I like it, is 'world class'.

We don't have the highest mountains. We don't have the longest rivers. We don't have the biggest lakes. We've got no Mediterranean beaches, a dearth of tropical rainforests, and precious few polar ice caps. Mainly we've got drizzle and dykes. *The Reasonable British Countryside* – that would have been a more apt title. *The Perfectly Serviceable British Countryside. The It-May-Not-Be-Much-But-It's-Ours British Countryside.*

And if it sounds as though I'm doing Britain down – well, hey, that's 'very British' too.

29 April 2001
The Countryside is Another Country
David Sexton

Why are all the 'countryside debates' turning out to be so peculiarly useless? Radio 4 had its roadshow *Countryside Debates* earlier this year, to no great purpose. Radio 3 took its turn on Wednesday night with one of its leisurely, themed evenings, titled *In a Green Shade*. It was, in many ways, even worse.

The evening was hosted by the 'cultural historian' Patrick Wright, chairing a panel of experts in the studio: the 'environmentalist, writer and campaigner' George Monbiot, the 'rural historian' Alan Howkins, and Caroline Davies of the 'Rural Stress Information Network'. They all talked around a set of feature programmes, for no less than three and a half hours.

In *Rebuilding Jerusalem*, Wright himself presented a documentary about utopian groups who had moved to the countryside, from the Salvation Army to the 'Bruderhof'. In *The Echoing Green*, Jonathan Bate took a look at the role the countryside played in the work of writers such as Jane Austen, distilling the argument of his recent book of 'ecological criticism', *The Song of the Earth*. In *From Cottages to Cowsheds*, the architecture critic Jonathan Glancey looked at recent building in the countryside, calling for more innovation and fewer dreary estates.

It was obvious from Wright's opening remarks that the entire evening would have remarkably little connection with the everyday realities of life in what remains of our countryside. Instead, it was to be another excursion into the world of 'images' and 'issues'.

'For generations, evocative images of country life have served to fire dissent, to sustain the public will at times of dispute or warfare, and to measure the health of the nation at large.' So there we were before we had begun, in the land of images where no man lives.

Wright went on to say without qualms: 'We're going to be reviewing the countryside, its virtues and crises, its historical traditions and its future prospects.' The countryside, he told us, is 'a symbolic repository in which many generations have placed their hopes and fears'. That's true in one sense. In another sense, it's completely untrue. The countryside is not symbolic, it's a fact. Or it was.

Off he went, asking his guests what 'that word "country"' brought to mind. The rural historian replied: 'A divided image, really.' The rural stress lady more or less agreed: 'I think the word that comes to my mind is "diversity".' George Monbiot was, as usual, fluent in the pursuit of his own political agenda. 'I see the countryside, I guess, as a place of suppressed conflict in which the class and economic divisions which you see more clearly in the towns tend to be smothered by a culture of deference, really. There's a false consensus which is pretty well built around a cultural and political edifice built by landed power originally, and increasingly by financial power . . .' And so on.

Wright seemed pleased. 'We'll be unpacking these images in the programmes to come,' he promised, unpacking images being very much the kind of thing that cultural historians do for their supper. There was no end of such talk. A woman from the Countryside Commission told us that the countryside had 'a deeply intricate cultural freight on it'. We were invited to look at 'other latencies' and 'constant resonances'.

All that was agreed, repeatedly, was that there was no single countryside, but diverse countrysides. Or it might more simply be said that there is precious little real countryside left, in England at least, compared even to the countryside of living memory. That, perhaps, is why all these countryside debates are so unreal too.

Among all this chatter, there came a voice speaking clearly in one of the letters from the sticks. The novelist Rachel Cusk now lives on

Exmoor. She argued that if her version of the country life was a fiction, it was none the worse for that. 'Landscape is a construction now in English life: it is defined by its perilous innocence, by the negatives of "unspoiled" or "untouched". The spoiling forces teem at its boundary, casting their shadows.' This is the countryside we all recognise.

Just down the road, beyond the National Park, ordinary countryside begins, with its caravans and development. 'If Exmoor is a fiction, then that perhaps explains my feelings of sympathy with it . . . Exmoor breathes on like a lung, green and empty, life-giving, for the moment at least safe. Its realities are not those of the world around it but then again, neither are mine,' said Cusk.

Most people who talk about the countryside are talking about their own countryside, their own lives. It's just too amorphous to do otherwise. Here was somebody doing so openly. Cusk's reward was to be reprimanded later in the evening by one of the earnest trolls on the panel.

'I quite honestly was quite horrified by one of the earlier contributors who was talking about caravans and holiday camps which seems to me the worst kind of snobbery . . .' he grumbled. Actually, anybody who visits our coastline knows well that one of the quickest ways to improve its looks would be to burn caravans in those great pyres, instead of cattle.

14 November 1993

A Memory as Old as the Century

Byron Rogers

Our Oldest Inhabitant leaves us tomorrow. He is 93 years old and it will be the first time, apart from during the Great War, he has been away from the village. With his usual neatness, he has arranged his photographs of streets, school and church, adding some of his old garden, so that his memories can be indexed in the residential home 40 miles away.

He is full of enthusiasm, being tired, he tells me, of cooking for himself. Also, slowly over the last few years, he has begun to appreciate how very old he is.

Recently he had a photograph printed in the newspaper, which he had taken in 1931, when he and some colleagues from the motor trade went on a day's outing to Fort Dunlop. He hoped it would prompt some response, but there was none. 'That's when it dawned on me they were all dead.'

Four years ago he went to a reunion of Royal Air Force mechanics at which everyone was given a number referring to his year of entry – but his own was so much earlier that nobody had thought to include it. Those who turned up in 1989 at RAF Halton were startled to see a small gentleman ambling round with a badge with a large zero attached to his lapel.

He was born here in a farmhouse in the fields, now in ruins. He courted his wife in the house I now occupy; she lies in a churchyard I can see from my window. He opened the first village garage and wrote the first village history, of which he is part, for in the old school records his name recurs.

Across 80 years he has kept his exercise books, all in immaculate copperplate, even a rare mis-spelling. Manoeuvres. Manoeuvres. Manoeuvres. Each one was written out 10 times, for this was when teachers cared about such things.

In the spring of 1914 Europe was a parade ground but the Oldest Inhabitant was writing over and over 'Representative Government. Representative Government. Representative Government.'

But then there were no more worries about representative government for it was September 1914. 'The Austrians have been badly beaten by the Serbs and the Russians are on their way to Berlin. The Germans are in full retreat.'

He was 14 and believed what he read in the papers.

There is more of this, with a song about General John French also on the road to Berlin, that crowded thoroughfare. He copies out a hair-raising poem, in full, called 'Fall In' by Harold Begbie, about girls who will ignore men who haven't enlisted – all part of the pressure which was exerted on the young in village schools.

But in the midst of it one young man was planning his future with the care of a moon shot. There would be an apprenticeship in the motor trade first, he writes in an essay, then a small shop, a bigger shop, a garage. And that is how things turned out.

'If I got plenty of money and got too old to do much business, I should get a large house in the country and keep a motor and several horses and a carriage . . .' The Oldest Inhabitant, as he now is, must have been struck by his own *folie de grandeur* for he adds, in parenthesis,

'Or get a little cottage and have the old age pension and go about on a tricycle'. It is not meant as humour for this was a very serious young man.

Yet curiously, in his later years, when he began to find walking difficult, the Oldest Inhabitant bought himself an electric carriage on three wheels in which he trundled from his bungalow to the shops. 'Very true,' he said, not being one given to self-pity.

He has seen so much go in his time, that whole world of horses and blacksmiths, and a village in which everyone worked on the land or was in service ('only I branched out').

He has known 10 vicars and almost as many schoolmasters. The village railway station has gone and also the Methodist chapel ('which I then desecrated by turning it into a car showroom').

Even the strange old squire has gone: 'Funny, mousy little man with a shifty look,' who used to address the small boys on the duties of being a good citizen ('which he never was').

Even now the Oldest Inhabitant will not be drawn on the squire's little weakness, though once, badgered by me, he totted up a whole cricket team of his bastards. None of this went into his village history.

The greatest change in his long life has been the coming of strangers, for with the car came commuting, and with commuting a whole society of villagers no one sees, who are gone with the morning and return at night. The Oldest Inhabitant is leaving a village where people no longer know him, though, as he acknowledged, the irony is that, in his business as a motor trader, he has been responsible for this.

He insisted in checking every line of this column, which did take me aback; that the small boy of the exercise books should still be there, as careful as ever. 'I know you, you rascal,' said the Oldest Inhabitant. 'And I want three free copies of the paper as well.'

His name is Philip Kingston and he can now spell representative government.

2 September 2007

How *The Archers* have Been Priced Out of Ambridge

Chris Hastings and Beth Jones

Roy and Hayley Tucker's struggle to find an affordable house in a picturesque rural village illustrates a growing problem faced by young families across Britain.

So desperate are the couple to buy a property in Ambridge, the fictional setting for Radio 4's *The Archers*, that Roy's father Mike is even considering selling his own home to provide funds to help them climb on to the expensive rural housing ladder.

But according to a study carried out by *The Sunday Telegraph*, in real life neither the Tuckers nor most of their fellow villagers could afford to live in Ambridge, where the main characters boast a property portfolio worth almost £40 million.

The astonishing value of the 26 properties featured in the programme, respected for its accurate portrayal of rural life, has surprised fans of the radio soap first broadcast in 1957.

'The residents of Ambridge are unbelievably lucky in the property sense,' said a spokesman for Archers Addicts, the show's largest 'unauthorised' fan club. 'All the characters manage to stay in the village, even if they can't afford to live there.

'There is definitely a house fairy in Ambridge, who magically appears and makes houses available to people when they need one. How they afford it is anyone's guess.'

The value of the houses was calculated by estate agents working in Inkberrow, the pretty Worcestershire village that provided the inspiration for Ambridge and where house prices have soared by 159 per cent in the past six years. Provided with detailed descriptions of the properties owned by the characters, they were asked to calculate what those homes would cost if they existed for real in Inkberrow.

The three firms – Timothy Lea and Griffiths in Evesham, Knight Frank in Worcester, and Allan Morris in Pershore – concluded that a third of the properties would cost more than £1 million and that, in total, they had a value of £37.5 million.

Ambridge's most expensive property, the 1,585-acre Home Farm, owned by Brian and Jennifer Aldridge, is valued at £6 million. Other valuable properties include Brookfield Farm, owned by David and Ruth Archer, which has a price tag of £2.5 million, Grey Gables Country House Hotel, bought by Oliver and Caroline Sterling, at £3 million, and the £2 million Lower Loxley Hall, home to Nigel and Elizabeth Pargetter.

Some of the characters own more than one property. Lilian Bellamy, who lives in the £2.5 million Georgian Dower House, also has a half share in The Bull, the village pub, which is valued at £600,000. In addition to Grey Gables, the Sterlings own the 50-acre Grange Farm which would fetch £1 million.

The high prices would also affect those who rent in Ambridge, making it difficult to save enough to keep up with the rising costs of buying a home. For example, tenant farmers Tony and Pat Archer would find it impossible to raise the £2 million needed to buy the 172-acre Bridge Farm which is their home.

Audrey Steel, a district councillor in Inkberrow, where the new health centre has just been named Grey Gables in honour of Ambridge, said local people could not compete with the property portfolios of their fictitious counterparts. 'People do love the programme but £1 million for a property is stretching it a bit,' she said.

Explaining how the difficulties faced by the Tuckers were shared by many in Inkberrow, she said: 'Young people have had to move away and are being pushed into the towns. It's emptying our village of young people.'

Earlier this month, a report by the Halifax bank revealed that house prices in the country were 14 per cent higher than in towns, with the average price of a rural property now standing at £246,104.

Adam Sampson, the chief executive of Shelter, the homelessness and housing charity, said: 'There are spiralling property costs in the countryside which means that property in many people's areas far outstrips their means. Young people especially are being driven out of the villages in which they grew up in a search for accommodation.'

7 August 1982

Those Who Don't Poke
Their Noses

The telephone kiosk came late to our village. Even then it was not conceded to an automatic exchange. A village woman plugged up the calls as they came in. As a boy, if I wanted to speak to my father, the operator would quickly tell me that he was not at home. She would also tell me where he was going and what he intended to do when he got there.

She blatantly listened in to everyone's conversation. It was not that she was poking her nose into other people's affairs, she was part of the village's unpaid-for social service. After all, why make a fruitless call when the information was freely available.

I do not recall ever hearing the word 'alcoholic' until I was at least 20 years old. We did not have alcoholics in our village. We had more than our share of drunkards. My great uncle Rainbow was not given that name for his drab way of life.

We then lived in a world in which there were no finger-wagging agents of the Nanny State telling them about brain damage caused by loss of logic capacities, oxygenation of the blood and the death of the non-regenerating liver. The village watched over Rainbow and his wastrel friends and guided their footsteps, but only when absolutely necessary. (They said the drink would get Rainbow in the end. It did. He died at 94 with a countryman's indifference to which direction he might next travel.)

A visit from the district nurse – heavily moustached, puffing and wheezing like an asthmatic badger – was a combination scandal sheet newspaper and the wireless. She was paid to participate in everyone's life, from the cradle to the grave. It was an unlimited licence to poke her own nose. Like little pigs with big ears we hung on her every wheezed word.

I live half my life in suburbia now. My neighbour, who has lived in this street for 40 years, prides himself that he does not know all the other residents by name – there are only 26 houses in the street – and that he has never spoken to some families even though they have lived here as long as he has.

As the summer ripens and the columns of weekend cars trundle out of the cities, some to weekend in country cottages, I have begun to realise that the attitude of urban insularity is being insidiously exported from town to country.

Cars numbered in thousands an hour hurtle down the Birmingham–Taunton motorway. The people in the motorway cars seem to believe, in increasing numbers, that because they have brief access to the country they have a right to say how it will be managed. But not from the countryside they visit; from the urban centres where all the big decisions are made.

Take another point: Sir Harold Wilson, as Prime Minister, removed tax relief from second homes. The idea was to penalise the rich. But the rich have continued to buy their country cottages.

And into this condition, where the gap between town and country is measurably widening, comes the person with temporary residence. They come, they appear to see very little, and they do not participate. They do not poke their noses.

Certainly the weekenders patronise the village shop, and I use the word in its less pleasant sense, and they like to have a pint in the local with the village 'characters'. But would they guide the latter-day Rainbow home? I doubt it. They are also offended if you want to know too much about their personal lives. It is not that we really want to know if that silver-haired man is married to that young woman. It may be envy, or vicarious living. Or poking our noses.

In the countryside a village jumble sale is not a means of redistributing local wealth. It is an informal parliament where often fiercely conflicting views are traded and important local issues aligned. The weekenders do not attend jumble sales. They do not want three size-15 collarless shirts with the wartime economy label, and I did not want a plated asparagus dish. But it was a small price I paid for knowing that 22 red hinds were resting up on a certain pasture. And note that precision: not a herd, but 22 specific hinds.

The village shop is not simply the place where you leave your cottage keys. You should also leave your most personal and intimate secrets there, secure in the knowledge that everyone in the entire parish will know them by morning.

A new vicar arrived, an Oxford graduate with four children at public schools. We were all deeply impressed and knew in an instant he would never get on. In the country the rich and the poor have a deep affinity because they know who they are; they do not have problems of identity. It is the middle classes, the socially aspirant and the weekenders, who irritate because they have too much of too little consequence to hide. Hiding requires isolation and secrecy, a sort of emotional drawbridge which keeps them in but does not necessarily keep us out.

The vicar's wife took a large box to the home of an elderly gardener. 'It is to put your clothes in,' she said. 'And me sit on top of it all naked and cold?' he replied.

If only she had asked. It is not that we ever poked our noses into his private life. It was the most natural thing in our world to know he was the sort of man who needed life to provide him with just one suit.

Participation is not always organising the local ecologists to clean out the pond, remove the bikes and the bedsteads. It may be just in getting closer to your neighbour even if you can smell that one suit while it is still in the next parish. Incidentally, that box is still empty. I know it without crossing his threshold . . . or poking my nose.

28 December 2006
Thank the Lord for *The Vicar of Dibley*
Gerard O'Donovan

For many of us, the most idyllic place to spend Christmas would be a peaceful English village: tiny, picturesque, with a fine church at its heart and a cast of quirky characters, from the squire of the manor down to the resident idiot, to welcome us into its midst.

And so it was this year, that more than 11.4 million viewers visited that national treasure of a village, Dibley, as *The Vicar of Dibley* emerged as the nation's most watched programme on Christmas Day. While the 2006 Yuletide television line-up certainly won't go down in television history as one of the most memorable, this was no mean achievement, overshadowing the demise of the long-serving, long-suffering Pauline Fowler in *EastEnders* by many hundreds of thousands of viewers, and knocking presumed front-runners such as *Doctor Who*, with a comparatively miserable 8.7 million viewers, into a cocked party hat (despite the draw of big name guest stars such as Catherine Tate). Even the multi-award winning *Little Britain*, which for this episode went Abroad, managed just 8.4 million.

So what is it about an enormous-bosomed lady vicar with a bob and a greater passion for chocolate than the Good Lord above that can make so many turkey-bloated, port-addled people want to spend a precious hour with her on Christmas evening? Is it just a case of festive easy-viewing, something for the generations to sit down together in front of, put up their gouty feet and enjoy one last collective giggle before the irritations common to families held at close-quarters start to make themselves felt? Or is this a true comedy classic, re-runs of which we'll be enjoying in 20 years' time?

Peter Fincham, controller of BBC1, modestly put the channel's triumph over ITV down to his 'wonderful schedule of programmes that audiences love . . . which proved an irresistible combination and show that family viewing is alive and well and in excellent health'.

Of course, scheduling plays a big part, and doubtless the show's pole primetime position, sandwiched between a milestone *EastEnders* episode and the promise of *Little Britain*, helped greatly. As for family viewing, *Dibley* did indeed deliver something for everyone, offering romance and absurdity in more or less equal measure. The Rev Geraldine Granger, 'always the vicar, never the bride', found love, lost it and then found it again (the conclusion to her romance will be broadcast on New Year's Day) and, along the way, performed a rousing version of Gladys Knight's 'It Should Have Been Me', which is bound to feature in any future line-up of Best Ever Comedy Moments.

Meanwhile, the verger Alice displayed new depths of dim-wittedness after an encounter with 'that new book of the Bible – *The Da Vinci Code*', and meekly accepting an exasperated Geraldine's instruction to go search for Narnia as she locked her in a wardrobe. The episode finished with a rather rude joke about pencils and accountants' bottoms – with luck Grandmother may have dozed off for that last one.

Of course, this wasn't a one-off rating's success. The show's enduring popularity goes deeper than that. It has been pulling in big audiences on and off since 1994, thanks largely to the sure hand of writer/creator Richard Curtis who, despite moving into a rather bigger league with such films as *Four Weddings and a Funeral* and *Notting Hill*, has always found time to return to one of his favourite characters. In a recent interview for *Radio Times*, he attributed much of the show's success to Dawn French's performance as Geraldine.

'It's pretty clear she's always been the heart and soul of the show.

Geraldine had to be very funny but also a very good person – and that's a tricky combination.'

In a nationwide viewers' poll for the television series *Britain's Best Sitcom*, *The Vicar of Dibley* surprised many by roundly beating such perennial favourites as *Dad's Army*, *Porridge* and even the critically revered *Fawlty Towers* for third place (behind *Only Fools and Horses* and *Blackadder* – another Curtis co-write). And this despite the handicap of having the less than cool Carol Vorderman as the show's advocate.

In her thesis for its supremacy, Vorderman argued that '*The Vicar of Dibley* stands alone in that at its heart it's about the struggle to be good, to be tolerant and patient and still be funny . . . and that's not easy. But it never gets overly sentimental. There's a dash of whisky in the bedtime drink, a suspender belt under the cassock. Geraldine Granger is a fantastic comic creation – and she's played by one of the greatest comic actors Britain has ever produced.'

All good points, with the definite exception of the one about sentimentality. Dibley can get decidedly treacly in places. But Vorderman went rather more astray when she suggested that the show, in its early years at least, was 'a cutting-edge social satire'. Nothing could be farther from the truth – it may have introduced, even humanised the idea of women priests at a time when their ordination was still controversial, but the intent was hardly serious.

Unlike, say, *Little Britain*, there is nothing remotely cool about *The Vicar of Dibley* and there never has been. In fact, you'd be hard pushed to find its loyal fans or even anyone under the age of 50 who will happily admit to watching it. But what it does have is all the elements of the classic situation comedy that have worked over the years, be it written in the British style by one or two writers – Curtis, or Marks and Gran, for example – or American style by a team of executive writers pumping out episodes of such classics as *Frasier* or *Friends* from a high-tech suite somewhere near Los Angeles.

At the core of any successful comedy is a strong cast of diverse, often hackneyed characters: add to Dibley's female vicar a village idiot in the form of Alice and her nice-but-dim husband Hugo, who in turn is linked (son of) to the sharp buisnessman/squire of the manor David, mix with a couple of strong personalities and the stage is set for all sorts of classic comedic goings-on. In the case of *Dibley*, it's a very middle-class stage.

In fact *The Vicar of Dibley* is a quintessentially English comedy that speaks to old, conservative middle-class values in an unscarily contemporary way. It follows in a long line of village-based situation comedies (from *Last of the Summer Wine* to *Dad's Army* and *Open All Hours*) that poke fun at the curious mix of social intensity and tolerance of life in small, often rural communities while, at the same time, clearly insisting that this way of life is to be cherished as among the best that anyone in this country could aspire to.

Above all though, *Dibley* represents an asbo-free world where really bad things never happen and kind people co-exist in harmony, disrupted only by misunderstanding and mind-boggling stupidity; where people don't feel the need to abandon centuries of tradition, just because of a clergyperson's sex, or even sexuality. Could there be a better place to spend Christmas?

The Wonders of Nature

The Oldest, Widest and Tallest
Juliet Clough

In a churchyard in Perthshire stands an ancient yew. A former editor of these pages, who disapproved of adjectives, would have blue-pencilled out that 'ancient', and, for once, I would have agreed.

Confronted with the Fortingall yew, 'ancient' seems a feeble word. Botanical experts, having wavered between estimates of three to nine millennia, have settled on about 5,000 years as its most likely age.

That makes the tree, or the two remaining fragments of its outer shell, the oldest known living thing in Europe. It was already 1,000 years old when the pyramids were built, and 3,000 years old at the time of the birth of Christ, and is still putting on a healthy flush of new growth each season.

Mike Strachan, woodland officer with the Forestry Commission in Perth, has promised me a whirlwind tour of Perthshire's arboreal champions – more of a breeze, really, in a county that includes Britain's tallest tree, widest conifer and the world's highest hedge. I could go on: tallest sitka and larch, biggest leylandii screen, widest lime. You get the picture . . . it's a big green one.

Already, I have notched up another adjective-defeater – the 100-foot high, 580 yards long beech hedge at Meikleour, planted in 1745 and officially recognised as the biggest hedge on the planet. In the sunshine, its zillion young leaves shaking off points of light like a green Niagara, it is a boundary to silence the most intractable of disputes.

En route to Fortingall, we stop at Cluny House Gardens, memorable for their own Himalayan profusion but also home to Britain's widest conifer, a monster Wellingtonia with a 36-foot waistline.

In a county well endowed with large estates, most of Perthshire's highest and mightiest trees stand as monuments to the landowning aristocracy of the 18th and 19th centuries. It was their creative efforts that, bent on improving nature both in looks and productivity, spawned these botanic giants.

At Scone Palace, near Perth, I stand spellbound among avenues of Noble firs, Wellingtonia and Western hemlock, their young needles ranging in colour from aquamarine to palest jade. The Scone Pinetum feels tranquil as a cathedral, its pillars soaring skyward to a vault of shifting, sun-filtering greens.

Nearby, its bark subsiding in rings like the ankles of a tired elephant, stands one of the Scone celebrities – a colossal Douglas fir raised from the first seed sent home from North America in 1826 by the man after whom the species was eventually named.

If there is one figure who contributed more than any other to today's Perthshire treescape, it is David Douglas. Born in Scone, he began his career as an under-gardener at the Palace, says Crawford Taylor, the estate's current woodland manager. He travelled to north-west America and as far as Hawaii, and introduced more than 200 plants to Britain – including the noble and grand firs, as well as the rather less admired sitka spruce.

Douglas's home county provided a mild climate in which American conifers could grow at twice their usual rate. Few visitors to Scotland realise how much of the greenery they view as typical is a construct, says Strachan – the result of foreign imports and forestry schemes dating from 400 years ago.

Our next sighting is a slender Douglas fir, topping 212 feet, on the banks of the River Braan, near Dunkeld. Reputed to be Britain's tallest tree, it holds sway among fellow giants in the Hermitage woodlands. Far from natural, their landscaping demonstrates the theatrical lengths to which the Romantic movement would go to manipulate nature.

Strachan explains that Ossian's Hall (the little, classical pavilion from which we admire a tumbling cataract) was originally hung with mirrors. Visitors to the 'wilderness' – contrived in 1758 by the son-in-law of the second Duke of Atholl – stood with their backs to curtains that swept open to reveal, reflected and in the round, what the poet James Thomson called 'the negligence of nature, wide and wild'.

Without my guide, I might not have given a second glance to the European larch towering over the west end of Dunkeld Cathedral. Indeed I spent several years of my childhood at school in Dunkeld, scarcely noticing it during Sunday services. In forestry circles, however, this tree is a patriarch of Old Testament venerability. The last of the five Dunkeld 'parent larches', planted in 1738, it was to become one of the forefathers of 14,096,719 larches established by the 'Planting Dukes' of Atholl in the course of the next century.

At Blair Castle, Diana's Grove makes a striking monument to the

Dukes whose initiative earned Perthshire its reputation for forestry. The late Alan Mitchell, doyen of British tree recorders, said of its two acres that it was unlikely any other area in the world contained so many different conifers of such height and volume at such a young age. Like the Hermitage, this artificial wilderness is only a minute or two from a busy main artery, the A9 from Perth to Inverness.

What about the future of Perthshire's heritage trees? It's all down to pound notes, says Strachan, surveying the amount of pruning and clearing that needs to be done. 'These trees aren't going anywhere.'

Is that so? Our last stop is in Birnam, by an arthritic oak, its limbs propped on crutches, its trunk decorated with slug trails and bracket fungus. Next to it flourishes an equally aged and enormous sycamore. They stand together, reputedly the last survivors of the forest whose branches, nearly 1,000 years ago, camouflaged an advancing army, fulfilling the prophecy of Shakespeare's three witches: 'Macbeth shall never vanquish'd be until Great Birnam Wood to high Dunsinane hill shall come against him.'

3 August 1997
Pilgrimage to Watership Down
Christopher Somerville

'A real rabbit is a terribly boring animal,' said Richard Adams. 'I'm afraid they don't sit around, like mine did, telling each other stories or helping each other out of difficulties. Quite honestly, I continue to be surprised at the success of that book.' Adams, his wife, Elizabeth, and I were sitting at the edge of a beech hanger on Watership Down. Buffeted by a strong wind, we perched on a bough fallen from a tree the trunk of which had been carved with familiar names: Bigwig, Fiver, Hazel, Silver, Pipkin.

The author of *Watership Down* had been looking forward to his favourite 'country walk and a few pints' to celebrate the silver jubilee of his classic novel. But he was still unsteady on his pins having had a new hip fitted (his third). However, it required only a few steps from the trees to command a stupendous view over 20 or 30 miles of Hampshire and Berkshire – the woods, valleys, streams, meadows and commons immortalised by Adams in 'that book'. The story about a group of rabbits in search of a safe haven, which the then-civil servant invented for his two daughters to while away tedious car journeys, was turned down by seven publishers. Rex Collings, a genial eccentric and small publisher, took on the book and, as Adams gratefully acknowledges, 'managed to get a review copy on to every desk that mattered'. It took two more years, but when the American public fell in love with the modest hero, Hazel, psychic Fiver, bluff and tough Bigwig, the 'crack-brained slave-driver' General Woundwort, and all the other rabbits of Watership Down, Adams was able to retire from the Civil Service – suddenly, and unexpectedly, a famous author.

On his beech-bough perch, Adams was musing on the appeal of his book. 'It's much easier to invent a red-blooded villain, like Woundwort, than a credible hero. I suppose what people like about Hazel is that he is ordinary and fallible. As for the book as a whole – well, my rabbits are anthropomorphised, of course; but I tried not to make them do anything that would be physically impossible for real rabbits.'

I must have read *Watership Down* a dozen times – out loud in class-rooms, to each of my four children at bedtime, and every year or so to myself for the sheer enjoyment of re-immersion in those beautiful descriptions of landscape, wild flowers, birds, water, wood and weather, all meticulously drawn at rabbit's-eye level. Now I had come on a pilgrimage to the rolling chalk downlands and lush valleys of the Hampshire–Berkshire border, the corner of English countryside where Richard Adams has lived most of his life, and which he insinuated so effectively into millions of readers' inner eyes and ears.

Hunting down the settings of *Watership Down* was not going to be difficult. A 15-mile walk along lanes and public footpaths would put me close to, or actually at the location of, almost all the book's best and most exciting episodes. A few of the settings are off-limits to a walker, sited as they are on private land – undoubtedly a contributing factor to their preservation so close to the ruthlessly developed M4 commuter corridor. As for direction-finding, the book contains its own topographical sketch map which, when teamed with OS Landranger sheets 174 and 185, is all a Watership Down pilgrim needs.

'As far as I can see,' Adams said, before we parted, 'there have really been no significant changes to the landscape in these 25 years. Even the rate of theft for new buildings and roads has slowed – although that bypass round Newbury is pitiful to see.' In the opening chapters of *Watership Down*, Hazel, Fiver, Bigwig and a handful of companions flee from their native Sandleford Warren after Fiver experiences a vision of a field full of blood. Shortly afterwards the warren is destroyed to make way for a new housing estate. Here, on the outskirts of ever-expanding Newbury, it might very well have happened during the past 25 years. But, miraculously, it has not – although the bypass works lie only just to the north.

The greatest change to the *Watership Down* landscape is in the character of its main roads. The A34 has been widened, straightened and laden with signs. The slowly moving 'hrududu' – as Adams's rabbits call every kind of motorised vehicle – has been superseded by speeding cars and lorries. Any animal trying to cross that road today would be a furry pancake within a second. The roaring and rushing A34, however, is the only busy road a *Watership Down* pilgrim comes across. Newtown Common remains as the fugitive rabbits knew it – a dark, dry, peaty world of heather, birch scrub, broom and gorse. But the growing trees of the common have blocked off the southward view that Fiver described to Hazel: 'High, lonely hills, where the wind and the sound carry . . . That's where we ought to be. That's where we have to go.'

I had to wait for my own first glimpse of Watership Down until I had followed a flinty track past Frith Wood, site of Cowslip's strange, degenerate warren of effete rabbits doomed to die in the farmer's snares. Seen from here, the downs rose like a dun-coloured wall, topped with a monstrous communications mast at Cottington Clump – what would Fiver and friends have made of that? Further to the west, Watership Down was crested by a clump of trees – the beech hanger among whose tangled roots Hazel and company excavated the Honeycomb, a communal chamber where they could gather to enjoy each other's company and tell Lapine tales and legends.

Richard Adams, the son of the local doctor, knew the area's farms and houses well. Many are woven into his tale, none more memorably than Nuthanger Farm, at the foot of the down. Here, Hazel and his companions come raiding for spare does; in the lane Hazel is shot by the farmer's man, and saved through Fiver's intuition. In the farmyard Hazel is rescued from the clutches of a cat by the farmer's daughter and returned to Watership Down in the 'hrududu' of Doctor Adams – an affectionate portrait of Richard's own father. And it is from Nuthanger that Dandelion and Blackberry entice the farm dog, in the book's denouement, up to the down to complete the destruction of General Woundwort.

The house at Nuthanger Farm stands exactly as Adams describes it, 'like a farm in an old tale . . . built of brick with a stone-faced front looking south towards the down. On the east side, in front of the house, a barn stands clear of the ground on staddle stones'. The farm lane leads to a short, sharp climb up the 'coombe', or dry valley, to meet a flinty upland track at the top of the down. One way leads to the beech hanger; the other, a grassy ride between thick thorn hedges, runs south towards the territory controlled by that uncompromising lapine overlord, General Woundwort.

Woundwort must be the most memorable villain in animal fiction. Of hare size and fox-like cunning, this formidable rabbit established and arranged the strictly run warren of Efrafa so that every tiny detail of organisation was under his own claws. Woundwort is part dictator, part soldier, part savage schoolmaster – and wholly terrible. I kept looking for him, as I crossed the long, tree-lined Roman road called Caesar's Belt and went on south along ancient downland trackways. In the vicinity of Efrafa a particularly big rabbit did dash across the track – but the Woundwort of my imagination would have made mincemeat even of this burly specimen.

General Woundwort's domain was sited by Adams where an agricultural track crosses Britain's oldest road – the ridge track called the Harroway, sunk in a wonderful and ancient tangle of oak, ash, beech, birch, elder, sloe, apple, cherry, sycamore, yew, field maple and hazel. Sadly, though, there is no sign today of burrowing anywhere around Efrafa. From the Harroway, however, I could see the railway arch and the field beyond where Bigwig and his ally, the black-headed gull Kehaar, had confronted and outfaced Woundwort. And through the valley below ran the clear, shallow River Test, down which the Watership Down rabbits escaped from the astonished General – on board a punt.

From Sandleford Warren to the Test, Richard Adams's *Watership Down* landscape remains almost wholly unaltered. So do the age-old principles of his storytelling, where heroes triumph over villains and virtue is rewarded at last: just the way a thundering good yarn ought to turn out.

25 September 1993
A Shock Wave on the Bright Water
Brian Jackman

It is 25 years since the author Gavin Maxwell came to live in the lighthouse keeper's haunted cottage on Kyleakin Island, in the narrows between Skye and the Scottish mainland. A brilliant, complex, troubled spirit, he arrived in July 1968 with a pet tawny owl and a tame otter, to pick up the pieces of a life that had little more than a year to run.

Behind him lay a long trail of sadness. His marriage had ended four years earlier. His finances were in disarray. Despite the books that had won him worldwide renown, it seemed as if his life was cursed. The latest blow had fallen in January that same year. Camusfearna, his old home at Sandaig, immortalised in *Ring of Bright Water*, had burned down; and Edal, his favourite otter, had perished in the flames.

In September 1969 Maxwell died of cancer. His ashes were buried by the shore at Sandaig, close to the cairn that marks Edal's grave, and Kyleakin Island, marooned in the mill-race tides that go churning down the Kyle of Lochalsh, was left to its ghosts and eider ducks. Now, a quarter of a century later, the same dark forces that pursued Gavin Maxwell in life are still at work. Plans are afoot to build a giant road bridge over the sea to Skye and – by the cruellest of ironies – it will run straight across the author's last retreat at Kyleakin, destroying the wild otters that have colonised it since his death.

Gavin Maxwell was only 55 when he died, but he had played a host of colourful roles. Grandson of the Duke of Northumberland, he became a wartime secret agent, shark-hunter, portrait-painter, adventurer, racing driver, traveller and naturalist. But above all he became a writer. His first book, *Harpoon at a Venture*, described his days hunting basking sharks in the Hebrides: it was an instant success. A critic acclaimed him as 'a man of action who writes like a poet'. He went on to write more bestsellers, including *A Reed Shaken by the Wind*, based on his travels with the explorer Wilfred Thesiger among the marsh Arabs of Iraq, and *Lords of the Atlas*, a historical tour de force set in Morocco.

But it was *Ring of Bright Water*, describing his idyllic days at Camusfearna with Edal the otter, which placed him firmly among the most popular authors of the century. 'The timing was perfect,' says Douglas Botting, who knew him well and whose splendid biography of

Maxwell was published this week. *Ring of Bright Water* came out in 1960, when the public was thirsting to escape from the dreariness of the 1950s, and sold more than two million copies. 'He rather resented the fact that he'd been typecast as the otter man,' says Botting. But the fact remained that Maxwell did for otters what Joy and George Adamson did for lions.

Through the evocative power of his writing he did more than anyone to focus public attention on their plight. 'Gavin's contribution to saving the otter is immeasurable,' says Botting. 'It was probably the greatest achievement of his life.' Yet there was little trace of the conservationist in his early life. He came from a class whose customary pursuits were hunting and fishing. After the Second World War he harpooned basking sharks for a living – huge, harmless fish longer than a London bus – selling the oil from their 60-gallon livers for £100 a ton.

In 1954, during his expedition with Thesiger in the marshes of Iraq, his conversion took place. He was given an otter cub, a tiny creature no bigger than a kitten. Maxwell called her Chahala. They became inseparable. Maxwell, whose private life was a constant torment, always said he got on better with animals than with people. Here at last was something he could love unreservedly. Two months later, Chahala died – but not before Maxwell the shark-butcher had unwittingly become Maxwell the conservationist. 'What he was to call his 'thraldom to otters' had begun. He returned from Iraq with another otter, a male cub called Mijbal – Mij for short – and took him to Camusfearna, his lonely house on the shores of Sandaig Bay, facing the Isle of Skye. In 1957, Mij was killed accidentally by a road-mender at Sandaig – and replaced two years later with an African otter, called Edal. By now, the story of *Ring of Bright Water* was under way.

It is one of the many ironies of Maxwell's life that in 1960, when the book was published, the conservation movement had not been born. 'At that time he had no awareness of what conservation was about,' says Botting. 'When he arrived at Sandaig one of the first things he did was to destroy all the hooded crows' nests he could find.'

But by the end of the 1960s he had become all too familiar with the threats facing Britain's wildlife. It was from Kyleakin in the last year of his life that he launched, at the suggestion of Sir Peter Scott, an appeal called the Edal Fund, to raise money for otter conservation under the umbrella of the Worldwide Fund for Nature (WWF). At that time, otters in Britain were unprotected and still legally hunted with packs of hounds. But the hunters were never their worst enemy. In the late 1950s, otters faced a far more insidious menace. Pesticides – the same toxic chemicals that were simultaneously bringing down the peregrine falcon – had begun to wipe the otter off the map. All over Britain, except in the far north and west, otters were disappearing from our rivers. In time, the most persistent poisons such as dieldrin and DDT were banned. So, too, was otter hunting, when the otter became a protected species in the late 1970s. But by then the damage had been done. In the war on wildlife the otter had become the major casualty, losing 95 per cent of its traditional territories in England and Wales.

Even today, toxins let loose more than two decades ago are reaching the otter at the end of the food-chain, and the species remains absent from most English rivers. Only in the West Country have wild otters made a promising comeback. Since 1977 they have slowly extended their range, spreading out from the Tamar, Taw and upper Torridge to reclaim former haunts on the rivers of east Devon. Elsewhere, captive-bred otters have been successfully re-established in East Anglia by Philip Wayre, who runs the Otter Trust at Earsham, on the Norfolk–Suffolk border. For 10 years, Wayre has been releasing otters, and claims complete success in parts of north Norfolk, where numbers are now back to what they were before the disastrous population crash of the 1960s.

But the chief hopes for the otter's survival in Britain rest in the Scottish Highlands and islands, where the greatest numbers remain. Yet even here they are vulnerable – the oil spillage from the supertanker *Braer* threatened to overwhelm Shetland's otters. Now, once again, the otter is under siege as plans for the new Skye Bridge go ahead. The development is highly controversial. Most of the islanders don't want it, and even some that do are critical of the choice of a concrete box-girder bridge instead of a more elegant cable bridge that would avoid Kyleakin.

The only hope for the otters of Maxwell's island lies with Dr Bruce Stevens, an Aberdeen businessman, and his wife, Veronica, who have set up a group called Save the Otters of Scotland. They believe the bridge chosen by the Scottish Office breaks the 1979 Bern Convention and the 1981 Wildlife and Countryside Act, both of which protect the otter, and have lodged an appeal with the European Parliament.

What would Maxwell himself have done? Douglas Botting is in no doubt. 'He would have been outraged. He would have taken up arms against the bridge. He would have drummed up a massive resistance and fought to the end.' But, failing a miracle from the European Parliament, the Scottish Office will have its way. The bridge will go ahead, driving deep into one of the otter's last European strongholds, casting a permanent shadow over Gavin Maxwell's bright waters and setting back the cause of otter conservation for years.

16 April 2000
Flights of Imagination
Richard Mabey

All this coming week isolated swallows, exhausted by their long flights from Africa, will be flitting in low over the beaches of the south and east coasts. 'One swallow doesn't make a summer' goes one of our best-known ornithological proverbs; but the fact is that anyone who does catch a glimpse of one of these early birds will take it as an exhilarating sign of spring, however strongly the chill easterly winds are gusting.

There is a Greek vase in the Vatican collection that shows a man and two boys watching the first swallow, with words coming from their mouths. 'Look, there's a swallow,' says the first boy. 'By Herakles, so there is,' replies the man. The other boy, his arm raised in greeting, says 'There she goes, spring has come.'

For the poet John Moat, 2,000 years later, swallows mean even more, carrying with them a vision of all they had seen on the way – 'the great rivers, the curve of the blue stratosphere, the smell of a continent burning, the thunder and drumbeat of names like Ngorongoro'.

Although we are one of the most urbanised nations on earth, we still celebrate birds in our everyday lives, both at a social and a personal level. We write letters to national newspapers about the first cuckoo, prophesy weather from the calls of woodpeckers, and good or bad luck from gatherings of magpies. We eat pheasant, race pigeons, and ornament Christmas cards with winter robins.

Birds have inhabited our prose and poetry on a vast scale, often as metaphors, as far back as the swans and nightingales of Anglo-Saxon riddles. The humble sparrow, no doubt familiar to prehistoric man, picking about the middens, appears in the Venerable Bede.

In their literary history, as well as in their personal association, birds are, above all, emblems of place and moment, reminding us of childhood homes, love affairs, golden summers. Skylarks seem to be part of the spirit of the open fields, just as dippers, with their pebble-white breasts, are the familiars of fast-flowing upland rivers and piping redshanks of salt-marshes.

At a more mundane level, birds have been emblems of football clubs and army regiments. Pubs are named after them, and among the innumerable Swans, Eagles and Falcons there is a Firecrest inn near their nestling heartland in Wendover Forest, Buckinghamshire, and a Mother Redcap (redpoll) in north London.

In St Mary's church at Selborne in Hampshire is a stained-glass window of St Francis, featuring every bird mentioned by the 18th-century naturalist Gilbert White in his *Natural History* . . . of the parish. And, right up to date, there is a strictly contemporary mythology about, for instance, the pigeons which commute on the London Underground and the bizarre industrial materials which are woven into the nests of many urban birds. The government has even included the population levels of birds as one of the indicators of the quality of life in modern Britain (and should be depressed about some of the results).

Birds Britannica, my forthcoming book, is about all these things – how intricately involved birds are in our cultural and social lives, and especially how their folklore is not something nostalgically tied to the past, but a living, evolving narrative. How is it that birds have built up such association? What is it that makes folklore such a seemingly inevitable outcome of our relationship with nature, in the face of the evidence of modern science?

At an anecdotal level, much is simply a consequence of sharp and witty observation. But human beings seem to have an inherent drive to think metaphorically, and many of the most telling stories and allusions seem close to being ecological as well as literary metaphors, to be attempts to understand how we all fit together in the natural scheme of things.

Owls, for instance, as birds of the night, have always been creatures of mystery, wisdom and foreboding. The barn owl, especially, with its flat, anthropoid face and unearthly shriek, has always been attributed with special and not always benign powers. Because it haunts ruins, it was believed to bring ruin, and from this it was a short step to the owl becoming a creature of doom in a more general way.

At the heart of bird folklore are birds' common English and vernacular names, which, as for plants, are an immense catalogue of often highly local namings which comment on appearance, sounds, habits and habitat. So there are the pied wagtail, peewit, tree creeper and marsh harrier. The long-tailed tit collected more than a score of local coinings, which chiefly commented on the remarkable coincidence of this pert, squat, mouse-like bird tucked inside an almost spherical nest made from moss, lichens, feathers and spiders' webs. It was a long pod, Jack-in-a-bottle, mumruffin, pudding bag, feather poke and in Northamptonshire, as noted by the poet John Clare, the delightful bumbarrel.

With the nightjar, a summer visitor to heathland and forest clearings, the quality of its song is its most distinctive feature. This is a far-carrying churr, uttered chiefly at dusk and dawn, and resembles a distant two-stroke engine, or a fishing reel being slowly unwound; or, as one more fanciful writer suggested, wine being poured into an empty vat. The whole performance catches the aura of hot summer twilights. The birds start reeling about 40 minutes after sunset, always from a stationary position stretched out along a branch. The song starts abruptly, seeming to come from first one direction then another as the bird turns its head from side to side. Suddenly it stops, and the bird launches itself out against the night sky, wings held tilted upwards as it glances over the heath, like a kite tugged by a child. Sometimes, if a pair are courting, they may clap their wings above their backs. So the bird was called an eve churr in Hampshire, a wheel bird in Surrey, a Jenny spinner in Cheshire, and a scissors grinder in East Anglia.

There are collective names too, such as a watch of nightingales and a charm of goldfinches (one definition of a charm is 'a blended sound of many voices': and the term may refer to the bell-like tinkle of a calling flock). Some of these collectives, like a murmuration of starlings, are bookish and probably quite modern. Some, such as a wisp of snipe and a parliament of rooks, have just a hint that they may be authentic ancient coinings. But the question has to be asked whether these vernacular names are now any more than museum pieces, remembered in books but not in use. You can still hear tom tit for blue tit, sea-pie for oyster catcher and bonxie for the great skua. But does anyone in Scotland still call a lapwing a wallopie weep?

The robin has been through several changes in its common English name. The Anglo-Saxons called it the ruddock, because of its red breast. In the 15th century it was the robin redbreast, which was shortened first to robinet and then, during the 19th century, to redbreast. Robin only came back into fashion comparatively recently, and it was not until 1952 that the British Ornithologists Union accepted it as the more or less 'official' name.

But the connection with the colour red has remained constant. The first postmen, who wore bright vermilion waistcoats, were known as 'robins', which is one of the reasons why they feature on Christmas cards, and why the robins are sometimes shown with a letter in their beak. Perhaps this also owes something to the tradition of the robin as a benign, charitable bird. It is a robin which covers the children in the *Babes in the Wood* legend with leaves, and which is the luckless victim in the 'Who Killed Cock Robin?' rhyme. In Britain, there has always been a belief that to harm a robin will bring bad luck or even death to the culprit – unlike on the Continent, where they are widely caged or killed for eating.

The magnificent cinnamon-and-cream plumaged bird of prey, the red kite, has kept its name, but has been through dramatic changes in its status and identity. In the medieval period it was common throughout England, and in early 15th-century London it made such a contribution to public health by scavenging carrion from the streets that it was made an offence to kill one – the very first conservation enactment not solely concerned with protecting hunting rights. But by the 17th century the tide had turned against the red kite. Despite being principally a scavenger, it doubtless snatched a few young chickens and game birds. And it certainly stole washing to ornament its nest. (Autolycus in *The Winter's Tale* – himself 'a snapper-up of unconsidered trifles' – warns that 'When the kite builds, look to your lesser linen').

Some idea of how common the kite was and of the scale of the slaughter is given by the churchwardens' accounts for the village of Tenterden in Kent. In just 14 years from 1677 they record the killing of 432 kites. With the spread of keepered shooting estates from the late-18th century it is no surprise that the kite was driven into extinction across England and Scotland by the end of the 19th.

But in the wilds of central Wales, where there were no shooting estates, the kites found a last refuge. Only a handful of birds had survived, but in the 1950s a group of committed Welshmen formed the Kite Committee, and were able to push the population up to 100 pairs by the beginning of the 1990s.

So kites, embattled in this small but expanding colony in the hanging oakwoods of Ceredigion, became a symbol of Welsh nationalism, a satisfying snub to the English gentry, which had exterminated them on the other side of Offa's Dyke. But the growth of the population was laboriously slow, and there was some evidence that interbreeding was contributing to this. It seemed unlikely that they would ever repopulate their old haunts over the border. So in the late 1980s the Royal Society for the Protection of Birds and Nature Conservancy Council began a project to reintroduce the kite in England and Scotland using nestlings imported from the large populations in Sweden and Spain. The project has been a great success, especially in the Chilterns, and kites sailing over the beechwoods, their plumage seemingly fringed with ermine, still seem undeniably Celtic.

But, astonishingly, the kite has again fallen foul of farmers and keepers, and many of this new population have been shot or poisoned, sometimes accidentally, but often, no doubt, because they are still seen as competitors for prey with human beings. The scapegoating of birds of prey (and many others, including naturalised immigrant birds) is the most flourishing means by which they are mythologised today. Golden eagles are demonised by sheep farmers, peregrine falcons by pigeon-fanciers, and hen harriers by grouse-shooters. Sparrowhawks, having recovered their population levels to pre-DDT days and often showing off their hunting skills on garden birds ('They use my bird table like the Ritz bar,' complained the Duchess of Devonshire), now have a Society for the Protection of Songbirds marshalled against them.

Nothing, however, can match the enmity that is raised against the magpie, which is blamed for the demise of just about every declining small bird, from the song thrush to the London spadger. People have seen magpies looting eggs and young birds in their gardens, and believe the evidence of their eyes, even though every one of the many surveys done on magpies proves that, except at a highly local level, they have no impact whatever on song-bird populations. The irony is that, outside gardens, bands of clacking, burnished magpies are still relished, and still start off the luck-chant, 'One for sorrow, two for joy . . .'

But then bird folklore, alive and well in 21st-century Britain, has always been defiantly, delightfully irrational.

9 May 2011
Letters to the Editor
Birdsong

SIR – Here in Gloucestershire our wood pigeons (Letters, 7 May) continue to sing: 'I can't say cuckoo. I can't say cuckoo. I can't say cuckoo. No.'

Alan Heywood
Eastcombe
Gloucestershire

SIR – We must have very badly behaved wood pigeons here in Shropshire because, after cavorting on the ash tree branches just outside our bedroom window, they call to each other: 'It's your fault, you know.'

Pam Wheeler
Kenley
Shropshire

SIR – My grandfather told me that Taffy was waiting by the farm gate deciding which cow to steal, when a pigeon came along and said: 'Take two cows, Taffy.'

Richard Goodbourn
Keymer
West Sussex

SIR – The wood pigeons in this part of the Midlands are evidently more censorious than those in other parts. As I often find myself translating for my husband, their song is: 'The lawn needs cutting.'

Sylvia Holt
Sutton Cheney
Leicestershire

SIR – Every year on our farm we were visited by a pair of ring doves. Their conversation was always the same and went: 'I just don't want to.

So please don't make me. I told you dar–ling. No!' The reply in a lower key: 'Now come on sweet–ie. And don't be sil–ly. You know you want it. Now!' Various pairs came and went but the talk was always the same.

Elizabeth Higgs
Badlesmere
Kent

SIR – I can't help feeling that this correspondence suggests that birdsong is the acoustic version of the Rorschach test.

Ronald Walford
Darenth
Kent

1 February 1997
The Ministers for Birdsong
Michael Waterhouse

I was alerted to the pleasure of birdsong in my early thirties by reading a remarkable book by a remarkable man – *The Charm of Birds* by Viscount Grey of Fallodon, statesman, naturalist and, as of today, our longest-serving foreign secretary.

Grey was an enigmatic character. He was one of a small group of Liberal Imperialists who, at the turn of the century, formed one of the most talented administrations that Britain has ever enjoyed. But at heart he was a countryman and a reluctant politician: he took days to make up his mind whether to accept one of the most powerful political appointments and he went abroad only once during his 11-year tenure as foreign secretary.

His private life was full of tragedy. His first wife, Dorothy, died in a driving accident. Both his brothers were killed hunting game in Africa, and his two beloved homes in Northumberland and Hampshire were burned down. He started to go blind in middle age.

The Charm of Birds is a wildlife classic. It was first published in 1927 and was reprinted every year until the outbreak of the Second World War. For me both it and its author have been an inspiration. I have happy childhood memories of that wild Northumbrian coastline where his family lived for many hundreds of years and my parents-in-law lived close to the site of his cottage in the Itchen Valley in Hampshire. About 15 years ago I embarked on my own diary of nature notes which developed into both a tribute to Grey and a celebration of birdsong.

In *A Wandering Voice* I have tried to retrace Grey's footsteps a century or so later, whether in Hampshire, Northumberland or Scotland, and to examine the birds he wrote so colourfully about. In writing it, I soon became aware of the devastating effect man has had on bird habitat and population in the years since Grey's book first appeared. At the same time I came to realise just how big a role the love of birds has played in the lives of men who have shaped the great events of the 20th century. It is not too fanciful to suggest, for example, that Grey's passion played a key part in the creation of the 'special relationship' between Britain and the United States.

On the morning of 9 June 1910, Grey, then our foreign secretary, set off into the New Forest for his famous 'Bird Walk' with ex-President Theodore Roosevelt. Having taken a train from Waterloo the two men began their journey down the Itchen valley from the little village of Tichborne and then moved on into the heart of the New Forest. During their walk they saw 40 different species of birds and heard the songs of 20 of them. They discussed politics and poetry.

The two men became firm friends and remained so for the rest of their lives. That friendship reaped rich rewards. It was, of course, American support in the First World War a few years later that ultimately secured an Allied victory. There is also an interesting parallel to the 'special relationship' developed a generation later between Grey's old Cabinet colleague Winston Churchill and Theodore's cousin, Franklin Roosevelt.

A surprising number of our prominent politicians have shared a love of birds. In the inter-war years, there was Neville Chamberlain and his Parliamentary private secretary Alec Douglas-Home, who went on to become one of the shortest-ever serving Prime Ministers. More recently two Chancellors of the Exchequer, Norman Lamont and Kenneth Clarke, have thrown themselves enthusiastically into the same extra-political pursuit.

Some people may dismiss these men as amateurs playing at ornithology and say that their observations have no serious scientific basis. There is some truth in the charge but it should be remembered that today we can draw on a wealth of modern scientific findings in analysing precisely why birds sing that was not available to our predecessors. What people like Grey possessed was a profound understanding of birds, born out of years of loving observation.

Nevertheless, birdsong is much more than a delightful gift from nature. For the birds themselves it provides an essential and extremely sophisticated communication system. In his book, *Vocal Communication in Birds* (Edward Arnold, 1979), Clive Catchpole makes a subtle point. 'Communication,' he writes, 'is rather a difficult term to define, but in general it is the process whereby the behaviour of one animal alters the probability of some behaviour in another.' On a recent visit to the Edward Grey Institute of Ornithology at Oxford University – a lasting memorial to the man – I heard Professor Chris Perrins put it more pithily: 'Birdsong is a method of attracting the girls and keeping the boys at bay.'

As a leisured Victorian country gentleman, Sir Edward Grey might have been offended by Perrins's snappy soundbite, yet *The Charm of Birds* shows that instinctively he understood the point the modern professor was making. It would be no bad thing if a few more of our present-day politicians showed the same feeling for birds and nature. Our countryside today is all too thinly represented at Westminster.

The Charm of Birds tell us a great deal about the subtle – and not so subtle – changes taking place in our rural areas. The rise and fall of different bird populations are increasingly posing vital questions for modern decision-making. At a time when we have destroyed so much of their habitat, their voices deserve to be heard – and not just for their beauty. They have something to contribute to the acrimonious debates over, for example, road-building, housing development and agriculture.

In their different ways the old romantic bird-lovers and today's more scientific ornithologists are pointing in the same direction. Take the willow warbler, one of Grey's favourites, whose song was so common round Fallodon, his home in Northumberland, that he referred to it as 'the everlasting bird'. Listen first to Grey's lyrical description: 'The notes have an endearing quality of their own, they suggest something plaintive – as if the bird were pleading. "A cadence as soft as summer's rain" has occurred to me when listening to the song, which is particularly touching.'

Now hear the voice of modern science. The willow warbler is our most numerous summer visitor, with more than three million pairs migrating from Africa to nest in Britain and Ireland. A density of two singing males per acre is not unusual. Females arrive here a week or so later and are attracted by the singing males in their established territories. A female will choose the best performer for a mate and in this way selects the fittest partner with the strongest genes for breeding purposes.

Recent studies in the Netherlands have demonstrated that this delicate communication system can be thrown into disarray by a continuous human-originated noise. Research on a local nature reserve has shown that a territorial species such as the willow warbler has a lower breeding density in areas adjacent to main roads. Three zones were designated and the road zone (within 200 metres of the traffic) demonstrated a combined density of territories 35 per cent lower than the other zones. The distortion of the male's song in the 'road zone' led to difficulties in attracting or keeping a female.

Birdsong provides us with a long list of unforgettable moments. There is, for example, the blood-curdling scream of the jay when a human enters the private world of its oakwood, unerringly described by W.H. Hudson: 'A little late a jay screamed at me as only a jay can. There are times when I am intensely in sympathy with the feeling expressed in this ear-splitting sound, inarticulate but human. It is at the same time warning and execration, the startled solitary outburst of uncontrolled rage at the abhorred sight of a fellow human being in his woodland haunt.'

Similarly, many people are familiar with the 'mink-mink' alarm call of the blackbird, warning perhaps of a foraging cat or weasel. Then there is the glorious medley of the great dawn chorus in May, a nightingale singing on a moonlit night, the annual arrival of the cuckoo and chiffchaff, the bubbling spring notes of the curlew . . .

All these have been part of the natural fabric of life in Britain for centuries. Nobody appreciated the gift of birdsong more than Sir Edward Grey. Some, at least, of his political successors recognise it, too. The rest of us forget it at our peril.

10 July 2004
It's a Bug's Life in Deepest Essex
Peter Marren

'It's an RDB1!' The entomologist deftly flicked the unsuspecting fly into a tube. RDB1s, otherwise known as endangered species in the *Red Data Book*, are the rarest of the rare, so rare that their extinction is a near-certainty unless whatever is ailing them is identified and removed.

This particular RDB1 was *Gymnosoma nitens*, a medium-sized fly. As an adult it hangs about on hogweed heads. Its larva is a parasite that eats caterpillars. From the inside. While they are still alive.

We were on the shore of Canvey Island in Essex on some rough ground by Safeways' car park. Unlikely as it seems, this plot of grassland and scrub, measuring no more than 70 acres, is the richest place for insects in Britain. 'It has more invertebrates per square foot,' says Buglife's conservation director, Matt Shardlow, 'than any other site.' It has even been called 'Britain's rainforest'.

I had joined an outing organised by the British Entomological Society. Nearly everyone had a net of some sort: tough canvas jobs to sweep insects from the grass; muslin butterfly nets for flyers and miniatures for pouncing on small fry. The bee expert had a tube fitted with a padded plunger. The spider man carried a tray fitted with a mesh lid for sifting his prey from dead leaves and soil. The fly folk used a device called a pooter for sucking unsuspecting beasties off their perch and into a tube.

Nearly everyone found at least one RDB within minutes. There are at least 30 here, including the shrill carder bee, which weaves a neat nest out of moss and whose high-pitched hum sounds like a dud light bulb just before it pops. There are also plenty of wasps, including a leggy sort that specialises in hunting spiders, and another that carries unconscious bees back to its lair, strung underneath like a helicopter carrying ammunition to the front.

And then there's Morley's weevil. Canvey Island is the only known site for this stout, snub-nosed beetle, said to be named after the environment minister, Elliot Morley.

Yet, if this bug-heaven is a rainforest, it can only be in terms of its natural diversity. There are no full-grown trees, and it doesn't rain very often. Canvey Island has a lower annual rainfall than much of the Mediterranean. And, far from being a virgin wilderness, it is a brownfield site, vacant land wedged between the oil refineries of the Thames estuary and a new superstore. The soil that supports so much wildlife is not nature's own but a mixture of dredgings from the Thames estuary and chalk brought in as top-dressing.

Why, then, is this place so extraordinarily rich in insects? Matt Shardlow believes the answer is partly where it is, and also in what it is. Canvey Island is not only one of the driest places in Britain, but also one of the sunniest. It is a natural place for warmth-loving insects that find a bare foothold in Britain. But, more than that, it boasts an unusual variety of insect-rich habitats within a confined space – warm, crumbling banks on which solitary bees can nest and bask; wet hollows and ditches where dragonflies and other aquatic insects congregate; and above all the right kinds of wild flowers – vetches for bees, sweet-smelling nectar flowers for butterflies and moths, and flat-topped hogweed, beloved of hoverflies.

You find chalk plants, heath plants and salt-marsh plants growing within a few yards of one another. This kind of close-packed variety is rarely found in the wild. It happens here because the place is effectively man-made. It wasn't designed to be a nature reserve, but that is what it has become.

Buglife is campaigning to preserve as much of the site as possible as a green open space. Planning applications to develop the site have been turned down on the grounds of its importance for rare species (it contains at least three Biodiversity Action Plan species which the government is committed to conserving as indicators of environmental health), but even so it is earmarked for development by the local authority.

As Germaine Greer, Buglife's vice-president, points out, there are plenty of business parks but only one Canvey Island. The idea is to preserve two-thirds of the site and develop the remainder as 'wildlife-friendly offices and workshops' – a plan Buglife 'cautiously welcomes'.

Walking in 'England's rainforest' feels strangely like visiting a foreign country. Apart from the hop, hum and buzz of insects, there is an unusual assortment of exotic plants among the native ones. Perhaps the goat's-rue, bladder senna, rose campion, bastard cabbage and other strays from southern Europe were brought here in soil dumped from the London docklands. Whatever their origin, they add to the dreamy atmosphere – Essex with a generous helping of Genoa. Or maybe we should see it as a homespun version of the ruins of Angkor Wat or the Mayan temples, of the proud monuments of the past swallowed up by the advancing jungle. We need such places, not only for the likes of the shrill carder bee but to sharpen our own sense of nature.

3 September 2005

Meet the Crays

Julian Rollins

If you know anything about crayfish at all, it is probably that they go very nicely between two pieces of bread with a little rocket. The crayfish has been the runaway success of the takeaway food industry over the last few years, or so they told me in a posh sandwich bar in London this week.

Apparently they are a summer thing; we eat more of them at this time of year. So next time you are enjoying your crayfish and rocket spare a thought for crayfish nearer home.

Our native crayfish is so small, growing to little more than an inch long, that it would hardly take the edge off anybody's appetite. It has also proved too small to hold its own in what is an unequal struggle with an unstoppable alien invader, the American signal crayfish.

At a meaty nine inches long, a signal crayfish dwarfs its British cousin. That is why they were brought here to be farmed for meat. A few were either released or escaped and, since the 1970s, have been enjoying their freedom, moving into rivers and canals in southern and eastern England as well as parts of the west, the Midlands and Wales.

That has been a disaster for our native crayfish. They are comprehensively out-fought every time they meet signals and are also highly susceptible to a fungal disease that the newcomers carry.

Signals have made their presence felt in other ways, too. They burrow with such enthusiasm that riverbanks collapse and no underwater plant or animal smaller than themselves is safe from their voracious appetite.

The Basingstoke Canal in Hampshire and Surrey is just one of many waterways with signal crayfish problems. The canal's angling association secretary, André Grandjean, says that as numbers of what he calls 'the Crays' have reached plague proportions, anglers have deserted the canal.

Fishing with hungry signals around is difficult, Grandjean explains. As soon as a baited hook sinks into view beneath the surface, crayfish swarm over it, fighting for a meal.

'We have been losing members because of this,' says Grandjean.

'When anglers get a bite they want to know that it is a fish on the end, not something with two great claws.'

The presence of crayfish has also changed the character of the canal. 'The little monsters eat just about everything and, over a number of years, they have stripped out all the weed,' he says. 'We used to have some beautiful big water-lily beds on the canal, but they are long gone.'

Now, however, a change in the law may be about to shift the balance against the new arrival. Catching crayfish has been illegal in England and Wales except on the Thames and its tributaries, where a special bylaw has allowed trapping on licence.

But at the beginning of June new bylaws were approved that allow crayfish to be trapped wherever they can be found. The Environment Agency is issuing 'consents' for trapping.

On the face of it, catching and eating signals has to be a Good Thing, as it takes pressure off the native crayfish population and freshwater eco-systems. But the Environment Agency is keen to stress that the law change is more about tidying up legal inconsistencies than controlling the invader.

Veterans from the crayfish frontline are inclined to agree. Tired of putting up with the crays' strong-arm tactics, Grandjean's angling association decided it was time to fight back.

Armed with a licence and crayfish traps, the Basingstoke anglers began catching signals in earnest in April 2004. A year later the canal had offered up more than a ton of crayfish.

In the early days Grandjean and colleagues were hauling out crayfish that were big enough to sell to local restaurants. Now only tiddlers are emerging in the traps, too small to yield any useful meat.

The effort has bought the canal's fishermen a respite, but Grandjean is under no illusion that it will be much more than a brief lull in a long war.

And it turns out that what the Basingstoke trappers have discovered by trial and error sits comfortably with the best available science on the subject. At the Environment Agency, Julie Bywater, an ecologist, admits that she and her colleagues are largely in the dark as to the lifestyle of the signal crayfish: they like to live in muddy water and even making an accurate population assessment is almost impossible as they retreat into burrows at the first sign of a net.

One of the few known facts of crayfish life may be important, however: they are cannibals. 'They will eat just about anything, and that includes any crayfish smaller than themselves,' Julie Bywater explains.

'So the worry is that by taking out the biggest specimens we may actually be fuelling an explosive population growth.'

Stopping this alien will evidently take something more than a sandwich or two. The best bet may be to use the species' own taste for crayfish meat against itself, she suggests.

If big male signals could be fished out, sterilised with a blast of radiation and then returned to the water, they could do the job of controlling their own kind. They would be around to cannibalise smaller signals but could not make babies of their own.

'It is an approach that has worked with other species,' says Bywater. 'But we don't yet know whether it could be done with signal crayfish. If it could it would be very costly – but that might be a price worth paying if they could be removed.'

14 February 2010
Animals Dig in for the Big Freeze
John Lister-Kaye

It is winter in the Highlands. In the marsh and the trackside ditch, in the loch's peaty mires, in the pinewood, the pulses of life have slowed and stilled. The nature of the Highlands has shut up shop; the signs have all come down. It is winter. The bugs and weevils are hiding now, the worms, the millipedes, the caterpillars and leatherjackets, the frog and the toad, adder, slow worm, wood mouse and vole, the squirrel, the hedgehog and the fat snoring badger are settled in for the long, dark cold.

This has been a Scandinavian winter and it isn't over yet. The last week has been below zero at night, struggling to 3 or 4°C by day under a weak sun. Here in the Highlands of Scotland we may be better prepared for snow and ice than further south, but we have become complacent of late. Some years there has just been a dusting of powdery snow, sometimes none at all, and the thermometer has barely dipped below zero.

For some of our wildlife this has been misleading. In warm winters hedgehogs have emerged from hibernation far too early, only to find there is nothing to eat or that the ground freezes again. While they can duck back into hibernation, it is risky and can consume too much energy too quickly so that they don't make it through to spring. But not this year. They're still tucked up in their leafy and mossy dens.

I found one quite by accident a few weeks ago. I perched on a stump almost completely rotted, a deep moss-filled crater and a rim of wood just wide enough to support my backside. I peered into its dark, fungal interior – something wasn't right. It had been recently disturbed. I pried further, carefully lifting a thick green hassock of moss. Underneath was a bed of soft, dry, fibrous and needly litter, with the sort of heady, mother-earth scent you'd expect from someone practising aromatherapy in a potting shed. I pushed my fingers into it and came to fresh, dry oak leaves. How could fresh leaves get underneath moss? Now I knew someone was at home. A finger teased gently into the leaves withdrew smartly – it was very prickly.

I couldn't resist taking a peek, so I half uncovered the fat, large hedgehog curled as tight as a clenched fist. She didn't stir, although I fancy I detected a slight firming of the furry aperture where her head and legs were tucked together, but whether this was a reflex tension that performed regardless of her torpor or whether she was not yet fully in hibernation, I couldn't say. Frosts were then nightly events, so she may have been in there for some time; although the fresh leaves she took in with her impaled on her spines as a winter wrapping seemed to suggest that it can only have been after the November leaf fall. What I found so intriguing was how she had managed to close off her entrance, somehow blocking the tunnel with leaves and pulling the moss door closed behind her.

I covered her up again, tucking her nest in around her and doing a slightly better concealment job than she had done for herself. I gathered some extra moss from another stump and laid it carefully over the top. Foxes and badgers will unroll a hibernating hedgehog and leave only its spiny skin as the evidence of their efficiency. We have plenty of both foraging through our winter woods, and while I don't believe in interfering with nature – a complicated ethic I have often struggled with – I certainly didn't want to be the cause of her demise. I finished off with a couple of dead spruce branches across the top for good measure.

So she is well out of the way, below the cold, then below snowdrift, breathing barely detectable and only a flicker of a heartbeat, down from 190 beats per minute to 20 or less. Hedgehogs' body temperatures fall from 35°C to 10°C, only the area around the heart retaining its normal temperature. Metabolism falls by 75 per cent, which is vital so that it can eke out the consumption of its precious fat reserves. Hopefully this year she will stay where she is until April.

Our winter hit in a big way back in mid-December. Suddenly we had

56cm (22in) of heavy wet snow immediately followed by a freeze. Not a fridge freeze, this was a deep freeze – actually, colder than your deep freeze. At its moonlit nadir it crashed to −18°C. That's −0.4°F in old money, what we used to call 33 degrees of frost. And it lasted for four weeks, cold sufficient to turn snowdrifts into rigid ramps and pyramids of impenetrable ice, to freeze the loch to 27cm (11in).

Power lines and trees burdened with frozen snow came down, pipes froze and avalanches of ice cascaded down roofs, bringing with them slates and guttering by the yard. Farm buildings crashed to the ground. But that is nothing compared with what happened to the poor old woodcock. This most elegant of all woodland waders survives by probing the leaf litter with its bill for insects, worms and bugs. It couldn't. For weeks they found nothing to eat at all.

My friend Peter Tilbrook picked up three dead woodcock in his garden at Cromarty and I found one in our woods so weak that I could pick it up. Wrens have been clobbered, too. Very sensibly they congregate in huddles to keep themselves warm. But many wrens, tits and tree creepers will not have survived the cold; it isn't just that they can't maintain body heat, even if they could there are no insects to eat.

On the foreshore waders have had a hard time as the sea edge and the mudflats froze like concrete. I found dead oystercatchers, and where I usually see turnstones they were absent – sensibly headed south for unfrozen stones to turn. Our grey geese, normally overwintering here on the Moray Firth in tens of thousands on the fertile stubble and potato fields, cleared off to England or the Low Countries.

Last night I went to see if our badgers were out and about, and they were. I was pleased to see two animals in good condition, perhaps helped by the peanuts we put out for them. And I saw one pipistrelle bat chasing a moth, but then the pips are remarkable. They have a much more mobile hibernation than the hedgehog. They can switch their heterothermic torpor on and off, so if it warms up in mid-winter and a few moths emerge, they can pop out for a night bite.

Many of the flying insects are dead, like the corpses of dragonflies gripped to the stems of rushes in a last embrace. Their work is done; their future lies in the eggs now secure among water-lily leaves frost-browned and rotting beneath the ice. The long-eared bats vanished from the roof long ago, migrated south in pursuit of warmth and insects; dozens of twitching bundles of fur and membranous ears jammed into the apex under the slates, there one minute, gone the next.

All but the toughest birds have headed south: the golden plovers are long gone from the hills, their plaintive calls faded away, down to the estuaries and the mudflats where they gathered in flocks before pressing on south. The high hills are empty but for the golden eagle and the snow-white ptarmigan; above the loch the buzzards scream back at the croaking jeers of ravens and hoodie crows, the only sounds, the only movement to be seen.

Our eagles will do well this winter. Red deer are starving right across the hills: an abundance of carrion dots the snowfields, and hill sheep will have succumbed too if shepherds couldn't get hay to them in the deep snow. So the eagles will come through well and we may even see an increase in chick production this spring. It's an ill wind that blows nobody any good.

30 March 1996
Prime-Time Weather in Spring

Our ancestors in their wisdom have told us that the weather in April and May is the key to the whole year: they named it the Prime Time. So what are the crucial signs?

There are many to guide us, such as 'Should it rain on All Fools' Day it brings good crops of corn and hay'. As March came in like a lamb, it is likely to end in rough weather, so All Fools' Day next Monday may well be showery.

The sayings go on with 'April cold and wet fills the barns best yet', 'when April blows his horn, 'tis good for hay and corn', and 'east wind in spring, a brilliant summer will bring'. So, what we need is cold, wet weather with an east wind – not a very attractive prospect.

Another old saw tells us the weather on Easter Day foretells the harvest. Sir Thomas More, that great sage whom Henry VIII executed, declared that the weather in the second half of April foretells the summer. And although Good Friday is another variable date, it is one of the most reliable days of prediction of all.

More immediately, the *New Book of Knowledge*, from the 16th century, tells us: 'If on Palm Sunday there be rain that betokeneth to goodness; if it thunder on that day, then followeth a merrie year.' But another belief holds: 'If the first three days of April be foggy, rain in June will make the lanes boggy'. You will find all these sayings surprisingly reliable: they have stood the test of time.

Watch the migrant birds. If the house martins build on the north side of the house, you may be sure of a hot summer. Then they say that if the cuckoo lands on a bare bough, sell your hay and keep your cow, but if he lands on the green may, sell your cow and keep your hay. As to the long-term prophecies, last September's oak apples were full of flies, which Erra Pater says foretells a meetly good year. Those oak apples have a very good track record.

Already this year the grass is late in starting to grow and it will be all the better for that. The continuing frosts of February and early March have delayed the setting of the blossom but they will also be found to have killed many spring pests to the benefit of the blossom. It could be an excellent fruit year.

It is too early to try to forecast the summer weather but, if one watches for nature's signals during the next two months, one will have a very good idea by the end of May. So far – but only so far – the signs are promising. Keep your fingers crossed.

27 April 2011
Letter to the Editor
Weather

SIR – Having enjoyed four days of splendid bank holiday weather during a family canal boat holiday, I feel compelled to write a thank-you letter. To whom should I write?

Andrew Goldstone
London N8

10 April 2004
Restoration of a Poet's Corner
Peter Marren

If only the land could speak what a story it could tell. And there is a patch of land that can be said to have spoken, through the poetry of John Clare. Swordy Well is a disused limestone quarry near Peterborough, where Clare worked as a farm labourer. In the 1820s, this was a wild landscape of bumps and hollows, a skin of soil and natural grassland over old stone workings said to date back to Roman times. It was precious, also, as home of the wild pasque flower.

Swordy Well itself was a deep pool in which someone had once found a sword. Watching his flock nibbling the thyme-scented turf, Clare was entranced by the richness of the plant life, particularly the insect-mimicking bee orchids: 'where nature's skill/ Doth like my thoughts run into phantasies'.

Swordy Well eventually became Swaddiwell Field, no longer a common but a commodity. Its transformation by plough and pick inspired one of Clare's best poems, 'The Lament of Swordy Well'. 'I'm Swordy Well a piece of land,' he declares, before describing how the land was made a pauper, no longer capable of supporting orchids, songbirds and butterflies:

> When grain got high the tasteless tykes
> Grubbed up trees, banks, and bushes
> And me, they turned me inside out
> For sand and grit and stones
> And turned my old green hills about
> And pickt my very bones.

Nearly a century later, the Society for the Promotion of Nature Reserves, inspired by Clare, rented the field as one of the first nature reserves in the country.

However, it could not prevent the land from being sold and reinstated as a quarry. After the Second World War, the quarry became a munitions dump. A nearby pit was filled with waste from a paper works which leaked rainbow-coloured dye, to surreal effect. Canisters of herbicide were buried in a third.

From a place that once revealed, in many small ways, 'great nature's plan', Swordy Well became what is said to be one of the most polluted corners of rural England. Duly filled up with rubbish, then levelled, its very contours have been planed away, its identity lost. Power lines now cross the site which, from the road, looks like any other field. You wouldn't look at it twice.

But all was not lost. The Langdyke Countryside Trust, formed to rescue sites associated with Clare, has been managing Swaddiwell for a year now, and plans to open it to the public.

And the field, it transpires, has begun to heal itself. Though the remaining quarry had become an unofficial car racetrack, its shallow pools were home to crested newts and water beetles. Swordy Well's scars, the rock faces of limestone and estuarine sand, reveal enough of its prehistory to have been labelled as a Regionally Important Geological Site. The Trust has stripped away the hard standing and race tracks and hopes to introduce sheep to maintain the grassland that is slowly re-colonising the quarry. Butterflies – such as the Chalkhill Blue – should follow.

But the real miracle of Swordy Well lies outside the quarry, on a bank overlooking a stonecutter's yard. The limestone grassland has lots of flower seed heads and enough moss to match Clare's description of 'mossy steeps'. And among the moss there were compact leaf rosettes next to dead stems, which could only be one thing. Incredibly, they were bee orchids.

It appears that the topsoil of Swordy Well had been piled up in banks while the tipping was going on, and afterwards spread back over the site. In the process, it preserved the seeds of many wild flowers, including the hardy, dust-like seed of wild orchids. Bee orchids are rare in this corner of England and are unlikely to have spread here from another site. They are probably descendants of the same plants that Clare saw in the pastures of old Swordy Well, 'mimicking at will/ Displaying powers that fools the proudly wise'.

In Clare's sense, Swordy Well was not just a piece of land. It was rather a living tapestry of plants and animals, almost an embodiment of life itself. Physically the land has changed for ever. But the impulse of life is stronger than mere contours. For me, at any rate, the bee orchids have transformed the story from a lament to a reaffirmation of nature's extraordinary resilience.

17 June 1995

Bring Back the Beaver
Matt Ridley

Scottish Natural Heritage wants to reintroduce the beaver to the Highlands. This giant aquatic rodent became extinct there in the Middle Ages, having been hunted for its fur; but the same species survives in Russia and has been reintroduced to France. Although sea eagles have been restored to Britain from Norway, the reintroduction of the beaver would be the first time we have brought back a mammal that has died out. Is it wise?

Few countries are as biologically impoverished as Britain. We have lost almost all our native large mammals: moose, boar, wolf, bear, bison, giant elk, aurochs, mammoth, wild horse, woolly rhino. The last five are extinct, of course, but the other five are not. Because they do not live in our woods and on our moors, the ecology of Britain is different. There are, for example, no large grazing animals in our woods, except red deer in Scotland and Exmoor, with dramatic effects on vegetation and insects.

To bring back our native mammals would not upset the balance of nature as the disastrous introduction of exotic animals from Asia and America – mink, grey squirrel, muntjac, sika deer – has done. Indeed, there are ways in which it would restore the balance. For example, there is little doubt that if wolves returned to Scotland they would reduce or disperse the concentrations of red deer that prevent the regeneration of native Scots pine forest. More important, wolves are efficient killers of foxes, and the present vast overpopulation of foxes – fed by recovering numbers of rabbits – is disastrous for many ground-nesting birds, such as the declining black grouse.

But Scotland is not a wilderness. It supports sheep and hikers, as well as deer and foxes. Scottish wolves would quickly learn to ignore deer and foxes for the easier game of killing sheep. Though they might not kill hikers, they would certainly dampen the enthusiasm of parents for letting their children go on school camping trips. After much politicking and debate, wolves have recently been released in Yellowstone National Park in America, where they were exterminated earlier this century. They refused to leave their pen at first, but have now taken to the wild. The first dead cow on the park boundary is anxiously awaited. Ranchers expect to be heavily compensated and, if necessary, allowed to shoot the culprit.

There was some enthusiasm, a few years ago, for the idea of reintroducing wolves on the island of Rhum, in the Inner Hebrides, since it is a nature reserve. But the island is now reckoned too small to support a population of wolves without risking them exterminating the deer. So, until the Common Agricultural Policy collapses and sheep farming ceases in Scotland, the wolf will have to wait.

So, too, will the wild boar, because boar are great destroyers of crops, and compensating farmers is unlikely to appeal to the government. The moose and the bison are unlikely to return for similar reasons. Brown bears and lynxes would probably kill lambs and scare hikers, so they are unlikely to come back soon, either.

That leaves the beaver. Beavers are good for rivers. They dam them, which traps silt, moderates floods and creates ponds for fish and other wildlife. Old, silted-up beaver ponds make fertile meadows. In Tierra del Fuego, where beavers were introduced decades ago, the effect has been dramatic: newly fertile valleys, raised water tables, expanded wetlands. There is a myth abroad that European beavers do not build dams, but this is not true. I recently walked along a ditch in Latvia that had beaver dams every few hundred yards. Beaver-watching in Scotland could one day be as rewarding and popular as badger-watching is becoming in England.

Who can object to having back this busy, clever, harmless, water-loving civil engineer? Foresters and river managers, that's who. Chopping down trees to eat and build dams with, beavers can make a mess. The Forestry Commission is not going to take kindly to a tree-eating mammal, even though beavers are as little enamoured of the forester's favourite sitka spruce trees as the rest of us.

But if beavers are going to annoy people who work for quangos, that seems to be a reason for having them, not against them. We have spent enough of the taxpayer's money making giant, dull forests of exotic conifers; and besides, beavers are remarkably easy to control because they live in one place. So, it would be vital if they were introduced that they were not made a protected species. The right to cull them should be vested with the landowner, as it is in the case of foxes, and not with the state, as it is with sparrowhawks. Otherwise, the first time a house is flooded because a beaver has dammed a nearby stream, there will be the ridiculous sight of the house owner either facing prosecution for destroying the dam, or demanding compensation from the state. The way to make people love beavers is to devolve the right to control them. Otherwise, they will come to be resented as sparrowhawks and even badgers are coming to be resented by countrymen because it is a crime to disturb them.

The issue of reintroduction, however, touches a deeper debate: what are the Highlands for? Judging by the letters page of the *Scotsman*, Scots seem increasingly to be demanding that Highland estates be taken into public ownership, or given by the state to collective bodies, as the Mar Lodge estate has been. They are then to be used for subsidised recreation, not commercial gain. Whether that vision appeals to you or not, it is coming, and there is little doubt that one of the first acts of a putative Scottish Parliament would be to increase the public ownership of land in the Highlands, whether by purchase or confiscation.

At the same time, the wild land lobby is determinedly pursuing its dream of a true Scottish wilderness. In many parts of the north-west Highlands, sheep farming and grouse shooting are already money-losers, deer stalking is marginal and the only reasons for owning land are to collect the government grants for planting it with exotic trees, or just to do nothing and enjoy its beauty. Restoring the original fauna of the Highlands would seem to follow logically as part of that.

I once walked up a valley in the Rocky Mountains armed with nothing but binoculars and a fly rod. There were bear tracks by the tiny stream, I saw a moose browsing in a pond and every half mile there was a beaver dam, behind which was a pond inhabited by tasty, cut-throat trout for which I fished, mostly without success. One day, Scotland could be like that.

3 April 2004
An Eye for the Gulls
Peter Marren

I realised I was never going to be much of a birder the day I thought I spotted an Iceland gull. These snow-white polar gulls get about a bit and you wouldn't be surprised to see one arrive on the north wind at some frozen port in the far north. But this one was sitting in a haystack in the middle of a field on a fine day in Leicestershire. And it was exceptionally white, even for an Iceland gull, indicating, according to my trusty Collins field guide, that it was a young bird that had lost its mother and had wandered hopelessly off course on the way to Reykjavik.

That would also explain why it was just sitting there, staring into space. This was one sad gull. It didn't move as I walked up, which wasn't surprising because by then I could see that my Iceland gull was actually a milk bottle. That's the thing about birds. There's the image that you see and the image in your head. If you want to see a bird badly enough, your mind can play the strangest tricks: exotic finches that turn into crisp packets, rare ducks that become yachting buoys or fishing floats.

If only I'd had the excellent book that was published this spring. I could have jumped on a plane to Lerwick sometime between October and March, taken the road to Boddam, turned right just before reaching Scousburgh and parked the hire car by Loch Spiggie. And if I didn't spot an Iceland gull inspecting the litter bin, there would almost certainly be plenty more nearby, along with a great northern diver, long-tailed duck and, in the dunes, the rare snow bunting.

The author to whom I owe this news is David Tipling, a birder and professional photographer. He has produced a guide for the discerning birder, indicating 300 of the best birding spots and all the birds you might hope to see when you get there.

Britain's million or more birders have never had it so good. Field guides are numerous, often of excellent quality, and available for most of the frequently visited countries of the world. Bins and scopes are lighter, optically better and more affordable than ever before and, best of all, there's no shortage of where-to-go books telling you exactly where to find the bird of your dreams. The facilities are improving, too. At Welney, on the Ouse Washes, you can watch wild swans land on a specially floodlit field from a heated observatory. At Rutland Water, where birders migrate in late summer for the annual bird fair, you can swig coffee on an elevated viewing gallery and watch ospreys catching fish. The London Wetland Centre at Barn Elms even has a tower hide with a lift.

Birdwatching has become a serious leisure activity. At the more dedicated end, it has generated its own folklore and language. Twitchers, the birding equivalent of trainspotters, talk of jizz and stringing, dipping out and bunking off. They have year lists, life lists and even day lists, in which they compete to tick off species.

Particular birds are known by nicknames such as 'icky' (an Icterine warbler) or spreddie (a spotted redshank), often seen at Dunge (Dungeness). Tools include not only scopes and bins but pagers and phone links, such as Birdline, which gives last-minute information on the latest rare birds.

With these advances at their fingertips, small armies of twitchers gather at the exact spot where some transatlantic or Siberian vagrant has checked in and tick it off. Veteran twitchers reminisce about the '76 sapsucker or the '66 thrasher. They enjoy yarning about the elusive lanceolated warbler that everyone was looking for and which was sitting under a twitcher's tripod. Or the White's thrush that was carried away by a cat with the twitchers in full pursuit.

Like fishermen, birders enjoy telling a good tale. Unlike the egg and skin collectors of yesteryear, they have nothing but notebooks and memories to show for their time and money. You make up for it by yarning in the pub afterwards.

But there's no getting away from it, birding is hard. The skulking habits of many birds are bad enough, but there is the added problem of light, ever flickering, often inadequate and invariably from the wrong direction and tending to reduce your bird to a silhouette. The writer Mark Cocker has summed up birding as a battle between you, the bird and the light. Often the moment of recognition passes in a flash. Then you spend a lot of time with your notebook trying to remember what you glimpsed.

Where-to-watch guides are useful, but by their nature they are biased towards places where birds congregate regularly, such as seabird colonies and reservoirs. David Tipling gives a great deal of space to the coast and islands, especially Shetland and the Isles of Scilly, where you can expect the unexpected. His home county of Kent receives fairly generous coverage, but mine, Wiltshire, which he thinks is in the Midlands, gets short shrift.

A common failing of birding guides is their exclusivity. Do users care for nothing but birds?

For example, Prawle Point in Devon may well be the best place in Britain to see cirl bunting, but no one would know from this that it is also one of the best places to watch dolphins and migrant butterflies. Even birders must occasionally want to look at something else.

So three cheers for British birding and at least two for David Tipling. With his concise directions, lists of key species and pretty photographs, Tipling's book will doubtless find its way on to the back seats of a lot of lightly addicted birders and day-release spotters. The more ardent will require the greater detail of the similarly titled book by Simon Harrap and Nigel Redman.

But no one can make birds perform to a timetable. Probably no guide will prevent me from confusing milk bottles with stray gulls. But they do make it easier to find where birds congregate, even if the birdwatchers may outnumber the birds.

6 August 2009

Amorous Birdwatchers Get Back to Nature

Birdwatchers have been told to report unsuitable behaviour to the police after reports of visitors having sexual encounters in hides.

Lincolnshire Wildlife Trust asked visitors to remember that there are rules to be observed while birdwatching, that noise can disturb the animals and that the hides are for 'quiet enjoyment only'. The misuse of the structures, which remain unlocked all night, came to light after a birdspotter heard loud sounds emanating from a hide in the south of the county.

Rachel Shaw, from the trust, said: 'There are certain things that happen at nature reserves that really shouldn't.'

Famous 'twitchers' include Sean Bean, the actor, and Mick Jagger of the Rolling Stones.

3 July 1999

Tougher Than Ever on the Wildlife Beat
Maureen Paton

Whatever you do, do not call Paul Henery a bunny-hugger. 'It's dangerous to anthropomorphise animals,' says the Northumbria-based police constable, one of only seven full-time wildlife liaison officers in the police force. 'Bunny-huggers infiltrate animal-activist groups and release mink from farms because they are blinded by their love for the animal. They don't see that the mink can't exist in the wild and will harm other species.'

His sensible lecture proves timely. I have just emitted the typical sheltered city-dweller's cry of distress when Henery's police Land Rover drives past a squashed rook. 'That was someone's accident, not an indictable offence,' he points out.

A nature-lover who doesn't believe in keeping pets, he is giving me a six-hour guided tour of badger setts, rare birds' nests and other favourite targets of the law-breaking fraternity.

Eleven years ago, this former country-park warden was pounding the streets of Newcastle as a young police constable, arresting former schoolmates for car theft and even being stabbed in the head on one occasion while trying to break up a 'domestic'.

But by 1989 he had realised where his true vocation lay: outside the city in the surrounding countryside, the deceptively tranquil scene of what is now becoming the fastest-growing area of crime in the world. With a huge internet market in endangered species, illegal trafficking in exotic animals is a money-spinner second only to the drugs trade – and often involves the same people.

Following profiles in the Channel 4 documentary *Wildlife Cop* in 1995 and in Channel 5's *Ecowarriors* series in 1996, and a feature in this newspaper, the next step will be a television drama series based on his life. Henery is acting as consultant on the forthcoming BBC1 series *Badger*, with Jerome Flynn as a Northumbrian detective specialising in wildlife crime.

An intriguing mixture of the sporty and the artistic, this brawny-armed, 6ft 2in son of a miner boxes regularly in the gym and is studying part-time for a fine arts degree at Northumbria University. He is also a member of the Society of Wildlife Artists. Some of his paintings are used on the set of *Badger*. He revels in his contradictions. 'I don't look like a twinky-winky officer – all open-toed sandals and David Bellamy beard,' he says. 'I don't fit into anyone's stereotype.'

We are joined on our tour of the Northumbrian coastline by his colleague Rebecca Sinton, from the Royal Society for the Protection of Birds. Sinton's nearest equivalent in *Badger* is portrayed by actress Rebecca Lacey in the role of an intrepid RSPB investigator. Usually, the television version glamorises its real-life inspiration beyond all recognition, but Henery and Sinton turn out to be even better-looking than their counterparts Flynn and Lacey.

Little wonder that *Hello!* seized the opportunity to run a photograph of him when *Wildlife Cop* was chosen as the magazine's documentary of the week.

'My wife Lynn was amused, but she doesn't really like all the publicity,' says Henery. 'And many of my colleagues in the police are frightened of the media. It's not that I enjoy it, I just realise what a powerful tool it can be.

'But I wouldn't be a policeman if I wasn't endowed with common sense. If you come from a mining community, you keep your feet on the ground and don't go believing all the hype.' As he points out, public recognition can make undercover work difficult.

He works alone most of the time, meeting informants or conducting surveillance operations. The rich fauna of Northumbria makes it a prime county for wildlife crime, especially when city gangs descend upon what they think of as an unpoliced land of opportunity.

'The problem with wildlife crime is that there are no injured parties,' says Henery. 'You don't get Mr and Mrs Peregrine turning up at the police station, saying: "Someone has stolen our eggs." So we have to rely on intelligence.'

His workload is extraordinarily diverse. Police raids on suspects often need an animal expert on the team, since drug dealers increasingly stash their wares among tarantulas, pythons or alligators on the assumption that such exotic pets will deter searches.

Some of Henery's toughest cases involve badger-baiting, for which it is notoriously hard to secure convictions. Farmers often fear that their barns may be torched or their families harmed if they inform on the culprits, who commit their crimes in broad daylight. Even vets who treat the injured dogs won't necessarily inform on the owners.

Henery considers badger-baiting one of the most urgent areas of wildlife policing because of the immense cruelty involved.

'I don't want to stereotype anyone,' he says, 'but there are a lot of badgers in the north-east and a certain kind of person from a working-class community thinks of it as their equivalent of fox-hunting. It's hard physical activity to dig down into a badger's sett and tough, working men have traditionally been involved in that.

'The practice is steeped in history. It's part of my job to know that. But I come from a mining community and I don't go badger-baiting. We make it one of our priorities because of the strength of public opinion against this abhorrent crime.'

This is the cue to visit a Northumbrian animal sanctuary run by one of Henery's best contacts, Lisa Bolton, in order to check on the health of Emma and Henry. Rescued from the baiters, the badgers curl up together at night as if bonding because of their terrible shared experience. Among the other patients is Hazel, a blind roe deer shot and left for dead by poachers who took her mother.

Their progress helps Henery put some of the inevitable frustrations of his job into perspective. 'I'm first and foremost a public servant, so I can't comment on controversial things that I'm personally outraged by and that I think the public would be outraged by. I've got to be neutral in order to do my job professionally.'

11 September 1992
Obituary
Maurice Burton

Maurice Burton, the naturalist, who has died aged 94, delighted *Daily Telegraph* readers for more than 40 years with his weekly 'Nature Note'.

His newspaper writing was a by-product of his prolific literary output of more than 70 books and 60 scientific papers. When he finally retired at the age of 92, having contributed 3,000 or so of his idiosyncratic commentaries on the natural world, it was fitting that he should have handed over the baton to his son Robert, whose column, like his father's, appears in the *Telegraph* every Saturday.

The son of a shunter at King's Cross, Maurice Burton was born on 28 March 1898, when the smoke-blackened streets of north London sustained little in the way of animal life beyond horses, household pets and vermin.

With no thought of studying the ways of nature, young Maurice won a scholarship to Holloway County School. He hoped to read history at university, but the First World War intervened and he joined the Army instead, serving as a gunner on the Western Front.

When recalling what followed, Burton maintained that his career would have taken an entirely different course had it not been for an anthill, a talking cadaver, a suit of tails and a girl from Littlehampton. He explained that these apparent ingredients of a story by P.G. Wodehouse in fact represented the major turning points in his life.

Burton resolved to become a zoologist after a chance study of the ant in the trenches. The scurrying activities of this insect, so like that of human beings, were forced on his attention one warm May afternoon in 1918 during a lull in the fighting.

Burton watched the ants for several hours as they rushed about on the parapet of his trench, and, thus inspired, begged his mother to send him books on nature.

After the war he took a zoology degree and doctorate at London University, specialising in sponges (marine invertebrates). He tried a spell as a schoolmaster at the Latymer School at Hammersmith, but sponges had by this time become an obsession. He used to lay the world's literature on the subject on the floor of his room so that he could read it as he walked about.

It was around this time that Burton suffered a nightmare, in which a corpse he was dissecting sat up and started to speak. He remembered reading a paper by Professor Vosmaer of Leiden University, noting a correlation between the study of sponges and insanity, and determined to branch out.

He decided to give zoology lectures, but this plan faltered when he found that he could not afford the full evening dress which he believed was necessary for this line of work.

Then, in 1927, an opportunity arose to supplement his income when a girl he had met on a sponge-hunting expedition to Littlehampton introduced him to the editor of the *West Sussex Gazette*.

Burton was contracted to write a nature column for the paper at a penny a line, and he gradually saved enough for a suit of tails. It turned out that he did not need one after all, but his secondary career as lecturer and journalist was launched.

In the meantime, Burton's reputation as a serious scientist had won him the post of sponge expert at the Natural History Museum, where he remained for 31 years.

In 1933 his observations on the locomotion of sponges aroused great interest. One writer in *Punch* confirmed the phenomenon from personal experience. His own sponge, Fluffy, had disappeared from the bathroom and was later found in the garage where his son's car was kept. 'You will readily accept that this is an extraordinary instance of a sponge's locomotory powers,' wrote the man from *Punch*.

After the Second World War, Burton moved to a large house and garden at Albury, near Guildford, where he established a large menagerie. From then on, there was always copy to hand. From his family of foxes he made the first recorded observation of the split personality of the dog fox.

He also discovered that hedgehogs could trot at three miles an hour.

Burton retired from the Natural History Museum in 1958. From 1946 to 1964 he was science editor of the *Illustrated London News*, and he contributed the 'Nature Note' in the *Daily Telegraph* from 1949 to 1990.

Although a scientist of distinction – he was a Fellow of the Zoological Society and worked out that he had spent some 12,000 hours peering at sponges through a microscope – Burton never disdained nature's homelier manifestations. His observation that water voles do not like rain was one of countless insights which brought his writing to life for non-specialist readers.

He received numerous letters from his readers, many of which formed the nucleus of the next week's article. The devilish cunning of dogs was a favourite topic. One correspondent, rushing to investigate the sound of the Sunday joint crashing to the floor, swore he saw his dog trying to incriminate the cat by pushing it towards the scene of the crime.

Burton declared that at one time he might not have believed the story, but now thought it was probably true.

Maurice Burton was a man of unfailing curiosity, and his journalism was as fresh in his nineties as it had been more than 60 years before.

He married, in 1928, Margaret Maclean; they had two sons and a daughter.

21 March 1992

Nature Note: Hares and Science
Robert Burton

After my note last week on the antics of hares, my agricultural friend and *Weekend* columnist Robin Page complained that I was 'demythologising' nature.

The problem with science is that, while giving a more accurate picture of the natural world, it can make it appear so dull. I do not think this is the case with explaining the madness of March hares. The pleasure of watching them is not diminished in the least.

For me, the attraction of science is that it reveals a world that is richer than we imagined, although at the same time there is a delight in finding that it is so well-ordered. However, I heartily sympathise with my friend for the loss of romance in the countryside.

Before the scientists started their patient inquiries into the habits of common animals, the countryside was full of marvellous tales of magpies' weddings, badgers' funerals, rooks' parliaments, rats carrying eggs, hedgehogs milking cows and other wonders. I fancy that Robin Page's real complaint against scientists is that the fox is no longer the romantic Reynard or Charlie but the prosaic Kevin that he introduced last week.

Yet demythologising nature need not be negative. The 'mystery of migration' used to be a fashionable phrase but, as we learn the secrets of how these frail scraps of life cross oceans and deserts, we can talk instead of the marvel of migration. I do hope that the sight of birds returning from their amazing travels will brighten the dull days of my friend as he steers his tractor along its appointed course.

11 November 1995
Nature Note: Mole
Robert Burton

A story that harks back to the long, hot days of the summer concerns a mole that lived on a lawn. Note that it was on the lawn and not in it. Mrs J.S. Edrich of Stowe watched it spend a good part of the day foraging on the surface of her lawn over a period of four or five weeks. The mole was so unconcerned at her presence that she could hand-feed it earthworms and she was able to see that it was foraging for leatherjackets.

It seems that this mole had been affected by the dry weather. Sun-baked soil is difficult to dig but it may be more important that earthworms and other soil animals become inactive so they will not fall into a mole's tunnels and get snapped up.

A mole outside its system of tunnels could be described as a fish out of water. Yet it seems to manage. When young moles cut the apron strings and leave their mothers' tunnel systems they often live above ground for a short time until they can find an untended patch of ground in which to set up home.

On three occasions, Mrs Edrich says she placed her mole in the vegetable garden (which had been kept moist) yet it returned to the lawn each time. The vegetable garden already had a resident mole, which presumably drove out the interloper. The latter was lucky that Mrs Edrich's lawn was infested with leatherjackets and that she gave it earthworms as an extra benefit.

6 January 1996
Nature Note: Weasel
Robert Burton

There used to be a belief that the British Isles were inhabited by a second species of weasel, smaller than the familiar one. It was known as the cane weasel, or sometimes the mousehunt or miniver. For all I know, there are still people who hold this notion.

Country people, including gamekeepers who handled hundreds of small carnivores in the course of vermin control, swore to the existence of this animal, yet museums never obtained specimens. The mystery reminds me of the 'beasts' that are reported to roam the countryside, yet never yield cast-iron proof of their existence.

The root of the cane weasel story probably lies in the great variation in the size of weasels. The female weasel is only half the weight, on average, of the male. Also the average size varies from place to place. In continental Europe, weasels progressively get larger from north and east to south and west.

Two explanations have been put forward to solve the problem of the cane weasel. Weasels have two litters in a year and one theory suggests that cane weasels are the young of the first litter which breed before they are full grown. The second idea is that the young of late litters pass the winter at less than adult size.

17 July 2010
Beware the Devil's Darning Needle
Peter Marren

Is that a monkeypede on the carpet? Are those hairy Mollies on the cabbages? Is this a bad year for snartlegogs? They sound like the zanier side of science fiction, but these are country names for woodlice, caterpillars and cockchafers respectively. And there are many more, up to 100 each in the case of certain groups such as woodlice, dragonflies or ladybirds.

Many such names are forgotten, but others are still in use, especially around the edges of Britain – in Cornwall and Devon, for example, or in north-east England and the Borders. The earwig is known in the Newcastle area as 'twitchbell', a name that takes us straight back to the Tudors. 'Bell' is a polite abbreviation for 'bellocks', and must have arisen from nipping encounters inside the codpiece.

Ladybirds have always had a wholesome reputation. Their name dates from the Middle Ages when the little round beetles were seen as winged messengers from the Virgin Mary. Red was a colour worn by Our Lady in memory of the blood of Christ, while the spots on the most familiar ladybird formed the mystic number seven, corresponding with the Seven Joys and Sorrows of Mary.

In south-east England, however, ladybirds are also bishy barnabees. Apparently nonsensical – there is no known 'Bishop' Barnabee – it is probably a pun on 'burn' and 'bee'. Ladybirds are the colour of flame, hence the rhyme, 'Ladybird, Ladybird'.

Country names for woodlice, too, are surprisingly affectionate. They are Billy buttons, cheesy-logs or chizzle-bobs, chucky-pigs or bibble bugs. Many of these delightful names are very local, prompting the speculation that if an expert were lost in England he would know roughly where he was from the name of a woodlouse. Perhaps we are still inventing them. Two Berkshire children told me they called them 'wigglemice' or 'Dougal spiders', after Dougal, the apparently legless dog in *The Magic Roundabout*.

Other insects had an unfriendly, if not hellish, reputation. Dragonflies are popular now, but not so long ago they were feared for their imaginary stings and called 'hoss-stengers'. Their shape and markings were signs of their nature. Dragonflies were seen as animated crossbow bolts or flying snakes, especially adders, hence names like 'snake-arrow' or 'penny adder'.

One memorable name was the 'devil's darning needle'. They said that if you fell asleep by a brook, the devilish darner could sew your eyes shut. Others believed that dragonflies bothered only bad people. Good ones had nothing to fear, and the dragonfly would show them where to fish.

Generally speaking, 'devil's' insects were those that stung, like wasps, or looked as though they could, like dragonflies and the devil's coach-horse beetle. Spiders were doubly wicked since not only could they 'sting' but they were considered deadly poisonous. A centuries-old spider name that is still used in Yorkshire is 'attercop' or 'poison-head'.

Certain insects are best known for the sound they make while flying. Large moths buzzing loudly around the lamp were known as 'buzzards' and beetles as 'buzzard-clocks' or 'bum-clocks'. The big cockchafer beetle or maybug sounded like the noise of the pilotless jets or V-1 bombs during the war, and hence for a while shared their nickname of 'doodlebugs'.

The folknames of bumblebees, too, are mostly about humming sounds. They are droners or drumbees, dumbledranes and bummiebees. One bee is known in parts of Scotland as 'foggie toddler', the bee that 'toddles' about like an infant among the 'fog', another name for grass.

Other names echo more high-pitched sounds. We normally hear the whine of a mosquito before we spot the thirsty insect trailing through the air. The name mosquito, which means 'little fly', ultimately comes, via Spanish and Latin, from the Greek muia – a word that imitates the sound the insect makes before it bites.

During the research for my book, *Bugs Britannica*, I found to my surprise and joy that moths are still known as 'bob-owlers', at least in Worcestershire, and that their hairy caterpillars are woolly bears or oubits, just as they were 500 years ago. Dragonflies are still edders and stengers; the dumbledore or dor beetle is alive and well, and has lent his name to the wizard in Harry Potter.

It is good to know there is a subversive subculture out there, stubbornly insisting on our right to call beetles mitchamadors or starfish cassock-cats. In this age of uniformity and standardisation it seems there are still pockets of resistance, even if it is confined to the folk-names of ladybirds.

28 May 2009 – 1 June 2009
Letters to the Editor
Painted Ladies

SIR – I'm sure it can only increase the pleasure your correspondents have taken in the sight of painted lady butterflies to be reminded that the collective noun is a rabble of butterflies.

Graham Weeks
Barcelona

SIR – These painted ladies may well have come from France. We saw hundreds of them flying low over the Somme battlefield at Beaumont Hamel last Thursday.

Very poignant. Many people believe that butterflies represent the souls of the departed.

Maureen Kirby
Hazelbury Bryan
Dorset

SIR – During my naval career, I saw painted ladies in Bugis Street, Singapore.

However, they were not butterflies and some of them were certainly not ladies.

Dennis Whitehead
Gosport
Hampshire

30 March 2011
'Miss, Are They Pigs?'
Clive Aslet

'Marvellous,' said my friend at the Countryside Alliance. 'Kate Humble says that children should get out more, and it's all over the media. We've been on about it for years.'

Yes, that's true. The *Springwatch* and *Lambing Live* presenter isn't, and doubtless wouldn't pretend to be, searingly original; her observation this week simply reflects what more or less any educationalist, any parent, any adult with half a brain would think. It's a truth so blindingly obvious that it ought to be written in 10-foot-high letters of flashing neon on Westminster's rooftops. Every child should have some exposure to nature.

And yet, for all the SATs and national curriculum, the proliferation of paper qualifications and inflation of grades, many young people grow up in a state of unabashed ignorance of the countryside. They never see a butterfly's wing, or hear the rapture of a skylark. They don't know the joy of floating sticks in streams, or making daisy chains; they're allowed to reach adulthood in a state of shocking deprivation, as disconnected from the fields upon which we all depend for our food as a rickety-legged Victorian chimney sweep.

They'll go out into the world with something missing – a whole area of their inner selves which ought to be there, but isn't. Emotionally if not physically stunted, they'll crawl through their days, unable to connect not just with the natural world itself, but also with the poetry of Keats, the symphonies of Mahler, the art of Monet. They may say they're happy eating fast food on an urban street corner, with the blare of traffic and amplified music in their ears. But they can't truly know, because they've never experienced an alternative.

Every survey, including one I commissioned when editor of *Country Life*, confirms that many children wouldn't know a beech trunk from a mobile phone mast. A colleague once stood beside some beagles at a country show and heard a schoolboy ask his teacher: 'Miss, are they pigs?'

Admittedly, that child came from a struggling London borough, but I don't think country children are much better off than townies. Although their postcodes may locate them in a village, their lives will probably be suburban. Parents, worried about paedophiles and motor vehicles, won't allow them to bicycle along country lanes. Instead, they'll drive them everywhere by car.

Shopping will be done at a supermarket that looks exactly like the ones in cities, except for being bigger and surrounded by more concrete. If the family goes on an outing, it will be to somewhere stage managed, with parking, toilets, noticeboards and disabled access. Research by Hertfordshire University has shown that adults don't want to risk a country ramble because they can't read a map and have an abhorrence of muddy clothes.

Schools already have to dispense so much sticking plaster to the broken society that I am reluctant to add to their load. It's parents who ought to show their offspring lambs and primroses, stag beetles and bluebell woods. However overworked and impoverished we've become, most people in Britain do take a holiday, which could just as well be spent in the British countryside as overseas.

Teachers, though, might find that their charges learn better in the countryside than in the classroom. It is as relevant to Shakespeare ('There is a willow growes aslant a brooke') as to science. While the present generation may be content to live in ignorance of farming and land management, these subjects will become hugely important to their children and grandchildren, living on a planet that has to feed a population of 9 billion, with ever greater tensions over water. That's quite apart from the moral and ethical questions posed by GM crops, cloned animals and TB-infected badgers.

Schools should value the rural environment as much for the effect that it can have on pupils as what they can learn about it. The celebrity teachers in Jamie Oliver's Dream School may struggle to get through to today's angry, dissocialised yoof, but farmer Roger Hosking doesn't. This year he was awarded an MBE for his work with disadvantaged youngsters, often with criminal records. When all the support services are in despair with what to do with them, Hosking invites these youngsters to spend time on his Derbyshire farm, Highfield Happy Hens. There even the toughest nuts collect eggs.

'At first the kids who come here will crush them,' says Hoskings. 'They're so bottled up and tense that they'll pick up three eggs and they're squashed. Within a day or two – certainly within a week – I can guarantee that anyone can collect eggs without breaking them. Those angry hands have become gentle hands. They've never thought gentle before. Thinking gentle means I can have a decent conversation with you without swearing.'

Gary Richardson of the Countryside Foundation for Education takes his Labrador with him to the educational days that he organises for schools. The dog will twirl round and kiss on command. 'I'm going to teach mine at home to do that,' said one boy. 'It's a Rottweiler.' Perhaps he had begun to think gentle, too.

The countryside is rather like history. The less that it is taught adequately as part of the curriculum, the more an appetite grows for other sources of information. So the countryside has boomed on television. BBC *Countryfile* has gone prime time. Hugh Fearnley-Whittingstall and *Edwardian Farm* produce rich rural smells. Hardly a week goes by without the *Today* programme urging listeners to look for some creature in their gardens. Ms Humble's career is a product of the phenomenon. But goggling at nature on the small screen doesn't necessarily make viewers go outside to interact at first hand. Cookery programmes are said to be similar in this respect. We now have an audience of rural voyeurs.

Which is strange, because never has the countryside been more welcoming. Rural England is as marbled with footpaths as a rib of beef. You can roam at will across Scottish moorland and through Welsh forests. Farmers are delighted to welcome visitors. I stayed in Devon the other day, where the farmer and his wife spent all night lambing: I was rather ashamed when they served a breakfast that was better than the Savoy. Landed estates and many farmers almost fall over themselves to attract school groups.

I say almost: any actual falling might constitute a health and safety hazard. The Countryside Alliance has found that one of the principal obstacles to schools visiting the countryside is a fear of being sued. I can believe it. When building wigwams out of twigs at a rural location, the children of my son's primary school had to wear yellow builders' hats.

But how many schools have had damages awarded against them as a result of a countryside accident? Precious few. We have become creatures of our fear. We're breeding children who don't even know the smell of May blossom as a result.

5 September 1998
Country Diary
Robin Page

An astonishing story comes from an English primary school. A pupil picked up a 'deadly fungus' on the school playing field. The child was rushed to Addenbrookes Hospital in Cambridge after touching such a hazardous object; the school's annual sports day was postponed because of the threat to the school, pupils and parents and the playing field were sprayed with fungicide as a matter of urgency. At the end of the day the child was released fit and well and identification of the 'deadly fungus' came from the Plant Sciences Department of Cambridge University. It turned out to be a common, edible mushroom.

I could understand such over-reaction at an inner-city school, or a holiday home for neurotics – but this happened in a village on the edge of the Fens. Thus the hysterical urban mind continues its conquest of rural Britain.

19 April 2009

A World of Natural Wonder

Stephen Moss

As a child, back in the sixties, I always seemed to be outdoors. Collecting tadpoles in jam jars in spring, paddling around rock-pools on summer holidays, playing conkers in autumn, and building snowmen during the winter were simply part of the seasonal rhythm of growing up.

By the time I reached my teens, I had developed the passion for nature that has since shaped my whole life. I am one of those very lucky people whose lifetime's passion is also their job – making television programmes such as *Springwatch* and writing books about the natural world. But I owe all this to one simple thing: that when I was growing up I was given the freedom to explore outdoors – a freedom that so many of today's parents now deny their children.

And in case you're assuming that I lived in the deepest countryside, nothing could be further from the truth. I was brought up in a single-parent family on a suburban housing estate on the fringes of west London. My mother went out to work, leaving me in the care of my grandmother, who decided when I was allowed to go out, where, and with whom.

Understandably protective, she nevertheless allowed me to walk to school from the age of six, play ball games in the street and clamber over the fence at the back of our garden into the piece of scrubby elm woodland we called the 'forest'. Later on we fished for tiddlers in a nearby ford, wandered for hours around the gravel pits, and rode our bikes all over the neighbourhood. These experiences were typical for all my schoolmates – yet just 40 years later, they make our childhood sound like something out of *The Famous Five*. Nowadays, our children are growing up in a different world. A recent survey by Natural England discovered that the most popular place for children to play is at home – which, as any parent knows, means in their bedroom. As a friend of mine pointed out, when we were kids, if you went to your bedroom during daylight hours it was as a punishment, not to watch television and play computer games.

As a father of five myself, I understand the very real fears that prevent parents allowing their children to experience the outdoors in the way we did. But the consequences of failing to give our children natural play are very worrying.

Simply exploring the natural world has so many benefits: not just physical, but emotional and social too. Climbing trees and building dens encourages teamwork and risk-taking, both vital elements in child development. From an environmental viewpoint, if our children are never exposed to nature, why would they ever want to care about it? And where will the next generation of naturalists come from if they are never allowed to play in the wild, and learn about the natural world first-hand?

My own experience confirms this. With my two older sons, David and James, I went along with the consensus that children should be supervised, rather than free to explore outdoors on their own. As a result, both grew up without caring much about the natural world.

I still remember an incident, when David was about 12, which shows how attitudes have changed since my childhood. He came home one day full of excitement, having built a den in the local park. I am ashamed to say that my first reaction was to ask if anyone had seen him – knowing that he was more likely to be reported to the police as a vandal than be commended for doing what boys have done for generations.

Now, I have been given a chance to redeem myself. Three years ago my wife Suzanne and I moved to Somerset with our young children Charlie, George and Daisy. With more than an acre of 'garden' (a former cider orchard rapidly turning into a meadow), and plenty of wildlife to discover, they are rapidly turning into budding naturalists.

I have discovered that the key to enthusing them is to be as hands-on as possible – catching butterflies with a net, picking wild flowers and getting hands dirty at every opportunity. Not surprisingly, they absolutely love it – and while I occasionally have to drag them away from the television, once outdoors they lose themselves in the natural world in a way that is a joy to see. But they are the lucky ones. Over the years I have been able to guide them and fire their enthusiasm. Not every child is lucky enough to have a naturalist as a parent, yet every child deserves to enjoy 'going wild'. That's what prompted me to write *The Bumper Book of Nature* – a realisation that these outdoor activities are unknown to a generation of parents and their children.

I hope the book will kick-start a movement to get families back in touch with the pleasures of the natural world. A world where climbing a tree, building a den or simply mucking about outdoors will no longer be the preserve of a privileged few, but something that every child enjoys.

Most of all, I look forward to a world where, as children go out to play, the words they hear as they leave home are those my mother used to say to me: 'Be good, enjoy yourself and be back home for tea!'

2 January 1999
Birds: Now for the Good News . . .
Malcolm Smith

It was difficult to know what to focus my binoculars on first; a flotilla of different duck species feeding at the water's edge or three svelte, brown and cream marsh harriers hunting low over the fringing reed-beds seeking out a hapless little reed warbler for tea. But when the woman next to me asked, somewhat nonchalantly, 'Have you seen the two spoonbills over there?' I didn't hesitate.

We were, after all, a long way away from the Danube Marshes on the Black Sea coast, the headquarters of the spoonbill in Europe. This was the very much less exotic Leighton Moss Reserve, run by the Royal Society for the Protection of Birds, in Lancashire.

Snow-white spoonbills, which stand the height of a heron and use their flattened namesake to probe mud for food, have been visiting this wetland in ones and twos every year since 1992. So far, they haven't nested. But soon, they will.

That assertion may seem wildly optimistic, given the experts' repeated cries that an ever-growing list of Britain's birds are in rapid decline – anything from tree sparrows and song thrushes to yellowhammers and lapwings. Only last month the Worldwide Fund for Nature (WWF) warned, in a widely publicised report, that the skylark, song thrush and grey partridge could die out here within the next 10 years.

But consider this fact, rarely mentioned by the prophets of doom: we now have 42 more species of breeding birds than we did in 1800. In the same two centuries, just four species that were known to be breeding in Britain in 1800 have given up the ghost. (Another six species could be counted as losses but none of them was breeding here in 1800 and they have been recorded as breeders only intermittently over the years. In other words, their fortunes have fluctuated wildly.)

The list of losses does not contain any former breeding species that has packed its bags within the past few years, the attractive red-backed shrike being one of the very few examples. After all, unless a bird has been absent for some years, it's impossible to be sure that it isn't just about to return.

This detailed information on the fortunes of Britain's breeding birds – almost certainly the best-documented in the world – comes from an analysis done by Dr David Gibbons and Dr Mark Avery, respectively the RSPB's head of monitoring and director of conservation; and Dr Andrew Brown, English Nature's ornithologist. They used a scoring system to assess the general population trend of each species that bred in Britain in five time periods from 1800 up to 1995.

Why 1800? Simply because there are very few reliable accounts going back further. Accurate statistics are a more recent phenomenon which reflects the huge amateur and professional interest in Britain's birds and the veritable army of BTO (British Trust for Ornithology) members supplying information.

They also found that less than a third of these 42 new species are escapees from captivity or birds released here in the hope that they would settle down to breed. So the majority arrived of their own volition, found the place to their liking and stayed. Some – like the collared dove – are today incredibly abundant even though they didn't arrive here until 1955. Others, such as the elegant common crane, remain very rare.

No one disputes that a number of bird species, many of them abundant as recently as the sixties and seventies, are declining, some rapidly. According to a recent analysis by David Glue of the British Trust for Ornithology (BTO), of 73 species monitored by its Common Bird Census, 33 have been declining over the past 25 years. But another 17 species are holding their own and no less than 23 are increasing in numbers.

Most of the declines are of once common farmland birds like partridges and skylarks (the latter down by 60 per cent since 1970) and some birds of wet grassland and woodlands. The species on the up include birds of prey – the now common sparrowhawk, for example – which have recovered after the banning of the most toxic pesticides; some birds of wetlands and open water, and highly adaptable species such as wood pigeons, avid feeders on cereal crops.

'Some of this increase in species might be due to better recording,' suggests Dr Jeremy Greenwood, director of the BTO. 'Huge numbers of people are on the lookout for new species these days. Just imagine what would have happened in Victorian times to the first avocets (the black and white wading birds long since adopted as the emblem of the RSPB) to return to re-colonise marshes they had disappeared from years before. They would have been shot.

'Wetland birds in general have increased, partly because of better management of the wetlands that remain and also because shooting pressure has fallen. There may be just as many, or more, wildfowling clubs but there is so much less informal shooting for the pot. It's less indiscriminate, too. And the best places, wetlands and others, or most of them, have been protected as reserves.'

John Marchant, head of the BTO's Census Unit, adds another reason for these remarkable gains. 'Climate warming may well be helping certain species to spread up from southern Europe. Cetti's warbler (a small, noisy, brown bird fond of dense vegetation) has established itself in southern England, having gradually spread north from the Mediterranean. Another comparative newcomer is the serin, a lovely yellow songster of gardens and parklands, which was a very occasional visitor for years but has more recently stayed to breed, albeit in small numbers.'

While the total numbers of birds of all species is almost certainly much lower now than it was in the past – because of huge reductions in the areas of key habitats such as woodlands, moorlands and wet grasslands – our bird fauna has become much more diverse in species. What's more, it may diversify yet further as climate warming pulls in some southern species.

Marchant suggests several new birds that we might begin to see in Britain before long. Little egrets – attractive, snow-white, heron-like wetland birds – have already started to breed in very small numbers in southern England in the past few years. They are likely to spread.

The cattle egret – its white and yellow cousin with a habit of following livestock or tractors in open fields – could also fly our way from its Spanish strongholds.

Black kites, duller cousins of the more colourful red kite, might also set up shop. Their visitation would be less spectacular: they already breed as close as northern France.

Climate change could, of course, have its downside, too. Birds such as snow buntings and ptarmigan, which breed on high ground in Scotland, could leave for more northern climes – Scandinavia, for instance.

Inevitably, conservationists have focused on the losers. The steep declines of once abundant farmland birds – almost certainly due to changes in farming practices since the fifties – has grabbed headlines time and again.

But should we be so concerned about farmland birds, anyway? After all, the fields and hedgerows that form their habitats are relatively recent and entirely man-made. Until Roman times and the early Middle Ages, extensive forests clothed much of Britain, while extensive wetlands filled many a lowland valley. Both, sadly, have been desecrated.

Viewed over a longer timespan than a mere 200 years, perhaps we should be less bothered about the likes of skylarks, the numbers of which must have shot up as forests were felled and open land created. In the long term, it is broad-leaved woodland and wetland birds which have suffered most from habitat loss – woodpeckers, songsters, such as thrushes and nightingales, and marsh dwellers, such as herons and bitterns. And woodland and marshes are far richer in all sorts of species than open fields.

Conservationists must not lose sight of this longer perspective. They should pay as much attention to recreating more woodland and wetlands as they do to making farming more environmentally sensitive. That way, we are more likely to continue to enjoy a richer set of birds than ever.

14 May 2001

Rare Birds Return to Peace of Greenham

A.J. McIlroy

After nearly a decade the 'churring' song of the nightjar has replaced the roar of American nuclear bombers at Greenham Common.

The call, likened to 'the noise of a distant lawnmower', has been recorded on the 1,200-acre site at Newbury, Berks, along with the songs of the Dartford warbler and the woodlark, among Britain's rarest birds.

Andy Waters, of the Royal Society for the Protection of Birds, said: 'As we remove the concrete and restore the heathland the wildlife is coming back.

'We have recorded the churring of eight or nine male nightjars as well as the presence of seven woodlark pairs and three singing male Dartford warblers.

'The calls are territorial, and the nightjars make their churring sound around sunset as they catch moths and other insects on the wing. It would be difficult to miss this lawnmower-engine sound, which vibrates so much on the ear and reminds us summer is not far away.'

The RSPB says the common is part of the national network of heathlands that is crucial to the revival of rare birds.

'After being an integral part of the west's nuclear deterrent in the Cold War, and nearly a decade after the last American war planes left, the common is part of the international programme to save threatened bird species,' said Mr Waters.

Greenham became synonymous with the nuclear age during the 1980s when women peace campaigners camped outside the nine-mile perimeter fence calling for the removal of Cruise missiles.

Five years after the United States Air Force bombers left in 1992, the common was formally handed back by the Ministry of Defence to Newbury council and a trust of local businesses and community interests.

Their £7 million programme to return the site to heathland is now in its final stages after the recycling of more than one million tons of concrete, metals and tarmac from the airfield.

29 October 2005
Who's Afraid of the Big Bad Wolf?
Martin Hodgson

Clouds scud across the face of a full moon that hangs low above the glen. In the half-light, skeletal pines and silver birch glimmer eerily against the dark hillsides. The wind whips over the heather, carrying the distant roar of the river. On a night like this, it is not hard to imagine that the Highlands could once again echo with the untamed music of a wolf pack in full howl.

Wolves once roamed most of the northern hemisphere, from Portugal to China and from Mexico to Alaska. Today, they have been exterminated in most of their former territories: trapped, shot or hunted to death – driven back into the tangled thickets of legend and fairytale.

Britain was one of the first places in Europe where wolves were eradicated. They had disappeared from England and Wales by the end of the 13th century, but survived for several hundred years more in the rugged terrain of the Scottish Highlands. Legend holds that the last wolf in Scotland was finally hunted down in the upper reaches of the River Findhorn in 1743. Since then, the only wild wolves in Britain have been those that stalk hungrily through folk tales, devouring grannies, blowing down houses and menacing girls in red riding attire.

So when landowners or conservation activists propose bringing the wolf back to Scotland, it is perhaps not surprising that many people fear the worst: an invasion of ravening beasts with an insatiable appetite for sheep, deer and hill-walkers. But a growing body of wolf supporters argues that returning *Canis lupus* to the Highlands would boost tourism, help restore the depleted ecology and offer a lifeline to communities no longer able to survive on the meagre returns of farming and hunting.

Paul van Vlissingen, a Dutch businessman who owns the 80,000-acre Letterewe estate in Ross-shire, believes there is also a moral argument for bringing back the wolf. 'We are ruining the environment just by the way we live, so wherever we have the smallest chance we should try to redress the balance,' he says.

Van Vlissingen is financing a three-year study to examine the viability of reintroducing the wolf. He plans to present his findings to the Scottish Executive in the hope of stimulating a nationwide discussion. 'It will be a heated debate, I'm sure,' he says. 'But if there were still a dozen wolves roaming the countryside, perhaps causing a bit of trouble here and there, would anyone want to kill the last 12 wolves in Scotland? I'm sure the answer would be no.'

The conservation of existing animals is not the same as bringing a species back after hundreds of years, however, and species reintroductions inevitably provoke controversy. In September, the Scottish Executive turned down a proposal to reintroduce the relatively unthreatening beaver, after 10 years of often bitter argument. Even so, deputy environment minister Rhona Brankin insisted that the decision did not close the door to the possibility of bringing back other species.

If the wolf is to return any time soon, it seems more likely that it will be thanks to another millionaire landowner: Paul Lister, the son of MFI founder Noel Lister, and owner of the 23,000-acre Alladale estate in Sutherland.

He has already launched an ambitious plan to 're-wild' the former hunting estate, transforming it into a fenced wilderness reserve, where he hopes wolves, lynx and even brown bears will eventually roam free.

According to Lister, the carnivores are just one part of the plan, which will also involve replanting native flora to encourage the return of insects, birds and smaller mammals. 'The habitat inside the fence will be as wild as possible,' he says.

Lister's model is the Shamwari game reserve in South Africa, whose owners rehabilitated a series of overgrazed cattle farms, re-stocking the area with everything from prairie grass to elephants.

For the plan to succeed, Lister will need to convince neighbouring landowners to join forces with him, doubling the size of the reserve to some 50,000 acres – large enough, he believes, to accommodate two packs of wolves (12 to 15 animals), three pairs of lynx and up to 30 bears.

He has enlisted a team of conservation experts and wildlife managers, but there are many hurdles to overcome before the wolves can return. For a start, there is no legal provision for the kind of reserve that Lister plans; under current legislation, predators and their prey cannot be kept in the same enclosure. The project also faces opposition from ramblers over the idea of a 50-mile electrified fence, and from farmers and gamekeepers who fear an escape.

'Our ancestors worked like hell to get rid of wolves because they were devastating their livelihoods. To reintroduce them just seems bizarre,' says David Thompson, the vice-chairman of the Scottish Gamekeepers' Association.

'There will be some groups which will resist us till they're in their graves,' admits Lister. 'But there will be other people – hopefully the majority – who want it to succeed. Because if the majority don't want it, it isn't going to happen.'

Down the glen from Alladale, the villages of Ardgay and Bonar Bridge face each other across the Dornoch Firth. Opinions here have been divided since news of Lister's plan broke this year. 'We're farmers, so if any of those beasts break out we'll have our guns ready,' says one woman. 'But if it brings jobs, it'll be the best thing that's ever happened here.'

On a late-summer evening, some 400 people, from weather-beaten crofters to newly settled English retirees, squeeze into the Ardgay community hall for the first public meeting with Lister and his team.

'I'm pursuing a vision,' Lister tells the audience. 'One that will create jobs and restore the ecology. I think the benefits will outweigh any inconveniences, but this whole project will not go ahead unless we as a community want it to happen.'

There is a polite round of applause, and then the questions begin. Will the project stop ramblers walking up the glen? Will the fence be strong enough to hold the animals? Will it be strong enough to withstand a heavy snowfall? What would happen if an animal escaped?

Lister replies that many African reserves safely contain elephants and lions. 'But how much snow do they get in Africa?' one man asks. 'It gets so deep here, the beasts could just walk over the fence.'

The animals will be tagged with tracking devices so park rangers can monitor their movements, says Lister. 'In the unlikely event that an animal escaped,' he says, provoking a ripple of nervous laughter, 'it would be recovered within hours.'

By the end of the meeting, only a handful of speakers have expressed outright hostility to the plan, but many people are still uneasy at living near a wolf pack. 'It's a real worry,' says Stephen Gortan, a company director who lives nearby. 'We need guarantees of safety, not just promises. I've got a little boy – if he's playing in the garden it'll be snack time when the wolf's around.'

According to the naturalist Christoph Promberger, who spent 10 years studying wolves in the Carpathians, our fear is out of proportion to the threat they actually pose. Although they will prey on livestock if they can, they do not normally attack humans. 'Wolves simply avoid people. You're much more likely to die of a wasp sting than from a wolf.'

But the idea of the wolf's hostility and appetite has been cemented by centuries of folk tales, in which the wolf is invariably big, bad and ravenous. Michelle Paver, author of the *Wolf Brother* series of children's novels, traces this idea back to the moment when our ancestors gave up the nomadic life of the hunter and settled down to become farmers. Farming communities from Sámi reindeer herders to Montana cattle-ranchers detest the wolf, but hunting peoples such as the Inuit respect its prowess on the trail and include it in their rituals and creation myths.

'Hunter-gatherer cultures identify with wolves, because they're clever, they form strong family bonds, they communicate, they play and they're terrific hunters,' says Paver. 'But once livestock becomes your property, the wolf is regarded as your enemy rather than your brother.'

To early farming cultures, the wolf represented all that we had left behind in the woods, she says. 'Everything bestial in man – all the appalling drives and unmentionable urges – was projected on to wolves.'

This, coupled with the fear of rabies, was the likely origin of the werewolf – now the staple of creaky horror movies, but once seen as a real danger. In medieval Europe, laws against werewolves were passed, and suspected lycanthropes were burnt at the stake. As recently as 1933, the English clergyman Montague Summers wrote a book treating werewolves as a demonic historical fact. 'A werewolf is possessed of all the characteristics, the foul appetites, ferocity, cunning, the brute strength, and swiftness of that animal,' he wrote.

If the werewolf expresses a fear of the beast within man, there is a parallel tradition portraying a humane quality in the beast. The figure of the child raised by wolves looms through history, from the legend of Romulus and Remus to Kipling's Mowgli. But true or apocryphal, these stories tell us more about human dreams than about actual wolves. Centuries of legend and fairytales have obscured our knowledge of the wolf's biology, and the complex web of ecological relations that link it to other species.

In 1995, grey wolves were reintroduced to Yellowstone National Park in the US, despite the opposition of a powerful ranching lobby. Ten years later, the benefits, both ecological and economic, are clear, says spokeswoman Cheryl Matthews. 'The data we've gathered suggests that wolf reintroduction is leading to a greater biodiversity across the whole ecosystem, not just inside the park,' she says. Scraps of meat left by wolves have provided valuable food sources for eagles and other scavengers. The wolves have also helped the recovery of over-grazed woodland by flushing elk from one area to another.

Lister believes that a similar effect would be felt in Scotland, where the intensive rearing of deer and sheep has stripped the hills of heather and stopped the regrowth of Caledonian pines. And just as the Yellowstone wolves have reduced the park's coyote population, wolves in the Highlands would cut the number of smaller predators such as foxes, polecats and stoats. This, in turn, could aid the survival of endangered ground-nesting birds such as black grouse and capercaillie.

Tourist centres near Yellowstone have also seen a surge in revenue, thanks to the thousands of visitors coming to see the wolves. The financial argument may be the one that rings loudest in the Highlands: stalking and fishing no longer provide enough employment to keep youngsters in the region, and Lister thinks his project will generate at least 100 jobs and create trade for hotels and other businesses.

Central Europe – especially Romania, which is home to a third of the continent's wolf population – has already seen a boom in wolf tourism. In many areas, shepherds still lose stock to predators, but humans – at times grudgingly – have found a way to share their landscape with the wolf.

In Britain, however, it has been more than 250 years since large carnivores roamed in the wild: we no longer know what it means to live with the wolf at the door.

And perhaps we have forgotten more than that. On our overcrowded island, we have lost the sense of wilderness. Even the remotest corners of Scotland have been shaped by centuries of human intervention. 'A mountain with a wolf on it stands a little higher,' wrote the American author Edward Hoagland. How much richer would the British landscape be if the Highlands were once again to echo with a wild lupine howl?

15 April 1995
Kites Flying High
Roger Dobson

Forget the goose; it is the red kite which is laying the golden egg for rural mid-Wales. The kite, much protected and prized, and guarded for a decade or more by groups of volunteers including a squad of Gurkha soldiers, SAS members and a band of Watford ornithologists, has suddenly become big business.

Thanks to such protection over the years, the numbers of the birds have grown, and so too has the range of entrepreneurial activities of people living in the Welsh communities which make up the area that will, from next month, be marketed as 'Kite Country' – the only region of the principality where the dragon gets second billing to a bird.

There are kite minibus tours which travel beneath the flight path of the birds as they fly from nests to local refuse tips scavenging for food, and there are kite treks, walking holidays and mountain-bike tours.

There is now a watch-the-kite-eat attraction, kite farm walks at £2 a time, hotels offering kite holidays, and a 'Stay on a Farm in Kite Country' project which has so far attracted around 130 farmers happy to tell guests about the bird that was almost wiped out at the turn of the century, reduced to a handful of breeding pairs in Wales.

There are also souvenirs like kite videos and CDs; kite badges, postcards and T-shirts; kite books; kite label jam, kite key fobs, and kite kites. No one steals the kite eggs any more, but other souvenirs do disappear.

The sheer scale of the bird's value to mid-Wales is revealed in a request for financial assistance for the Kite Country Project made to the Welsh Office by Powys County Council and a consortium of other local authorities, most of whom have adopted some form of the kite in their logos.

Measured in tourist income alone, the kite is now reckoned to be worth about £4 million a year – the equivalent of nearly £10,000 for each of the 457 birds. It is also estimated to be providing nearly 60 jobs in the hotel and leisure industry in an area of the Cambrian Mountains which has been vulnerable in recent years to agricultural decline, low wages and depressingly high rural unemployment.

All these predictions on income do not include other activities linked to the lure of the rare bird, like the Red Kite Cafe at Llywernog, Red Kite Mountain Bikes at Llanwrtyd Wells, and the Red Kite minibus tours.

Kite Country co-ordinator, Tony Walker, heads the project, which is being formally launched on 22 May. He said: 'The red kite has made a big difference to this area. It is bringing in income and in a sense that is a reward for the protection it has had from the people here. The kite has become the accepted image for this area and we are now going to market that image under this one project. When you come to this area you see more kites on logos than dragons.'

Kite mania may also have been responsible for the disappearance from the Red Kite Café, a mecca for bird buffs, of a red-kite sculpture of the bird that had been carved from a block of North Wales slate.

'It just disappeared. It was very big and heavy and they unscrewed it from the wall,' said Tony Hawtin, the proprietor. 'We are now going to get a new sign which can't be stolen – we are going to paint it on the roof.'

At Aberystwyth, Peter Davies, a member of a kite-observers team, has logged 24 businesses and councils which use the kite logo. They range from an estate agent to a film company called Baracud – Welsh for red kite. 'The kite seems to have become an image for the area. Several also use it on promotional brochures and that sort of thing,' he said.

Two new visitor observation centres at Rhayader and Nant-y-Arian, near Aberystwyth, are the top attractions for kite connoisseurs. Nine cameras will be permanently trained on kite nests and within the next few weeks live pictures will be screened in the centres.

'In this way people can get very close to the birds without disturbing them and without giving away the locations of the nests. The centres are as interactive as possible. Visitors can use and direct the cameras themselves, and then they can go outside and see the real things flying above them,' said Walker.

A new attraction at Gigrin Farm near Rhayader means that between November and April tourists can watch the kites eat food put out at 2 p.m. each day. Admisssion to the farm kite trail costs £2.

The promotional literature says that the birds come within 10 metres of special hides built at the end of last year.

There is also an interactive computer centre at Llandovery, a red-kite museum at Llandrindod Wells, and several book shops boasting red-kite books, posters and postcards. Tony Walker's project offers enamel kite badges whose numbers are limited to the number of red kites there are in the region.

And if all that wasn't enough, the new marketing plan for Kite Country shows that the aim this year is to attract 100,000 visitors, with particular emphasis on attracting more people over winter.

'Attracting visitors at this time fills empty beds and extends the season,' says the strategy report.

For those worried about exploitation of the kite, the report gives the assurance that the environmental impact of increasing numbers of visitors is being monitored to make sure it does not affect the bird.

After all, mid-Wales does not want to kill the bird that lays the £4m-a-year egg.

10 October 2011

Feeding Red Kites 'Will Make Them a Menace'

Red kites risk becoming a 'menace' in urban areas as birdwatchers leave out food in the hope of seeing them at close quarters, researchers have warned.

The birds of prey have made a comeback in some parts of the countryside after three centuries of being hunted to the point of extinction. But there are fears they will become a dangerous pest if lured into gardens, and a study on the urban feeding of red kites is to be conducted by Reading University's biology department.

Reading is not far from the Chiltern Hills in Oxfordshire and Buckinghamshire where the birds were reintroduced in the 1980s.

Cathy Rose, from the Chilterns Conservation Board, said: 'The kites become accustomed to coming close to people and while for some that's a great experience, for others it's terrifying.'

30 May 1998

Eagle Eyes on the Egg Thieves
Matthew Gwyther

John Dodsworth is a lucky man. If the Royal Society for the Protection of Birds (RSPB) had its way, he would be behind bars this weekend. Last week, Durham magistrates found him guilty of the possession of 1,100 wild birds' eggs, but gave him only a conditional discharge.

The RSPB, which is lobbying hard for custodial sentences to be imposed for all serious cases of egg theft, was outraged. 'We were livid,' says a spokesman. 'If he'd been found guilty of badger-baiting, for example, he could have well ended up in prison. Some of his eggs came from incredibly rare species where we're down to the last few pairs in the UK.'

Dodsworth, of South Shields in Northumberland, is no isolated crank. Egg thefts go on the whole time. Over the Easter weekend, for example, some were stolen from two rare pairs of sea eagles nesting on the island of Mull in Scotland.

There are only 15 pairs of sea eagles in the country and, although the RSPB had kept a watch on the clutches, the eggs were spirited away, probably in the early hours of Good Friday. Egg collectors are strongly suspected because both trees showed signs of having been climbed.

The struggle between the RSPB and Britain's 'eggers' has been continuing for many years, part cat and mouse, part bitter guerrilla war. The charity goes to great lengths to protect the nests of endangered species. Included in its arsenal are automatic time-lapse photographic equipment, infrared night sights, pressure pads linked to alarm systems, observation vans with one-way glass and even barbed wire wrapped around the base of tree-trunks.

When sufficient evidence is gathered, police prosecute under the 1981 Wildlife and Countryside Act, which forbids the disturbance or collection of the eggs of any wild bird.

Guy Shorrock, an investigations officer with the RSPB, is like a cross between Inspector Morse and Doctor Dolittle. A former policeman, he has done his time crawling through the undergrowth in camouflage paint and has nothing but contempt for the eggers.

'These are ridiculous, obsessive individuals,' he says. 'We estimate there are about 300 egg collectors, of whom a small proportion – say 30 to 40 – are actively and illegally adding to their collections. They are all male. We have never come across a female egg collector.'

So not a million miles away from trainspotters? 'Yes, except that what egg collectors do is socially completely unacceptable.'

With the RSPB's intelligence nets spreading nationwide, the heat is now on collectors – so much so that many use 'safe houses', with hidden compartments and false panels, to store their trophies because they know the risks of keeping eggs at home. There has even been one case of a disgruntled woman shopping her boyfriend to the RSPB because she grew weary of his hobby.

The oldest established egg collectors' club is the Jourdain Society, against whose members the RSPB has conducted a remorseless campaign over the past 15 years. It is named after the Rev F.C.R. Jourdain, who died in 1940. He was a leading light in the British Oological Association and an egg collector with a notorious temper that earned him the nickname 'Pastor Pugnax'.

His public rows about tufted ducks and Corsican nuthatches with P.F. Bunyard, an oologist who was stone deaf, were apparently a sight to behold.

The Jourdain holds three dinners each year at which they get together and talk eggs. A while ago the RSPB, in conjunction with a film crew, bugged a room at the Fleece Hotel in Gloucester in an attempt to gain evidence of wrongdoing against Jourdain members. Another dinner at the Red Lion in Salisbury was raided by 14 police officers and two RSPB staff: eight trays of eggs were removed.

The Jourdainians' loathing for the RSPB is surpassed only by their disdain for the press and they very rarely assent to interviews. One broke ranks and agreed to talk to *Weekend* on the strict understanding that his identity would be kept secret.

The essence of his argument was that, although the RSPB did some good work, it had been taken over by zealots – 'little Hitlers', he called them – who had forgotten about the true welfare of birds. The scientific value of egg collection had been overlooked and innocent individuals with collections taken legally before 1981 had been subjected to harassment by the charity.

'My own collection, which was started by my grandfather and continued by my father, has become like a millstone around my neck,' he says. 'I've had to have affidavits sworn of its legality and sometimes I feel like just smashing it up to avoid all the hassle.'

But wasn't it true that more than a dozen Jourdain members since 1981 had been found guilty of unlawful egg possession? 'Yes, but we have expelled people when it was necessary. One individual kept on at red kites. You cannot do that here. For red kites, you go to Spain.'

In fact, collecting red-kite eggs is also illegal in Spain, but arrest is less likely on the Continent so many collectors now travel abroad.

It was clear that our informant believed the law to be an ass and cited the example of the meadow pipit as a bird that would re-lay eggs within 10 days if relieved of them by a collector.

'Taking a clutch of sea eagles' eggs is unforgivable, but removing common eggs does no harm at all,' he says.

Most in the bird world disagree. Ian Lycett of *Birdwatch* (not an RSPB publication) says: 'It's an old-fashioned hangover from the Victorian era. Very few birders are interested in eggs these days. Most find their collection abhorrent.'

As recently as last year, James Whitaker, the Jourdain Society's dining secretary, was found guilty at Otley magistrates of offences under the 1981 Act. Out of a collection of 2,895 eggs, it was found that 148 had been illegally gathered, including seven from the rare merlin. He was caught out by discrepancies in his documentation: some had collection dates 45 years apart, but appeared to be written in the same handwriting and ink.

Whitaker did not go down without a vigorous fight. Guy Shorrock, who gave evidence for the RSPB, says: 'They had me in the witness box for 10-and-a-half hours and the trial went on for 12 days.' Whitaker was fined £1,480 – £10 per egg – and made to pay £1,600 costs.

These penalties were nothing compared with those handed out to Jamie and Lee McLaren. Known in the ornithological world as the Abbott and Costello of egg-collecting, the brothers from Portsmouth were caught red-handed in the Orkneys last year with 31 eggs, including clutches from hen-harriers, red-throated divers and merlins.

'They were nothing to do with us,' says our member of the Jourdain. 'Jourdain members are first-class field naturalists who carefully study breeding habits. Those two were just cowboys.'

The McLarens' big mistake was to video each other robbing nests: one scene even showed a fulmar vomiting the contents of its stomach over their shoes in a last-ditch attempt to protect its offspring. The Sheriff at Kirkwall demanded that the McLarens be fined £90,000 each – a tall order as Jamie, a labourer, earned only £130 a week and Lee, a part-time taxi-driver, an even more modest £53.

The bird world was aghast, but the fines were reduced to £6,000 and £4,000 on appeal. Nevertheless, the McLarens will still be paying off their fines in 2004.

Meanwhile, there is more welcome news from the Lake District. Under close guard, next to Haweswater after years of barrenness, England's sole pair of golden eagles have finally produced some eggs. This week, as *Weekend* went to press, the cheep of taloned chicks was expected at any moment – God and villains willing.

23 September 2006

The Waders That Inspired a Lost Art

Peter Marren

Robert Gillmor reaches the hide at about eight o'clock on a bright morning. The cool light floods across the reed-fringed pool, backlighting a huddle of wading birds sifting for food in the shallow water. As usual he sets up his mini-studio in the corner, attaching his telescope to a clamp in the corner of the hide. It has an angled eyepiece that allows him to draw with one eye on the bird, the other on his sketch pad.

He sketches rapidly, one eye screwed up against the brilliant light. 'I often spend the day sketching a single species, trying to capture its movement,' says Gillmor. 'The first drawings are often tentative. There may be pages of starts and stops. But then you get your eye in, and things seem to slow down and it starts to come together.'

One of the delights of this hide at Titchwell on the Norfolk coast is that the light changes all the time. Gillmor remembers one particular morning when the early sun caught a group of avocets. 'The water lapping round their bellies was streaked with gold, while the birds themselves were silhouetted a dove-grey colour outlined in white. It made a beautiful picture that I later turned into a linocut, a four-colour print of gold, two greys and black. An unlikely combination you might think, but absolutely true to life.'

Gillmor has been illustrating birds for more than half a century now. A keen naturalist from boyhood, he learnt about printmaking by watching his grandfather, the wildlife artist Allen William Seaby. His own first published illustrations, ink drawings of the Manx shearwater, appeared in British Birds in 1952, when he was still at school. He has illustrated more than 100 books since then, as well as a steady flow of watercolours, scraper-board drawings and linocuts, all based on close observation of living birds in their natural habitat.

'Gillmor's work is always immaculately executed,' says Andrew Stock, president of the Society of Wildlife Artists. 'It's usually bold in design, often with subtle yet vibrant colour patterns.'

Lino-cutting is Gillmor's favourite medium, and one he has made his own. His new book, *Cutting Away*, contains 90 of his avian linocuts, each accompanied by a commentary by the artist. Some have the feel of a Japanese print: a flight of swans behind a curtain of reeds or a gaggle of preening spoonbills in the dove-grey evening light. There is a lyrical cut of sparring hares in the March moonlight. And a wonderfully bold display of migrating lapwings.

Long-legged birds with contrasting colours work best in this medium. That is why Gillmor spends so much time in hides on the coast watching waders, swans and shelducks. 'Little brown jobs' in gardens are less linoleum-friendly.

His favourite bird is the one that best resembles a living linocut. 'For me, avocets are the most fun to watch,' says Gillmor. 'The chicks totter around on too-large legs, exploring this and trying that. Every so often mum calls her chicks to be brooded. They pile under her loose belly feathers, her wings drooping on either side, and all that can be seen are a mass of little legs jostling for the cosiest position.'

Cutting Away works on two levels, says Gillmor. Literally the title refers to the way the artist works a sheet of linoleum, scoring and gouging the surface into a kind of negative of the subsequent print. But it is also about getting down to basics. 'Lino-cutting forces me to select and simplify,' he says. 'It's about bold, flat patterns and colours. You have to consider the relationships of shapes and the spaces between them, and add detail only where it is relevant.'

Back in the 1960s, when Gillmor was making his mark, very few people earned a living from drawing and painting birds. It was Gillmor who, in 1960, wrote to all the best artists of the day – Peter Scott, Keith Shackleton, Eric Ennion and others – and persuaded them to participate in an all-bird exhibition. It proved to be a showstopper and toured the country for two years.

That success led to the formation of the Society of Wildlife Artists, which held its first exhibition in 1964. Today it shows around 500 works by 80 or more artists from Britain and abroad, reflecting a worldwide renaissance in wildlife art. Gillmor is now seen as the 'godfather' of modern bird art, encouraging traditional artists to develop, while welcoming the more progressive and innovative.

At 70, his energy and imagination show no sign of slackening. According to Stock: 'It is Gillmor's gentle hand on the tiller that has steered the successful course of wildlife art in this country over the past four decades.'

17 September 1977
The Last Rites of Summer
J.H.B. Peel

The landowner who says he is too busy to trim his hedge is like the helmsman who says he is too busy to steer his ship. Hedges in a farming country are necessities, not ornaments. If they run amok they fail to provide an adequate windbreak for livestock and crops. Hedges ought to be leafy and close-knit to a height of 4 or 5 feet; above that level they rob the adjacent soil of sunlight and ventilation.

Many of the lanes near my home are only just wide enough to take a car, and by the end of July the branches and briars need to be cut back. If this is not done, vehicles get scratched while cyclists get wounded. One of my own small fields overlooks just such a lane, and in midsummer the hedge is trimmed by a farmhand. During September it is re-trimmed by myself. The task occupies less than an hour, and is time well spent, as anyone knows who, at 10 o'clock in the morning, has watched the sun disperse an autumn mist. Choosing an auspicious day, therefore, I proceed to tidy-up, armed with leather gauntlets and a sharp blade.

The lane itself is steep as well as narrow. In fact, the field overlooks the stiffest contour of a 1-in-3 gradient. The lane leads (as we say) from nowhere in particular to nowhere in general. It was made in order to serve a few remote cottages and farms. The far side of it dips to a combe and then climbs a lofty ridge of woodland and pasture. To say that nobody ever uses the lane is a colloquial way of stating that in autumn the traffic averages two vehicles a day: the milkwoman in a van and the farmer on a tractor. During August I did once count as many as three vehicles in six hours, but such congestion is neither seen nor heard from the house.

There is something modesty complacent in the performance of a duty whose results are private. Few people have ever seen me trimming the hedge. Strangers might never notice that I had done so, were it not for the unkempt hedges on some of the other lanes which have been neglected for decades, and are now as high as a house.

So, under the hot sun and to the tune of humming insects, the grass and briars are slashed away, leaving a green-and-brown tidemark in the lane. A certain amount of amateur botanising takes place during the work. One identifies the common plants – bracken, nettles, docks, blackberries – together with the relics of dog's mercury, herb robin, snowdrops, anemones, celandines, violets, daisies, primroses, bluebells, foxgloves. In short, the lane is a kind of calendar, recording the birth of spring and the death of winter.

How easy it is to recognise, yet how difficult to define, the look of the land in late September. A quick glance may deny that autumn has arrived, for the shaded beech and the riverside meadow still glow as green as in August. Garden flowers still span the spectrum, and a white cloud enhances a blue sky. Closer examination, however, tells the truth. Trees and bracken bear the brown marks of age. The grass, too, may be brown, especially on hillsides during a dry spell.

Every shadow is a sundial, showing Earth's progress round the sun. And where are the birds of yester-spring, those tireless food-ferries? They are in the shade, silent after an August moult and the last brood. Some of them will soon migrate like rich men wintering in a warm climate. Only the robin has much to say, cocky as a member of the choir who suddenly finds himself singing solo. Next month his voice will sound above the sigh of falling leaves and the moan of rising wind.

'Golden' is a favourite September adjective among the poets. The dust itself seems golden; and if the landscape shows a field of standing corn, then the yellow radiance really does catch the eye, distracting it from all other colours. But the gilt is very thin on a season whose sunsets may unfold Mary Webb's vista:

When autumn winds are on the hill
And darkly rides the wasting moon . . .

After half-an-hour the trimming invites a rest, so I lean against the bank, sampling the silence. Far away on the opposite hill a farmhouse glistens white. In the middle distance a red stag strolls leisurely into a coppice. Midges tread the mill of a sunbeam that slants like an intangible pillar across the lane. Three feet above my head, a robin sits astride a spray of holly, quizzing the debris.

Now the pungent smoke climbs like an Indian rope until, breasting the bank, it meets a breeze and is zig-zagged away. Everything is so dry that a single spark may start a fire. However, the hedge has been shorn back-and-sides, and no passer-by will complain that a briar has grazed his cheek. Meanwhile – standing guard over the bonfire – I lose count of time, but when I look up at the sun, I see that I have spent more than a dozen minutes alternately feeding and compressing the blaze. When at last the smoke subsides, the ashes in the lane resemble a pyre from which the autumn and the winter will evoke another spring.

Some people regard hedge-trimming as a trivial task, on a par with brushing one's teeth: necessary, no doubt, but scarcely a topic of conversation. The world, they say, would soon be in a sorry state if we spent our time wandering up and down the country lanes of Britain. True; yet true also that the world would soon be in a less sorry state if we could rusticate some of those people who now spend their time wandering up and down the corridors of power. When set in its proper place, trimming a hedge gives an active answer to a famous question:

What is this life, if, full of care,
We have no time to stand and stare?

19 November 2001
What Would Gilbert White Say?
John Humphrys

A thousand years ago, a yew tree forced its way above the ground in the churchyard of Selborne. It may have been three or four centuries earlier – there is no way of telling – because yews become hollow with age and a ring count is not possible.

But now, it is gone; laid low by the savage storms of 1990. All that remains is a hunk of dead wood, smooth as paper to the touch, and a plaque to mark its existence; a monument to the past. Selborne, home to the great 18th-century naturalist Gilbert White, is the poorer for it. But at least it was the force of nature that destroyed it, and not mankind.

I went to Selborne because I was angered at what man is doing there: at recent reports that planning officials had allowed mechanical diggers to rip out huge chunks of the land, disfiguring precious water meadows to create three man-made ponds. It was being done, it was claimed, in the sacred cause of environmental improvement.

The aim was to create greater biodiversity. But this, surely, was vandalism of a high order. If they could do this to Selborne, how else might this precious preserve of England's heritage be at risk from the improvers and the ravages of passing centuries?

As the Selborne Yew was the nation's most famous tree, so Selborne became the nation's most famous village – its life chronicled in painstaking and exquisite detail in White's book, *The Natural History of Selborne*. For generations, almost every child who ever won a prize at school has had White's book thrust into his grubby little hand by the visiting speech-day dignitary. It is said to be the fourth most published book in the English language and White's many fans say that he was the first real naturalist.

White immortalised a world that has been preserved over the centuries – or so it has always seemed to many of his disciples. His home has become a museum, a model of its kind, unpretentious and welcoming. His gardens are lovingly tended by men and women devoted to his memory. Even his vegetable plot has been recreated to grow the melons of which he was so fond. Villagers still worship in the church of which he was a humble curate.

Close your ears and eyes to the traffic that tears through the main street and it is, indeed, just possible to imagine that Gilbert White still wanders the deeply rutted lanes of Selborne.

In fact, everything has changed. Not just the holes for the ponds. Not just the ancient yew. Not just the modern houses tacked on to the end of the village. The history of Selborne has been re-written.

Take the most mundane of those changes – the new houses – and compare them with the cottages White strolled past. They are utilitarian boxes. They have none of the charm of the old thatched cottages with cobbled paths and clinging honeysuckle. No Japanese tourist would bother unslinging his digital camera from around his neck to snap them.

Yet Selborne, like so many villages in rural England, had been dying. Young local people could not afford the prices of this punishingly expensive corner of Hampshire and were moving away. No young families means no new children and that means no need for the village school. Selborne was on its way to becoming a dormitory village, the preserve of wealthy weekenders or commuters – precisely the opposite of how it was in White's day, when most of its inhabitants scarcely set foot outside the parish. The new houses are reserved for local people and are described as 'affordable'. The village has changed in order to stay alive.

The gardens of White's home have changed, too. There is a pond where none existed in his day. Sacrilege perhaps, but the pond is alive with newts and frogs and water beetles.

In another corner of the gardens, workmen are completing a field centre that will be used mostly by visiting schoolchildren.

The view from White's house has changed even more. In this part of the world they do not call a wood a wood. If it clothes an escarpment, they call it a hanger. The slope that rises from the rear of White's house is, today, as thickly wooded as any hanger in Hampshire: there are great beeches, whose leaves are turning in the cool autumn weather, and dark and brooding yews.

What Gilbert White saw when he was studying a flight of martins in 1780 was land that was 'clothed with beechen shrubs which, being stunted and bitten by sheep, make the thickest covert imaginable; and are so entangled as to be impervious to even the smallest spaniel'.

Then came the industrial revolution. The shepherds left the hills to find work that paid more than their pittance and the sheep went, too. With no sheep to nibble at them, the saplings became trees. Their canopy closed over the hills, cutting off the light to the scrub, and now even the largest spaniel can scamper to its heart's delight.

It was the next revolution that was to bring the most profound change to Selborne: the agricultural revolution of the fifties.

Farming in this country had changed remarkably little until the last world war. England was still largely a patchwork of mixed farms with small fields. The hedges offered shelter to the livestock and a home to the birds and beetles that feasted on the insects attracted to the crops. When the crops were harvested, the soil kept its stubble until it was ploughed for the next sowing in the spring. Most of the chalk downland with its thin soil was never ploughed. It was used, instead, as grazing for sheep or suckler cows. Nor were the water meadows ploughed.

But then came the war and the U-boats, blasting British freighters and their cargoes of grain to the bottom of the sea. At the start of the war, we were importing more than 22 million tons of food and animal feed, most of it carried across the North Atlantic by a fleet of 3,000 merchant navy ships. Three years later, that had fallen by more than half. It was a terrifying time in our history and the politicians swore we would never be held hostage again. British agriculture had to become efficient.

If that meant ploughing the downs and draining the water meadows, then let it happen. If ancient hedges or copses made it difficult for the vast new machinery to operate, then the diggers were brought in to rip them out with scarcely a tear shed. Farmers no longer needed the birds and the beetles to act as predators; the insects they had been eating were killed off by the new pesticides. Small mammals that had sheltered in the winter stubble disappeared as spring wheat gave way to winter sowing.

And for any farmer who might have had a twinge of regret for the old ways, there were generous new subsidies to compensate.

So England changed and Selborne changed with it. The downs around the village that had given White such pleasure, and such rich material, fell silent as the birds and the butterflies began to die out.

The lapwings and the skylarks are now a rare sight. It was White who discovered how the flycatchers kept their young cool on hot summer days by fanning their wings above their nests. He learnt how the nightjar produced its song, listening to him night after night. These days, it is rare to see a flycatcher or hear a nightjar at all. Some birds, such as the stone curlew, have vanished entirely. Many of the wild flowers that thrived on the downs and in the meadows around the village have gone.

Now, this is all grist to the mill of a journalist with a mission. Mine, remember, was to sound the tocsin about how they have been destroying this most precious jewel in England's rural crown. It is easy to do that; there is much to be alarmed about. But it misses the point of Gilbert White and his life's work.

White was more than just a simple chronicler. Yes, he was intrigued by every chirrup of a grasshopper and whether the swallows really did – as was believed then – hibernate in some local hideaway during the winter. But he was equally interested in celebrating 'the miraculous way that the world fitted together and worked'.

Would he have been appalled at the lack of respect shown to habitats once so rich in flora and fauna – or would he have recognised the need for change?

I had expected the good people who guard Selborne and struggle to raise the money for it to stoke my anger at the changes, but they did not. The local ornithologist, Dr John Eyre, is naturally dismayed at the disappearance of many birds, but welcomes the appearance of new ones: White had never seen a collared dove. As we talked over a splendid lunch in White's tea parlour, one perched on the roof of his old brew house.

Real conservation is not about paralysis. It is not about freezing a moment in time, but managing the changes that happen over the years. Gilbert White – his writings and his home – gives us a base line. We can marvel at what we once had, but instead of wringing our hands in despair, we can value what is left – and try not to make the same mistakes again.

18 June 2011

The Tragedy of the Gold-Crested Humble

Clive James

For more than a month now, *Springwatch* (BBC2) has been back, its main aim obviously being to see how thoroughly a perfect format can be screwed by burdening Kate Humble with help. Until 2009, she had all the help she needed. Bill Oddie supplied the kind of facts that even Kate, at one with nature though she is, could not be expected to have at her elegant fingertips. But Bill Oddie, unwell and needing a rest, moved on; and the Beeb panicked, wondering what they could do to save Kate Humble from the dangers of solitude. Her status as a threatened species has been signalled by surrounding her with assistants, advisors, scientists and clowns. Ah, my snow leopard. If you're in there, can you wave a paw?

The reader will correctly deduce that Kate Humble speaks to my heart. I doubt if the same is untrue for any male viewer of whatever age. Recently the last soldier to have fought in the First World War died smiling and I bet he was thinking of Kate Humble. It isn't just that she's so wellspoken and finely formed, it's that she has a merry way of convincing you that nature is a good thing, really, even though some of the new clutch of fluff-tit chicks might not make it through the night. And if nature is a good thing, then doubly must she be, for she is nature at its best.

Or she was, but then the improvements started. The format fiddlers moved in and got busy. In previous years, apart from Bill Oddie searching for an elusive fact in his jacket made of pockets, there was nobody to distract from Kate except a guy in the far north who spotted otters. Up there on some Shetland or Orkney, he had given his life to climbing around the rocks at night whispering 'There they are!' or, more commonly, 'Where are they?' But now he is gone, and by my count he has been replaced by at least two other guys that can be cut away to at any time when you are just settling down to hear more from Kate about the fluff-tit chick in peril of its life.

One of these guys has beaver fever. He is convinced that we will be enthralled by the reintroduction of the beaver, even though there are plenty of locals on tap to say that beaver dams kill salmon, and even though the beavers themselves soon convince you that their colleague who ended up mounted on Mel Gibson's hand was the only one with any talent. The guy who spotted otters looked like one of the Heroes of Telemark: a striding Viking worthy to share the screen with Kate.

The guy with beaver fever looks like a man deeply interested in beavers. This week he wasn't there. Search the dam.

But there is yet another guy who penetrates deepest Wales armed with special permission to mispronounce 'wild-life' so that millions of children will grow up talking about 'why-life', unless they listen to Kate, which there is increasingly less opportunity to do. Back at base, Kate has to cope with Chris, Martin and the Fun Doctor. Chris is formidably knowledgeable but he has an unfortunate taste for banter, as if what we wanted from Kate were a comedy routine instead of eye-to-eye contact across the steaming surface of an Irish coffee. And as for the new recruit Martin, he is afflicted with a nervous snigger, as if he can't believe that he is on screen for minutes at a stretch with Kate nowhere in sight.

I can't believe it either. It's not as if Martin has anything to tell you that Kate couldn't, which is the chief argument against putting any of these chaps into the programme at all. But the job of distraction is not down to just them: there is also a Fun Doctor figure who jumps out of a doorway and runs around frantically so as to signal to anybody in the audience under the age of two that a joke is on the way. For if there is not a quiz, there must be a joke. There must be anything except a straight narrative from Kate about the ailing fluff-tit chick. Not that Kate is undone by compassion. She is a realist. In fact she might be something even tougher than that. Last week it took a baby barn owl three and a half minutes to swallow a wood mouse and Kate was laughing all the way.

Perhaps it is better for younger male viewers, while still in short pants, to face the possibility: you could be a wood mouse, upside down in the throat of a baby barn owl and going down nastily to oblivion, while the most beautiful adult female human being in the world throws back her honey-coloured curls and laughs her head off. There is always a chance that *Springwatch*, *Autumnwatch* and all the other regular nature shows for the whole family don't show us quite enough of that. About a month ago, on BBC Four I think, there was a very good nature programme about nature programmes. Adorned with the family-friendly title of *Welly Telly* and narrated by Bill Oddie, happily back on the case, the show traced the development of the why-life show as a genre.

With due allowance for entertainment requirements, there was always an emphasis on red in tooth and claw. There was just a question about how much of the bad stuff to show. The question grew more acute as the cameras got better at seeing everything. David Attenborough was there to say that the really bad stuff has always been left on the cutting room floor. What we were allowed to see was dreadful enough: a lioness, say, eating the insides of an antelope while the antelope was still alive. The antelope looked more puzzled than pained, but it would still have been a tough one to explain to the kids.

Yet explain it to them we must, in preparation for the even worse news that human beings do these things too, and not just to animals but to each other. But not always; and by the end of their lives, having gone through every stage from babyhood to decrepitude without having encountered a predator like Ratko Mladić anywhere except on television, they might have learned that being human is to love life. The correct lesson, but our haunting doubt must always be that they might learn it too easily. Shouldn't we be out there with a spear like a young Masai warrior, killing the lion to earn our cup of blood and milk? Damn me, but I never did it; and now it's too late. The corn flakes got me, and 70 years later I'm still eating them. Even the processed version of existence, however, has turned out to be pretty thrilling. Why life? Why, so that it can be loved; and if you doubt that, just look at Kate Humble, briefly visible amongst her swarm of helpers, like Botticelli's Venus caught in a rugby scrum.

Disappearing Worlds

13 June 1992

The Village Pub: an Endangered Species

Byron Rogers

You have heard old men talk about such things; you may even have noted the odd absence yourself when the developers have gone. But until now very few had actually seen it happen – the sheets of chipboard nailed to the window frames of Georgian buildings and of brick bunkers at the edge of town – when, in 1992, all over Britain, the pubs started to shut up shop.

Two went within the last few months, four miles from where I live; I mention this only because it is impossible to get national figures. One was a village pub 200 years old. The other, the Brave Old Oak at Towcester, probably dates from the late Middle Ages. In other words, something very ancient is ending abruptly in our time. There's nothing new about pub closures. A small town will have half the number it had 150 years ago, when pubs were small. What is new is that we are seeing it happen now, not in cities, where nothing comes as a surprise, but in the villages, where we take notice. Villages have survived so much: the end of the bus service, the sale of council houses, their time-share in the new vicar; they have survived even the closure of the school. But when the pub goes, the one communal meeting place goes, and the village becomes a housing estate on a B road.

Why are they closing? If you ask people, they are as mystified as Beatty at Jutland ('There's something wrong with our bloody ships today . . .'). Is it the recession? There have been other recessions. No, the answer is to be found in an extraordinary sequence of events starting with the only really successful consumer revolution there has ever been. In the 1970s the Campaign for Real Ale changed public taste, and consequently made the brewers change their minds about their products.

But that was only the start, for beyond lay the 'tied house' monopoly by which a pub could sell only what its controlling brewery wanted it to sell.

Public pressure in the 1980s prompted something remarkable:

referral of the matter to the Monopolies and Mergers Commission by a Tory government.

The commission reported in 1989. No brewery was to have more than 2,000 tied houses. Choice. Competition. Bliss. Some 11,000 free houses created at a stroke. And in addition, an old wrong that few of us knew about would be put right. Pubs had been excluded from the 1954 Landlord and Tenants Act, which gave protection to people in rented accommodation. Now the uncertainty of their tenants would be removed. Just like that, as the late Tommy Cooper used to say.

But two things were overlooked. The first was that the trade secretary at the time was Lord Young, who had never done anything just like that. The second was the position of the tenants.

Bowing to pressure from the brewers and his own backbenchers, Young watered down the proposals. Only half of the tied houses over 2,000 would have to go – but what caused the trouble was that Young gave the brewers a breathing space: 1992 is the year of their deadline. The pubs will have to go before 1 November. More to the point, the change to the Landlord and Tenants Act will not come into force until 11 July. So the brewers were given the opportunity to send out notices to quit, in some cases to people who had spent their entire working life in a pub. The brewers had three choices: to sell, to lease, or to carry on renting with the monopoly removed. If they sold, the tenant had to go, which was easy enough given the short-term nature of their agreement. But sell what? It was a chance to offload the worst pubs, and blithely over the fields the would-be licensees came, clutching trade magazines which were suddenly full of exotic food recipes and mark-ups (400 per cent on a curry). Alas, there was a recession. In 1990–91, the brewers put the price up by an average 18 per cent. Some old tenants persuaded to sign a long-term lease found they couldn't make ends meet. The pubs began to close.

Still, new companies were quietly formed to lease blocks of up to 300 pubs from the brewery, a system known as 'parking'; the fact that these pubs then went on to sell only the brewery's products was pure coincidence. Which left those tenants who went on renting their pubs, but at a rate five times what it had been. They had little choice: the pub wasn't only a workplace, it was their home.

In their defence, the brewers claimed that the old rents had not been commercial, but that this hadn't mattered so long as the monopoly survived (one Midlands brewery estimated that only four per cent of its profits came from rents). But then, the brewers had changed. Most had become part of big conglomerates – some had even stopped brewing beer – and to them, pubs and the men who ran them were merely figures on a balance sheet reviewed by accountants. The brewers had moved away from their roots. So had some licensees, who were now businessmen, restaurateurs, impresarios of the live performance and the quiz evening, men who could read a balance sheet. They talked a lot about what the public wanted, and they will survive as publicans in cities, though theirs may not be a pub you recognise.

So what will happen to the village pub? This has to survive, otherwise the present police policy on drink and driving will result in what will effectively be a large-scale form of house arrest throughout the shires. But survive as what? The only hope for the village pub is for it to go back to its roots, to become the shop it once was and some canal pubs still are.

Conceivably it could be a post office as well. There will need to be a new flexibility in licensing policy, but there is no reason why this shouldn't happen.

As for pubs pure and simple, I have a place in mind as I write this. There is no jukebox and no piped music, just whitewashed walls, a black-leaded range and two settles drawn up beside the fireplace. Nor is there a bar, for the pub is from a time before this, and beer is bought from the barrel.

People talk to each other here, and to the landlord, for whom the pub in his front room and being a publican is a part-time job.

It is like this because the chairman of the brewery lived up the road and considered it his local. He saw to it that nothing changed. He is dead now, and his family brewery has already been taken over twice, but the pub survives. Where is it? Travel west along the A40 from Carmarthen, and after three miles turn right along the B4298. The pure of heart will find it, and I would like to think that they will find themselves looking at the future.

20 June 2009
Obituary
Flossie Lane

Flossie Lane, who died on 13 June, aged 94, was reputedly the oldest publican in Britain, and ran one of the last genuine country inns.

For 74 years she had kept the tiny Sun Inn, the pub where she was born, in the pre-Roman village of Leintwardine on the Shropshire–Herefordshire border.

As the area's last remaining parlour pub, and one of only a handful left in Britain, the Sun is as resolutely old fashioned and unreconstructed today as it was in the mid-1930s when she and her brother took it over.

According to beer connoisseurs, Flossie Lane's parlour pub is one of the last five remaining 'Classic Pubs' in England, listed by English Heritage for its historical interest, and the only one with five stars, awarded by the Classic Basic Unspoilt Pubs of Great Britain.

She held a licence to sell only beer – there was no hard liquor – and was only recently persuaded to serve wine as a gesture towards modern drinking habits.

With its wooden trestle tables, pictures of whiskery past locals on the walls, alcoves and a roaring open fire, the Sun is listed in the *CAMRA Good Beer Guide* as 'a pub of outstanding national interest'.

Although acclaimed as 'a proper pub', it is actually Flossie Lane's 18th-century vernacular stone cottage, tucked away in a side road opposite the village fire station.

There is no conventional bar, and no counter. Customers sit on hard wooden benches in her unadorned quarry-tiled front room. Beer – formerly Ansell's, latterly Hobson's Best at £2 a pint – is served from barrels on Flossie Lane's kitchen floor.

Since she began to ail after a fall in 2006, her customers have helped themselves. There is no till. People put the money in a row of jam jars, one for each denomination of note and coin; although she was never observed to be watching, from her command-post in her favourite armchair she could distinguish between the different clinking sounds they made.

The broadcaster Jeremy Paxman once described the pub as his discovery of the year. 'Flossie, the landlady, sits in the middle of the room, wearing a pair of surgical stockings. The only food is a pot of eggs, which Flossie pickled several moons ago.' Her regulars have formed themselves into a Flossie Lane Society, run as a kind of guild, and are known as Aldermen of the Red-Brick Bar. Every year they appoint a mayor, nominated by the outgoing one, who wears a squirrel-skin cape made by a local butcher.

The mayoral handover involves the eating of squirrel pie and a parade through the village, led by the new mayor wearing the honorary mayoral chain, hat and staff which bears a symbolic sun in homage to the pub.

When Hobson, the Rhodesian ridgeback belonging to the Fiddler's Elbow fish-and-chip-shop owner next door, was appointed mayor, the dog was quickly found to be not up to the job and in turn appointed a successor.

Although they are intended as harmless fun, the rituals at the parlour pub are seen by some villagers as strange and off-putting.

'There are still some people in the village who think it's a secret society,' one regular admitted, 'but it's not a closed shop, even though it is a bit different and off the wall.

We welcome people here.' Visiting the pub in 1996, the *Guardian's* food writer Matthew Fort noted: 'There was no sound but for the ticking of the clock and the conversation between the landlady and the only other customer, which had five-minute pauses between sentences.' Like Paxman, Fort fudged the pub's exact location: 'The landlady said that she didn't want a lot of folk coming along and disturbing the peace.'

Florence Emily Lane was born at the Sun Inn, Leintwardine, on 10 July 1914, the only girl in a family of five. Her father had been a policeman at Ross-on-Wye and her mother was the first member of the family to hold the licence.

Educated at the village school, as a teenager Flossie waited on the customers and helped out in the kitchen by washing bottles and glasses.

After the death of her parents, her brother Charlie took over the licence in 1935 – the year of George V's silver jubilee – and held it jointly with her until his death half a century later. Flossie Lane had run the pub singlehandedly since 1985.

Both she and her brother were particular about who drank there: sons of the village were preferred, although some approved non-rustics were tolerated. The pub is still the base and meeting point for the local cricket club, bellringers and fly fishermen drawn to the River Teme which runs through the village. Although popular, there are concerns for the pub's future: over recent years, Leintwardine has lost four of its pubs and inns.

During her infirmity Flossie Lane's regulars rallied round to keep the Sun going, manning it on a rota basis. The owner of the neighbouring chip shop ordered the beer from the brewery, served the customers, and delivered chip suppers which were washed down with pints of Flossie Lane's ale.

Although her name remained above the door, latterly the pub was effectively run for her by its devotees, all of them locals. The accounts, the washing-up, the laying of the fire and even the sweeping-up were undertaken by the volunteers.

Flossie Lane was proud of not having kept up with the times, and did not hold with modernisation. In an age of lager louts and binge drinkers, no one at the Sun Inn can ever recall the slightest hint of trouble there.

'The pub hasn't changed in all the years, and they are all good people here – I won't have no rough,' she insisted. Although she had been serving ale since the twenties roared, Flossie Lane's secret recipe for a long life was simple. 'I'm a teetotal,' she said. 'I like a nice cup of tea. I leave the drink to the others.' A chronic agoraphobic, Flossie Lane was never known, within living memory, to have ventured outside her pub (other than to take the air in the rear garden). She never learned to drive and took her holidays at home. She enjoyed a reputation as the best-informed person in the village, and every evening cheerfully dispensed local gossip to her customers.

In her advanced old age, Flossie Lane's regulars converted a downstairs room into a bedroom to spare her the stairs, but for at least the last 10 years she had slept every night in her customary armchair.

The last person out tucked her up.

Flossie Lane, who never married, is survived by five nieces.

15 April 1995
Stand-Up for This National Anthem . . .
Robin Page

The song of the skylark is the national anthem of the British countryside. For generations it has come pouring down from above moor, mountain, marsh, heath, down and open field. It has been heard from the Shetlands to the Scillies, from St Kilda to Scolt Head. It has been the inspiration for poets, painters and musicians.

Now the sky is empty, the song has gone. Now, almost unbelievably, it is possible to stand at the centre of a large farm field in the middle of spring and hear not a single, solitary skylark. The anthem that has soared and tumbled down the centuries has been all but silenced in a mere 15 years. Why? Why?

The day I first noticed the change came seven or eight years ago. On a summer's day I was walking with the dogs along a farm track by a field of winter wheat, its green ears looking full of promise for a good harvest. There was blue sky, a warm breeze and the wild roses were beginning to bloom, but something was missing.

All I could hear was the sound of the breeze on the nearby leaves and the distant drone of traffic. I went on and then – through a hedge, across grass and alongside barley – I heard it: that song. But briefly, just once. And this on a walk when the music should have been gently washing over me the whole way.

According to the British Trust for Ornithology, skylark numbers have fallen by more than 50 per cent in the past 15 years. There is no single, dramatic cause: the changes in the countryside have been subtle. Chemicals sprayed on to cereals and livestock are not affecting the creatures at the top of the food chain but those at the bottom. Certain fungicides, herbicides and insecticides are removing the food supplies of insects, as well as destroying insects themselves, while herbicides are killing all weeds before they can produce the seeds that the seed-eating birds depend on.

Consequently, there has not been widespread starvation, a sudden holocaust; rather, there has been a gradual denial of food, meaning less chick survival and a steady decline in the population. And now it has left me feeling bereaved.

The music of the lark has been with me all my life; I was born in May and larksong has been almost constantly around me ever since. Even as I sit writing this, my mind can accurately reproduce the harmony, so constant and familiar has it been.

I remember nature walks at the village school when the 'drift' and the fields leading from it would be awash with the sound of summer larks. There would not be a single skylark but many. Often they were impossible to count – they were too high and the sky was too bright. We just accepted the constant fall of music – pure, clear and as much a part of the summer air as the scent of blossom and the sounds of the swallow and the cuckoo.

The larks were there at harvest-time, too, as we picnicked in the fringe of shade at the field's edge. In the autumn they were still singing, as if in the middle of a false spring, mapping out their territory in song, ready for the next year.

But now that reassuring reference point has gone. So what has happened to the skylark? What has happened to bring silence to the heart of the country – a silence that even in the environmental gloom of the sixties seemed unimaginable? Inevitably it is related to agriculture. Despite over-production, farming is still becoming even more intensive and every year brings new changes, together with new chemical pesticides.

But the decline, however serious, is not irreversible – if we can only discover the will. Let the skylark's music play again.

7 March 2002
The Last Cuckoos
Leader

If falling numbers of cuckoos are anything to go by, spring has been cancelled. The population of the bird that heralds the new season is in free fall: down 20 per cent in farmland areas, and 60 per cent in woodland, over the past 30 years. The reason is a sharp decline in the number of caterpillars, the favoured food of cuckoo chicks, after some cold springs, combined with a decline in other species: the cuckoo is unique in its practice of secreting eggs in the nests of other birds.

As if the loss of their gentle call was not enough, there will be a terrible knock-on effect in other fields. People who write letters to newspapers will be disconsolate: the competition to be the first to hear the bird each year is such a familiar ritual that a collection of letters to Another Newspaper was called The First Cuckoo. Swiss clockmakers will down tools, and poets will be left twiddling their quills in mid-air. Wordsworth brought up the cuckoo in several poems, writing fondly of the 'darling of the Spring', 'Breaking the silence of the seas, among the farthest Hebrides'.

People will have to look elsewhere for signs of spring: a correspondent to this newspaper referred yesterday to a fledgling collared dove appearing in the garden as early as last month. For future reference, if you hear its coarse, rapidly delivered, three-part cooing – 'kuk-koooOO-kook' – warmer weather is on the way.

28 April 2001
Letters to the Editor
Cuckoos

SIR – As I walked my dogs along the pavement today, all of us looking wistfully at the empty green fields and burgeoning trees behind the hedge, I realised that I had not yet heard a cuckoo this spring (Wild Things, 21 April). Could this be because the bird has decided not to come to England this year, having got the message that the countryside is closed?

Sally Bowes
Wisborough Green
West Sussex

SIR – I have waited and waited to hear the cuckoo, and, just as buses, three called together at once. It was extraordinary – an asylum of cuckoos. Actually, here in rural Suffolk, you have more chance of cuckoos than buses, but that is another story.

Heather M. Tanner
Earl Soham
Suffolk

13 March 2004
Is it Goodbye to Old Big Bum?
Sandy Mitchell

Hares are beyond strange: they are downright spooky. You can be walking across a bare field in which a single bright stone is visible in the distance, when a hare materialises suddenly at your feet and zips off on a long-legged sprint. As soon as it stops and squats, it vanishes. Binoculars and sharp eyes are no use. These creatures become invisible with a twitch of their magic cloaks.

What's more, hares don't burrow a home deep in the ground. They prefer shallow scrapes on open land where they lie in a supernaturally watchful state. The only time they are easy to spot is at this time of year, when crops have yet to grow. They sit up on their haunches and showcase their boxing skills, making moves as mad as Mike Tyson.

So it is easy to see why there are as many ancient superstitions about hares as there are odd local nicknames – such as 'wood cat', 'dew flirt' or 'old big bum'. They grow so big in the sugar-beet fields of East Anglia they are known as Fen donkeys.

Exact scientific details about hares have been hard to get until now. The last national survey is out of date, and guesses about their total population range from 800,000 to 1.25 million. No one can quite agree on how far their numbers have fallen since farming monocultures first pitched them into decline after the Second World War, although English Nature suspects their numbers have dropped two per cent over the past decade.

And that is why the government made hares a 'priority species for nature conservation', setting a target under its Biodiversity Action Plan of doubling their numbers by 2010.

Dr Nancy Vaughan, a mammal specialist at Bristol University, has just completed a five-year study, watching hares, radio-tracking them with individual collars and quizzing more than 1,000 farmers in England and Wales about sightings. She found that almost half saw them rarely or never. The hope was that her project – one of the most comprehensive surveys of its kind – might suggest ways of increasing numbers.

One of the greatest mysteries was why hares are quite so scarce on grassland compared with areas where crops are grown. Is diet to blame? Or predators such as foxes and buzzards? Neither, it turns out. 'Hares from pastoral areas were able to obtain a good-quality diet, but unable to maintain good body condition,' says Nancy. Yet her computer models reveal an extraordinary difference in average lifespan between hares in arable areas, and those subsisting on pure grassland: arable hares can live for more than five years, while the others survive for only two.

One explanation she proposes is that hares on grassland are so hyper-alert in order to spot possible threats that they are constantly put off their dinner or burn up energy running away from perceived dangers. So neurotic are these poor animals that they even show less interest in breeding than their cousins elsewhere.

Dr Vaughan was forced to reach a dismal conclusion: 'The changes needed in habitat management in order to achieve large changes in populations in hares are either unfeasible, or detrimental to other species of conservation value.' In a nutshell, the biodiversity target of doubling hare numbers by 2010 is hopelessly unachievable.

Although doubling hare numbers may be impossible in a short time, not everyone is as gloomy about more modest increases. New environmental schemes for farmers due to be introduced next year should be extremely beneficial for hares, believes Dr Stephen Tapper, of the Game Conservancy Trust: 'Hare populations in East Anglia and the West Midlands saw a 20 to 30 per cent increase where farmers benefited from a pilot scheme of incentives to introduce such things as beetle banks, conservation headlands and over-winter stubbles. Those incentives will be available in 2005 to all farmers. Farming will change radically and it will benefit all farmland wildlife, although it will take a few years for the numbers of hares to come through.'

But even if hares are not entirely beyond the help of farmers and biologists, it will still take a good shrink to fathom the workings of their crazy little minds.

7 August 2004
Cursed Be the Slipper Stealer
Peter Marren

Sometime in the evening or night of 10 July, someone stole the lady's slipper. The place where this most gorgeous of wild orchids grew has been an open secret for the past few years. Each season saw up to 3,000 people making the journey to Silverdale in Lancashire to see the plant in bloom. Its setting was dangerously accessible and surprisingly suburban – a disused lime pit at the edge of a golf course.

The plant itself was older than any of its admirers. It had been known about for the best part of a century, and was probably approaching its 100th birthday. Latterly it had produced several flowering stems, each one crowned by a golden slipper held in the clasp of four long, purple petals.

Hardly another wild plant in Europe approaches the lady's slipper in sheer glamour. It looks like a jungle plant transported by some miracle to the cold dales of northern England. When I saw it for the first time, I thought I was dreaming.

It is also our rarest wild flower. Before 10 July 2004, there were two. Now there is only one. Once there were hundreds. The 400-year history of the lady's slipper orchid in Britain is an object lesson in greed and desire.

Its first appearance in print was in 1629, in John Parkinson's *Paradisus Terrestris*, a compendium of 'all sorts of pleasant flowers which our English air will permit to be nursed up'. Parkinson's 'Earthly Paradise' has been called the first gardening book. Yet, even in the company of Parkinson's stocks, gillyflowers and early tulips, this particular flower stood out. Helpfully, he told his beruffed reader exactly where to obtain it – not from a garden centre, but a wood.

A certain Mistress Thomasin Tunstall had supplied Parkinson and others with roots looted from 'a wood or place called the Helkes', three miles from Ingleton in the Yorkshire Dales. A local trade had sprung up, centred on the marketplace in Settle, and a one-way traffic of lady's slippers poured from the craggy woods of the north Pennines into the flower pots and semi-shaded borders of country houses. It was popular enough to acquire tradenames that tend to speak for themselves: 'the Great Flower Prize of Craven' or 'the Pride of Yorkshire'. Proud indeed was the Dalesman who could point to a row of nodding purple-and-gold blooms in his rock garden.

But the plant was rare, far too rare, to sustain the fashion for long. The 'wood called Helkes' gave up its last golden slipper in 1790. As the gardening writer Reginald Farrer expressed it: 'Helkes Wood is an oyster forever robbed of its pearl'. It was the same story everywhere, from the coastal denes of Durham to the heights above Matlock. By the mid-19th century, the lady's slipper was considered a great rarity, so rare that a different kind of orchid lover began to appear – no less zealous, but now dedicated to preservation rather than transportation.

In Arncliffe, for example, the good angel was the vicar who saved the plant from plunderers by the simple expedient of cutting the plant's stems before it could flower. Without flowers, the lady's slipper is virtually indistinguishable from the much more common lily-of-the-valley. At Castle Eden Dene, which became a popular attraction in Victorian times, another guardian secretly transplanted some of the seemingly doomed lady's slippers to a safer place. Significantly, this refuge was not a garden but an inaccessible limestone ravine. Unfortunately it failed to survive.

A wiser measure was secrecy. From the 1880s onwards, authors were becoming deliberately vague about the whereabouts of the last few flowers. Readers were even allowed to believe it had become extinct. Only a few were in on the secret, which was that just two plants had survived the holocaust, one in Yorkshire, one in Lancashire. There have been rumours of others, but none has been substantiated.

On those two, all the panoply and weight of the modern conservation industry has at last descended. Seed from the Yorkshire plant has been nurtured at Kew. The performance of the wild plants has been monitored assiduously and the plants themselves protected by round-the-clock volunteer wardens. Access to the Yorkshire plant is discouraged. During the past 10 years, seedlings cultivated at Kew have been planted at six wild sites, though it is too soon to say whether the attempt has succeeded.

In the meantime, analysis of the DNA extracted from the wild plants and garden plants of wild descent has revealed a surprise. While the Yorkshire plant is beyond doubt a *carte blanche* native, the stolen Lancashire one is not. It seems to originate from the Alps, possibly from Austria. Most likely it was secretly planted in its lime pit around the turn of the 20th century by a botanist returning from a continental holiday. But, while that disclosure must lessen the scientific value of the Lancashire plant, it was still the nearest thing to a wild lady's slipper orchid in Britain that was both accessible and thriving.

If ever a flower has been loved to the edge of extinction, it must surely be this one. The last lady's slipper, 'somewhere in Yorkshire', is perhaps a testimony to the precarious position of any exotic wild flower in a crowded land of acquisitive gardeners. Like Henry V, it was 'too famous to live long'.

As for the unknown thief, the latest and hopefully the last in a long line of sneaky slipper pilferers, more words by Reginald Farrer seem particularly apposite. The lady's slippers of Arncliffe, for long guarded by the good vicar, were eventually dug up for gold, to be paid by 'a professor from the north' who offered a reward for every plant he could lay his hands on. 'And so,' wrote Farrer, 'the valley was swept bare.' And the consequences for the perpetrators of the crime were weighty: 'Accursed for ever more into the lowest of the Eight Hot Hells, be all reckless uprooters of rarities, from professors downwards'.

To escape this dire fate, all the thief has to do is to return the plant to its home.

28 September 2003
The Village That Died
Christopher Jones

It's the silence that chills. Not the shrapnel on the roadside, the exploded tanks in the grassland around, or the blood-red signs warning of danger. No, it is the stillness of this autumn day – no cars, no machinery, no human sounds.

At the bottom of the dusty hillside track I can make out the tower of a church and the outlines of greystone houses, a dark copse shrouding what must be the village centre. Closer to, though, the buildings have neither roofs nor windows, weeds weave through the walls and fireplaces, and the ponds are thick with lily-pads. The figures drifting around are sombre, contemplative as at a funeral.

For this is Tyneham, a forgotten field that will be forever 1943. This *Domesday*-listed village, tucked into a fold of swooping Dorset countryside, became a casualty of war unlike any other British community. Its misfortune was to be situated near the gunnery ranges attached to the Royal Armoured Corps Gunnery School based at Lulworth Camp, an area used as a tank firing range since 1916. By the middle of the Second World War the Lulworth range was judged inadequate for the more powerful weapons being developed. To expand the range the area occupied by the village of Tyneham and surrounding farms had to be evacuated.

The villagers left almost 60 years ago, just before Christmas 1943, with the assurance of the government – 'Churchill's pledge' – that they would be able to return after the war. A note was pinned to the church door: 'Please treat the church and houses with care. We have given up our homes where many of us have lived for generations, to help win the war to keep men free. We shall return one day and thank you for treating the village kindly.'

They never returned. When the war ended the continued military occupation of the area was deemed still necessary and the villagers remained forever resettled. A public enquiry upheld the occupation, despite protests and reviews that rumbled on amid controversy and recriminations until the 1970s.

The MoD did, though, allow access to the village and the surrounding land when live firing is not taking place. At weekends the village sees human life of a non-artillery nature. The Church of St Mary the Virgin, to which the plaintive plea was pinned, is almost as the villagers left it. There are stone monuments to ancient squires and faithful servants, a medieval piscina, an altar. But the Jacobean pulpit is on loan to Lulworth Camp, and the bells and organ have been relocated to other churches. Display boards inside add flesh to the bare bones of the village, explaining which family lived in each house. The ghosts begin to take on names, occupations, characters – the Pritchards, the Millers, the Bonds.

Inside the raftered schoolhouse, the realness of the former inhabitants is inescapable. Restored to its earlier condition, the single schoolroom is just as the children left it. Benches are lined up in neat rows with ancient inkwelled desks; coat pegs are labelled with names of the classmates; a vase is filled with wild flowers. Lessons in the village would have been fitted around the farming and fishing. An inspector's report of 1921 noted frowningly that the school's sanitation was deficient, and that sheep and ducks roamed freely outside.

Along the unmetalled roads there are no street lamps, no signs, no shops, no drainage or water pipes – none of the urban furniture of the last 60 years. A tree planted in 1911 commemorates the coronation of George V. A tap of spring water and drinking trough remain where villagers filled their pails. The telephone box outside the former post office is the only touch of modernity. A reinforced concrete box with finial is a pre-Gilbert Scott kiosk in the post office's 1921 Kiosk No. 1 design. Signs inside warning 'I am on war work. If you must use me, be brief' are one of the few signs of this village's wartime fate. Mostly it seems to belong to an even earlier age.

Not all the village has survived. The Elizabethan manor house – home of the village squires – was demolished by the MoD and parts incorporated into buildings elsewhere. Its 17th-century panelling, wooden overmantel and ancient glass are on display in the Dorset County Museum in Dorchester. The grandest house left in the village is the rectory. Stone pediments above the doorway and a paved courtyard still mark its social distinction. In its sheltered garden a palm tree suggests the last vicar's green fingers. Touches of domesticity – a washing tub, the twisted metal remains of fireplaces; some lead drain piping – remain in the other houses too, a reminder that life was far from a Ruritanian idyll.

Visitors to the village can usually wander farther afield, taking a circular walk through the surrounding valley down to Worborrow, providing they don't stray off the marked paths. Rare plants such as the dark green fritillary and wild cabbage flourish in the ruins and medieval fields; kestrels, sika deer and skylarks grow up in the wilderness.

It is an irony acknowledged by those angry about the village's fate that Tyneham's closure was the very thing that ensured its natural survival – no modern deep-ploughing methods have disturbed an ecological order untouched for centuries.

Inside the church the Great War memorial is dedicated to the six Tyneham men, aged between 21 and 38, who gave their lives – a toll that can have left no family in this tiny community untouched. 'All men must die. It is only given to the few to die for their country.' When the whole village gave up its existence 25 years later, it was a bitter-sweet privilege.

20 November 2007
Closed All Hours
Clive Aslet

There used to be a railway station at Heads Nook in Cumbria, seven miles east of Carlisle. But one night during the 1960s, a gang of workmen arrived and secretly dismantled it. Dr Beeching had wielded his axe. That was the first in a series of closures to smite Heads Nook, a process brought to grim conclusion this year when its sub-post office cum village shop was sold to a builder-developer, following the earlier demise of a pub and chapel. This is the story of the English village in our times: its life-support systems are being slowly but inexorably switched off.

Go back 40 years, and Heads Nook was a prosperous village. There was a tweed mill in the valley, and Rebecca Nicholson, now a snowy-haired 90-year-old, was top weaver. ('Just put weaver,' she tells me in the front room of her immaculately kept cottage, 'we mustn't boast.') She and her husband moved from nearby Talkin in 1940. It was 'sheer heaven' in the horse-and-cart days. She remembers the chapel – or, as it has always been known, the church room – as a busy place of worship, full to overflowing at Christmas. Her daughter, Barbara, was christened there. It has now been converted to a house. 'It was a great little village. Two bus companies served Heads Nook. My husband, Eddie, worked on the railway as a porter, then as a signalman.' But today she feels Heads Nook is a very different place. 'If I couldn't drive, I don't think

I'd want to be here . . . It's sad, that's the only thing I can say.'

Recently, 'localism' has become a buzz word with all political parties. 'Walkable' communities, where basic services are no more than a stroll from the house, are seen to be more cohesive – and generally happier – than commuter suburbs. But, all too often, country villages have gone in the other direction. According to Pub is the Hub (an organisation dedicated to improving rural services by maximising the role of pubs), country pubs are closing at a rate of six a week. Six hundred rural filling stations close every year. 'Communities need at least one focus point to preserve a sense of identity,' maintains John Gardiner of the Countryside Alliance. In places like Heads Nook, that identity is slipping.

Farming helped keep the community together, because the farmer – like the vicar and the village bobby – was a full-time presence. Heads Nook used to have several farms, with farmers taking eggs and potatoes to the village shop to be sold. But like many other villages, the only farmers living in Heads Nook now are retired.

Families and young people once gave life to the village. The international event rider Ruth Edge, 28, who keeps horses in Heads Nook, held her wedding reception at the Coach House. But even this 'brilliant' pub closed, and the youth of Heads Nook find little to keep them. 'They go to university in London or Manchester,' comments Steve Griffiths, a Scouser who found his way here 20 years ago and, bucking the trend, wouldn't live anywhere else. 'Once they've gone, they rarely come back. I can't think of any who were brought up in the village who are still living here.'

After the Coach House closed, the only place for villagers to meet informally was the post office, which doubled as a shop. 'When you walked through the village you always saw someone going to the shop,' says Allan Davidson, a former policeman who chairs the village hall committee. Today, on his walk to meet me, he has seen nobody. 'Maybe 10 years ago, people would buy all their vegetables at the village shop. The difference in basket price between Tesco in Carlisle and the village shop can be a lot of money.' I meet one woman loading bags into an estate car. 'Sometimes I say the village has no soul, but there are some lovely people living here,' she sighs. 'I feel guilty because I used to go to the village shop and then stopped using it.'

That is the nub of the issue, says Jim Robinson. He owns the post office – or, as it's now called, The Old Corn Mill development, a terrace of three houses (two with two bedrooms, one with three), on the market at between £180,000 and £210,000. He emerges from the white builder's van that has brought him from his home a few miles away. 'When the shop is open, nobody wants to go in. When it's closed, everyone wants to go in,' he comments. He bought the post office after the previous owners had divorced. 'Nobody has complained about the development. Why should they? It's fantastic – absolutely brilliant – a centrepiece for the village.'

Certainly the work has been done well, and the owners of the three houses will be able to luxuriate in en suites, where en suites never existed before. (According to Cumbrian Properties, which is marketing the houses, purchasers are likely to be investors or second-time buyers working in Carlisle.)

Yet not every village in England has suffered their reversals of fortune quietly like Heads Nook; some have taken up arms and started a community-owned store. According to Virsa (the Village Retail Services Association), there are more than 170 in existence. The economics can work for villages with as few as 200 inhabitants. Flintham in Nottinghamshire is not even deterred by the absence of premises, having taken advantage of Nottinghamshire Rural Community Council's 'Shop in a Box' project where a portable, temporary building is delivered to the village.

The Plunkett Foundation is one of a number of bodies that can help with grants. Mr Davidson acknowledges that there have been successes, some near to Heads Nook. In Hesket Newmarket, locals have teamed up to buy the micro-brewery behind the Old Crown pub, threatened with purchase by parties thought to be more interested in redevelopment than in brewing. Despite producing a beer named Great Cockup, the enterprise makes a £15,000 profit on a turnover of between £68,000 to £95,000, according to the Social Enterprise Coalition. The Black Swan at Ravenstonedale has converted a barn to sell locally sourced food and other products. Hesket Newmarket, however, is 'in John Peel country, and far enough from a town to work', observes Mr Davidson, and Ravenstonedale is similarly remote. But Heads Nook is too near the bright lights of Carlisle. Even Mr Davidson, for all his affection for the village, would not be tempted to invest in a community shop here.

'People in the countryside feel so bludgeoned,' explains John Gardiner. 'It needs leadership, drive and commitment to keep services alive.' Not everywhere has those resources. It may take only two or three single-minded people to provide a nucleus around which others may cohere. Successful community enterprises, he says, often depend on 'a number of people who have the guts and determination to drive something through, and that inspires other people to join.' But without a quorum of dynamic spirits, villages like Heads Nook give up.

Heads Nook is not totally bereft. The village hall survives, offering a botanical art group, Scottish country dancing and bowls. The Women's Institute have started a 'drop in and chat' event once a month. A mobile library comes once a month from Carlisle. Buses call four times a day. But visits by a mobile police station have been cancelled and the adult education service has stopped yoga classes.

Beside the recreation ground, a man with pronounced ginger eyebrows is cutting the hedge. This is Billy Fleming, who represents Heads Nook on the Haydon Parish Council. Recently, he was behind efforts to reopen the railway station, but the plan fell foul of health and safety regulations. He is as fatalistic as everyone else. 'If you have to make money, you can't keep these places open. It's all to do with money, isn't it?' Not quite. Village spirit has something to do with it, too.

18 January 2009

Post Office Raid Foiled . . . By Closure

Adam Lusher

Two armed robbers overlooked one detail when they targeted a village post office – it had already fallen victim to Royal Mail's closure programme.

Two men, who are still at large, hit Village Stores in Stanton St John, near Oxford, armed with a gun and a machete. They told Dennis Ingrey, 58, to open the post-office counter in the hope of escaping with thousands of pounds. Mr Ingrey said, 'I told them they were six months too late.' They made off with just the shop's takings.

2 October 2004
To Conker the World
Charlotte Mackaness

Next Sunday, cries of 'iddley, iddley ack, my first crack' and 'hobily, hobily honker, my first conker' will reverberate around the village green in Ashton, Northamptonshire, the venue of the 40th World Conker Championships. The competition, which was started in the 1960s, attracts players from around the globe who are cheered on by thousands of spectators.

'This year we have competitors from Germany, Canada, the US, Australia, South Africa, Ukraine and the Czech Republic, as well as a large French contingent,' says John Hadman, secretary of Ashton Conker Club. 'People travel huge distances to play. One year we had a Dutch chap who cycled all the way from Holland.'

Vic Owen, a local man in his seventies, leads the proceedings as King Conker. His ceremonial attire includes a bowler hat and strings of conkers. Many of the contestants come in fancy dress or protective clothing. 'Although we've never had what you'd call a proper injury, it's easy to give your forearm a nasty knock if you swing and miss,' says Hadman. 'Players in gloves, cricket pads and full American footballing kit are not uncommon.'

Despite the eccentricity, the championships are run under strict rules. Each game is overseen by two stewards and players draw for a new conker after each round of the knock-out competition. Club members collect the conkers from Ashton's trees, and string them with bootlaces. 'Not allowing players to use their own conkers gives everybody an equal chance because we know that none of the conkers has been hardened through pickling, varnishing or other illegal methods,' says Hadman.

Sadly, conker cheats are the least of the organisers' worries. Hot, dry weather meant that conkers were few and far between last year. 'It was hard to find conkers of a decent size, and we had to extend our collection area to a 25-mile radius around the village,' says Hadman. 'But most worrying of all is a leaf-mining moth that weakens horse chestnut trees and threatens conker harvests.'

The horse chestnut leaf-mining moth (*Cameraria ohridella*) was spotted in Wimbledon two years ago. Since the half-centimetre-long moths were first noted in Macedonia in 1985, they have swept across

Europe. In severe cases of infestation, 700 miners have been found on a single leaf.

'The moth can produce as many as five generations. The miners burrow into the leaf, eating it from the inside,' says Andrew Halstead, principal entomologist at the Royal Horticultural Society (RHS). 'The insects damage leaves, causing them to fall early. This loss of vigour weakens the tree and affects conkers.'

According to Dr Nigel Straw from the Forestry Commission, it's too early to know what the long-term impact could be. 'Two studies from the Continent have looked at the effects of defoliation,' he says. 'Both found that in severe cases, conker numbers appeared not to be affected, but their size was reduced by up to 50 per cent. However, these studies were only conducted over a year. Defoliation over a longer period might cause a reduction in the number of conkers.'

Treatment by spraying with insecticide is unviable because of the size of most horse chestnut trees, and the reddish-brown moths have no natural enemies. Although leaf miners prefer the warmer conditions of southern Europe, the pupae have survived winter temperatures as low as minus 23°C in Hungary.

The Forestry Commission suggests that to prevent the moths spreading, infected fallen leaves should be collected and incinerated rather than being left in compost heaps.

Despite such precautions, the moth is moving up the country at a fast rate. Since 2002, it has been reported as far north as Cambridge and Stratford-upon-Avon. 'Although it isn't a strong flier, the moth's small size means that it can be carried easily and spreads rapidly. It's probably already in Northamptonshire,' warns Andrew Halstead.

'I've been in touch with the RHS and the Forestry Commission,' says John Hadman. 'They have advised on what to look for, although identifying an infestation isn't easy. The brown patches caused by the moth look similar to a fungal disease, and this summer the leaves turned brown prematurely because of the cold, wet weather.

'Although this moth isn't as drastic as Dutch elm disease, the prospect of poor harvests of undersized conkers is worrying,' Hadman adds. 'At some stages we have 10 games going on at once so we need a lot of conkers. Each year we pick 5,000 for the competition. They are around 35mm in diameter. If necessary, we'd have to reduce the size of championship conkers or look a long way outside Ashton for our supply.'

The reigning world conker champion, Brian Stewart, a print technician from Corby, is looking forward to defending his title, but fears for the sport's future. 'It would be sad if conkers was jeopardised by these moths,' he says. 'The game is under threat as it is. It's been banned in many schools because it's considered dangerous. If conkers comes to an end, I'll have to train for something else – maybe the marbles world title.'

2 March 1974
A Doomed Landscape
Paul Johnson

The life of a freelance writer is a precarious one, but it has one enviable compensation: it gives you, to some extent, freedom of movement and location. I intend to spend most of the rest of this year working on a book in a remote glen in the Scottish Highlands, and to use my spare time exploring that enchanting countryside, much of which is still unfamiliar to me.

It is, of course, a doomed landscape. Until a few months ago, I had foolishly supposed, along with many other people, that the discovery of prodigious quantities of oil around Britain's coastline would transform only parts of the east coast of Northern Scotland, and that the stain of industrialism would not creep far inland.

But now we know that much of the north-west coast, with its unique juxtaposition of island seascape, sea-loch and mountain, glen and moor, is also threatened. There, the oilmen and the engineers intend to create dramatic shapes on a scale to disturb the contours even of that mighty skyline. The precise size and areas of the depredations are yet to be determined; bitter controversy is raging, and local men and women are banding together in fierce groups to repel the invaders. But all recent experience shows that, where the money at stake is large enough, no local interest, however well organised and militant, and no planning law or regulation, however empathic or precise, can in the end withstand the forces of change. Those of us who live in London's green belt have become painfully aware, in recent years, how the revolution in land-values has succeeded in eroding territory once thought sacrosanct.

Already, in the north of Britain, the gigantic vision of the wealth to be found – a vision which expands almost daily as fresh discoveries are reported – has led Whitehall to project legislation which, in effect, will hurl down the protective walls of planning procedure, and surrender the Highland fortress to the oilmen and their auxiliaries. By the end of the century it seems likely that Britain will again be one of the wealthiest countries of the world. But in the years between, the Highlands will undergo the greatest transformation in their history! More brutal, perhaps more poignant, than the clearances which drove the clansmen from their glens at the beginning of the 19th century; more radical even, in social and moral terms, than the arrival of the Irish monks, who first brought Christian faith and civility to those wild parts. For not just people but the very physical structure of the land and sea will be re-cast; and the process, already begun, will move forward with irresistible force, and accelerating pace, to an end which no one yet can possibly calculate.

Nor is Scotland alone threatened. The oilmen are now at work in the Celtic Sea, where similar, perhaps even greater, discoveries are expected. There are already the early, ominous hints of activity off the coasts of Cornwall and Devon, around Pembrokeshire, in Cardigan Bay and North Wales, off Cumberland. These are the last jewels in our crown of wild nature. Change, indeed, has already come to Anglesey. That magical island, when I first knew it, with its low valleys which led nowhere, streams which wandered without purpose except to delight, mysterious groves and quiet villages, was still an apt setting for the shades of the Druids who once frightened Agricola's legions. Now it is fast becoming an offshore launching-pad for the new Titans, more awesome and destructive than any Magus. I know a cottage, directly on the shingle of the north-east coast, still untouched, from which you can see, across the straits, the whole majestic range of Snowdonia. Although I have travelled all over the world, I have seen nothing, for my taste, to equal this splendid panorama. Nor even Byron, gazing down from Marathon on to the Isles of Greece, could have wished for a more inspiriting vision of beauty. I fear that this, too, will soon be obscured.

So I intend to look about Britain, while there is still time, and store up visual memories; luxurious rations, carefully preserved, against the Age of Iron to come. I shall make drawings too. It is one of the tragedies of our time that we no longer possess a school of English landscape painters, to record our fast-dwindling heritage for future generations.

When in the early 16th century Renaissance men like John Leland first realised that nature was a friend of man, rather than an enemy, and travelled about the country to describe its glories, there were no painters of landscape here. Thus, for all practical purposes, we know the appearance of Tudor England only from words. Happily, when the Industrial Revolution dealt the earliest blows to the north and Midlands, we had a galaxy of talents to capture for ever the scenes, that were lost. Now we have the camera, but it is not the same thing; for only painting can combine the physical elements with the aesthetic and moral response of the beholder. There is no substitute for the co-ordinated eye, brain and hand of a Constable, a Girtin, a Richard Wilson.

How much time we have got, who can say? I would guess less than a generation. The speed of historical change increases with every year. In our own day, Britain has forfeited its status as a great imperial power and threatens to become little better than an economic colony. The erosion of landscape will be no less swift. We shall be richer at the end, but we shall have lost something which no ingenuity or power of man can ever restore or replace. So we must travel and observe now, around the condemned kingdom.

4 September 2004
Elegy for a Vanishing Way of Life
Robin Page

The other day I was asked what I thought was an odd question: 'What qualifications have you got to write about the countryside?' Well, I haven't got a degree in anything, let alone agriculture or, horror of horrors, environmental studies. My qualifications are far simpler: I live next door to the house where I was born, on the farm where my father worked for 60 years, in the village where I went to junior school, in the countryside that gave me a pet owl, jackdaws, fox cubs, newts and tadpoles, and near the hedge where I want my coffin to go when I finally fall off my perch.

In other words I have been part of the same chunk of countryside all my life. I don't need sociologists, economists, politicians, or environ-mental studies graduates to tell me what has happened in rural Britain – I have seen it myself.

I was born at home in May 1943. (I have always had a talent for doing things differently, and apparently I tried to enter the world sideways.) Water came from a pump outside; the lavatory was a bucket across the yard. There were hens at the bottom of the garden (at that time we didn't realise they were free-range). Our milk came from the small herd of dairy shorthorns on the farm. The milk was neither pasteurised nor homogenised, but we never fell victim to E.coli, listeria or hysteria. In the summer my mother would let some milk sour, then put it in a hanging muslin bag to drain and become milk cheese. Made from the extra thick milk produced after a cow had given birth, it was like the curds and whey of 'Little Miss Muffet'. Heated in the oven, with sugar, it set like egg custard and was delicious. Now such foods are labelled 'unfit for human consumption'.

Where the cows grazed, barn owls quartered the meadows at dusk, bee orchids flowered in the roadside verges, cuckoos called throughout the spring, and farming and nature seemed to be in harmony.

I had to walk half a mile to school, passing houses left unlocked all day. Burglary was unknown, though the bobby from the next village of Grantchester did a daily round on his bike. Just before the Victorian school buildings we passed the chapel and the church; God still played an important part in the life of the village and local farmers did not cut their corn on the sabbath.

At times the village schoolmistress was a frightening tyrant, cajoling and shouting and sometimes losing her false teeth. But on other occasions her mood changed and she became lovely. Her aim was to get as many ordinary village children through the eleven-plus exam as possible, but she also wanted them to appreciate where they lived. 'Who wants to go for a walk?' she would suddenly ask on a sunny June afternoon. Then, forgetting any curriculum, she would take the whole school on a nature walk – stopping to look at the newts in the village pond, listening to the birdsong along the hedgerows and allowing us to pick wild flowers.

One thing she did not teach, teeth in or out, was sex education. Today's children are not so lucky, being given the clinical facts almost before they can write. For me, the teacher was the frisky bull in the yard.

Gradually, however, change came to this idyll. We moved into the farmhouse with flush toilets and piped water; water mains came to the rest of the village, along with street lights and new houses. With tractors and combine harvesters, fewer men were needed to work on the land, and the production of monoculture cereals became more financially attractive than milk and cows. On new housing estates, rootless incomers arrived and the word dormitory began to compete with community.

In 1974, I documented this ever-increasing pace of change in a book *The Decline of an English Village*, which was called 'a social document relevant to the whole of the English countryside' in the *Times Literary Supplement*. Some 30 years on, a second edition of the book is being published. For it, I have written a new epilogue outlining the rural vandalism that has occurred under the guise of progress, and warning of more future acts of political idiocy – otherwise known as planning.

But this new edition is not just a grumpy old man lamenting the past. It contains, too, a foreword by Zac Goldsmith showing that an appreciation of what is happening in today's countryside crosses generational boundaries.

As he writes: 'Today's engineers of progress are pushing us blindfold from a past they refuse to acknowledge towards a future that they cannot define.'

This 30-year period of progress has been alarming. The Common Agricultural Policy has led to farming becoming industrialised – and a wildlife wipeout. Lark song and cuckoo calls have disappeared. 'Britain has a milk lake and a butter mountain,' we were told. 'You can help by getting rid of your cows.' It was a lie: Britain was self-sufficient in dairy products. It was Germany and France that had created the over-production. So, as part of the agreement for Britain's entry into Europe, our politicians calmly and cynically slaughtered 300,000 healthy British dairy cows to allow butter and milk to be imported from Germany and France.

To the north of the parish the Cambridge Western bypass has been bulldozed in a great curve of dual carriageway. The new road was sold to the locals as a bypass, but that was another lie: plans shown to a local farmer years ago showed that the road always was meant to be the M11 linking the Midlands with the future Stansted Airport. So the Public Inquiry for Stansted was pure farce.

Dutch elm disease then swept the parish, taking the landscape's dominant trees, including those where I climbed to see kestrel chicks. In the village itself changes have happened too. God has lost His popularity and reality in the form of *Big Brother* and Sky Sports has replaced spirituality. The old squire's house has gone to a *Sunday Times* rich-list developer and even my semi-detached farm worker's cottage is said to be worth an astonishing £250,000. To me, however, it is worthless simply because I still want to live in it.

When, three decades ago, I wrote about the decline of the English village, I didn't know the half of it. The whole of our rural culture, it turns out, is under threat.

6 April 2009

Perhaps We Need to Bail Out the Countryside

George Pitcher

If the collapse of Lehman Brothers and the fire-sale of Merrill Lynch were powerful symbols of the end of the City as we had come to know it, then the demise of the Royal Show, the premier farming event of the British calendar at Stoneleigh in Warwickshire, is a totem of the end of our countryside. Just as the thundering herd of flash American investment bankers turned out to have galloping foot-and-mouth and terminal blue-tongue, a voice on BBC Radio 4's report on the Royal Show confirmed that if it 'was a horse, you'd shoot it'. It's a timely metaphor; if RBS was a horse, we'd have shot it too.

But, while a thousand dinner parties have squelched to the hand-wringing of urban middle-classers down to just a single BMW, the long-term decline of countryside industries has largely gone unlamented. Sure, television news crews have filmed various Ruperts marching on Parliament to claim, not always entirely convincingly, that fox-hunting is an essentially working-class occupation; but the suffering of British agriculture has elicited far less national anguish than the plight of the banks.

Perhaps that is no surprise. The banks have taken the nation's pensions down with them. And so long as our butternut squash was being flown in from Nicaragua or wherever during the years of plenty, no one much minded that our indigenous growers were being driven to the wall by supermarket groups that have eyes only for their competitive margins. The urbanites gorged themselves on New Zealand lamb and Argentinian vegetables during the boom years, amusing themselves with gags about the difference between a British farmer and a jumbo jet engine (the jet engine stops whining when it gets to Florida). But it is axiomatic that we don't know what we've got until it's gone. Soon the Royal Show will be gone and we can only hope British farming doesn't follow it.

If it does, some will blame our farmers for the loss just as they do the bankers for the financial crisis. This equation between essentially honest tillers of the land and greedy financiers in suits may have farmers reaching for their 12-bores. But just because we'd rather spend a weekend with a farmer than an hour in the company of a banker doesn't mean we should absolve the former of any blame for their circumstances.

The Royal Agricultural Society tells us that the Royal Show has to go because it's no longer economically viable. It also solemnly informs us that part of the reason that it can't pay its way is that the countryside has 'changed'. Well, you could knock me down with a mangelwurzel. I guess that might be why there are fewer blacksmiths around, because our modes of transport have altered somewhat over the past century too.

The Royal Show has been staged for an unbroken run of 170 years. Are we seriously meant to believe that it has been operating the same model since 1839, only to discover that some insuperable 'change' had occurred in agriculture in the first decade of the 21st century that meant it had to be called off?

More likely is that somewhere along the line the organisers have messed up. They haven't changed their pitch sufficiently to match the market. There are other country shows around Britain that remain popular, even lucrative. I have friends who go to the Royal Cornwall. The Bath & West has undergone various re-incarnations. These shows aren't any more about red-faced, burly farmers looking for a new bull and horny-handed sons of toil trading harrows. Gabriel Oak no longer plies for hire. They have an obligation, if they are to survive, to entertain as well as to trade. And, sad as it may be for those who have farmed the land for generations, that is a rubric for the countryside itself.

If farming is in terminal decline, or at least farming as we have understood it for the past couple of centuries, then other uses for the countryside have to be developed and encouraged, beyond building new homes across swathes of it. And that requires both imagination and a new covenant between town and country.

As matters stand, the two are more estranged than ever. Country dwellers despise the townies, the weekenders and second-homers with their pristine 4x4s and truculent children. And it's a two-way motorway:

the government since 1997 has viewed the countryside, at best, as a museum. Village post offices have gone, pubs are decimated or have been gastroised, bus services have disappeared. The church as a hub of community is hobbled by its own economic crisis.

The new appointment of the South Downs as a National Park only serves to show how the government believes that rural beauty is to be corralled, rather than integrated in to the rest of our economy. As a nation, we need to decide what we want from our countryside. Country votes don't win elections, but you might suppose that the Conservatives would think there was something worth conserving here.

After all, there can't be a Royal Show if there's nothing whatever to show.

4 October 2003
Guides to a Lost World
Peter Marren

Television spin-offs aside, the only books about wildlife you see on the shelves of WH Smith are the field guides. Even these are books only in the sense that they have pages.

In form and function, they are closer to manuals – the words are subordinated to the pictures, and information has been honed for a particular purpose. You snap open the guide and swiftly identify that insect or flower. You use the guide like a pair of binoculars, to spot a bird and move on to the next one. They are not books so much as kit.

How different from the first generation of field guides, the *Wayside and Woodland Blossoms* volumes, published 100 years ago by Frederick Warne (which was also Beatrix Potter's publisher – *Peter Rabbit*, her first book, came out in 1902). The series was written for a more leisurely age, when people often collected or reared the objects of their curiosity and wanted to know how to find them and how they lived, as well as what they looked like.

The 30-odd titles, now sadly out of print, ranged over most of the wild animals and plants found in Britain, but were particularly strong on insects, with volumes on such esoteric subjects as *Pyralid and Plume Moths*, *The Spider's Web* and *Land and Water Bugs*. In their familiar chunky format, designed to slip into the pocket of a Norfolk jacket and with their, by modern standards, drab monochrome jackets, they served British natural history at a time when naturalists were generalists, rather than specialists, and studied life in ponds and ditches on the doorstep instead of travelling to the tropics.

The guides scored a number of publishing firsts. They were among the first nature books to make full use of photographs. *Butterflies of the British Isles*, published in 1906, used a three-colour printing process to reproduce mounted specimens in lifelike colour. They were the first affordable pocket guides to include all the British species of larger moths, grasshoppers and bugs, and they probably hold a record for longevity, with nearly 70 years in print.

And they were recognisably books – books that bookworms love, with their fussy gilt-blocked bindings, illustrated endpapers and speckled page-ends. Distinguished scientists have told me that it all started for them with a birthday copy of T.A. Coward's three-volume *Birds of the British Isles and their Eggs* or Richard South's two-volume *Moths of the British Isles*. Perhaps the key to the books' charm lies in that phrase 'wayside and woodland'. It was coined by the first writer of the series, Edward Step, a London naturalist whose many books have the flavour of a nature ramble through ordinary countryside, rather than nature reserves (Step's stamping ground was London's parks and commons). There is an air of Sunday-school innocence in titles such as *By the Deep Sea* and the *Come With Me* books about wildlife in the garden and through the seasons.

These were books you could read with pleasure for their scientifically accurate, fascinating accounts of the intricate lives of bees and ants, or information about which trees made the best firewood or how plants acquired their names. Step generally wrote from first-hand observation, so the reader had a sense of looking over the writer's shoulder and seeing something through his eyes.

To naturalists of a certain age, the *Wayside and Woodland* books may, as they do for me, conjure up a lost world of cycle rides down lanes and byways, a knapsack over the shoulder and a butterfly net strapped to the back; of country rambles and jam-jars filled with pond life or caterpillars; or of camping out and hearing the dawn chorus echo around the tent.

I have written three books about books: the Collins *New Naturalist* series, which married cutting-edge science with natural history for the post-war generation; the *Observer's* books, a set of pocket encyclopaedias at five bob a throw; and now the *Wayside and Woodland* guide. Written for the book collector and nostalgically inclined naturalist, I have tried to convey something of the era they served and why they were such a success.

We have presented it as an *Observer's Book of*, with the blessing of Frederick Warne & Co. for the use of that name. It forms a companion volume to my *Observer's Book of Observer's Books*, published four years ago (and still in print). It even has a number, and a nice round one: No 100 – a happy coincidence for the centenary of the series is just around the corner.

7 October 2007
When the Wind Stopped
Clive Aslet

Twenty years ago, colleagues were in mourning. It was not that the Great Storm, sweeping in from the Channel Islands, had driven a Channel ferry aground, or torn the roofs from houses like Christmas wrapping paper from a toy. In the *Country Life* office, the ancients were lamenting the disappearance of landscapes they had known since youth. I went to Kent to report on a county that in places resembled Flanders during the First World War. In London, majestic plane trees had toppled across the railings of Georgian squares and on to cars. In the country, lanes were blocked. A nation that had barely come to terms with the elimination of elm trees from the countryside was in shock.

Charles Gooch, a land manager for Savills, remembers one client at Boughton Monchelsea, in Kent. 'Out of a stand of 88 high beech trees there were just eight left. He was so shocked and horrified we couldn't persuade him to allow the contractors in to clear up.' It was a tragedy for historic landscapes. While the storm, like an avenging angel, passed over the head of some woodland, leaving it unscathed, it gathered speed in the spaces between the clumps of country-house parks. Stately avenues were left in tatters.

For much of the 20th century, owners were too strapped for cash to plant young trees. They continued to glory in stands of timber that were in some cases centuries old. But everything in nature has a natural span. These trees, which had reached maturity decades previously, by

1987 were naturally dying back and would have gone at some point over the next 30 years; the Great Storm brought them all down together. Capability Brown's landscape at Cadland Manor, on the Solent – pines, planted in light soil – was turned, in the words of the owner Maldwin Drummond, into 'pick-a-sticks'.

Mature beeches are among the loveliest of trees but, with their wide-spreading, shallow root system, almost absurdly vulnerable: there had been no frost, persistent rain in the weeks prior to October 15 had turned the ground into porridge, their tops were still heavy with a dense canopy of leaves. At Knole and elsewhere, the wind plucked them up as though they were seedlings. They fell still attached to great discs of root and earth. Toys Hill, at the highest point of Kent, lost 98 per cent of its trees in some places.

All of southern England, it seemed, was desolation: there were many who could not envisage it ever returning to its former leafy splendour. But if country lovers had turned their eyes northwards, they would have found cause for hope. By a meteorological freak, Bramham Park in Yorkshire, with its important Baroque landscape, had been hit by a strangely localised hurricane in the 1950s. Visitors to the horse trials held there each June will know that the *patte d'oie*, or goosefoot, of radiating rides, lined by tall beech hedges, has now been completely restored.

And so it has proved in the south. In fact, 20 years on, the devastated landscapes are now looking remarkably healthy, and in some cases – particularly commercial forestry areas – they actually look rather better than before.

The Great Storm of 1987 not only removed a great number of trees long past their prime, it also served as a call to arms for estate owners. English Heritage, the Countryside Commission and even Nicholas Ridley, the otherwise not notably green environment secretary of the day, came up with grants. With their help, more trees have been planted in the past 20 years than at any time since the 18th century, though it will take time for the youngsters to grow to the proportions of their fallen predecessors.

The great landscape parks owned by the National Trust, such as Nymans, Chartwell and Sheffield Park, are sparer than they were before 1987, but in better heart for the future. Indeed, Britain was fortunate in the timing. Had the Great Storm struck in 1947 or 1917 the country would have been much less able to respond.

Like the parks, woodland was damaged, particularly on the ridges of hills, but here the priorities were different. Stands of closely planted commercial timber did not have the same aesthetic value, nor was there the same need to recreate particular landscape features. The Great Storm coincided with a change of thinking in forestry. After the two world wars, timber was regarded as a scant national resource, in a country that has one of the lowest proportions of forest cover in Europe. The hillsides of northern England, Wales and Scotland were planted with single-species conifer blocks.

By 1987, the environmental impact of such monocultures was being widely deplored. It was, besides, becoming cheaper to import wood from Scandinavia than grow it at home. Even the Forestry Commission, once the champion of sitka spruce, was coming to a different view. Woodlands were for walking in, as well as growing telegraph poles. The public demanded a greater proportion of broadleaves, even though they rarely have commercial value.

This required a different approach. Rather than planting trees of the same type and age, to be clear-felled in blocks, the doctrine of 'continuous silviculture' was evolved. Young trees should be encouraged to grow up among their older brethren, according to this new policy, then, when they have reached maturity, extracted without damaging the surrounding wood.

This is working with the grain of nature, rather than against it. One of the lessons of the Great Storm is that nature herself has recuperative powers beyond the scope of human intervention. While many traumatised landowners instinctively rushed to replant their woods, others appreciated the benefits of untidiness. 'Once cleared up, Boughton Monchelsea regenerated itself and we now have a wonderful stand of beech trees again,' observes Mr Gooch. The National Trust, too, has moved away from the ideal of aesthetic perfection. It is more likely to leave tree trunks to rot gently on the ground, where they become a Ritz Hotel to insects and fungi.

In Richmond Park, the assistant manager, Adam Curtis, talks of 'phoenix trees which have blown over and resprouted. The water filling in the root crater creates an ecological niche'. Ground that is no longer shaded by a dense tree canopy becomes quickly colonised by bluebells, orchids, mosses and other species. Very soon saplings will spring up. Foresters have come to realise that selecting from the dozens of plants that regenerate naturally is better than choosing from three or four that have been specially planted.

Fortuitously, in 1987 there had been a heavy crop of acorns and beechmasts, many of which have indeed sprouted into now tallish trees. It was not, however, always the same species that regenerated. A survey by Forest Research, part of the Forestry Commission, in 2002, showed that while ash remained abundant at sites where it had previously been dominant, oak and beech woods tended to be overtaken by birch, the equivalent to a pernicious weed in forestry circles. Another survey showed that fallen conifers were spontaneously replaced by broadleaves, including coppiced hornbeam, alder and sweet chestnut (managed long ago but since forgotten).

The Great Storm was not the last. Winds have been higher in subsequent storms, and we shall experience more such 'extreme weather events' if climate predictions are correct. A diverse woodland should be better able to withstand them. Meanwhile, what seemed to be the cataclysm of 1987 is a continuing boon for one group in the population: cabinet-makers. In Surrey, Senior and Carmichael saved two dozen specimens from the hundreds of trees that crashed down around their workshop at Betchworth. They continue to make small numbers of their Hurricane Chair, a harlequin of the fallen incorporating oak, ash, sycamore, yew, walnut, chestnut and holly.

The wind blew, and it ruffled the face of southern Britain, but there were no permanent scars – and the old girl is looking pretty good again.

22 August 2010
The Final Bough
Mark Seddon

When I was growing up, the English elm was coming down. Towering hedgerow giants that once cast a dusty shade over countless country lanes suddenly began to shrivel and go yellow and brown; and the summer landscape across lowland Britain became first wintry, then barren. For the early seventies saw a new, virulent strain of Dutch elm disease take hold which, within the space of a couple of decades, had wiped out between 25 and 30 million elms, transforming the British countryside forever.

But in Brighton, Eastbourne and parts of East Sussex, it was a different story. Partly protected by the Channel and the South Downs, the elms received some initial protection from the fungus-carrying, beetle-born disease. Here, pioneering tree specialists and the swift response of the local authorities, combined with a good deal of local pride in saving the trees, meant that a programme of sanitation felling and surgery largely contained the disease.

Today this region has the largest and most diverse population of elms anywhere in the world. Brighton is home to the National Elm Collection, and the jewel in that city's crown is Preston Park, home to the world's oldest English elms, leviathans that are known and loved locally as the Preston Park Twins. A mighty row of Wheatley elms fringe the park, and all around are the colours, shapes and beauty associated with a tree that, to the amazement of visitors, can still be found here. If ever there is a campaign worth launching, it would be to achieve Unesco World Heritage status for this place.

Brighton was my epiphany as a boy. The streets were lined with Jersey elms, the parks had an astonishing array of elm varieties, and – joy of joys – there was the Hollow Brace Tree, an English elm planted in 1776, the year of American independence, possibly as Brighton's first amenity tree, which to this day stands in the grounds of the Royal Pavilion. This tree is the pride and joy of Royal Pavilion gardener Robert Hill-Snook, who told me that he hears 'gasps of delight' from visitors when they see it. 'They didn't realise these trees still existed,' he said. 'They say it is like travelling into the past.'

But it is a very different story for the English elm amid the small valleys of the South Downs, to the east of Brighton. Here, as I discovered, they are on the very cusp of fighting a losing war against Dutch elm disease. Almost every hedgerow and line of trees is showing the tell-tale signs of aerial beetle attack.

In the village of Litlington, a champion English elm whose billowing, cloud-like shape once inspired artists such as Constable and Turner, is surrounded by younger trees that have been hit by the disease. How much longer does this mighty tree have? The totemic Cathedral Walk, a stand of towering English elms near Alfriston in the Cuckmere Valley, has also been hit, and in the village of Berwick, I witnessed a team of tree surgeons tackling dead and dying trees behind the local pub.

As Mary Parker, a Dutch elm disease field officer, explained, the elm beetle carries with it a deadly fungus that, once inside the tree, spreads rapidly and blocks the water-carrying vessels. If affected trees aren't removed quickly, the beetle breeds and moves on – and the fungus spreads through the root system of the elms to attack neighbouring trees.

It is the English elm's misfortune to be descended from rootstock brought to Britain by the Romans 2,000 years ago to prop up their vines, unlike more disease-resistant British natives such as the wych elm or smooth-leaved elm, still to be found in many parts of the Midlands and East Anglia. Claims from some nurserymen that they are successfully growing disease-resistant English elm should be treated with extreme caution.

But why the resurgence of the disease this summer? And what is new about the threat facing our last remaining stands of rural English elms? The dry, hot summer may have only aided what's been going wrong in recent years, and which now risks undoing 40 years of hard work. Last year, new charges of up to 50 per cent were brought in for private landowners for diseased tree felling. Some irresponsible landlords have left dead trees standing. Others simply cannot afford the charges. East Sussex County Council has legal rights of enforcement – after all, this is a Dutch elm disease control zone – but locals point to new layers of red tape, all slowing up a process that used to be fast and efficient.

And there are deeper concerns about what the Autumn Spending Review could bring. Next April, the new South Downs National Park comes into existence, and although the county and district councils will continue running disease-control programmes, many I spoke to hope the new authorities will get behind the battle for the English elm.

Sadly it may be too late to save the tree in the ancient Friston Forest, not so long ago relatively disease-free. Here, locals say, the Forestry Commission has all but given up and, looking around at the dead and dying trees, it is hard not to disagree. A local resident, Gay Biddlecombe, says: 'I've contacted them repeatedly, but never get anywhere, and now my trees have got it. It's a disgrace.'

The Forestry Commission told me that they intend to send in teams to tackle the outbreak, but added that they don't see 'a healthy future for the elm in the Friston Forest area'. If the Forestry Commission takes this view here, there will not be a healthy future for the surrounding areas, either.

Those landscapes, paintings and poetry inspired by the elm, which still remain here – just about – could soon be lost forever. What is needed, say the experts, is an emergency sanitation programme of tree-felling that carries on through the winter and works up from the coast and into the valleys. There needs to be less red tape, and all bodies – including the Forestry Commission – need to show the same dedication as the local authorities.

Saving the English elm comes at a cost, but these trees have a national significance, woven as they are into our history and culture. Yet those costs are surely marginal when compared to what we could yet lose. 'If we lose the elm, what next?' Gay Biddlecombe asked, as I left her home in the forest.

What next, indeed.

Town and Country

22 August 2009
Not a Rum Baba in Sight
Jane Alexander

It's a hot sunny Sunday in the small Exmoor town of Dulverton. The crowds have spilt out of the Bridge Inn and people are lounging on the grass next to the river. Children are paddling and bodyboarding, dogs are splashing in the water, swimming after sticks, and there is a gentle hum of laughter and conversation. Then someone wanders up waving a copy of a Sunday paper and the mood shifts.

'What's she said this time? Who's she got her teeth into? Whose husband is she after now?' Exmoor isn't happy with Liz Jones. Actually that's an understatement: Dulverton is positively fizzing with fury. Since moving to a house a few miles outside the town about 18 months ago, the newspaper columnist has solidly and consistently run down the countryside in general and Exmoor in particular.

Exmoor, according to Jones, is cold and dirty, smelly and vicious. The yokels who live here are even worse: we kill things and eat them; we farm and forage; we are old, smelly, hairy and toothless. We don't wear Prada and our pubs are stuck in the seventies.

If ever there were a blueprint of how NOT to move to the countryside, this would be it. Now Jones's book, *The Exmoor Files* (Weidenfeld & Nicolson, £12.99) has been published and Exmoor is bracing itself for another attack. Frankly, we don't need it: the countryside is already battered enough without Jones kicking it when it's down. Our farmers have suffered foot-and-mouth, bovine TB and cascading prices. Pubs and restaurants are closing hand over fist.

Schools, shops and services are doomed when there simply aren't enough people to use them on a regular basis as swathes of the countryside become second-home enclaves. So we rely on tourists to keep our little town going and Jones is single-handedly putting them off. 'We nearly didn't come after reading her column,' says one woman from Yorkshire. 'She made the food sound awful and the locals a real nightmare.'

Jones is just one of the teeming hordes of people who are leaving the city in search of the Good Life. According to the Commission for Rural Communities, around 110,000 people a year move out of cities to the countryside and the figure is increasing every year. Some do their homework and slide carefully, sensitively, into rural life. Others – sadly – don't. They fall in love with a Merchant Ivory dream of the countryside and then get petulant when it fails to live up to their romantic expectations.

'I had this dream of what it would be like living in the countryside, but the reality is about a million times harder,' Jones says. 'There are days when I long to be back in my warm, clean house in London with my nice things and Space NK up the road. I want to be all dressed up and meet my friends for a drink in a trendy hotel bar. I want my car not to be full of mud and bits of wood. I want to be warm and clean.'

I understand the warm and clean bit. In winter, I sit at my desk with a hot water-bottle on my lap, a grubby dog at my feet, trying to type with fingerless mittens to keep my fingers from freezing. But that's the price you pay for living in draughty country houses. I will freely admit that the countryside is smelly and muddy, and yes, people here hunt and shoot and fish and farm. But, truly, what did she expect? It's not *The Wicker Man*; we don't keep our proclivities a secret.

If you're going to move to the country, wouldn't it be wise to do your homework? If you're a fashionista vegan who's vehemently against field sports, surely it's insanity to move to a place mainly famed for its hunting, shooting or fishing?

Cynical locals suggest it was all for the sake of the book – after all, country nasty makes much better copy than country nice. Exmoor simply isn't country 'lite' or country soft and sensual, not by a long (well-aimed) shot. We don't have Daylesford Organic on our doorstep. You can't pop into Cheltenham for a few cocktails. Sorry, but it isn't Kensington with cows.

This is the real countryside: it's a bit Wild West; more than a little 'nature raw in tooth and claw' and, to my mind, all the better for it.

Jones presents a clichéd, stereotypical and, frankly, lazy image of the countryside. She is clearly an intelligent woman and her opinion pieces can be smart and lucid, yet when she writes about Exmoor, she really loses the plot. We're not naïve here – we know that every journalist uses people for their raw material and she's simply the latest in a long line of writers who have mocked country ways. But, here in Zummerzet we're bored to our back teeth (yes, some of us do still have them) with that tired old image of bumpkins glugging back the scrumpy with bits of straw in our ill-coiffed hair.

If Jones actually bothered to get out and join in, she'd find rich material in spades. Exmoor is blissfully odd. Where else would you find people obsessed with the arcane practice of bolving (imitating the sound of a stag in rut with the aim of getting it to bellow back to you)? Where else could you watch wide-eyed and slack-jawed the Riphay Scuffle, an insane *Mad Max*/Armageddon version of beaten-up 4x4s hurtling their way through streams and revving up vertiginous banks?

Yes, the deep moorland is isolated, wild and remote. It can be a harsh life and underneath the picture-postcard prettiness lies serious rural deprivation. Chris Wynne-Davies of the Commission for Rural Communities says that west Somerset (which encompasses a large part of Exmoor) is 'the 10th most rurally deprived local authority district in England'. Many people live close to the poverty line: some don't have mains electricity, let alone broadband.

No wonder that, if you ask farming people out on the moor what they think of Jones, playing like Marie Antoinette with her pet lambs, buying Evian for her horses and spending thousands on a handbag, they shake their heads in bemusement. Her waxing bill alone would probably keep a moorland family in food for a year.

The weirdest thing though is that Jones isn't living in the middle of Exmoor, she isn't even living on the moor at all. The book talks of Jones 'burying herself alive in the middle of the bleak, unforgiving wilderness that is Exmoor National Park'. But she actually lives outside the park, swathed in soft rolling farmland while her 'wreck of a farmhouse' is drop-dead gorgeous (or it certainly was before she moved in). But then I suppose her version makes a better story.

Moving to the countryside is a huge seismic shift. If you're sensible, you test the waters by renting or stick within kicking distance of a large town. When we moved to Exmoor, we knew it would be a steep learning curve. We accepted we would have to tread carefully, to watch, listen and learn, and above all to adapt.

The first thing we did was to introduce ourselves to our neighbours, including a wonderful countrywoman called Elaine. 'In the countryside, you need your neighbours,' Elaine says firmly. 'You might not agree with them, you might not even like them, but you should never upset them because you just don't know when you'll need them.'

Yet Jones firmly ignored hers. One poor soul finally took the initiative and went over, pot of jam in hand, to say hello. She was greeted with an irritated frown. 'I can't talk to you now, I'm doing a photo shoot,' Jones said, firmly shutting the door in her face. Meanwhile her farming neighbours (lovely people, one and all) are routinely slated for, well, farming mainly.

She seems to believe in some Disneyesque vision of the countryside with herself cast as Snow White. 'I rescue the mice and shrews Sweetie [her cat] insists on bringing into my bedroom,' she trilled in one column. 'They reside in a row of shoe boxes (Manolo Blahnik, Bottega Veneta).' She feeds organic muesli to the rats in the stables and lambasts farmers who send lambs off for slaughter, particularly when 'they are still breastfeeding'.

At first people smiled indulgently at another daft townie who thinks we shoot pheasants on Sundays (it's only clay-pigeon shooting). They gently rolled their eyes when she couldn't reverse up the lane in her BMW. The consensus was that she'd soon 'come round', loosen up a bit and start to muck in. But she didn't. She swooped into our local bar, Woods, without even glancing around. No tentative smile, no hint of a hello. A few people tried to make friendly overtures but were abruptly rebuffed.

Then the shrugs and amused smiles turned to puzzlement, hurt and finally anger as she started attacking the area. 'I have given up trying to eat out in restaurants here on Exmoor,' she said. 'It is still stuck in the seventies, with only things in baskets and rum babas on the menu.'

Not true, not remotely true. Woods, to take just one example, serves seriously smart food and stunning wine. It's been fêted in every paper going (including this one). We've thought long and hard and can't think of a single place where food comes 'in a basket' and the search is on for a rum baba because nobody around here has tasted one in decades.

Dulverton itself is blessed with great small shops – both of the everyday useful variety (such as greengrocers, hardware, newsagent, chemist) and the totally frivolous but delightful variety. You can buy everything here from a saddle to a pair of sky-high slingbacks, from an antiquarian book to a fishing rod, and from a set of Sophie Conran cookware to a sack of dog biscuits.

OK, we don't have a vegan café or an avant-garde cinema, Harvey Nichols hasn't decided to stick an outpost here and yes, you may have to travel a little if you want a Brazilian or a fancy facial. But it is not the benighted backwater she describes and the people who live here are not the hairy, straw-sucking peasants she depicts.

'I will never, ever meet a man here in the middle of a moor, where even to be in possession of your own teeth is a bonus,' she moaned in one column. No, Liz, you will never, ever meet a man here because you're not getting out, not making friends and not joining in.

If Jones had come to Exmoor with an open mind and open heart, she would have been made hugely welcome. Exmoor loves mavericks and eccentrics, and would have indulged and fêted her. But all she has done is moan and gripe and poke fun at her neighbours and her town.

She clearly fell for that age-old idea that things will be better in the country than in the big city. Well, they can be, but you have to make an effort. You have to meet people halfway. You have to pitch up to things. Above all, you have to adapt. You simply can't expect the countryside to change itself just for you. If you read Jones's book please take it with a hefty pinch of salt (or a salutary lesson in how not to move to the country).

Better still, ditch the book and discover the real Exmoor and Dulverton for yourself. I can guarantee a warm country welcome, great food, good company and not a rum baba in sight.

Incomers' Guide to Moving to the Countryside

DO

Accept that it isn't just the city with fields – it's another world with a whole different set of rules, mores and even language. Be friendly. Introduce yourself to the neighbours; smile when you walk in to the pub or down the street. Be open-minded and willing to try new and even odd things. Fêtes, ferret racing, nettle-eating competitions? Give them a whirl. Never judge a person by their clothes, car or appearance here – the scruffiest old codger could be a Lord; the farmer's wife could have a PhD in astrophysics. Live and let live: you may not agree with hunting, farming, pottery figurines or baggy sweatshirts but just keep your mouth shut. Let your hair down a bit. Loosen up, have a laugh.

DON'T

Expect the countryside and its inhabitants to change centuries of lifestyle to fit around you. Allow your pet dog to savage the local stock. Move into the heart of farming country and moan about mud/ smells/noise/tractors/farming in general. Be overly sentimental. The countryside is a working place not a theme park. Wild animals die occasionally; farm animals die a lot — get over it. Make it public (especially in national newspapers) that you fancy other people's husbands. Poor form. Moan when your automatic sports car gets stuck in snow. Drive a 4x4 Suzuki or Subaru like everyone else.

30 March 2009
Letter to the Editor
How to Make Friends in the Countryside

SIR — How lovely to read some common sense from Matthew Taylor MP about second homes (report, 25 March). People moving to the countryside, expecting to live happily ever after, seem to forget that we have laws, just as in the towns. One of the good ones is: don't let your dog run loose unless you know it does not chase sheep. The countryside is not a big play park.

You should also support your local church, school and shop, even if it does not stock every brand of coffee. Taking down Devon banks and putting up chain-link fencing and lights is not a good move. The countryside is supposed to be dark and the banks are for keeping in animals.

In our part of the world £6 is considered a good hourly wage, so please don't tell us you bought your house with your annual bonus. It does not endear you to us.

Manners are also important. If you drive in the lanes you must be prepared to pull over and reverse. If we reverse for you, please say thank you. Everyone coming into Devon and Cornwall should take a reversing test at the border and stay there until they have got the hang of it.

Sally Hamilton
Cornwood
Devon

18 September 2008
Disposal of Capital
Cathy Salmon

With its village pond, ancient stocks and immaculate cottage frontages, the Hertfordshire village of Aldbury is the epitome of rural tranquillity. Thoroughbred racehorses clip-clop elegantly from the nearby stables. Tractors rumble towards sloping adjacent fields. The village post office and shop buzzes with morning chatter.

In the cellar of the Valiant Trooper pub, Biraj Parmar, 40, is checking the levels in his beer kegs in readiness for 11 a.m. opening time. A fresh London Pride barrel needs to be tapped and the new keg of local Tring brew Jack O'Legs is ready to serve.

This is new territory for the former senior risk manager with Deutsche Bank and, before that, Barclays Capital in London. It is a far cry from his previous domain. As head of UK Corporates for the global investment banks, Biraj was responsible for clients who would trade in excess of £12bn of foreign exchange and interest rate derivatives a year.

Leading a team of 12 risk specialists, his daily mix was one of 7 a.m. dealing-room meetings, presenting to plc boards – some of them FTSE 100 giants – and constant phone calls to clients as he structured complex financial products in order to manage his customers' risks.

Three nights a week after writing detailed reports on the day's proceedings, he would leave the office at 8 p.m. for dinner with clients in the capital's most exclusive restaurants. He'd return home around midnight, before rising at 5 a.m. the next morning to start again. The pace was relentless – 16-hour days meant he only saw his children, Mica, nine, Emmie, six, and Xavi, five, at weekends and holidays. It required huge professional and personal commitment, but the rewards were immense – at Biraj's director level, his bonuses were multiples of his six-figure salary.

But that was his old world – a world now dramatically collapsing. Earlier this week, Lehman Brothers, America's fourth largest investment bank, filed for bankruptcy protection on the same day that Wall Street giant Merrill Lynch agreed to a Bank of America takeover.

As he absorbs the news, Biraj feels he's had a lucky escape. For in February of this year, after 12 years in the City, he made the monumental decision to turn his back on the Square Mile with its lifestyle and accompanying benefits. Instead, he and his wife Beth, 37, decided to realise a long-held desire to downshift from the corporate rat race and enhance their quality of life.

Biraj recalls the tipping point for his decision. He was busy prioritising customers with a colleague a few rows across the dealing-room floor when he saw the flashing red light on the dealer board – his phone was ringing. He knew it was a key customer. But as he reached out to take the call, the light turned green – someone else had got there first. He stood up, locked eyes with the team-mate holding his phone and watched, startled as his colleague – without shame or conscience – waved him nonchalantly away, before snaffling the £50k deal himself.

He says: 'I knew then that it was time to get out. The City is known for its philosophy of aggressive competition between staff – this kind of thing was happening all the time. Over the years I've seen the emphasis on customers as the priority diluted. It's far more about aggressive selling with little regard for what the customer needs. There was an increasing drive to sell more complex products with less transparent profit levels and I was uncomfortable selling them to customers who, to my mind, required something simpler.'

His stomach still churns at the memories of close colleagues discarded at a moment's notice 'like broken computers' in a climate of mass sackings. 'One minute they'd be chatting to the secretary about the weekend – the next she'd be handing them their belongings in a bag downstairs. It was carnage. Some of the things that were going on were just unbelievable. The City has become a nasty, unpleasant place to work.' It was time to move on.

A joint hospitality venture had always been his and Beth's preferred option, given that some of his City clients had been hotels, brewers and restaurants, and Beth's background was in human resources.

In June, the leasehold of the Valiant Trooper became theirs. But running a pub in these turbulent times is certainly not the easy option. Just last week, the British Beer and Pub Association (BBPA) announced that 36 pubs are closing every week across Britain – that's five a day – as drinkers choose to buy cut-price alcohol for consumption at home. A total of 936 pubs ceased trading in the first six months of 2008, according to figures compiled by CGA Strategies, and the BBPA fears closures will gather pace with the imposition of above-inflation rises in beer duty. So in a slump that has seen beer sales plummet to their lowest levels since the great depression of the 1930s, has Biraj jumped out of the proverbial frying pan into the fire?

'You could say that,' he reflects. 'It's a terrible situation, but if you look at where those 36 closures a week went wrong, customer service would be top of the list, followed closely by poor food.

'People are going out less – if it used to be six times a month, now it's maybe three. But they're eating where they know what they're going to get and we have to make sure that's here at least two out of those three times.

'With the downturn gripping the UK economy, pubs have to offer consistently high standards of service, food and drink, at a price customers think is worth paying. Customer service is an easy phrase to use, but you need genuinely to focus on customers and understand that having a relationship with them will ultimately drive whether you make any money.

'Our customers are our first priority. My customers come in and I know which glass they need, what beer they drink, what kind of head they need. I know what to say when I hand it over and I know what they'll say when they take it. That's what relationships are.'

But do the regulars at the bar inspire him as much as the four rolling screens screaming information at him at his old desk in the City? 'More,' he says, without hesitation, 'because this is much more real life.'

Since first clapping eyes on the historic 18th-century freehouse, the couple have seen the potential to build its ambience and broaden its appeal. 'It's a really exciting opportunity to turn a well-known pub in a beautiful setting into a real gem,' says Biraj. 'It's a combination of being commercially interesting and a lot of fun.'

The couple have carried out some interior and exterior refurbishments. They've lost some staff, taken on others, hosted monthly curry nights, a comedy night, a wine-tasting dinner and mini beer festival and are promoting their family-friendliness with free Sunday afternoon face-painting and 'after-school' suppers. The beer – always good – is now 'excellent – even better than before', according to local Mid-Chiltern CAMRA (Campaign for Real Ale) members.

By way of advice, the BBPA is urging pubs to concentrate on the 'Five Fs' – food, families, females, forty-somethings and fifty-somethings. The Trooper seems to have them all covered. 'We're starting to attract a true mix of people now,' says Biraj, enthusiastically, 'walkers, cyclists, tourists, young, old, affluent, hard-up, professionals, blue-collars and families – not just locally but from all around.'

Significantly, they have just recruited a new award-winning chef, whose 'innovative but classic' culinary style has immediately made an impact. 'In terms of frequency of visit and new customers we're really starting to gain,' says Biraj. 'The same couple ate here three times last week.' Compared with what the pub's previous incumbent was making, turnover has increased by more than 100 per cent and, with relish, Biraj reports that locals are telling them they've brought the heart back to the village.

Beyond his strong customer focus, it's clear that some of Biraj's other City skills migrate naturally to running a pub. To 'mitigate risks', he and Beth have done a range of courses covering pub management, cellarmanship and personal licensing. Biraj's negotiating know-how ensures the best deals with suppliers, and at the end of every day they appraise the business – assessing everything from performance to figures.

While there are some similarities to his former life, for the most part the two realities are poles apart. 'I still get up early, but at 7.15 a.m., when my team and I would have been having a five-minute huddle, updating each other on markets and client activity, I'm walking the dogs [Jack Russell sisters Milly and Lucky],' he says. 'I have breakfast with my children and we chat and play games before I take them to school. I realise now how much I've missed out on. It's great to spend real time and have real conversations with them.' Some days he does the school pick-up too when he chats to the 'yummy mummies' in the playground – 'because I'm trying to persuade them to come to the Trooper', he smiles, wryly.

'My commute is now a 10-minute drive through the National Trust forest of Ashridge, past deers and badgers, and virtually every morning I say hello to a dozen jockeys riding past on some of the most expensive horses in the world.' (The former jockey and racehorse trainer Walter Swinburn has stables in the village.)

'Beth and I work really long hours, but they're really long hours that we're together and we're really enjoying it. It's a different pace, a different stress, but our quality of life has definitely improved and I feel very optimistic about the future. Given what's happened in the global financial markets this week, I feel a massive sense of relief that I chose to do my own thing. I'm in control of my life, which is something that can't be said for the thousands of people at Lehmans in London,' he adds with regret, 'who don't even know if they'll be getting this month's salary.'

14 March 2009

City Boy Finds His Place in the Country

Christopher Middleton

Four years ago, Harry Mosley went on a day trip that changed his life. Only 12 at the time, he was one of a group of young south Londoners who travelled to the 7,000-acre estate of Lord Normanton, in the New Forest, to experience the fresh air of the countryside and to try clay-pigeon shooting.

Organised by Vauxhall MP Kate Hoey, and covered by the *Weekend Telegraph*, this unlikely outing left such an impression on young Harry that, at the age of 16, he has left school and become a trainee gamekeeper. We meet him at Sparsholt Agricultural College, near Winchester, where he is halfway through a one-year diploma in game management.

Dressed in jeans and trainers, he looks no different from any other Lambeth teenager, but an hour later, he stands beside a Hampshire trout stream, utterly transformed. Gone is the urban gear (and slouch), and in its place the sturdy green clothing and upright bearing of the rural gamekeeper. Plus a large shotgun, slung over the shoulder.

Now it's fair to say that the original *Telegraph* article caused quite a stir, with its portrayal of inner-city teenagers at the business end of a double-barrelled firearm. But whereas some youngsters might see a gun as a glamorous accessory, Harry views it as a working tool.

'You have to know how to use it, and you have to know how to respect it,' he shrugs. 'Last week, we were called out in the middle of the night to find a deer that had been hit by a car. We spent two hours following the blood tracks and, when we eventually found the deer, we had to put it down, because it was so badly injured. The way I see it, death is just a part of life. And it was much better to put that deer out of its misery than let it suffer.'

It's this kind of level-headedness from Harry that has impressed people, and has led to him being awarded a bursary from the newly set up Countryside Alliance Foundation. The CAF pays for his board, lodging and equipment, while the London Borough of Lambeth covers his fees.

'I should imagine this is the first time Lambeth have paid for anyone to go to agricultural college,' laughs Kate Hoey, chairman of the Countryside Alliance and one of the few Labour MPs to vote against the hunting ban.

'This shows that just because you live in the city, it doesn't mean you can't be interested in the countryside. Mind you, Harry has been very determined in the way he has followed up that initial trip in 2005.'

Soon after getting back to London, Harry made contact with Lord Normanton's estate, to ask if he could do work experience during the school holidays. The answer was yes, and he hasn't looked back.

'I've been amazed at the transformation,' says his mother Jenny. 'Harry used to be quite a home-orientated boy, never wanting to stay the night at other people's houses. Now he's the opposite. He comes home at weekends [in Waterloo], but he can't wait to get back to college on Sunday night.

'The fact is, he loves being outdoors in the fresh air. I think it's that boy thing: riding on the back of a truck one minute, up a tree the next.'

Not to mention chopping-up logs, herding deer, building game pens, rearing pheasants, protecting them from foxes, and carrying out all the other tasks a gamekeeper is called upon to perform.

'People don't realise it, but gamekeepers are responsible for managing roughly two-thirds of the entire countryside,' says Tim Bonner, head of media at the Countryside Alliance. 'The woods, the fields, the forests – the reason they look like they do is not because they've been left in their natural state, but because they've been managed. Take any wood, in any part of the country, and the chances are it was planted originally to serve as cover for game rearing.'

And where there are young game birds, there are foxes to be killed, usually by lamping.

'That's when you shine a bright torch, or lamp, into a fox's eyes and make this squeaking sound, so he thinks you're a wounded rabbit,' explains Harry. 'He comes down the light towards you, then you shoot him.

'The other night, I was really pleased with myself, because I squeaked one fox until it came right up to the window. Mind you, it wasn't in the countryside; it was outside my nan's house, in Tooting!'

15 February 2003

Reasons to be Fearful

Sinclair McKay

And so the bulldozers prepare to move in; thousands of new houses with irritatingly small windows will sprout all over the fields of the south-east like orange mushrooms. In the future, we are told, economic gravity will pull town mice away from the overpriced inner cities and into brand-new communities – from Thames Gateway onwards – all over the gardens of England. Poor suckers.

Well, I'm going to cling on until my fingernails bleed. No one is dragging me anywhere near a field. I'm not going to be woken by the menacingly Hitchcockian noise of the dawn chorus. For the truth is that, like a great many Londoners, I am frightened of the country.

Like many phobias, this one took root in early childhood. The memory flickers dimly: an infant-school outing; a smelly farmyard somewhere just north of London; a milking shed; and a cow leaning forward and licking me.

It may be false memory syndrome, but the phobia is a certainty. Village pubs, with their village locals, seem oppressive. Fields are too wide open. Why are those cows looking at me like that? Why are they now running across the field towards me? Who are those creepy teenagers taking turns on that quad bike thing? Where can I buy a packet of Silk Cut? That gate is open – should I close it? Am I allowed to walk on the edge of this field and, if not, is that farmer allowed to shoot me? And please, please, can we go back to London now?

I could try availing myself of a new National Trust countryside education scheme in the Midlands (of which more a little later), but the thing is that I am not alone. Many landmarks of English popular culture are steeped in the townie's antipathy to his rural cousin. The film *Withnail and I*, a comedy about two dissolute young actors in the late 1960s, is as much about fear of the countryside (both Withnail and the eponymous I are terrorised by a farmer who sports a polythene bag on his foot) as anything else.

The Wicker Man, a 1970s pagan horror set in the Hebrides (but based on a novel set in Cornwall) similarly plays on urban discomfort at all things remote.

A great many episodes of *The Avengers* are set in sinister villages where the entire parish is up to no good. These days, there is *Midsomer Murders*, which, as we townies know, is a documentary. And then there is Worzel Gummidge, who, despite being a scarecrow, has somehow become the iconic representation of all yeomen.

As inner-city schoolchildren, my friends and I sometimes wondered what children in the country did. After all, there's famously nothing to do there. We shook our heads sadly at the thought of the boredom they had to suffer.

And I know what you rural folk are going to say, so I will say it, too. This failure of imagination, this urban bafflement, is at the heart of this government as well – the whole Islingtonian lot of them. You can see the naked distaste playing on their faces as countryside matters come into the spotlight.

As a number of Londoners would agree, New Labour's stance on rural affairs is wrong and harmful. Hunting is one of those things country folk inexplicably enjoy, and sophisticated urbanites such as myself have no business stopping them.

But, like many townies, I cannot bring myself to take pleasure from any aspect of country life. How can people live like that? Those tiny supermarkets with their sparsely stocked shelves; that mud, getting everywhere; the vile smells; slippery stiles and creepy orange baler twine; sheep with hideously dirty bottoms; the non-stop exposure to terrible weather; and being stuck in a tiny community with those people.

The Londoner's fear of the country is a very old tradition, celebrated in music-hall song: one early-19th-century ditty involves a Cockney falling asleep on a tram and waking, to his horror, at the end of the line in the open country. There is a very fine passage in Melanie McGrath's recent book *Silvertown*, an account of the life of her East Ender grandmother. Jane Fulcher is evacuated, with her children, from Bow to a farmhouse in Essex. The whole thing is utterly beyond her ken. She cannot fathom why anyone would think it natural to live far away from other houses and in a place where the birds wake you at dawn.

The evacuation does not last long. Mother and children return swiftly to London, preferring to face the Blitz than the threatening presence of the farmer's cows.

Which is all very well, but what is to be done? After all, the serious point is that urban misunderstanding of the country has already had the most catastrophic consequences. The idea is to enlighten the next generation. There are various schemes for schoolchildren to learn about rural life, including the National Trust scheme called 'Making the Countryside Real' starting next month at Woolsthorpe Manor, near Grantham in Lincolnshire, the former family home of Sir Isaac Newton.

Here, and on the adjoining Birkholme Farm, children will 'learn about the history and future of farming, food and countryside management', says a spokesman. 'Pupils will be made aware of the important role farming plays in creating and managing the environment and producing quality food.' They can also see how the country worked in Newton's day. Surely, much as it does now?

Then there is the Forest School in Evesham in Worcestershire, which uses woodland to introduce parties of schoolchildren to greenery. The scheme's organisers say that, with some children, a day at the Forest School is the first proper glimpse of countryside they have had.

Obviously, it is all too late for me. I will never develop a taste for swivel-eyed horses or agricultural fairs, with their lethal farming machinery. By all means, continue with your fêtes, your village committees, your enthusiasm for food that still has mud on it and your weird ability to drink – without retching – milk that has just that minute come out of a cow. Long may these traditions flourish. But as far away from me as possible.

11 December 1999

The Countryside's Ambient Noises: Chainsaws; Dogs Yapping; Shotguns
Alexander Garrett

A plaintive cry in the middle of the night. A child awake? After a few moments' attentive listening, the culprit turns out to be a tawny owl in the back garden, completely oblivious to the notion of antisocial behaviour.

In the countryside, the silence can be deafening at times, and it certainly accentuates every creaking bough or slamming door. But anybody who believes that swapping an urban setting for a rural one guarantees peace, could be in for a shock.

Stories are legion of townies who have sought tranquillity in a country village, and then complained bitterly about the sound of cocks crowing or combine harvesters harvesting.

A couple of years ago, there was the case of 64-year-old Midge Mather, who cut the ropes of the bells in the neighbouring church at Compton Bassett, in Wiltshire, because the noise was driving her mad. In another episode, a couple moved to a house next to a village pub, then tried to get it shut down because it was too noisy for their liking.

For most country dwellers, the biggest noise problem is caused not by animals or farm machinery, but by traffic. Four years ago, when we were looking for a house on the borders of Somerset and Wiltshire, what we had in mind was a quiet country lane on the edge of a village.

It soon became apparent that a large proportion of villages are on busy roads, and that the older houses in a village tend to be in the middle, with cars and lorries speeding past the gate.

By contrast, most residential streets in cities are shielded from traffic noise by rows of intervening houses. Motorways pass through some of the loveliest areas of countryside, but make living there hell.

Even if you are lucky enough to find a house in the country away from the main road – for which you pay a premium – it is surprising to discover how far traffic noise can travel. We live half a mile from a trunk road. Most of the time it is peaceful, but sometimes the roar of a single lorry seems to crescendo along the valley, thanks to wind or atmospherics.

The countryside has its own ambient noises, too: chainsaws whining like a swarm of overgrown mosquitoes; dogs yapping to each other like the Twilight Bark in *101 Dalmatians*; and the sound of shotguns being let off in the cause of protecting local ecology.

If you live, as we do, near to Salisbury Plain, then to that list can be added the deep thump of shells exploding, which rattles the windows, supplemented by Chinook helicopters flying overhead and the occasional crackle of machine-gun fire.

And once a year, there is a festival on a hill a couple of miles away – the Big Green Gathering – which sounds like a moderately interesting party in a garden a couple of streets away.

But these are all relatively innocuous, and it is because the level of background noise in the countryside is generally quite low that the all-important sense of peace can be so readily and infuriatingly shattered.

Among the main culprits are those with mechanised toys – scrambler bikes, microlights and remote-controlled model aircraft – all of which are taken to the most scenic locations with the seeming objective of upsetting the largest number of people over the maximum possible area.

RAF jet fighters also deserve a mention for their unique ability to reduce country dwellers to trembling wrecks, by appearing from nowhere at Mach 1, and crossing the garden at leylandii level. I do not recall it happening when I lived in a city. I'm waiting for one to fly under my washing line.

Personally, I do not classify any natural sound, be it cows mooing or leaves rustling, as noise. They are why I moved to the country in the first place. And I think it would be churlish to complain about noisy milking machines – especially if you have chosen to live next to a farm.

It is the suburban noises of cars and recreational equipment that really upset the calm of the countryside. Even then, it may not be perfect, but I would sooner be woken by a vibrant dawn chorus than by my next-door neighbour's car alarm.

1 March 1998
The Country We Love
Joanna Trollope

There will be, I devoutly hope, between a quarter and half a million countryside supporters gathering in Hyde Park today. They will be a richly varied lot, in terms of age, occupation and class. But they will be, for all their disparities, united in a single, powerfully important purpose: that of demonstrating to probably the most metropolitan government we have ever had the value and significance of country life in England.

Not that the threat to rural life is really a matter of political colour: the English countryside and its people have suffered quite as much from Tory inertia as they are in danger of suffering from Labour incomprehension. And incomprehension it is, quite simply, of what the land and its way of life mean to a majority of the English, even to those liable to panic attacks beyond the inner zone of the London Underground.

There is something singular about the relationship between the English and their countryside. It is partly a romantic passion for the

Anglo-Saxon rural idyll, shared with other northern races, but it also comprises two other elements: a robust instinct for living in practical harmony with nature (resulting in that much admired social unit, the English village), and an almost pantheistic appreciation of landscape.

Historically, of course, landscape spelt power, in terms of the sheer numbers of tenant followers leasing land from a landowner. This is a far cry from our modern and much feebler notion of the landscape as a refuge from urban stress. The older, muscular approach to the value of the country meant that it remained powerful right up to the last century, and even when the economic balance did swing in favour of cities, the first thing the newly rich did was to buy a country estate. Even today, it appears more enviable and significant to possess a baroque house sitting in its own portion of, say, Wiltshire than to have the most splendid of town houses.

Enviable and significant, yes; sentimental, no. It is salutary to remember that living out in the sticks has, except for the very wealthy, only been tolerable from a practical point of view for half a century. Before that, in most English villages, and certainly out in the wilds, there was no piped water, no electricity or gas, no mains drainage. Even now, rural life is not for the faint-hearted. There is more weather out there, more inconvenience, more dullness, less culture, less society, more prurience, more mud.

Yet, for all the drawbacks of rural life and its tough and uncompromising history, the English continue to feel a determined union with the countryside. It is a sense of both belonging and finding salvation there, in a community – preferably consisting of church, pub, farms, cottages, a small school and a Big House. We have, we English, a national village cult; we cherish the myth that out there, among fields and woods, there still survives a timeless natural innocence and lack of corruption.

It is nothing new, of course, this yearning for an earthly Elysium: man has been searching for Eden ever since he lost it. But it is interesting that we should yearn for it so strongly now, at the end of a century of rampant materialism, just as the painters and craftsmen of the pre-Raphaelite movement sought it 100 years ago.

We know, at some deep level beyond reason, how much we need our countryside. Of course we appreciate its beauty – think of losing the Kentish Weald, the Yorkshire Dales, the Sussex Downs and the Cotswold hills to industry or housing or play-farming theme parks – but we need it at a more profound level, too. The Romantic poets, notably Wordsworth and Coleridge, identified the natural universe with some kind of spiritual force. They chose rural life as the setting for their *Lyrical Ballads*, 'because in that situation the passions of men are incorporated with the beautiful and permanent forms of nature'. The beauty of nature appears to be a visible expression of all those spiritual concepts for which we have words but no precise imaginative grasp: infinity, eternity, the soul, the spirit.

This pantheistic belief is what sweeps through the music of Elgar and Vaughan Williams, the novels of Thomas Hardy, the paintings of Turner and Constable, and the poetry of George Herbert, John Clare and Gerard Manley Hopkins. And now, to some perhaps unexpressed degree, it is sweeping through everyone marching into Hyde Park, even those with ferrets in their pockets. It is a quest to save something from whose degradation or loss the nation would never recover.

These fine feelings, however, are nothing without the practicalities. Country life, the human energy that keeps the land a living, organic thing, is harder and more important than ever. Farming in England has been on the decline since the 1860s, but the rate of failure has accelerated wildly in the past decade, for the ironic reason that, unlike farmers of the past, farmers of the present, with the help of industrial developed technology, have farmed too well.

Rural England can no longer regard itself as a jealously guarded agricultural workshop, but has to recognise that something more sad and savage has taken the place of harvest homes and gentle spring sowing: a bleaker picture of rising rural homelessness, decaying villages and farmers committing suicide in that quiet despair peculiar to country people.

The language of the modern countryside is now about diversification and environmental considerations. Rural communities are trying to adapt to non-agricultural ways of living, knowing that it is far, far better to adapt than to go under. The countryside has to find new ways of working, and the population will change along with the economics, as it always has done.

Yet, powerful as these forces are, and radical as the changes that they bring may be, they will not alter the fundamental feeling that the English have: that it is their innate, inalienable right to live in the countryside, a place where light and dark and sun and rain dictate a rhythm of life that no scientific sophistication can ever alter. Even in the depths of the economic recession of the early 1990s, the price of land did not drop as far or as fast as the price of houses. What does this tell us? It tells us that the crowds in Hyde Park today are not marching just for themselves and their way of life; they are marching for the nation.

8 July 1997

On the Trail with a Fox-Hunting Band

Tom Utley

It was clear from my first sight of the Countryside Marchers, gathered in the courtyard of Eastnor Castle, that these were not the sort of people who make a habit of joining protest marches.

There were a fair number of country gents and their wives among them, a great many farmers, a few solicitors, a couple of middle-aged chartered surveyors, a hairdresser, a postman or two, a nightclub owner and, perhaps most incongruously of all, a group of about 40 prep-school boys and girls.

Leading the marchers and dressed in yellow T-shirts printed with the slogans 'The Voice of the Countryside' and 'Listen to Us' were the 35 or so 'core walkers'. They had set out from Machynlleth, Powys, on our branch of the march six days and 110 miles earlier. They were walking all the way to London. The other 300-odd were mostly local people, with us just for the day in Hereford and Worcester.

I discovered later that Thursday morning that the marchers had all been given instructions not to talk to the press. It seemed daft to dress people up in T-shirts saying 'Listen to Us' and then forbid them to speak.

But the marchers themselves, without exception, were all too sensible to take any notice and over the next two days of hard slog through rain, mud and burning sunshine, dozens poured out their fears about the future of the countryside.

Most had joined the march particularly to protest against the bill introduced by Michael Foster, the new Labour MP for Worcester, to outlaw fox-hunting. But they saw the threat to hunting as only part of a broader attack by ignorant urban legislators on their way of life.

The most conspicuous of the core walkers was Richard Williams, 31, the master of his own pack of foxhounds, who farms half of Snowdonia – conspicuous because he was hobbling along on a crutch. His foot and the lower part of his leg had begun to stiffen and swell up on the second day of his march and it was painful to watch him trying to walk.

'I've taken painkillers and everything, but they just don't do a damn thing,' he said. 'But I am determined to get there.

'This is the most important issue facing us. If people like Foster are going to be allowed to ban hunting, it's the end of the British state that we know and cherish. We have rights for gays and lesbians and black people. But people in the countryside are a minority and we have rights as well.

'I am not a lawbreaker but if they wish to make me a criminal, that's a matter for them, and I'm prepared to go to jail and eat porridge for the rest of my life. I suggest that Jack Straw starts building his prisons now, because they are going to be very full of country people in five years' time.

'Fox-hunting in our part of the world is essential.'

Clive Ashby, 46, headmaster of the Elms school near Ledbury, said his maroon-uniformed pupils had chosen to join the march.

'A lot of the children here or their families are involved in the countryside or country sports,' he said. 'All country sports have an element of cruelty, but it is far better to have everything out in the open. Hunting gives the right balance to the countryside and it is our duty as human beings to give the best possible life to everything around us.'

Another marcher who stressed hunting's contribution to wildlife was Roger Hughes, 51, a farmer from mid-Wales who does not himself hunt. 'My main concern is if you are going to encourage ground-nesting birds and other wildlife to flourish, then you have got to have pest control,' he said. 'Where I live there is a lot of forestry and the only other way of controlling foxes, apart from hunting, would be by trapping or poisoning.' Foxes were also a grave threat to curlews and peewits, whose numbers were in sharp decline. Hunting kept the fox population down. Other methods of control would wipe them out completely. 'I am on this walk to save animals, not to persecute them,' he said.

As we puffed up the Malverns above Eastnor, I spoke to Barry Wade, 52, an ex-townie from Wolverhampton. Mr Wade is national chairman of the Working Terrier Federation, which polices a humane code of practice for treating quarry. 'Terriers are the only remaining legal method of controlling foxes underground,' he said. 'We breed them for intelligence, character and durability. All that will die if hunting is banned and terriers will be confined to the show ring. We don't regard terrier-work as a sport. We regard it as pest control.'

Another unlikely demonstrator was Bill Reid, 63, a club owner and former pop promoter. He staged Jimi Hendrix's first British concert and is now the joint master of the VWH Hunt. 'Hunting is in grave danger,' he said. 'But we are raising our heads at last and stating our case. Why is it wrong to kill a fox that's a nuisance, but right to kill a rat that's being a nuisance? I think we are going to win.'

My townie legs were beginning to ache when we stopped for lunch at Upton upon Severn, where the streets were lined with well-wishers. This was the first centre of population that we had come across, and many of the marchers thought it odd that they were walking mostly across country, where nobody could see them, rather than taking their case to the masses. The organisers explained that this was partly because of difficulties with the police, but also to spare the marchers' feet from the pain of walking on tarmac.

At Upton we had a vast buffet lunch. David Williams, 19, a fourth-generation hill farmer from mid-Wales and one of the core walkers, said: 'We have had more food than we know what to do with. I reckon I'll come off this walk fatter than when I started.' He said he was marching to London for the rally in Hyde Park on Thursday because the countryside where he lived was dying around him. 'I'm about the only youngster in the area,' he said. 'It's rapidly becoming a retirement home.'

In the afternoon I walked with Anabel Gill, 48, who farms in Shropshire with her husband, Johnny. She came up with yet another reason for saving the hunt. 'My husband and my 12-year-old daughter are passionate about fox-hunting,' she said. 'I can't contemplate the future with her father and her grounded for six months of the year.'

By the late evening, as we trudged painfully up Bredon Hill, eight miles south of Evesham, the rain was bucketing down. In my townie shoes, I had slipped and fallen into a lake of mud and ached in every limb after nearly 30 miles on the hoof. I was billeted for the night on Julian and Julie Barnfield at the Worcestershire Hunt kennels, in the constituency of Mr Foster. As I left the next morning, I counted on the Barnfields' dresser 25 current invitations to puppy shows and other social events connected with the hunt – evidence that in many parts of the country, the hunt is the centre of all social life.

The next morning the marchers were joined by more than a dozen leading jockeys, among them Willie Carson. 'I just support the country way of life,' said Carson. An inveterate townie, who had sat on a horse for only 20 minutes in his life, I joined the march supporting fox-hunting simply as a matter of civil liberty.

I left it after two days, footsore and aching, convinced that there are at least two dozen reasons why this integral part of country life should survive – for the jobs it supports, for the fun of it, for its contribution to farming and the balance of nature, for the horses and hounds which depend upon it – and not least for the foxes themselves.

22 February 1998

Walking Away from the Countryside March

Ross Clark

When the hordes of farmers, huntsmen and assorted malcontents march on Hyde Park next Sunday, I am going for a walk in the country. It will be a very good day for it because the self-styled countrymen won't be there. There will be no farmers shouting at me while I climb the barbed wire they have put across the public footpath, no patronising ladies on horseback telling me to back off and let their horse through else it might decide to kick me in the belly, no drunken farmhands racing their pick-up trucks home from the pub. They will all be making fools of themselves in London.

I have lived in the country most of my life, but you can count me out of the great Countryside March. You can also count out of it most of the other people who happen to live in the country. Posters for the march flutter in the back windows of the Range Rovers which fill the lanes at the weekends, but in my village in Cambridgeshire there has been little talk about it. The only people going are the self-appointed 'countrymen' – known derisively around here, as elsewhere, as the 'green wellie brigade'. They don't all live in the country, either. A disproportionate number of them seem to live in London and be employed as leader-writers for national newspapers, this one included.

Just like last summer's Countryside Rally, this march is a con. It was supposed to be about hunting, but the huntsmen quickly realised that most people who live in the countryside are either against hunting or don't care one jot about it, and that if their protest stuck to the hunting issue alone they would be able to hold their rally on top of one of the soap boxes at Speakers' Corner. So now it is about petrol prices, village shops and beef-on-the-bone as well.

It reminds me of those National Union of Students' marches I used to be invited on in the 1980s: you were supposed to be marching against Mrs Thatcher, against racism, against student loans, in favour of the miners, in favour of feminism, in favour of the Nicaraguan Sandinistas and so on. The fact that some people might possess minds subtle enough to distinguish between these issues never used to occur to the organisers. It is just the same with the Countryside March. One rambler who intends to join because she opposes green-belt development has been described as 'confused' by Robin Hanbury-Tenison of the Countryside Alliance – because she also happens to support a right to roam and to oppose fox-hunting.

There is another reason for bringing up the 1980s: the people behind the Countryside March remind me quite a lot of Arthur Scargill and his miners. Like all those trade unionists who used to defend the rust-belt industries, the Countryside Alliance seems to have lost all grip on political and economic reality.

I am sick and tired of hearing townspeople being told that they 'don't understand the countryside'. The truth is that they understand how it works only too well. They know that the arguments about hunting being a vital part of the rural economy are pure propaganda, even if, as I do, they support hunting on the grounds of personal freedom. They know they are paying over the odds for their food just to keep in business the would-be squires who bawl 'get orff my land' at them whenever they dare turn up for a weekend walk. They know that if it wasn't for the taxpayer farming would collapse – even if they don't know that in 1997 no less than 84 per cent of the £3.4 billion earned by farmers came in the form of subsidies as part of the Common Agricultural Policy. Countrymen really ought to stop complaining about the European Union. The body they accuse of ruining the beef industry is the very same body that has kept them above water for the past generation.

If there is anything townspeople fail to realise about the countryside, it is the other ways in which they are subsidising the people who live there. Farmland is exempt from inheritance tax; which helps to explain why so many wealthy urban people suddenly become countrymen in late middle age. The privatised utilities retain, by law, a pricing structure which amounts to a huge, hidden cross-subsidy which passes money from town to country. Every time you switch on an electric light you are helping to pay for the miles of cable which serve remote rural communities. You are paying over the odds for your water, too, in order to help the water companies service the pipes and pumps needed to fill Farmer Giles's bath. And when you stick a 26 pence stamp on a letter which is just going from one end of London to another you are helping to pay for a postman to deliver letters to remote addresses in the Scottish Highlands.

A large slice of local authorities' education budgets goes in the form of providing free transport to take country children to school. This is one of many examples of ways in which government policy is deliberately biased towards rural communities: urban children who live within three miles of their nearest school do not qualify for free transport. Rather than marching to Hyde Park to have a good moan, countrymen ought to be going there to fall on their knees and give townspeople a big thank you for being so generous in their financial support.

There is one way that countrymen could help repay their debts: that is to be a little more accommodating towards townsfolk who want to go to the countryside for a bit of fresh air and exercise. When I hear some of the landowner's objections to the government's proposed 'right to roam', I feel as though I am being transported back to some feudal past. Three years ago I went to interview the land agent who deals with Lord Romsey's lands in Hampshire. He was desperately concerned that a future government might want to allow ordinary people access to his riverbanks, saying it would deter people from paying large amounts to go salmon fishing there. Then, virtually in the same breath, he said that he was hoping the government would provide a grant to help the estate boost its salmon stocks.

I can't help observing that the squirearchy seems to expect its own right to roam. When a friend who owns some land in Sussex denied access to the local hunt, he was asked: 'Are you a communist?' He wasn't, actually; in fact, he worked in the City. But as far as the countryman's mentality goes, anyone who dares to challenge the feudal orders is a threat to national security.

What has amazed me most is the way that people whom I previously believed to be economic libertarians have been won over by the landowners who seem to me to stand for exactly the opposite. In its leading article two weeks ago this newspaper did at least acknowledge that farming is an industry like any other, which 'enjoyed special treatment under the Conservatives while others were left to their fate'. But I was quite alarmed by the assertion in the same leader that rural motorists are somehow getting a raw deal. Roads, like most things, involve a huge transfer of resources from town to country. There are thousands of miles of country lanes maintained for the exclusive benefit of a handful of countrymen who live at the end of them.

I was equally concerned by the claim in the same leading article that the government's plan to reduce the legal limit for drink-driving from 80mg to 50mg will undermine 'normal social interaction' in rural communities. Normal social interaction in the countryside disappeared long ago – as soon, in fact, as country drinkers took to driving. Cars allowed them to go to the towns, where the nightlife was infinitely more exciting, which is why my village had half a dozen pubs before there were motor-cars, and now has just one. Stricter drink-driving laws would help country pubs, not destroy them, because the only place country people would be able to go out to drink would be their local.

The onslaught of propaganda from countrymen has left many convinced that the government really is out to attack the rural way of life. It is untrue. In my experience the only people attacking the so-called rural way of life are country people themselves. Village shops are closing not because of hygiene laws imposed by Whitehall and Brussels, as the countrymen would have us believe, but because country people aren't shopping in them any more – they prefer to drive to Tesco. Most country people work in towns like everyone else these days. My neighbours include an accountant, a recruitment consultant and a translator. The only one who slaves away in the village all day is myself – over a computer. The traditional rural life – being paid a pittance to work yourself into an early grave and having no entertainment other than a few pints of gut-rotting cider at the end of the day – was something most country people were only too happy to turn their backs on decades ago.

Traditional country people don't even go in for so-called country sports very much. In the Kentish village where I was brought up I don't remember anyone going hunting or shooting. There was a hunt not far away, but like all hunts it consisted of a few old men on horses followed by several dozen people in 4x4s. Very traditional. The woods only began reverberating with gunshot five or 10 years ago when shooting suddenly became a big hobby among yuppies from London.

At least a lot of the huntin', shootin', fishin' lobby won't have far to go next Sunday. They might even be able to leave the Range Rover at home for a change and walk up from Fulham where, except at the weekend, they all seem to live.

3 March 1998
Letters to the Editor
The Countryside March

SIR – Granted, it was better behaved than a football crowd and a marvellous piece of politics. But where were the black faces, the gay foxhunters and the hunting rights for disabled groups? The march was just a display of conservative, frightened old England.

Martin Brandon
London N3

SIR – Isn't it typical of the country dweller that while protesting about townspeople's right to walk in the countryside they feel they have the right to snarl up the centre of London? They call themselves the protectors of the countryside yet destroy thousands of miles of hedgerow. They say townspeople should have no say in the way the countryside is run but expect them to subsidise the cost of providing gas, electricity and mail deliveries to their isolated villages.

Les Sharp
Walton-on-Thames
Surrey

SIR – I couldn't reach the West End to buy some records because of all these marchers. I am thinking about organising a rally in Shropshire for the disparaged urban community. We have a right to be heard.

Ray Johnson
London SE1

SIR – May I put in an appeal for the Countryside March to become a weekly event? It has been most enjoyable to walk in the countryside, even straying on to the perimeters of set-aside fields, heavily subsidised by the taxpayer, without being confronted by an agitated landowner demanding that recreational walking be confined to public paths, many of which have been ploughed through by his tractors.

William Buxton
Oundle
Northants

SIR – I hear the foxes had a field day on Sunday.

Martin Walford
London WC2

22 September 2002
The Real Countryside Alliance
Robin Chrystal

It was a strange place to hear such treacherous talk. In a quiet upstairs room of a West Country pub, four middle-aged men, dressed in checked shirts and ties, told me they were prepared to target ministers' homes, and even the Prime Minister's wife, to retain their right to hunt, writes Robin Chrystal.

Radio 4's the *Today* programme asked me a week ago to track down members of the so-called Real Countryside Alliance, a group that has claimed responsibility for a series of criminal acts across the country, including attacks on MPs offices and contaminating reservoirs.

Making contact was only possible through intermediaries from the hunting world who were wary of the programme's motives. But one promised to 'put the word about'. After that, I just had to wait.

When the call came, a man with a Somerset accent said that he was an associate of the group. And, even better, they were prepared to meet.

On Thursday, I greeted the smartly dressed and close-shorn men in a pub popular with those who hunt. The four, all between 40 and 50, refused to give their names but joked embarrassingly as they called each other 'John'. They looked like the last people who would break the law – so much so that I thought I was in the wrong place. I realised that I had the right men when the landlord casually remarked that he had arranged two coaches to go on today's march in London. They were scornful of the Countryside Alliance.

'We are all disillusioned Alliance members who have sat back and got more and more frustrated that they are not doing enough,' one said.

Another joined in: 'This was to be the summer of discontent when the Countryside Alliance would take on the government. It has been an absolute disaster.'

Two of the group claimed to work full-time in the hunting industry and said they would lose everything when the ban comes in. They said that they were part of a loose federation of activists running into hundreds across the country.

Their group, they said, had already organised its own illegal protests by dumping sheep carcasses. 'There were some dumped in the south-west area, at roundabouts and town centres. Reservoirs were targeted,' one said.

But that is mild compared to what these unlikely lawbreakers claim they will do next.

'We are prepared to do whatever it takes. We will intimidate ministers or local MPs, we will do it,' said one, keen to convince me that they were serious.

They warned that some of their associates were more extreme. 'We represent some people who are far more radical than what we are. We have got people that would quite happily use bombs and other things. We are trying to contain them.'

They suggested that some countryside activists – but, of course, not them – wanted to make fertiliser bombs similar to those used by the IRA.

'A lot of people are saying we have got a lot of fertiliser in the countryside. We have seen how people have used it in other countries and we ought to be using it here.'

The four said that they had been told that the Real Countryside Alliance would create chaos at this week's Labour Party conference in Blackpool. They claimed that a concerted attempt would be made to achieve gridlock in the town.

After that, they said they planned to carry out attacks on MPs' properties. 'Data on outspoken MPs is being compiled; there are a lot of prominent Labour MPs who have got property in the countryside. We are well aware of where a number of them live.'

With no sense of bravado, they openly warned that even Cherie Blair, the Prime Minister's wife, is at risk.

'He [Tony Blair] has been manipulated by Cherie Blair over hunting. She has made it quite clear that she wants it banned.'

I was shocked by the suggestion.

'You are not seriously telling me that you are going to target Tony Blair's wife?' I asked.

'Why not?' said one.

'I am prepared to target anybody who is not prepared to listen to common sense,' said another.

Any sense of waiting for ministers to bring forward legislation was utterly rejected. These men said they would not wait. 'We will stop at nothing,' they told me. 'We are committed. We are ready to do it now.'

19 July 1998

'You Don't Get Country Folk Moving to London and Demanding That They Stop the Buses'
Audrey Gillan

Tim Wood's neighbours don't like the smell. They don't much like him either, he has learnt over the past three years. During this time he has been involved in a wrangle over whether he should be allowed to add a free-range poultry unit to his farm. He says it will bring jobs and environmentally friendly eggs. His neighbours say it will bring flies and odours and disease.

This little row has consumed the picturesque village of North Cheriton in Somerset. It is a lovely place: home to working farms but home also to a large number of retired town dwellers who don't want to smell the country in their back yard.

'You would think I had put in an application to build an atomic power station,' said Mr Wood. 'People retire to this area, but they don't understand that it's a farming area and farming has to go on. When they live in the cities, it is us who feed them.'

Mr Wood's troubles are typical of the struggle between those brought up in the country and the increasing number of incomers who often want to sanitise it. This week such conflicts were again to the fore when Frank Sytner, a multimillionaire car dealer, failed in his attempt to sue Edward Baines, a neighbouring farmer, who had inadvertently spread mud on the road leading to the field where Mr Sytner kept his horses.

The former racing driver and his wife had bought a property in the village of Ridlington, Rutland. They were in search of the good life – the thing was they didn't much like the sheep, the noise of the cows or the muck that the animals brought with them.

Mrs Sytner told the court she could hear cows making a noise in a field and it was annoying. When the judge observed that it might be normal for cows to be heard in the countryside, she replied: 'Yes. It's unfortunate, isn't it?' The couple ended up paying their own legal costs as well as those of Mr Baines.

In the south-west of England, the National Farmers' Union has an acronym for people like the Sytners. They call them BANANAS, as in 'building anything near anyone is not allowed'. As more and more city dwellers move to the country, there have been tussles over planning permission, over cocks a-crowing, over the smell of manure and over pigs grunting. There have even been complaints about ringing church bells.

As the countryside lobby grows more vocal and more critical of the city invaders, with their strimmers and their four by fours, the frictions and fracas down among the hedgerows are set to continue.

Some urban dwellers have learnt quickly that they have bought into a dream that hardly touches on reality. Others have tried to turn reality into their dream, much to the chagrin of their neighbours.

Like many other Barbourians before them, the Sytners said goodbye to the rat race to pursue a life based more on the stanzas of a Romantic poem than founded in reality.

In 'The Deserted Village', Oliver Goldsmith wrote: 'Sweet Auburn, loveliest village of the plain, Where health and plenty cheered the labouring swain', but, for many so-called townies, life in the country is not so perfect.

'People come to the country and expect it to be a chocolate box,' said Mr Baines yesterday. 'I think there's the much wider issue of what you think is reasonable. Sheep make muck, that's what happens. If you come to live in the country you should be willing to accept country values and country patterns of behaviour at certain times of the year.'

Mr Baines, who is a local councillor in the area, pointed out that Mr Sytner had recently failed in a planning application to build a helicopter landing pad and an aircraft hangar.

Like others before them, the Sytners have learnt that, in spite of urban notions, country life is not very glamorous – it is not all home-made jam and dogs nestling by the Aga. For many in the countryside, it is cold, there is rarely any central heating, wall-to-wall carpets or the other accoutrements of a fitted life. Instead, there is the smell of silage and liquid manure; even the sounds of animals and working farm machinery.

Yet, increasing numbers of city dwellers are fleeing their homes in pursuit of rose-covered cottages either for the weekend or full time. A recent report by the Council for the Protection of Rural England found that Greater London is losing almost twice as many people to the shires as England's major urban areas combined.

'The perceived attractions of the 'rural idyll' are a strong influence on migration patterns and even those leaving relatively attractive suburbs cite problems of urban decay as a reason to move,' it said, adding that perceptions of this idyll needed to be replaced with more realistic messages.

Sometimes, the move doesn't work out quite as planned. Richard Jobson, a television presenter and former punk rocker, moved to Bedfordshire for the fresh air. He didn't get it. Instead, he became embroiled in a dispute with his neighbour, Sir Neville Bowman, who started a pig farm and built a manure mountain metres from the Jobsons' kitchen window.

'The sheer physical intensity of the smell just smacked you really hard in the face,' said Mr Jobson, and the court agreed. Sir Neville, though, was less than pleased.

Five years ago, Margery Johns became involved in a lengthy and expensive legal dispute when her cockerel, Corky, was accused of being too noisy by her neighbour in the hamlet of Stoke in North Devon. She found herself slapped with a noise abatement order.

'I feel there is a very important principle involved. Country life is country life, and to complain about a cockerel crowing is the thin end of the wedge,' she said.

'A mile away from us there is a farmer whose cows are being monitored for the noise they make. The whole thing is getting ridiculous. There are far too many restrictions being put on country people who are just doing things the way they have always done them. They're talking about smells, now. They want to deodorise farmyards. Well, I would rather smell cow muck than a London bus, but you don't get country bumpkins moving to London and demanding that they stop the buses, do you?'

In spite of the friction, many incomers bring in new money and employment. Some live a quiet life or get involved with the parish council or the village fête and become an active part of the community. Others simply get people's backs up.

By contrast, David Thomas, an author and former *Punch* editor, has moved from Fulham to West Sussex: he and his family are loving their new life and are trying to integrate. 'This is not the "real countryside", but, that said, you have to accept that you will be woken in the mornings by chickens and you will have a septic tank rather than drains.

'The country has to be allowed to have its life and its work. It's the worst kind of ignorance and snobbery to deny people who don't have money a way to make it,' he said. 'It's the arrogance of the nouveau riche. Their snobbery is far worse than the snobbery of the country gent, who at least understands the world that he inhabits.'

Tolerance and an understanding of both ways of life is what is needed, according to Ian Johnson, spokesman for the NFU in south-west England. 'These people move to the country but they don't want to be near the nasty niffs and noises,' he said, adding that some townies fitted in very well.

'They don't want any movement in the country. They want to ossify it, crystalise it or preserve it in aspic. They want their picture postcard there for immortality. What we need is compromise and being able to learn from one another.'

Raffaella Barker, the novelist, agrees. She and her family moved from London to Norfolk six years ago. 'You learn to love wellington boots in the country and if you can't hack that then you shouldn't even try it,' she says.

'You can't go poncing around saying you want parmesan cheese and fresh pepper. You have to be quite cool about the fact that all the vegetables have gone to London and back again. In the first few years everyone hates you, full stop, or you feel that you don't belong. But that changes and it's much friendlier than it is in London. I like the country idea, I think it's what society is based on.'

24 November 1973
Letter to the Editor
Environment

SIR — We have laws about everything nowadays. May we have one to limit the use of the word Environment? A score of five in your 40-line leader is quite a modest one.

I don't live in a rural environment myself. I just live in the country, where I am often visited by townsfolk who enjoy my lovely surroundings, although the countryside is sometimes spoiled by people whose pockets are not large enough to hold all the superfluous wrappings of the manufacturers.

Nancy Hewins
Willersey
Worcs

13 April 2002
The Townie's Guide to Country Life
Adam Edwards

The holiday season is just about upon us and so, therefore, is the time for the metropolitan classes to emerge from their halogen hibernation and start to favour friends and relatives in the countryside.

This is the start of a summer of weekends when urban man remembers his rural heritage and returns to patronise those of us who do not have a brushed steel cooker and a Tracy Emin bed. It is the season when the Tarmac sophisticate strolls through crops wondering aloud how much of the countryside to buy and shows astonishment when the local boozer doesn't have tempura of freshwater shrimp with a sweet Thai dressing.

These well-shod chattering townies will, of course, have forgotten that foot-and-mouth closed the countryside last summer. And that while it was shut, the nation experienced a *Gosford Park* moment.

The result is that there are now many misconceptions about how rural folk live in the countryside in the 21st century. For example, we don't, as a general rule, send our illegitimate children to work in our factories any more, get the butler to clean the silver by spitting on it or complain that the marmalade is not home-made.

However, just so there should be no misunderstanding on the part of our urban cousins as to how the well-bred countryman actually lives in 2002, here is a brief cut-out-and-keep guide to the manners and mores of the English shires:

Acceptable subjects of conversation are:

a) Tony Blair is a class traitor
b) Brian Aldridge is a heel
c) the price of lamb is a disgrace
d) the euro isn't working
e) the open fires in *Gosford Park* are fake

Sheep (the woolly ones that go baa) and cows (big fellows that go moo) still exist despite the best efforts of the government. The white paper jump-suit that was so fashionable last year is not in vogue with farmers this season.

It is common countryside practice to pour supermarket own-brand spirits into decanters and put tap water into fancy bottled-water bottles. It is not done to doctor the Floris.

The Aga does not do warm salads, foccacia, fondant tomatoes or anything on a mango tatin with Madeira jus.

Acceptable art is a painting of a dog, a horse or a photograph of a member of the family. There is always a slot somewhere for an oil painting or watercolour of the English countryside. The right place for Brit Art is the dustbin.

Thanks to Prince William, sunglasses may now be worn outside the M25.

Chintz is an interior decorating staple and never chucked.

It is important to learn to use a computer in order to converse with your children in their gap year. The internet is jolly useful for helping with the parish magazine. It also gives wayward sons something to do during the day.

A fleece is a unisex, classless garment worn for every occasion with the exception of church.

Local handicrafts – the chalkboard with a painted wooden cat on top of it, straw chickens, carved wooden objects – are an important part of our heritage and should be prominently displayed in the kitchen.

A stiff drink is three fingers of gin and one of tonic. You need at least two before eating. Nobody needs more than one lump of ice in a drink.

The downstairs lavatory is the right place for showing off. In the smallest room you may tell people who you are (school photos, snaps with dignitaries, awards, Oscars, etc.), where you are (framed one-inch-to-the-mile local Ordnance Survey map on the wall) and how rich you are (estate boundaries inked in on the map).

Do not walk if you can drive. If you must walk take a dog.

The fish that hangs on the wall and sings 'take me to the river' whenever you walk past is a hilarious joke that never palls. (So too is a life-size plastic model of a Jack Russell's bottom sticking into the air in the herbaceous border.)

A pork chop for a pork chop. (If you get invited to dinner you must return the invitation or lose a friend.)

You are automatically assumed to be C of E, whatever your religion. If someone claims to be C of E, it means he goes to church only on Christmas Day and Easter Day.

The local gay couple should be treated like everyone else. However, if they are staying overnight they are put in a room with separate beds.

Parking in a supermarket disabled slot without a disabled sticker is a capital offence.

The video is the most important electrical device in the house. Satellite television is puerile, vulgar and only acceptable if a decent signal is impossible from a regular aerial. Nobody in the country can get a decent signal.

Growing children need a regular intake of cheap pasta and supermarket tomato sauce, which is why it is the daily diet of all rural children whatever their background.

It is acceptable to interrupt any conversation to shout loudly at your dog. It is unacceptable for anyone else to do so.

The Range Rover is for going to town, the Cheltenham Festival, the point-to-point and Royal Ascot. The elderly estate car is for cross-country work.

Horses have right of way and should be ridden slowly in the middle of road every day except Sundays. Weekenders ride on Sundays.

'Trothing' (as in 'by troth landlord, a pint of your finest ale') is no longer a language in common usage in country pubs.

11 December 2004
Finding the 'One'
Mia Davis

There comes a time in every girl's life when it is important to find 'the one' – the kind of man who has strong forearms and can also read. Addressing this matter from the heart of the English countryside, however, is quite a challenge. Herein lies the problem. I am 32. I am in my prime. I am all woman. And yet, I am on my own. I ascribe this sorry state of affairs to the fact that I live in what could be described as a rural idyll, but which is, in reality, a desert bereft of men. In a small town, you are more likely to meet a rampaging cow escaped from an auction yard than an eligible man.

Where have they all gone? They seemed to exist at one time. The novels of Thomas Hardy and D.H. Lawrence are stuffed with them. Gamekeepers in braces and breeches abound. There are craggy, sensitive men living alone in cottages. Bathsheba Everdene had the pick of a thoughtful shepherd, a dashing soldier and a gentleman farmer.

But nowadays, there are no rugged gamekeepers striding around the woods, with rabbits jauntily thrown over their shoulders (indeed, the only rabbits I have seen have been flattened beneath the wheels of Ford Escorts driven by bored youths). I have tried wandering across the hills in a long skirt, looking winsome. I have strolled past the Forestry Commission hut in a bonnet. But I have yet to come across a handsome charcoal-maker in the woods. No. The rural splendour in which I live must be endured alone and I fear I must suffer life in the country as a spinster, with none of the distractions enjoyed by my city counterparts.

When the *Sex and the City* girls got bored, they went shopping and trampolining. In the country, there is nothing between you and nature. Like a character from a long and boring Russian novel, the winter finds me queuing for beetroot at the farmers' market and then returning home to make borsch for one. Even my Jack Russell, Beryl, hasn't met a dog of her own calibre and wanders the woods mournfully sniffing the ground.

I was enticed to the countryside six years ago by the quaint charm of a small market town in Shropshire in May. The idea of visiting the baker wearing a sprigged dress to buy a wholesome loaf of a morning seemed the antithesis of life in the city. And, more importantly, that was back in the heady days when I actually had a boyfriend. Had I realised that a few years later, I would be searching for a man among the livestock, I would have put the dream of a bucolic existence firmly on the back of the Aga. Yet I still find the countryside romantic. And this, I believe, is my problem: I can't give up on the hope of finding a gamekeeper in the woodshed.

I have made attempts to cast the net farther in the search for a man who does not wear an acrylic jumper splattered in slurry. The nearest big town is only 50 miles away, but a trip there requires a change of footwear, five gallons of petrol, emergency supplies (torch, blanket, compass, Kendal mint cake) and nerves of steel for night driving on country roads. As a result, I don't go often. The races, the auction yard, sheep-dog trials and the farmers' market have so far yielded no results other than the odd toothless grin.

For my many friends who live and work in London, returning to the countryside is a treat. But – to use a well-known country term – 'the grass is always greener'. How can anyone be expected to delight in clumps of primroses 24 hours a day? How can living in the middle of unspoiled countryside possibly compensate for the social life of a leper?

What about the tube, I hear the town mice cry? What about the dirt? The traffic?

Well, I reply from this bucolic idyll: what about the endless woodland? What about one bus a week? What about sheep, but no men?

I have become a shadow of my former urban self. I actually dream about shoe shops and wake among my twisted sheets with the words 'Harvey Nichols, sushi, and peep-toe Nubuck with a 4in heel' on my lips.

Life is so different that city life can seem as distant as the moon. Spend too long in the countryside and you find yourself marvelling at such a thing as street lighting. 'What good sense,' I found myself thinking the other day. 'Illuminating the roads at night.'

Yet despite the lack of street lighting – never mind bars, theatres, clubs and restaurants – the lure of the countryside remains. It seems that every urban couple wants to leave the city behind and spend their days growing carrots and picking blackberries for their rosy-cheeked children (who are positively thriving at the village school).

Good for them. What could be better for the family than growing up in the country? But for the single woman living in the countryside, the sight of Johnny and Isobel buying plums at the farmers' market is enough to make you weep, because Johnny and his metropolitan good looks do not exist in darkest Shropshire.

Being handsome is not the only clue that people are 'from away'. Just as their four-wheel-drive, rather than an old Land Rover held together with bailer twine, gives them away, so does their choice of carefully considered country apparel.

Country fashion is a peculiar thing, not least because true country wear consists of a pair of trousers with an elasticated waist, an old acrylic jumper and the sort of no-frills wellies now worn only in abattoirs. No one wears wax jackets or Hackett plus-fours. Tweed skirts and hunters are more likely to be seen in Chelsea than in the fields. A friend of mine boasted that she had found her cardigan in a hedge. This is hardly surprising considering the retail outlets available in a small market town. I live in a place famed for its butchers, so while I can choose between eight varieties of sausage, for clothes I have a choice between ladies' outfitters that could double as a set for a BBC post-war costume drama and a charity shop. Rummaging through the charity shops leads to an eclectic and varied style of dress.

'Hmm,' I found myself musing in one such shop the other day, 'if I buy this bobbly old beige jumper, will it go with the stout brown shoes on the rack?'

The success of the Boden catalogue can only be testament to the quest for fashionable outfits beyond London. A recent warehouse sale by Boden held at the local racecourse was very much like an upmarket jumble sale, where a scrum of women with basket handbags wrested £5 tea-rose skirts from each other. I have never seen such violence. If these women represent the Countryside Alliance, I would suggest the government tread very warily. They are quite capable of staging an uprising armed only with a rolled-up Boden catalogue and a Casual Linen Blazer.

Being a plucky gal, I have tried to make the best of things. I have been engaging in the community. Oh yes. I have attended every country event advertised. A ploughing competition, a duck race, ferret racing, a sheep-dog trial, a donkey day, various agricultural shows all featuring the largest marrow in the world, and a bat walk.

The local paper tells me I could go to the electronic organ society annual performance, a charity clay-pigeon shoot, a country music evening, an amateur production of *The Merry Widow* in the village hall and a talk on photographing miniatures (miniature what?).

Should none of the above appeal, there is always the green and pleasant countryside itself to turn to. Yet this, too, is myth. Just as everyone who doesn't live in London imagines life to be one big merry-go-round of concerts, theatre and galleries, the idea that country people spend their whole time wandering around woods, moorland and gentle hills, working up a ruddy glow before retiring to a cosy pub, has equally little basis in reality. Going for a walk in the countryside is not like a stroll in Kensington Gardens. Here, nature is out of control. It is dangerous.

There are no signs pointing to the tea rooms. A simple walk in the woods can get you seriously lost, and the ability to read a map is essential. Because my map-reading skills are bad – I thought the big blue squiggle on the road atlas was a river until a friend pointed out it was the M4 – I have decided that what may have been planned as a pleasant stroll could well deteriorate into something more alarming.

I have attempted many walks, but usually find myself hopelessly lost or pursued by excitable cattle. On one occasion, I discovered that I can run far faster than I ever imagined possible on 10 cigarettes a day, after Beryl inspired the interest of a herd of bullocks that decided to charge as one. Another time, I struggled through a forest that resembled the woods in *The Lord of the Rings* before I realised that I had been walking for two-and-a-half hours with no real idea of where the car park might be (one fir tree tends to look like the next). My only comfort was the thought of being discovered by a forest ranger, but they are never around when you need them.

Other than the Forestry Commission land, most of the countryside belongs to farmers who do not take kindly to trespass. The right to roam is an urban myth, because it applies only to open moorland and heath, so there is ample right to stride across Hampstead Heath or the Yorkshire moors, but should you find yourself anywhere near a ploughed field (of which there are plenty), you take your chances.

In this sense, finding a man has even greater significance. Not only could we go for a walk (one of us to provide cover, the other to tread in a field) but he could also identify rights of way and shout at stampeding cows.

The harsh reality is that there is virtually nothing to do in the countryside, unless of course you happen to be tilling the land. A normal day for me consists of taking the dog for a walk (see above), staring out of the window and thinking about writing something, visiting Spar to buy cigarettes and flicking through back copies of *Country Living* reading about 'rural' things.

Rural employment opportunities are so few that other than creating your own cottage industry – perhaps making rustic pots out of river clay for people who read *Country Living* – the chances of finding a rewarding career are roughly the same as managing to find a man who doesn't think broadband is extra-thick bailer twine.

Although the search for rewarding employment may be difficult in the city, there are jobs in the country that no one could even imagine existed. Take, for example, the turkey toenail trimmer. I hadn't even entertained the possibility that turkeys had toenails until I saw the job advertised. Could it be a nail bar for turkeys, where they all meet for a manicure and gobble?

With the turkey toenails trimmed and the Christmas tree in the town square leaning at its normal jaunty angle, I am reminded it is the season to be jolly. Quite how this is achieved when being single during the festive season is about as jolly as King Herod, I am not sure. I am, however, encouraged to try my luck at the Tenbury Wells mistletoe auction, where perhaps the whole bonhomie of the occasion and the presence of the romantic, if parasitical plant will produce results. Should this be in vain, I will have to reconcile myself to the now familiar prospect of Christmas alone.

Previous experience has taught me to be very wary of three things at Christmas: couples who tell you how lovely it is to 'spend time together as a family'; the Christmas *Radio Times* in newsagents; and trees wrapped in netting. The netting seems like a jolly good idea when you are of slight frame and attempting to wrestle the beast home, but, once removed, a tree the size of Scandinavia is unleashed.

Last Christmas, my front room was suddenly transformed into Narnia and I kept expecting a faun to appear in the undergrowth, which may not have been a bad thing, because even a faun would be better than spending Christmas in the company of Beryl dragging her lead around the house like Marley's ghost.

This year, it is highly likely that I will once again be spending the special day immured in my parents' freezing cottage, where I struggle to unwrap ethnic gifts with gloved fingers and try to resist the urge to stuff the whole Christmas tree into the creaking Rayburn, which has barely produced enough warmth to keep the ice from the windows. Only Tiny Tim is missing.

Again, the Christmas-card industry would have us believe that a country Christmas is spent in a snow-covered village where small children scamper in and out of houses with presents and cheer – but this isn't how it is at all. Why not produce a card depicting the single woman with her nose pressed against the snow-flecked window of a country-house party where inside couples cavort and celebrate their joy?

Because living in the country seems to have turned me into Bridget Jones without the luxury of Hugh Grant or Colin Firth to fall back on, I spend a lot of time wondering if I am now technically a spinster and consoling myself by thinking: 'At least they don't use the ducking-stool any more.'

After so long in exile from civilisation and life without a husband, I have decided the only answer is to embrace the situation. The call of the wild in the shape of a sturdy farmer seems to be beckoning. The only drawback is I have yet to find one who looks like Jude Law and smells of warm hay, rather than slurry. I can bake cakes in a farmhouse kitchen and stride across dew-flecked fields to check on the sheep. Jude (the name is pleasingly reminiscent of Thomas Hardy) throws open the rough-hewn kitchen door, pulls off my pinny with his strong hands and says 'Kiss me, wench' in a masterful manner. Whereupon, the cakes are forgotten and we enjoy a passionate embrace before he mounts his tractor and returns to the verdant fields.

Is this possible? Living in the countryside, I very much doubt it, but with the sort of courageous spirit not seen since I last went for a walk, I'm still looking. Should anyone know of such a farmer, please let me know.

17 December 2005
Please Keep Off the Mud
James May

It is time, now that someone has raised the truly preposterous notion of congestion charging in our national parks, to acknowledge a few painful realities about the countryside. There is a view that cars somehow do not belong in the countryside; I now put it to you that in fact the countryside belongs to the car.

Before anyone writes in with a volume of Rupert Brooke, I should make it clear that I understand perfectly the position occupied by the rural idyll in the English national consciousness; how its gently swaying fields of corn are instantly invoked by thoughts of home when abroad; how the memory of England endures not as a shopping centre or theme park but as an endless Arcadian vista who gave her flowers to love, etc. But how are we to enjoy all this, if not from the car?

You could go for a walk, say some, but have you seen the size of the place? It would take me two days to reach the edge of it from where I live, and even then there would be a few golf courses to negotiate before I arrived in the other Eden.

Cycling? Civilised bicycles only work on the road, and the road is only there because of cars. If you try off-roading on a so-called 'mountain' bike, farmers will shoot at you. And I have to say that if I were a farmer, and you rode across my field with an inverted polystyrene fruit bowl on your head astride £2,000-worth of unobtanium, I'd shoot at you as well.

No, the problem is not that people keep driving through the countryside, it's that people keep living there. If you're a farmer, tilling manfully on the land to produce the things I love to eat, then that's fine. Likewise a gamekeeper or some old toff, since they're not safe in the city. Also fine is running a country pub, as that's where I like to stop for a pie. But as for the rest – and especially those who think a 2in-high ribbon of tarmac is somehow 'ruining the countryside' – they can get lost, because their houses are spoiling the view from my Porsche.

If, for example, you're a merchant banker working in the city, you should live in the city near the bank. If you're the manager of a country bank, you should live in the flat above it or in a windowless bothy alongside. Similarly, working for a software consultancy and living in the sticks is as absurd as turning up for work at a software consultancy in a straw hat singing 'ee-aye-ee-aye-oh'.

I don't want to escape to the countryside in my car to be rewarded with an endless, rolling panorama of Barratt Homes. It's the ruin of England.

Everyone I know who lives in the cuds is, in terms of demands, aspirations and general lifestyle, exactly the same as my neighbours in London. They are separated from me by nothing more than a very, very big garden. They drive into town every day and complain about congestion, without stopping to think for long enough to realise that the road isn't there so that they can come in, it's there so I can get out in something with a flat-six engine and enjoy a world as Adam would have known it.

The harsh truth is that cod country living is a privilege bequeathed entirely by the roads and motor transport. So if you live in Chodford and despise all things automotive, you should live as I imagine country folk did before the car was invented. That is, like a chicken; in your own poo, driven mad by blight and at the mercy of wild animals. You should ride a donkey, and the road to your damp dwelling should be a rough track beset by bandits and deranged inbreds with huge hands and one eye in the middle of their faces.

Actually, I'd go further than that. You should not be allowed anything in life that is in any way dependent on road transport. So no fresh shittake mushrooms from the charming deli in the village, because they arrived in a van. You'll have to bake your own bread in the little cubby holes at the side of your Aga – the ones with the red-hot handles.

Anti-car sentiment is nowhere as incongruous as it is in the countryside. In fact, the beauty of the countryside in modern times is that you can drive through it, look at it, and then leave it alone. Its principal function is the growing of carrots, but after that, it's what sports cars were invented for.

Conflict

27 March 1999

Pity the Poor Lapwing – He Might Be Booted Out

Robin Page

If I have understood all the triumphalist ramblings of the ramblers properly, then I am unique. Apparently, I am the only person in Britain who has rambled over moor, mountain and meadow without being accosted by manic landowners waving shotguns. As a result, the government has come up with a right to roam over millions of acres of moorland. By so doing, New Labour has shown that it is no such thing: its attitudes on countryside issues remain firmly entrenched in Old Labour, and the right to roam is yet one more attack on the beleaguered rural community.

If the government really did understand the countryside, then the place for any right to roam to be granted should be on the thousands of acres of industrialised farming in lowland Britain. There, the policies of the CAP (Common Agricultural Policy) have allowed so much environmental damage to be done in the name of 'efficient farming' that it does not matter where people walk.

Moorland, on the other hand, remains one of Britain's most fragile and endangered habitats. It is the final refuge for some of our diminishing ground-nesting birds, such as the golden plover, lapwing, curlew, dunlin, merlin and black grouse: the last thing that they need is a right to roam. What is wanted is controlled, responsible access that allows interested visitors on to some of our most attractive areas without doing damage. The right to roam will allow the exact opposite: damage, disturbance and intrusion, all for the political anti-landownership baggage of the twenties.

Sadly, the problem of access is made more difficult by the way in which Britain has become urbanised, and so many visitors do not realise the damage they can cause. Over recent years on the farm, we have had electric fences flattened and barbed wire cut, simply to allow selfish walkers and mountain bikers to go where they like, regardless of the welfare of our cattle and sheep.

Two years ago, a gentleman with two buckets and two spades was digging up wild flowers, while last March I caught a woman chasing my pregnant ewes. To make matters worse, she was a veterinary student, who was trying to round up my sheep in *One Man and His Dog* fashion with an old collie and Labrador, neither of which had ever been trained.

It was one of the most stupid things I have ever witnessed. Yet if any of my old girls had aborted, who would have given me compensation – the Right to Roam Government?

That is one more problem: if people unused to the hazards of the countryside are exposed to deep rivers, the sharpness of brambles, dead branches that fall from trees and so forth, who is going to be legally liable for any accidents that occur? Does that mean that the countryside will have to be tidied up to make it safe? If so, wildlife will again be the loser. The government is good at talking eco- and wildlife-friendly policies, but in all its decisions connected with farming, field sports and access, it seems unable to grasp even the most basic facts.

Last week, I took part in a debate with Marion Shoard at Heffers bookshop in Cambridge; it coincided with the publication of her book *A Right to Roam*. Although the author appears to fill her pen with vinegar, she is, in fact, a pleasant and amiable person.

Oddly, she supports her arguments for a right to roam by comparing Britain with Sweden. What she fails to say is that, in Sweden, the population density is 19 per square kilometre; in Britain as a whole it is 238 (in England, 354). She also dismisses visitor horror stories as 'anecdotal evidence', whereas her conclusions are based on science. Surely the only difference between anecdote and science is that one is written down and one is not? That should not affect the validity of either.

Shoard seemed quite taken aback at the audience's reaction to the debate and the strength of feeling against the right to roam – not from landowners, but from ordinary people worried about the effect of ignorant feet on our disappearing wildlife.

21 September 2004

Letter to the Editor

Ramblers and Foxhunters

SIR – I am 60 years old, but when I read your leading article about so-called 'mass trespass' today, I felt young again. What harm are walkers likely to do to land? They are unlikely to achieve the despoliation and pollution that many landowners have caused with their destruction of hedgerows and wildlife.

Who is it that gleefully sells the land to developers? Not the walkers.

John Jones
Richmond
Surrey

10 March 1999

Letter to the Editor

Middle Classes' Right to Roam

SIR – In view of this bossy government's decision on the 'right' to trespass, I think all opponents should now organise a lengthy mass ramble, on the same day, in as many Labour MPs' gardens as possible. We could all take a picnic with us and really make a meal of it!

(Mrs) Rosemary Basden
Hatfield
Herts

21 March 1998

Munro Bagging

Peter Gillman

It was like a dream. The summit cairn was looming, lines of relatives and friends were clapping and cheering, my feet were moving forward as if self-propelled. As I neared the top of my final Munro, scenes of wildness and beauty, companionship and solitude, flashed before me, together with the pledge I had made, then broken, 10 years before.

At first I had sworn not to climb the Munros. The hill-walkers who commit themselves to step on to all 277 Scottish summits higher than 3,000 feet struck me as benighted souls for whom the term 'anoraks' seemed entirely appropriate. It seemed still more perverse that the man who sparked their obsession was an eccentric Victorian whose list – first published in 1891 – was riddled with arbitrary decisions over what constituted a full-blown summit.

For almost 20 years, therefore, I selected my goals without regard to Munro, not caring whether a mountain was above or below the 3,000 feet watershed.

The moment I broke my pledge and joined the anoraks can be precisely dated: it was on 8 August 1987, when I climbed the South Kintail Ridge. It was not just that I spent the whole day on a switchback ridge that dipped in and out of the clouds. I had also added seven new Munros to my name, boosting my total from 31 to 38 at a stroke. The arithmetic seemed tempting: just 25 peaks a year would see me to my target in 10 years.

And so I succumbed. I excused myself by saying that attempting the Munros would boost the motivation Londoners need to impel them up to the Highlands half a dozen times a year. And so I planned my campaign, recruiting friends and family as walking companions, scouring the maps and guide books, badgering editors for commissions that would take me to Scotland. I came to relish the idiosyncrasies of Munro's list and knew I was truly hooked when I attached a map of his peaks to my study wall so that I could record each new summit with a marker pin.

The rewards soon provided impetus enough. There are the sublime days, when Scotland extends beneath your feet like a map, the sky is unblemished, there are no navigation problems, and nothing else exists or matters. We had such days on the giant peaks of Torridon, Beinn Eighe and Liathach, when the rock was warm to the touch and our only burden was the weight of water we had to carry.

On Blaven, in Skye, we hurried to the summit in a summer twilight, to see the Cuillin range rising before us above a sea of cloud. In the Grey Corries, near Ben Nevis, we spent a magical winter's day, when our ice-axes rang out like tuning forks, as we followed the twists and curves of a glistening ridge festooned with ice sculptures fashioned by the wind.

More often, of course, Scotland is not like that. My record of climbs shows that fewer than half had afforded me a view from the summit. As my definition of climbable weather became more lax, I began to suffer the worst excesses of Scottish weather. There was the gale that blew me off my feet near the summit of Schiehallion, the thigh-deep torrent we had to wade on returning from Buachaille Etive Beag, the white-out we hit as we groped for the summit of Beinn Dorain.

I also learned to accept the possibility of failure. It took me four attempts to climb Gulvain, a modest peak in the Central Highlands, which included the frustration of being driven back by the wind when the summit was in our sight. Yet even these defeats helped boost the emotional charge.

It was also deepened through being shared, for the most part, with a cherished coterie of family and friends. Sometimes I climbed alone but my greatest reward came from climbing with my two sons. When they were young I would wait to shepherd them over any difficult stretches. Later our roles were reversed, and one of my sharpest memories is of my elder son, Danny – by then a father himself – patiently watching as I toiled up a slope he had already climbed, and then leading me over the kind of obstacle where I had once guided him.

The pins on my wall-map proliferated as the landmarks passed: 100 peaks in 1990, 200 in 1994, 250 in 1996. So it was, last May, that the end drew nigh. I had selected an improbable candidate as my final summit: Cairngorm, a 4,000-foot peak that occupies sixth place in the table, and is disliked by walkers because a ski-lift carries tourists close to the summit. But it meant that my three grandchildren would be able to attend the culminating moment.

The day was clear, the sky flawless. After the walking and ski-lift parties separated I took my time, savouring the memories that threatened to engulf me. I hardly noticed the tourists as I approached the summit, the honour guard parting to let me through, my wife Leni gripping my hand. I felt as if I had floated to the top.

There were hugs and tears and the popping of Champagne. One of my grandchildren had fallen asleep but the other two enjoyed the festive mood. We spent almost an hour beside the cairn then took the first steps back down, ready to celebrate again with a party that night.

I duly wrote to the keeper of the Munros list and duly received my certificate recording that I was the 1,726th person to 'complete' – the official term – the list. I looked forward to returning to Scotland in the same spirit with which I had begun, not caring whether a mountain was a Munro, and becoming re-acquainted with Scotland's lesser peaks.

A few days later a friend called from Edinburgh to ask if I had seen the *Scotsman*. Why, I asked? Because, he recited in a voice of doom, the Munros list had just been revised.

It was true. Unknown to me, the Scottish Mountaineering Club had been scrutinising the inconsistencies in Munro's list, even though most people felt they were integral to the absurdity of the whole enterprise. Indeed, there had been protests when a similar exercise had been attempted 15 years before, and a declaration that any further revisions should be resisted, 'otherwise the Munros would no longer be the Munros'.

Now two callow officials of the SMC had removed one of my Munros on the grounds that it was too close to another summit. Far worse, they had added eight more to the list, bringing the total to 284. True, I had climbed four of the new peaks already, but it still meant I had four left to do.

I was outraged. I was particularly incensed at the patronising tones with which the SMC's revisers had declared that although no one who had completed the former list was officially required to climb the new ones, it was a matter of conscience whether they did or not.

Despite my protestations, the siren called. I found myself scrutinising the map on my wall, locating the four unclimbed peaks. I began scheming the possible routes and asked my walking companions if they were interested. They were.

So next month, I shall be departing for Glen Coe, where two of the peaks are to be found. Later in the spring, I shall head for the last two. Although I tell myself I am doing so from choice and not a sense of obligation, there is something within me that will not be stilled.

One thing is certain, however. Nothing, but nothing, could dull the magic of that day on Cairngorm.

Why We Must Fight for Nimbyshire
Geoffrey Wheatcroft

Down here in Nimbyshire these are stirring times. Our shire stretches right across southern England and the West Country, and the Loyal Nimbyshire Yeomanry ride out wearing a cap badge showing an ecologically correct death's-head over the motto 'Not In My Backyard'. We are all Nimbies now – and quite right too.

Most prominent recently among the troopers of the yeomanry: Bel Mooney, Alistair Horne, Rupert Allason MP and Jilly Cooper. All are inspired by the memory of the late Lord Ridley, still revered as honorary colonel-in-chief. He was the acerbic but engaging politician whose wildly indiscreet remarks about the Germans led to his departure from office in 1990, and may have helped undermine Mrs Thatcher herself, for all his devotion to her.

Two years earlier he had been involved in another little, and much more local, difficulty. Nick Ridley was what Keynes would have called a *laissez-fairy*, of the most ardent sort. He believed that market forces should do their worst to do their best.

No one argued more eloquently that if the Old Rich could no longer afford to keep up their country seats then they should make way for the New Rich who could. No one was more critical of the selfishness of middle-class country dwellers who tried to stop houses, supermarkets, factories being built within sight or earshot of their backyards. No one condemned more crisply the 'send-em-away attitude' of those he himself called Nimbies.

Then it was proposed to build new houses on a meadow behind his own Queen Anne rectory in Naunton in Gloucestershire. The environment secretary, as he then was, decided that this particular piece of the environment needed preserving indefinitely.

Further south in my own corner of Nimbyshire, they have been demonstrating all summer long against the new Bath bypass, a dual carriageway running on stilts through a pretty neck of the Avon Valley and the Solsbury Plain.

One of the demonstrators was Mrs Jonathan Dimbleby, aka the journalist Bel Mooney. She camped out in a Mongolian yurt, swore to fast unto death if the road was built, and made friends with the

New Age travellers who were also protesting against the new road.

Even before Miss Mooney called off her hunger strike (having lost half a stone in weight) the unkind pointed out that she and her family drove to their country abode in Upper Swainswick from London every week on the M4. Where had she been when that mighty motorway cut its swathe through Berkshire and Wiltshire, chewing up pastures and parsonages as it went?

More embarrassment was to come. Some of the travellers were evicted from their camp site on Solsbury Hill and asked Miss Mooney if they could pitch camp instead on a field belonging to the Dimblebys – behind their house, not to say in their backyard. She said 'no'. 'No one in their right minds would put people in with animals and wild flowers,' as St Francis might have put it, but didn't.

Nimbyism is rampant on either side of the Thames. In this week's *Spectator*, Jeremy Paxman somewhat acidly describes a row in the Buckinghamshire village of Turville. The former village school stands empty and it is proposed to use it to provide holidays for children from 'inner city' primary schools.

It has been opposed by Alistair Horne, the historian and biographer of Harold Macmillan, with the support of other local Nimbies such as Lord Quinton, former head of Trinity College, Oxford, and a former (not as Mr Paxman suggests, present) chairman of the British Library.

Meantime, across the river in Berkshire, a plan to build six new dwellings in the village of Aldworth has been widely welcomed. But not by one local property owner, the Tory MP Rupert Allason, otherwise the intelligence writer Nigel West, who is fiercely opposing the development.

And to round it off symmetrically, the Queen of Bonkshire herself has donned the Nimbyshire uniform. Jilly Cooper's sex-and-saddles novels have brought her fame and a home in Bisley, Gloucestershire. There she has been leading the opposition to the building of 83 new houses near to her own des res, which would presumably become rather less des if they were built.

It is not so much easy as inevitable to make fun of the massed ranks of Nimbyshire. Whether it is strictly fair to do so, I am not so sure. Nimby-baiting is itself now a licensed field sport, set to take over from fox-hunting if that is abolished by Tony Blair after the next election.

But aren't we all Nimbies at heart? Surely we are – and can only be

– humbugs and hypocrites when it comes to the 'environment'. None of us wants to live next to a power station or an airport or a sewage farm. Yet we all use electricity, we all travel by air and we all go to the lavatory.

Anyone remotely observant and honest knows that we live in a great commercial nation, and that we owe our comfort and ease to Mr Gradgrind as he grimly toils (or his operatives toil) making unlovely but 'eminently practical things'. Having recognised that truth in the name of intellectual honesty does not mean that we are all obliged to spend our lives in the shadows of the chimney stacks of Coketown.

The whole school of, as it were, anti-Nimby historians has chronicled as what it sees as British decline in terms of a dominant aristocratic culture to which the once energetic bourgeoisie has been in thrall. Having made his brass where there's muck, laments Corelli Barnett, the successful manufacturer would flee the place of his and his wealth's origins and set himself up as a country gentleman.

Indeed so, and why not? What on earth is the point of making it if you can't enjoy it in a civilised way? What is wrong with the gentler civilisation of traditional country life?

Although the Nimbyshire yeomen I have described are all pro-fessional communicators, they seem curiously inarticulate when it comes to arguing this point and defending the Nimby position. Let me try for them, by way of quoting Lord Annan on the subject of E.M. Forster.

'He was unafraid of the contradictions in life which believed Liberals ought to face: that friendship may mean being hard on friends [and so say all of us who sometimes write about our Nimby neighbours]; that freedom and art depended on money and inequality; that his working-class friends needed houses but that the new housing estates meant the death of rural England and destroyed man's healing contact with nature.'

Lord Ridley could not have put it better, and indeed would not have tried. But I recommend it to Jilly and Bel and Alistair next time they are accused of intolerable hypocrisy.

9 June 2010

Phone Masts and Road Signs 'Cluttering Up Our Countryside'

The countryside is becoming increasingly blighted by 'clutter' such as road signs, pylons and phone masts, rural campaigners have said.

The Campaign to Protect Rural England said bad management and insufficient planning controls had made some rural areas look 'more like a scrap yard than the majestic green countryside'.

According to the CPRE, there are more than 52,500 phone masts and about 3.5 million telephone poles supporting 9.75 million miles of overhead wires.

In addition, up to 70 per cent of road signs in the countryside may be unnecessary, according to the CPRE and the RAC Foundation.

In the South Downs national park, there are 300 road signs in one seven-mile stretch – the equivalent of 45 signs per mile, the charity said.

17 January 1994

Sir Bernard Takes a Tilt at Windmills

Robert Bedlow

Sir Bernard Ingham, former press secretary to Lady Thatcher when Prime Minister, is opposing plans to build a 44-turbine wind farm close to his birthplace at Hebden Bridge, West Yorkshire.

He is leading protesters against proposals from National Wind Power to set up 200-foot modern 'windmills' at Flaight Hill.

Sir Bernard said: 'Wind farms are a monument to the "green" nonsense abroad in Britain. Any "green" who claims that wind farms are beautiful to behold is aesthetically dead. The farms resemble a cluster of lavatory brushes in the sky.'

The farms not only despoiled the landscape and the skyline, but they generated so little power that 'thousands of them will be needed if they are to produce anything worthwhile'.

Sir Bernard continued: 'Wind farms are not going to replace any fossil-fuel produced energy and you can't rely on them. Any wind below 11mph and they stop working, and in a gale they blow a fuse and have to be closed down. The consequences on the landscape are appalling. We have two wind farms around Halifax and they are not producing anything worthwhile. We are also concerned that the flora and fauna of the moor will be destroyed because the depth they have to dig the foundations will affect spring water supplies.'

22 May 1994
The Ultimate Nature Project
Joanna Ralphs

James Silk did not go to school on Thursday afternoon. Instead of the normal routine of piano, art, divinity, science and games, he presented himself before assembled worthies in Oxford's oak-panelled town hall and explained why they should not, under *any* circumstances, cut down the hedge in the field at the bottom of his garden.

He has earned the right to pronounce on such matters because it was he who first had the presence of mind to set about dating the disputed hedge, which Oxford's Wolfson College wants to bulldoze to make way for a sports field. After consulting his encyclopaedia, James painstakingly counted the number of trees and shrubs in a 30-pace stretch of the 250-yard hedgerow last Easter. He multiplied the result by 100 to calculate the total number, and obtained an approximate age of 400 years; a figure gratefully pounced upon by local residents and conservationists who are determined to save the hedge.

At Thursday's meeting, the latest planning enquiry into the hedgerow – now thought to be 1,000 years old – James modestly played down his role in the affair. He only did the project because he *had* to for school, he explained to the Department of Environment inspector.

But he does not mind admitting that among his school friends at Oxford's Dragon School he is becoming quite a hero.

'Some of them are so supportive that they have put posters in hedgerows saying 'Vote James Silk and not Wolfson'. One girl even carried one as a banner around the classroom,' he says, with evident pride, at his home in north Oxford.

Sitting in his short-sleeved grey shirt, his head of dark hair ruffled from a day of thoughtful scratching, he acts like a typical nine-year-old. He wriggles as he talks and when he loses interest in the conversation, stares out of the window. But his grave words bear little resemblance to the pronouncements of the average child.

When I ask him why he felt the need to address the inquiry himself, he fixes me with a steady look and says, in the measured tone of an accomplished politician: 'It needed a child's point of view. What a child thought. What someone under the age of 10 thought. I mean, it just seems *important* to me.'

Although the experience of addressing barristers, planning experts and a government inspector had made him 'slightly nervous', he had nevertheless felt 'very confident'. His parents both have a background in the law, and are adept at public speaking, so this is to be expected. Indeed, the law is one of the professions on James's own list of preferred career options, although he also fancies something 'to do with the movie or television business'. Spielberg beware.

James is a charming and intelligent child – and, it must be said, breathtakingly precocious. At his home – a lovely, modern, Georgian-style house on the affluent outskirts of Oxford – his mother, Hilary, a law lecturer at Oxford's Brookes University, greets me warmly after the hearing. Her husband Donald, a retired solicitor, paces dolefully around the living-room. He appears rather exhausted with the whole affair and periodically invites me to join him in a stiff drink. James's younger sister, Polly, sprawls next to her mother reading a book. She is rather put out, Hilary informs me, with all the attention her brother has been getting.

But she will have to get used to it, if James's current progress is anything to go by. He is already one of the top pupils in his class.

However promising his powers of reasoning and argument, though, James does have to accept that there is a slim chance his campaign could fail. Like any nine-year-old faced with the prospect of not getting his own way, this outcome spells nothing but gloom and doom.

'I would feel as if I had said goodbye to a very good friend and the feeling would probably go on for the rest of my life,' he says dramatically, and stares out of the window again.

1 May 1994

Barking Up the Wrong Tree
Matt Ridley

If you think political correctness and ethnic cleansing do not go together, you have never met a modern conservationist. Even as we celebrate becoming a multiracial society, environmentalists decry the presence of exotic and alien species in terms that would be positively racist if applied to human beings. Are they right to be so prejudiced?

In some cases, yes. Undoubtedly, the introduction of exotic species has been a far greater cause of extinction than chemical pollution. After Captain Cook had passed by, rats, cats and pigs wiped out hundreds of island species in the Pacific. New Zealand settlers formed 'acclimatisation societies' to bring out birds and animals from Britain to make the settlers feel at home, which was catastrophic for the native birds. Various American species have wreaked havoc among our native creatures (and vice versa): grey squirrels have all but exterminated red squirrels from southern England; mink are well on the way to wiping out water voles.

Yet eager bureaucrats are now becoming ridiculously over-zealous in their ethnic prejudice. A landowner acquaintance of mine in South Yorkshire applied to the Forestry Commission for permission (normal since the stealthy nationalisation of private forestry in the past decade) to underplant a mixed wood with young beech to replace senescent Capability Brown beech woods nearby. A young official visited him and vetoed the scheme. Reason? Beech is 'not native' to the Yorkshire limestone.

Quite apart from the effrontery of a government body – that, until very recently, urged and grant-aided the planting of little but sitka spruce (from Alaska) – telling people not to plant beech, the young man's sensitivity is absurd. Since the Ice Age, our forests have constantly changed as species shifted to adapt to the changing climate. Beech was one of the last species across the Dover land bridge and was still spreading north when history started.

Must we fossilise one glimpse of this ever-changing view? James Ogilvie, a more enlightened Forestry Commission conservator, points out that prejudice against the sycamore tree is the most bizarre. Among naturalists, the sycamore seems to be regarded by the environmental Gestapo as a desperate enemy, to be extirpated wherever it exists.

The sycamore's crimes are that its vigorous seedlings invade ancient oak woodland, shading out the flowers on the forest floor, and that it supports many fewer insect species than oak trees. These faults are the result of its supposed foreignness: it was allegedly brought here by the Romans.

Yet, according to Morton Boyd, a former director of the Nature Conservancy Council in Scotland, most of this is nonsense. Sycamores are probably natural invaders, which have spread across Europe later than other trees – of their own accord. Even if they did need man's help to get here it was the historical accident of the English Channel that made it necessary, not some divine decree that Britain and sycamores were incompatible. Come to that, many oak trees in British woods are descended from French or German acorns brought here in recent centuries. Should they be rooted out, too?

As for the supposed ecological poverty of the sycamore, Mr Boyd gives it short shrift. A sycamore supports a greater weight of insects even than an oak, and provides more food for birds than beech, ash or hazel. Since the decline of the elm, sycamore supports more mosses and lichens than any other tree and almost as many toadstools as oak. Its leaf litter is the richest of any broadleaved tree, which is why worms (and hence woodcocks) like it so much.

Sycamore will invade under a thin oak canopy, true, but oak invades under a thin sycamore canopy. So the spread of sycamore into ancient oak woodland is a natural part of the tree's historical arrival in these lands. There is nothing wrong with fighting it site by site to save wild flowers, but a general prejudice is absurd.

29 May 2005

Farmer Faces Jail for Disturbing Dormice

Roya Nikkhah

A farmer faces a six-month jail sentence after becoming the first person to be accused of disturbing a dormouse habitat.

Stephen Jones was charged under the Wildlife and Countryside Act when he attempted to erect a fence on his land near Caerphilly, South

Wales. However, he has never seen a dormouse on the 14-acre woodland site, and the only evidence of the animal's presence is a collection of hazelnut shells which appear to bear its distinctive teethmarks.

Mr Jones, 44, wanted to put sheep on the site to control weeds and undergrowth and drove his tractor through 200 yards of woodland in preparation for erecting the fence. He had previously informed a landscape officer at Caerphilly borough council of his plans because the site is protected by a tree preservation order and was told that there would not be a problem.

He was astonished, therefore, to receive a telephone call from Gwent police informing him that if he continued, his machinery would be confiscated. Shortly afterwards he received a letter informing him that he was being charged with five offences under the Wildlife and Countryside Act 1981 and the Conservation (Natural Habitats) Regulations 1994.

Under the act, it is an offence to 'intentionally or recklessly either damage or destroy, or obstruct access to any structure or place which a dormouse uses for shelter or protection'. If found guilty, Mr Jones faces a maximum fine of £5,000 or up to six months in prison.

Mr Jones said that he was unaware that the mammal – an endangered species that measures less than 3½ inches – might be on his land.

'I am absolutely stunned by the charges as neither myself nor anyone else who worked on the land had ever seen any evidence of dormice,' said Mr Jones.

'I certainly did not set out to intentionally destroy any dormice, and to accuse me of recklessness is ridiculous.'

He claims that a letter from the council which said that there might be dormice on his land was only sent to him after he had been charged.

Wildlife specialists from the council and the Countryside Council of Wales, the government body responsible for conservation in Wales, later inspected the site but no dormice were discovered.

Erica Colkett, the species officer for the countryside council, said: 'No dormice or their nests were found but evidence of their residence was discovered in the form of several characteristically opened hazelnuts on the site.'

Dormice leave teethmarks which are different to those of squirrels and common field mice. This is often the only way to detect their presence in woodland as they are nocturnal animals that hibernate for three quarters of the year.

Dr Pat Morris, a former senior lecturer in zoology at the Royal

Holloway University in London and a leading researcher in dormouse conservation, said that the animals are notoriously elusive.

'Dormice are extremely small creatures who spend all of their time either asleep or up in trees in the dark and are therefore incredibly hard to spot,' he said. 'It is difficult for conservationists to carry out surveys on them so it is very likely that many landowners have no idea that there are dormice on their land.' The Countryside Alliance, the pressure group which campaigns on rural issues, criticised the decision to charge Mr Jones. 'This is a ludicrous example of the increasing areas where farmers and landowners can potentially face prosecution for activities where they have absolutely no intention of disturbing wildlife or the environment,' said a spokesman. 'People seem to forget that it is individuals such as Mr Jones who are responsible for managing and protecting the countryside and its wildlife.'

31 January 2009

Set Your Sights on Our Glorious Wildlife

Simon Heffer

There are more deer now than at any time since the Middle Ages. The failure to cull them is causing severe environmental problems, affecting the balance of the countryside, and leading to the destruction of woodland. The problem is that many people, having watched *Bambi* once too often, think of such animals as superior to humans and requiring the sort of consideration normally applied to maiden aunts. Of course there should be a cull: and it should not stop there. Wild boar now cause havoc in some parts of the country – the celebrated vegetarian Sir Paul McCartney refused a few weeks ago to cull some on his estate that were running wild. Foxes are everywhere and need to be slaughtered in huge quantities, just when hunting is banned; and even badgers are spreading bovine TB. This is not Beatrix Potter, it's real life. Take aim, and fire.

7 June 2009
Red Alert for the Grey Squirrel
Harry de Quetteville

Rod Brammer, champion of country pursuits, has a substantial list of pet hates. It starts with the general – global warming ('a lot of tosh'), New Labour ('I have never hated anyone as much as I hate Tony Blair'), animal rights campaigners ('cowards . . . let them try') – but quickly moves to the particular.

In the bird world, magpies and crows ('with their horrible little black beaks') fare little better. Badgers ('tuberculosis carriers') and foxes ('it's only time before they kill a baby') are equally despised. But even in this lengthy list of loathing, a special niche of detestation has been carved out by the sturdy incisors of one particular creature: the grey squirrel.

'B— squirrels,' he says, lighting up his pipe in the gun room of his 62-acre farm in Devon, part of which he is turning into a bird sanctuary, though presumably not for magpies and crows. 'We should kill them all. I will be very happy when the last grey squirrel is under a glass canopy in a museum, stuffed.'

Such invective may seem the refuge of an eccentric, but Brammer, a 67-year-old who has successfully twinned the apparently exclusive roles of naturalist and firearms instructor, is by no means alone.

Earlier this week, the Prince of Wales joined the call for the grey to be wiped from these shores. 'It is absolutely crucial to eliminate the greys, which, as you know, are an alien species to the UK,' he noted in a letter to the Country Land and Business Association.

The Prince's logic for wanting to nobble the nimble nut-gatherers is straightforward enough. The greys, explains Brammer, are the bullies of the squirrel world – imported American bruisers who comprehensively out-punch our very own red squirrels. Not only are greys bigger, but they reproduce quicker and carry a pox which floors the reds. All in all, it's not a fair fight.

But calling for the 'elimination [of greys] in order to save the red squirrels and ensure their future in this country' is a tough ask. Grey squirrels already outnumber the diminutive reds by about 4 million to 150,000 or so.

Faced with such overwhelming odds, the red squirrel has mustered a decent band of champions. The Prince is the patron of the Red Squirrel

Survival Trust. The Save our Squirrels campaign has been granted hundreds of thousands of pounds of lottery money. The RSPB is no fan of the grey squirrel, owing to the animal's habit of raiding birds' nests for eggs and young. The Forestry Commission is equally disapproving of its capacity to strip bark from trees.

But while there is official distaste, there is little action on the ground. A countrywide strategy to take on the grey would require significant planning, and no doubt encounter stiff resistance from many city dwellers, for whom they are a welcome and rare taste of the natural world. And that's not to mention the RSPCA . . . which is where Brammer comes in.

He is not one for pressure groups, unless the pressure happens to be on the trigger of his 20-gauge shotgun. Brammer is to grey squirrels what the hardworking gardener is to snails: a driven, furious enemy.

'This,' he says, indicating a small cage equipped with a birdfeeder on the inside, 'is the "El Gecko" trap. It's bloody lethal.' Squirrels climb into the device, activating a simple mechanism which shuts a wire door behind them. Afterwards, he says, there is no escape – not even if the successful trapper has a sudden burst of remorse. 'They're vermin,' he says. 'You can't trap them and release them elsewhere.'

The squirrels, once caught in Brammer's traps, are usually dispatched with a rifle or air-rifle shot to the back of the head. He has the tokens of many such executions in his gun room: tails. Lots of them. In part, this is a hangover from times gone by, when forestry officials would pay the public to do away with squirrels; the tails were required as proof.

'I've been shooting squirrels since I had my first gun aged 10. It was one shilling a tail when I was a boy, and two shillings later on,' says Brammer.

But there is no mistaking the fact that the squirrels are the enemy, and their tails, kept in an empty cardboard box of shotgun cartridges, are also totems of each small victory.

With such expertise, deployed in the 20 or so years since Brammer acquired his farm, near the village of Shillingford, it is little wonder the squirrels are now a rare sight on his land.

In fact, he claims that they are a rare sight locally, because his cull of the greys has been taken up by friends and neighbours. 'Everyone round here is doing them in,' he says.

For those who are squeamish, like his octogenarian neighbour Jill, he is happy to install traps, and then send round Matt, his son, to do the dirty work.

But while there is a certain satisfaction in winning the battle locally, Brammer is looking for more. What he wants is all-out war. He wants to clear the country, county by county, using rivers, which the squirrels cannot cross, to secure the advance. 'They'll still be able to cross at bridges, of course, but we could really catch them there,' he says.

Of course, as with all ambitious generals, Brammer needs allies. Fortunately, he has just such assistance, strategically positioned in Northumberland, ready to sweep southwards. It comes from Rupert Mitford, the former hereditary peer, who is now (as the 6th Baron Redesdale) an elected life peer and Liberal Democrat environment spokesman.

Apart from being able to count the Mitford sisters as his great aunts, he also boasts the title Founder of the Red Squirrel Protection Partnership. Backed by £150,000 of Defra money, Mitford, with his hunting partner Paul Parker, claims to have killed more than 20,000 squirrels from his base in Rochester.

Now the RSPP is hoping to move south. 'We have asked landowners down there if they need any help,' said Parker, who is from Newcastle.

Back in Shillingford, Brammer, who reckons he has bagged 'thousands upon thousands of the b——', is equally keen to drive east. Between these two pincers, the grey squirrel, imported in the 1870s to adorn Victorian gardens, may finally meet its match.

'I know a bloke who remembers seeing a red around here when he was a nipper, and he was in the Home Guard, so that shows you how long they've been gone,' says Brammer.

Now he, Lord Redesdale and the Prince of Wales are pinning their hopes on a new Home Guard. A squirrel squad, if you like. 'Just get people involved,' says Brammer. 'There are 4 million squirrels. Pay people £4 a tail. Just £16 million, and it would be done.'

19 June 1994

Letters to the Editor
Saving the Reds from the Greys

SIR – The persistent encroachment of the American grey squirrel and the resulting destruction of our indigenous red squirrel has been with us for many years. It was particularly bad immediately after the last war when, after five years of inadequate pest control, the grey squirrel was posing a threat to forestry, and a campaign was launched to halt the danger.

This was done by offering a bounty for each squirrel tail, either in cash or cartridges. Many a schoolboy or forestry worker earned welcome extra pocket money, and the grey-squirrel population was significantly reduced.

Unfortunately the bounty system was discontinued, since when the grey squirrel has continued its invasion. There is no doubt that a similar incentive scheme would succeed now, especially if we started describing them as 'tree rats', which they are.

I am sure we all wish Scotland every success in repelling these invaders. We lost the battle in the New Forest years ago.

(Lord) Montagu of Beaulieu
Brockenhurst
Hants.

SO, some Lords think that squirrels should be shot or poisoned. We don't.

All squirrels are lovely. Surely everyone enjoys watching them skipping around in the back garden or in the park. And it is nice to look at them sitting down and nibbling at an acorn held between their paws. Hands off squirrels, red or grey.

Catherine Shelley and Terri Parsons
London E14.

16 August 1998

Why I Quit the Evil Animal Fanatics

Tim Reid

An activist with the Animal Liberation Front, which claimed responsibility for freeing 6,000 mink into the wild last week, has broken ranks with the organisation to tell *The Sunday Telegraph* of the 'unthinking madness' within the movement.

In a rare insight into the mind of the extremist, the man, who has just left the ALF and does not want to be named, said the decision to release the mink from a fur farm in Ringwood, Hants, was typical of fanatics who equated the plight of sheep with 'the Jews in concentration camps'.

Since the mink were let loose, thousands have been shot, hunted down or starved to death. Hundreds more have attacked local wildlife in search of food.

The RSPCA and other animal welfare groups have condemned the action and say the area faces a wildlife disaster. They describe the operation as a damaging own goal. The activist, who was involved in confrontations with police across the south and Midlands, said last night: 'The freeing of the mink has confronted us with the bizarre inconsistencies of the whole movement. They think anything that is caged should be freed, no matter what the consequences.

'Some people get involved for the buzz, but the majority really think what they do is justified. They believe the only bad species on Earth is the human being. They hate, absolutely hate, scientists. They have totally swallowed the propaganda that vivisection is a profitable industry. They view the scientists involved in animal experiments as the equivalent of Dr Goebbels. They hate being human and they hate humans.

'What they don't realise is that they are fascists. They believe the cause of animals supersedes that of humans. The feeling is that you have to be purer and purer, then you get more extreme and end up bombing people.

'The whole time I was with them, we never actually discussed animals. They are not really animal lovers. They don't watch wildlife programmes, or read books on animals. They know nothing about wildlife. They are anarchists who view the use of animals as a political conspiracy and human cruelty.

'Some of them even told me that they don't even like animals. They use the argument that you don't have to like black people to want to liberate them. It is a mindset that allows you to bomb people with immunity.'

The activist said the hard core of the ALF, who would appear at demonstrations wearing balaclavas, were mostly young men well informed about their legal rights, but quite prepared to go to prison.

They would mysteriously appear at mainstream demonstrations, outside laboratories or farms, often to return at night, when the dust had settled, to firebomb the buildings.

If a new recruit showed 'real dedication to the cause', the activist said, he would receive an anonymous call one day, out of the blue, asking him to turn up to a designated spot. That would be to take part in criminal activity. 'It is bizarre and extremist,' he said. 'I almost wanted to go out and kill cows by the end. Liberation is all. That is as far as they think.'

According to the Research Defence Society, in the past 20 years the ALF has caused an estimated £200 million of damage to organisations as diverse as schools, targeted for dissecting animals, department stores, charity shops and milk depots. At least another £200 million has been spent on improving security at hundreds of establishments.

The latest ALF manual, *Into the Nineties*, is an anonymous handbook which describes how to make timed incendiary devices, petrol bombs, damage vehicles, locks and telephone lines. It recommends tailing scientists, furriers and butchers to their homes, 'where pressure also needs to be put'.

'Animal abuse is everywhere,' it says. 'Butchers' shops, fur and leather shops, factory farms, vivisection laboratories, animal breeders, zoos, circuses, hunt kennels . . . Get the bastards. Don't let them get away with murder.'

The ALF, which has 2,000 official supporters, is made up of a number of animal rights groups who work in unconnected, local 'cells'. Police estimate that no more than 100 activists are involved in violent acts, such as bombing and breaking into farms.

The official ALF spokesman, Robin Webb, has remained unrepentant since the release of the mink. 'Even if one per cent of the mink are to survive in the wild it means that individuals of the species are living a life free from pain, free from exploitation and free from abuse,' he said.

'Even if mink are being shot, at least it is quicker than the way they are killed in the fur farms for coats that nobody really needs these days,' he said.

But Prof Roger Scruton, whose *Animal Rights, Animal Wrongs* was published by the right-wing think tank Demos two years ago, said that because animals are not, and never can be, independent persons subject to moral law, they have no rights.

'If animals have rights, they must have duties,' he said. 'It is stupid talking about their rights. We should talk about their welfare. Are you entitled to sacrifice 5,900 mink, and the other wildlife, so that 100 might survive? It shows completely screwy reasoning.'

12 September 1998
Symphony Out of Tune
Ross Clark

When W.G. Hoskins wrote *The Making of the English Landscape* in 1955, he imagined the countryside to be a vast symphony. Each age had contributed its own landscape features, its instrument line, which was then complemented by the music of subsequent ages. The oboes of the Iron Age, the trombones of the Roman occupation, the flutes of the Saxon settlement, the violins of the enclosures, the percussion of the railway age: the real beauty of the English landscape, said Hoskins, was in understanding how the individual parts added up to create the symphonic score that is an Ordnance Survey map.

But it won't be a symphony for much longer. Looking back from next century, it will seem as if the orchestra collapsed into a state of confusion sometime in the nineties. The flautists turned their score upside down and started playing backwards, the violinists mistook an inky smudge and started playing in the wrong key, and the trombonist got his finger stuck and began emitting an ear-piercing shriek.

The reason is that the countryside has suddenly been forbidden from evolving any further and is being turned instead into a twee theme park.

The landscape is no longer allowed to be a happy accident resulting from myriad uses: it has suddenly got to be 'restored' — that dreaded word that the Victorians used as an excuse to tear apart many a church.

There seems no end of quangos and other bodies that have appointed themselves as arbiters of taste over the countryside. At the heart of all of them is the mistaken belief that the landscape has one historically correct form to which it deserves to be returned and in which it must be preserved forever after.

They are driven by the kind of dripping sentimentality that comes from reading too much Rupert Brooke and drooling over too many of those old *London Illustrated News* prints of stagecoaches overturned in snowdrifts along some hedge-encrusted turnpike.

The hedgerow lobby is the most irritating part of the restoration movement. It is not enough simply to stop farmers ripping out hedgerows; we have got to start planting them all over the place. In my part of Cambridgeshire, National Lottery funds are being poured into the cause of covering the countryside with lines of mean little hawthorns that seem to serve no other purpose than to rip your trousers to shreds.

The justification seems to be a popular belief that the countryside was always steeped in hedges until the greedy farmers started ripping them out to squeeze a few more inches of profit from their soil. But it is a misguided belief. Over most of central England hedges only appeared during the parliamentary enclosures of the 18th and 19th centuries. Before that the countryside was made up mainly of open fields that strongly resembled those much-hated prairies of modern East Anglia.

The landless labourers who watched the original hedges being planted would have thought we were completely mad to drool over hawthorns and briars. For them, hedges were a symbol of oppression; the means by which landowners kept them out of the newly enclosed lands – land on which all locals had previously enjoyed the right to gather sticks and trap birds.

Hedges are really nothing more than the pre-industrial equivalent of razor wire. It is rather as if Berliners suddenly decided to cover their city with concrete walls to recreate what they saw as the traditional city landscape.

What is wrong with prairie fields, anyway? The openness of East Anglia is one of the pleasures of the landscape there. The joy of being in Norfolk and Suffolk is in counting half a dozen churches on the horizon – which will be impossible once the hedgerow lobby has had its way and covered the country with impenetrable thicket.

There is no reason why we should be ashamed of modern farming methods. It was, after all, a desire for agricultural efficiency that led to the enclosures, and, therefore, to the planting of hedges, in the first place. Watching a combine harvester smoking its way like a paddle-steamer across a great lake of wheat is an impressive sight, which the restoration lobby might enjoy too if it did not have such a prejudice against industrial civilisation.

What is noticeable about the restoration lobby's creed is that it reduces aesthetics to a handful of simplistic rules. New houses these days have all got to be jumbled about because irregular geometry is supposed to soften their impact on the countryside and make them look more villagey. But why should buildings be forbidden to make a visual impact? Some of the most remarkable and most visited villages, such as Milton Abbas, are those planned villages that consist of straight lines of houses.

Another annoying rule is that anything made from wood is natural and, therefore, good. Anything made from iron and steel is industrial and, therefore, bad. Hence the elegant iron railings and gates that used to line the parklands of southern England are gradually giving way to rustic wooden fencing. Most idiotic of all, mobile-phone companies have been forced to dress up what could have been elegant steel masts in the form of phoney trees just to please the aesthetic illiterates on local planning committees.

When the Forth Rail Bridge was opened in 1890, it was almost universally recognised to be an object of great beauty. So why be ashamed of electricity pylons, which, if placed sensitively, can add just as much to the landscape as did the great bridge?

There is a place in the Fens where there are a hundred pylons laid out in a straight line. Stand in the right place and you can see them vanishing into nothing, seemingly lined up inside each other like Russian dolls. It is a sensation in an otherwise featureless plain and never fails to impress people when you stop the car to show them. But, no, the countryside restoration lobby would still rather we all paid three times as much for our electricity just so that the cables are buried underground.

Its attitude towards wind farms is even madder. Here is an invention that promises virtually unlimited, renewable energy and yet still the lobby finds some way of being against it. It says it cannot stand the whirring and the sails ruin the skyline. Can you imagine 18th-century Dutchmen objecting to the thousands of windmills they watched being hoisted upon their own skyline? Of course you can't. The Dutch have long appreciated that there can be beauty in a man-made landscape as well as in a natural one – something that ought to be acknowledged by anyone who admits a fondness for those medieval peat workings now known as the Norfolk Broads.

Again, is there anyone other than the militant arm of the birdwatching lobby who sees merit in mudflats? They stink, they look awful, and since you cannot walk or play football on them they have no value as an amenity whatsoever. It is hardly as if estuarine mud attracts interesting birds, either – if you see anything other than a seagull you are doing extremely well.

Small wonder that in most riverside towns the mudflats were flooded with the aid of sluice gates centuries ago in order to create a cleaner, healthier, more impressive riverside. But these days you face the full wrath of the conservation movement if you dare so much as touch a mudflat. To listen to the reaction when Cardiff proposed to improve the appearance of its waterside by building a tidal barrier, you would have thought the city wanted to strangle every bird in Wales.

We shouldn't just flood Cardiff Bay; we should erect barrages up and down the whole Severn estuary and tap the enormous potential for tidal power. Given that the estuary enjoys the second highest tides in the world, it is environmentally irresponsible not to take advantage of such a huge natural-energy resource. In time, as with most impressive feats of engineering, tidal barrages would come to be seen as an important part of our heritage.

It is time we stopped the conservationists from making us think of our country as a bucolic backwater. If we have got money to spend improving the appearance of parts of the countryside, great. But rather than boring old hedges, rustic fences and pylons dressed up as trees, why don't we have some bold and original landscape architecture?

After all, when Sir Joseph Paxton was given *carte blanche* to stamp his imprint on the gardens at Chatsworth early last century, he didn't go for little hedges and dry-stone walls. But then he didn't have the countryside restoration lobby on his back trying to get him to turn the place into just another cattle farm.

23 January 2010
An Ill Wind Blows for Mr Badger
Geoffrey Lean

It was the good-natured Ratty, sculling down the river, who first warned against messing about with possibly Britain's best loved – and certainly its most overprotected – wild animal.

'Dear old Badger,' he mused to Mole in the first chapter of *The Wind in the Willows*. 'Nobody interferes with him.' And, then as Kenneth Grahame tells it, he added significantly: 'They'd better not.'

Britain's politicians have long taken this century-old piece of advice. No animal enjoys better protection than the badger, though few need it less. Uniquely, it has its own Act of Parliament to defend its wellbeing, yet – unlike hundreds of much more poorly safeguarded species – it is not at all endangered.

Badger numbers have been rapidly increasing recently, and so has the incidence of tuberculosis in cattle, devastating already hard-pressed dairy farmers. No one seriously denies that badgers harbour the disease and pass it on. Yet culling them has effectively been banned for the past decade, while rates of bovine TB have continued to soar. And, two years ago, the famously kind-hearted environment secretary, Hilary Benn, rejected plans to restart the killing.

For much of this, Mr Badger can thank one of history's greatest spin doctors. If Alastair Campbell had half Grahame's skill, we might still be having to endure Tony Blair's own particular brand of fiction. And if Gordon Brown had been able to employ him, perhaps his public image might, even now and against all odds, be closer to the gruff sage of the wild wood than to Mr Toad at his most despondent.

Yet the novelist's spell may be beginning to wear off. Last week, almost unnoticed outside the principality, the Welsh rural affairs minister, Elin Jones, announced a five-year cull, mainly in north Pembrokeshire, due to start this spring. 'Bovine TB is out of control and unsustainable,' she said, pointing out that the number of diseased cattle that had to be put down in Wales had risen more than 17-fold, from 700 to 12,000, since 1997.

In England, Stuart Burgess, the government's Rural Advocate, has called for Mr Benn's verdict to be 'revisited', adding that a 'tough decision' may have to be made 'earlier rather than later'. And Jim Paice, the shadow farming minister, has made it clear that a Tory government would encourage a resumption of culling.

There is now no conceivable conservation reason to object. True, at the turn of the century – when Grahame was writing – badgers were uncommon after a long history of trapping, snaring, shooting, digging and baiting. But the decline of the gamekeeper allowed them to start to recover, and the Protection of Badgers Act 1992 makes them inviolable. It is now not just illegal to kill or injure a badger, but to own one (dead or alive), to damage its sett, or to disturb it when in residence. You cannot do any work within 30 feet of a sett, even by hand, except with a special licence. You can go to jail for six months if your dog goes down one on a walk: if it gets stuck, you must wait at least 48 hours before trying to remove it – and then you may be forbidden to do so.

Partly as a result, badger numbers have soared. There are now thought to be at least 300,000 in Britain, and their only real enemies run on four wheels: some 50,000 die on the roads each year.

Yet culling has a snag – a big, if counter-intuitive, one. It may well not work in reducing bovine TB, and could even make things worse.

A giant, nine-year official study found that when badgers were killed to try to control outbreaks, incidence of the disease in cattle actually rose by about 20 per cent – because the badgers moved to escape the slaughter, infecting new areas. 'Proactive' culls which continue year after year, as is planned in Wales, were found to reduce the disease in the killing fields by some 23 per cent, but increase it by even more in surrounding areas as infected badgers moved out. And unless the culling continues constantly, they eventually return to their old haunts.

It helps if the culling zones have uncrossable boundaries, like rivers or the sea. Much of the one planned in Wales does, but it is exceptional. So, to be at all effective, killing would have to cover vast areas; by one authoritative estimate, more than half of Britain's badgers would have to be slaughtered just to get a minor reduction in the disease.

Other studies suggest that a more effective way of tackling TB would be to monitor and control livestock movements, given that most cases are caught from other cattle. And a badger vaccine against TB is almost ready, and could be administered orally, through bait, by 2014. So perhaps the problem may yet be solved, and in a way that even a nation brought up on Kenneth Grahame can stomach.

10 June 2011

Letters to the Editor
Badgers Must Be Culled

SIR – The majority of Britons oppose culling badgers to control bovine TB (Letters, 9 June). Just because a majority is in opposition does not mean it is not still the right thing to do; a majority supports reinstating capital punishment, but it is still wrong. One of the primary functions of democracy is to ensure that public policy is informed by evidence and reason, and not simply by whoever shouts loudest.

Mark Sanders
Minehead
Somerset

SIR – According to experts on *In Our Time*, tuberculosis in cattle evolved from the human form. So the logical next step in protecting cattle would be?

Alan Greenwood
Stoke-on-Trent
Staffordshire

SIR – I doubt that badgers are responsible for the decrease in the toad population (Letters, 6 June). The common toad has glands that secrete a poisonous chemical that a badger would find disgusting. My Labrador once licked a toad, then spent the next half hour frothing at the mouth. The toad walked away unhurt.

William Rusbridge
Tregony
Cornwall

Hunting, Shooting and Fishing

Ladies, It's Catching On

Fiona Armstrong

As the old gillie says: 'There are two things I like to see in my water: one's fish, the other's whisky.' One of my first teaching instructors was legendary angler Hugh Falkus who advised me to practise with a glass of whisky on my head. When I was able to cast out without spilling a drop, I would know I had mastered the art of fly-casting.

I don't like the stuff, so I didn't bother; which means I'm not a very good caster, even after 25 years. But what I lack in technique, I make up for in enthusiasm. It was my first husband who taught me the rudiments of the sport. I went on to catch more than he did – though I don't think that's the real reason our marriage failed. Fishing is traditionally a man's world, but statistics show some of the most phenomenal catches have been by women. The biggest fish ever caught on rod and line was taken by Miss Georgina Ballantine in 1922. After catching three good-sized salmon on the River Tay in Perthshire, the diminutive lady went on to hook a monster, and after a two-hour battle, a fish of 64 pounds was landed.

Let's face it, girls, we're naturals.

Which drives men mad – and makes them come up with the Theory of the Pheromones; yes, it is the female hormones which help attract the fish. This may or may not have basis in scientific fact, but I have to ask, if it were the men that caught the biggest fish, would anyone look for a reason why?

Women are not 'better' anglers, but unlike some of their macho counterparts, they do take advice and they do listen. They may also be more careful and thorough.

But I am not a fish feminist. I love men and have met some wonderfully helpful and skilled ones on the water. I first saw my now husband on the banks of a river in Alaska and there on the Alexander Creek we both caught more than we bargained for. Traditionally only one in 10 anglers was female. But according to the Angling Development Board, an increasing number of women are taking up and coaching the sport.

And with good reason, from the exercise and the fresh air, to the chance to unwind (excuse the pun).

Then there are the more frivolous ones: a girl can never have too many hats and, let's face it, those waders can hide a multitude of sins. Fishing for salmon, trout and sea trout is one of life's great joys. I have actually texted a friend from a boat on the River Tweed after catching my third salmon in an afternoon to say: 'This is better than sex or shopping.' (And it was, at the time . . .)

And despite its image, fly-fishing is not just for the rich or titled (though that can help). In Scotland and the north of England I've met money men and miners who do it, and butchers and bakers. I've yet to meet a candlestick maker, but there is still time.

We fishers are game and we have to be to swathe ourselves in green rubber and stand for days chest-high in a freezing river, with numb fingers and toes.

So, how to start? You need to find someone to take you to the water – so ask a friend or relative, or join a fly-fishing club. But beware going out with anyone too close. Getting your better half to show you the ropes is rather like asking them to teach you to drive.

Borrow someone's tackle until you know you're going to like it – then invest in a rod, a reel, some line and nylon and some gorgeous multicoloured flies. But beware: fishing flies are tied to catch anglers, not fish. Someone kindly invented a new fly for me and called it the Fiona's Fancy. Alas, nothing has fancied it yet.

Most important is to get some warm, waterproof clothes. I would love to tell you that most fly-fishing is done on balmy summer days, but I would be lying. So let's set the scene: it's slightly overcast, with a gentle breeze ruffling the water. You have found a good spot and waded in. You cast back and the line shoots out in front. The fly you have chosen so carefully swims tantalisingly downstream, when suddenly, there's a sharp pull!

Let's hope it's not a branch you have hooked, or a hot water bottle, which can be very fishlike. Now the temptation is to shout wildly for help. But landing a fish needs some calm. So do not ask nervous folk to help – or people who are shortsighted or with drink in them.

Whether you kill your first fish and eat it is up to you and the rules of the river. Wild salmon, trout and sea trout are in short supply, and many waters now operate a catch and release policy.

I can still remember the trembling hands, the fluttering heart and the utter joy as an 8lb silvery offering lay at my feet . . .

Ladies, I wish you screaming reels and tight lines. You will enjoy it, as long as you remember the only experts in this game are the fish.

14 June 2003
No Flies on Me
Adam Edwards

The flies are on the wing. It matters not a jot that most of these artificial bugs will snag on the hedgerows or be caught in overhanging branches before they get the chance to land on Britain's finest stretches of water.

For this is the season of the gentleman fisherman. These are the soft early-summer weeks when the chest-wading hunter-gatherer, fresh from Farlows in Pall Mall, pays through the nose to stand on the riverbank with carbon-fibre rod and magnesium reel to hook, and tell as many whoppers as he can.

However, there is more to fly-fishing than arriving at the gillie's hut in a company BMW. One must be aware of the many niceties of the sport. So here, for those with the Sage rod but the not-so-sage sensibilities, is a rough and ready etiquette guide to rod and reel:

1 Despite universal agreement that there is nothing finer than catching a wild brown trout on a dry fly, a worm may be used if nobody is looking.
2 The number of flies attached to a hat is in inverse proportion to the skill of the fisherman.
3 Dynamite, hand grenades and scuba diving are not part of the sport.
4 If you give the keeper £50, he will tell you where the fish are. If you give him another £50, he will lie about your fish.
5 If you want to be certain of fishing the best pool, get up while the rest of the party is asleep. Be back in your pyjamas and dressing-gown for breakfast.
6 It is traditional to take a swig from your hip-flask when you catch a salmon. If you are swanking about a fish you claim to have caught, empty your hip-flask before you tell the tale.
7 A squashed lunchtime 'piece' – sandwich – from the fishing bag

indicates gastronomic coarseness rather than enthusiastic sporting endeavour. Keenness is always indigestible.

8 It is not for you to judge whether the gillie urging you to fish in the middle of a bright sunlit pool has been drinking.

9 Whatever time of year you choose to fish a river, it will be wrong by a week.

10 The river you have been invited to fish will indicate your social standing. They are, in order of smartness, the Helmsdale, the Dee, the Spey, the Tweed and, finally, the Tay.

11 Sunglasses are for looking for fish, not looking like Bono. They should be orange Polaroid, not mirrored Ray-Bans.

12 Drinking heavily at lunch improves one's boasting.

13 The expression 'tight lines' – that old fishing cliché, rather like 'break a leg' – is used as a salutation only if you are a BT engineer.

14 If your multi-pocketed fishing waistcoat has more pockets than are needed, it will indicate to your fishing colleagues that you are an American.

15 If your neighbour fails to notice a fish rising, move gently downstream and try to flick your fly over it.

16 Since the introduction of 'catch and release', fishermen are expected to add a pound or two in weight to their report of the size of fish caught.

17 Remember that fish 'bite' for anglers, they 'rise' for fly-fishermen. Salmon are grassed, trout are landed and fish in general are killed not caught. You do not ask a fellow fisherman how many he has caught, you ask him if he's had any luck.

18 It is considered bad form to cut the fly off the cast of the day's best fisherman and use it yourself.

19 The admission that you don't like eating fish is liable to get you black-balled from the exclusive Fly Fisher's Club.

20 Never admit to using your rubber waders for anything other than fishing.

The gillie is a skilled artisan who knows every ebb, flow and fish in his stretch of the river. However, it is unreasonable to expect him to spirit up a fish for a newly arrived guest if other fishermen are watching.

He will open conversation with a new arrival with the observation: 'You should have been here last week.' This is his way of explaining to the guest that, thanks to his considerable skill, the fish were popping out of the water like corks seven days ago but the conditions may not be exactly right for him to work his magic now.

Despite his God-like powers, he will explain that he cannot control the wind, the rain, the sun, the rise and fall of the river, the clearness of the water or why the fish are or are not feeding on a particular fly.

However, shortly before he is expecting his tip, his awesome powers will return. Providing he is allowed to tie his 'fly' on to your leader, it is as certain as God is a fly-fishing Englishman that you will catch a fish.

20 October 2007
The Bart and the Bounder
Sandy Mitchell

If you were alone and came across these two men on a dark night on the bank of a river, you would bunch your fists ready for trouble. They are obviously poachers of the worst sort. The one who walks with a rolling swagger, with a thin belt lashed round his barrel of a belly, has wild grey locks and a hungry look in his eye. The other, more furtive, sports a camouflage cap ridiculously small for his head and trousers poked roughly into black wellingtons. Deckhands in *Pirates of the Caribbean* dress better and look more trustworthy.

And I think this description will delight the two men in question: Sir Richard Heygate Bt. and his equally well-bred but more disreputable cousin, Mike Daunt. After all, they refer to each other happily as 'the Bart' and 'the Bounder', like a pair of leery Victorian villains, and they have publicly confessed their sins in a wonderful book about their escapades with fishing rod and shotgun, titled *Endangered Species*. Roguish they may be, but these two are true countrymen above all.

Earlier this year, having somehow got their hands on a stretch of the glorious river Itchen in Hampshire, they decided to invite a group of non-fishing city publishers and booksellers to learn to catch a trout. It was mayfly season. The cows in the meadow, the pigeons in the oaks, even the dragonflies looked expectant in the June sunshine as if somehow they knew today would be one of nature's special days.

Our bookish Londoners looked completely bewildered, however. They turned up to fish wearing tight T-shirts and trousers in shades of beige along with woven straw hats, a style you might call

Gummidge-meets-Gaultier. The hardened countrymen (Richard is 67, Mike 65) and the townies looked at each other with blank amazement.

But Mike quickly marched his recruits to the riverbank, got them swishing fly rods and short lines to and fro nicely above the water, drilling them to practise their basic casting technique while repeating a short phrase out loud to give them the right timing. When I learned to fish years ago, I was taught by a retired major to do exactly the same thing while politely repeating the words 'Ladies and Gentlemen' to myself and, at this point, I should also mention a passage in the famous 16th-century *Compleat Angler* where the author Izaak Walton warns fishermen against using bad language on the riverbank in case the trout swim off in horror:

None do here
Use to swear
Oaths do fray
Fish away.

I mention this because Mike can't have read that bit. He had them hollering 'Cor! **** me now' every time they cast, and they obeyed him with a flicker of fear in their eyes.

Perhaps that's why no fish would oblige the beginners by rising to their flies. The trout kept themselves hidden well beneath the mirrored surface of the stream, fins pressed to their ears to blot out the vulgarity. Making matters worse, Richard was supposed to be helping Mike with the instruction but had disappeared. 'Where is he? Stupid bugger's always getting lost,' chuntered Mike.

The day was getting off to a messy start until Mike asked politely if he could demonstrate how to fish using my rod. And not since Dumbo flapped his great ears and suddenly took flight for the first time, and all the mocking circus animals 'ooh-ed' in amazement, has there been such a public turn around. Mike gave the 9-foot fishing pole a smart slap and sent the line zipping through the wind towards the far bank, farther and farther until – a fraction short of the deadly tangle of brambles on the far side – it floated down through the air and the fly pecked the surface a perfect yard upstream of a rising trout. It was sublime to watch, and the audience on the riverbank breathed an involuntary gasp of pleasure. Even the trout rose to applaud and soon there were fish on the bank. By lunchtime the Londoners could barely be prised away from the river and their newfound passion for the sport.

Mike, whose face had by now ripened in the sun like a giant raspberry, lead the way to the nearby Dog and Crook pub where he sank five whole pints of lemonade with his food. (I watched with morbid horror, sure his body would never survive the shock of so much non-alcoholic liquid.) And it was during lunch, between glugs of lemonade, that the cousins began to tell their stories.

Their mothers were sisters and best friends and their two boys 'met when we were still on potties'. The upbringing was outwardly conventional – Eton and Oxford for clever Richard; Cirencester and the army for hearty Mike – but they filled as many idle days as possible with fishing, shooting, boozing and chasing debutantes.

And it seems they never quite broke the habit. Between them they have now clocked up not two marriages, not four nor five, but six – a gluttonous three apiece – and the strange part is that divorce seems to have left Mike, at least, with a tender longing for his former wives. 'Lovely girl. Very rich. Should never have left her. Still the best of friends,' he said wistfully about one.

Although both men came from landed families, they had to earn their living. 'Car washer, male model, second-hand car salesman in the East End,' said Richard, ticking off the jobs he got through in his early days. 'Then I decided I had better get respectable when a prospective mother-in-law asked me how much I earned.' That was how he began a high-flying career in the serious business of management consultancy, which was only interrupted when he inherited a near-bankrupt ancestral estate in Northern Ireland that his father had done his damndest to drink his way through. (Apparently that glamorous old rogue, the worse for wear and carrying a bagful of the family silver, was stopped one morning on a London street by a suspicious policeman. 'Who do you think you are and where do you think you going?' asked the officer. 'I am Sir John Heygate and I am on my way to Sotheby's,' retorted the baronet defiantly.)

On the outskirts of Londonderry wasn't the best place during the Troubles to be living as a landed toff. Although a few Heygate ancestors had been hung in earlier centuries by the English as traitors, the IRA more lately took their turn to trim the bloodline, murdering Richard's cousin when he popped into a republican drinking den in Londonderry for a quick one and was taken for an army spy. Still, Richard did his best to restore the ruinous Irish pile with its 50 leaking rooms, and established a very successful salmon-smokery, before selling up the lot and returning to safer embrace of consultancy.

Cousin Mike, meanwhile, after his time as a soldier, found himself flogging the fresh game that he had killed on his regular sporting forays to director's dining-rooms in the City, and from there he ultimately built up a posh-food wholesaling company with a vast fleet of delivery vans. After cashing out relatively young, he fell into partnership with an old friend of the family, a revered fishing writer named Hugh Falkus, and the two of them taught fly-casting courses and led fishing expeditions to pursue salmon in unheard of corners of the Russian Arctic. (Incidentally, I interrupted the reminiscences to ask Richard, on the quiet, how much of a bounder his cousin really is. 'Oh, one hundred per cent,' he replied, affectionately.)

But before anyone gets the idea that this is a pair of relentlessly bloodthirsty old Bufton-Tuftons, here's a few stray facts. Richard, who likes to boast that on his curriculum vitae that he is descended on one side of the family from Celtic kings and on the other from the leading Victorian collector of Georgian pornography, doesn't shoot. In fact, he hates the sport: 'It's slaughtering and I don't like slaughtering. I did shoot rabbits a bit when I was in Ireland, and one day I shot one and it disappeared down its hole and screamed with pain and after that I never shot again.'

Mike shoots, all right, and claims on his own CV: 'He has shot since he was six years old when he was given his first air rifle. This, however, was immediately confiscated as his first target was his nanny's bottom on which he scored a direct hit at forty yards.' But he is even more scrupulous than his cousin in his own way. 'It is not really the conventional driven-bird stuff that I am about any more – I still love it, let's be honest – but I much prefer the wild shooting and, more than anything else, wildfowling,' he said.

And what makes their tales in their book such a treat is that the pair not only ransacked their long memories and old game books for anecdotes but actually went out on the road together last year for the best part of three months, travelling Britain, ferreting out old acquaintances – gamekeepers, gypsies, coal miners – and quizzing them about the secret ways of the countryside.

Thanks to this diligent pub-based research we learn about the inveterate Norfolk poacher, an old friend of Mike's, whose breathtaking record was to have poached 11 large fallow deer in a single day from the Holkham estate in Norfolk, belonging to the Earl of Leicester, and smuggled them back to his tiny cottage in a neighbouring village. What is more, he did it under the eyes of the estate's patrolling team of gamekeepers, who knew him all too well, with a subterfuge that in wartime would have made him a top secret agent. How? By dressing up as a woman pushing a giant old-fashioned pram, and bundling each freshly shot carcase into it, before trundling them slowly home one by one. 'Hah! Bloody brilliant,' puffed Mike, brimming with admiration.

It is not just terrific sporting history they have unearthed but social and natural history, too, of the kind that the school curriculum really ought to find a place for. One interview with an old Yorkshire miner reveals that when he began his working life 'every miner had a knowledge of birds and every pit had its own caged birds' society. It was a question of survival. The miners experimented with different breeding stock to find which one was best at showing the first signs of gas down mine. It was highly competitive and it gave us all an interest in the countryside.' He also tells, incredibly, how his school had a farm where every pupil had to kill their own turkey for Christmas.

But my favourite story of all is the one Mike tells about his duck-shooting expedition, on a sewage farm on the old East German border during the Cold War, when he was a young soldier in the Green Jackets. It is a wonderful account and illustrates better than I have heard the true sportsman's golden rule that you must never abandon wounded quarry – a rule much more sacrosanct to the Bounder than marriage vows or the laws of the land.

The story starts with him snatching a shot at a mallard at twilight and seeing it fall on a distant corner of the sewage farm. 'Like so much of Berlin in those days, the land was divided by the wire of segregation that ran between West and East and was patrolled by the East German Volkspolizei (Vopos) who had orders to shoot on sight any unauthorised person near the wire. My duck now lay injured on the wrong side. It was, at least, a very black night. I left my gun and cartridges against a tussock and crawled towards the wire . . .' The story ends with the Vopos firing a flare and a shot, but not before the young soldier has sprinted back to the West, slithering under the wire, duck in hand. Breathless stuff.

The Bart and the Bounder can never be accused of earnestness but in their research they did stumble on a significant hidden truth. Rural writers from Hardy, through Chesterton and Betjeman have taught us to accept with mournful certainty that we are seeing the final passing of a rural race along with their way of life. But have you noticed how this 'inevitable' dwindling has been going on for an awfully long time now, and still the supply of countrymen hasn't dried up? Anyone who remembers the great massed marches through London against the fox-hunting ban a few years ago will never forget the sight of those endless surging thousands of strong-boned, big-lunged men and women who fitted every rural stereotype.

'The English countryside is so magical that it makes new countrymen every generation, and the new countrymen are in every way as much a part of the country as those of 100 years ago. You don't have to be born there to be one of them; only find a way of enjoying it when you live there,' concluded Richard. Country people are not really an endangered species at all, and they will never die out – or at least not until England's very last green acre goes under concrete.

It is even possible, then, that the next generation will throw up a pair of exuberant aberrations like the Bart and the Bounder. Lord, help us.

24 February 2001
The Joys of Puntgunning
Jonny Beardsall

This is a big adventure. Squinting down the barrel of a puntgun, I am lying face down, freezing, in the bottom of a wooden punt, my left shoulder jammed under the gunwales, my right fist grasping the ludicrously simple toggle on a length of string which, when I yank it, will fire this king-size cannon.

Flat-out behind me, the helmsman, Mark Johnson, grits his teeth, working the rudder and a weighted 5ft pole with his bare forearm in the icy water, meeting the waves bow first as we come about stealthily and drift towards a large 'pack' of teal tottering on a mud bank in Cooper's Creek, three miles out in the Blackwater estuary, in Essex.

In its heyday in the 1800s, when there were no wildlife laws, puntgunning was a commercial operation supplying game markets. It was not until the 20th century that it became a field sport – but one that has never drawn a large following.

Johnson puts the number of active puntgunners in this country at no more than a dozen, who also operate on the Dee, the Solway and in The Wash.

Closing in on the unsuspecting birds, I turn my head a fraction, catching Johnson's eye. At 70 yards, we are in range when, suddenly, the birds begin to peel off the water's edge. 'Now,' he barks.

There is one big bang as a blue flash and then an orange flame burst from the barrel end. A pall of black, stinking smoke sweeps back into my face, which, happily, I still have because I remembered to keep clear of the 6-inch recoil.

Grabbing cartridges, I wade into the mud with a 12-bore shotgun. Four birds lie dead on the bank, while Johnson picks up another dead bird drifting off in the current.

That, according to Johnson, was the 'perfect punt shot'. Some birds were in the air, some were on the mud and some on the edge of the water when I fired.

Six birds is, for him, a satisfactory tally. The allure of puntgunning is in pitting yourself against a wild quarry on its own territory. It's about handling the boat, coping with the elements, the tides and the ballistics, while paddling close enough to the birds to take a shot without them scarpering prematurely.

'The thrill is that few other people do it,' grins Johnson, a director of a stonemasonry company in London, who has been puntgunning since he was 17. 'The drawback is that, because this gun is so big, everyone thinks you slaughter hundreds of ducks – which, as you have seen, is utter rubbish. You could shoot far more duck with a 12-bore. My average is four – half a dozen is brilliant. It's just a good day out on the river.

'I grew up here, so I'm drawn to the marshes. I enjoy the solitude. You won't see another soul out here.'

So who, I wonder, is that chap over there?

Frowning, Johnson raises his binoculars. Half a mile away, 75-year-old Mike Townsend is also at action stations – conditions today are too good to miss.

Dan Fairman is of this opinion, too. He had launched his 130-year-old punt alongside us at first light, so the estuary's three puntguns are all out on this overcast morning.

Leaving the boathouse at Maldon in darkness at 6.45 a.m., I discovered that one of my waders has a leak.

'Get your hands wet now and you won't feel the cold later on,' Johnson had advised, as we bailed out the punt with a sponge and steered the craft through the muddy shallows. Real puntgunners don't wear gloves.

His sea-going punt is 20 feet long and, like the gun, was built in 1986. The design was, he admits, 'heavily lifted' from the drawings of Colonel Peter Hawker, who wrote the definitive work on the sport in the late 18th century. The frame is oak and iroko, with a solid lump of oak in the bow section, and the decking is made of marine plywood. It is designed so that the stresses of the recoil are absorbed along its length.

Mounted between two metal gun trunnions, the 8ft weapon is secured by two pre-stretched ropes with 10 tons breaking strain, which run in a continuous loop around the bow.

'Every action has a reaction,' says Johnson. 'If you've got three tons coming back, then you've got three tons going forward . . . Without the ropes, the gun would throw itself into the water.'

Johnson rows for half a mile, where we halt on a mud bank to load the gun. There is a slight breeze and ice is forming on the bows. He unscrews and removes the breech plug, inserts the cartridge – 18oz of tungsten matrix shot with 3oz of black powder – and replaces the plug and mounts the breech. 'I make all my own cartridges, it's £15 a bang,' he says.

We scrub all the mud from the decking, painted battleship grey so that it will merge with the water, before Johnson picks up his two oars. Rowing is a one-man operation, but it keeps frostbite at bay, so gunners and helms do swap around.

'I prefer to helm, it's far more skilful because you must keep the punt close in to the bank and your angle of approach has to be spot on,' Johnson had said, as he watched me thrash about in the slob – the mud – picking up the birds.

'If you do get stuck, don't lean backwards, just keep moving forwards. Don't stop or you'll be stuck fast.

'A friend gave me a fright a few weeks ago when he sank up to his mid-thighs. I managed to pull him out of his waders and into the punt.

'You won't disappear, but the incoming tide could drown you.'

If you don't count the mud, sinking in deep water or getting lost in fog, the biggest danger in puntgunning is ice in the barrel. On a day like today, water slopping up and down the barrel can freeze and cause a breech explosion. 'That's when people die. Getting your head blown off is not unknown,' says Johnson.

1 December 2011

Pupil's Tears as 'Birdwatching' Trip Turns Out to Be a Duck Shoot

John Bingham

After waving his daughter off on a school 'wildfowling' trip, Ray Poolman expected her to return filled with the joys of a day spent birdwatching on the Cambridgeshire fens.

But he had not understood that wildfowling is rural shorthand for waterfowl hunting. Danielle Pooling, 10, arrived home in floods of tears after being taken along to a duck shoot.

Yesterday Mr Poolman criticised the school for putting his daughter through the 'harrowing' experience, and for not making the purpose of the trip clear to parents.

'I sent her off in the morning with a little chair and a pair of binoculars to view the birds. We thought it was birdwatching and she thought it was birdwatching,' he said. 'She wasn't expecting anyone to shoot ducks. It turned out to be a very harrowing trip for her.'

The school defended the excursion, part of a series of initiatives to teach the children about fenland traditions, and said the 'first-hand knowledge' was a 'fantastic experience' for children.

Parents of year-six pupils at Ashbeach primary school in Ramsey St Mary's, Cambridgeshire, received a letter earlier this month inviting their children on a visit to Welney Marshes in Norfolk, organised by Ely and District Wildfowlers' Association.

It said that children would be 'finding out about different species of wildfowl' in the wetlands and 'conservation of the landscape'.

It made no direct reference to shooting or guns but went on to refer to seeing dogs and 'equipment used for the sport' and reassured parents that the children would be safely out of the way during the 'wildfowling demonstration'.

'It talks about going to the Welney Marshes and seeing an "evening flight", which you would think would be birds all coming back in to roost, which probably looks nice, and seeing all the different species that inhabit the marshes,' said Mr Poolman, 49, a keen fisherman.

He added: 'This isn't about being anti-bloodsports or anti-shooting; this is about saying, "If you are going to do this with children the parents must know."

'The letter should have had words like shooting and live ammunition and made clear that birds could be killed, then a parent can make an informed decision. They allowed children to witness the death of an animal. Ramsey might be rural but we have a Tesco – people don't need to walk around killing animals to survive any more.'

Shirley Stapleton, the head teacher, said there appeared to have been a misunderstanding.

'This trip has run for several years. Parents were welcome to come on the trip,' she said. 'The children came back and no child told me that they were distressed. It is not just "let's go out and shoot ducks"; there is a whole conservation issue which the school deals with.'

She explained that the trip was part of a programme of events to educate the children about their rural heritage.

Next month children are due to take part in the village's Plough Monday traditions, dressing up as 'ploughwitches' and Molly Dancers and leading a straw bear through the streets.

'We try to provide the children with an awful lot of background knowledge which maybe other schools don't do,' she said. 'There is a lot of first-hand knowledge for the children. They have had some fantastic experiences. It is just disappointing that on this occasion it seems that we have upset a parent totally unintentionally.'

6 August 2005
Plenty to Grouse About
Jonathan Young

Elton John playing at your cousin's Krug-soaked wedding? Sorry. A week's cruising on Roman Abramovich's yacht? Still no good. A cosy weekend with Cherie at Chequers? Oh, come on.

No, if you want to cut it socially next week, you had better be boiling in tweeds, covered in spaniel hairs and grouse shooting on Friday – the Glorious Twelfth. Rather than Pimm's-sipping pretenders, you will probably meet piles of proper aristocrats with bloodlines stretching back to some Norman hoodlum, assorted multimillionaires and their intimate circle. And, this year, that circle is very intimate indeed, because red grouse numbers are expected to be at their lowest for 20 years.

But more of that later. First the good news. *Lagopus lagopus scoticus* is unique to the British Isles. It is actually a subspecies of the willow grouse. But while the willow grouse is sprinkled throughout the Arctic tundra, with local hunters bagging a brace or two, its red cousin is usually numbered in the hundreds of thousands. Here, they thrive on moors where the heather is managed to give them food and shelter, and the keeper protects them from fox, rat, stoat and crow.

The result is the most exciting game-shooting in the world, concentrated on 459 grouse moors in Britain covering 3.5 million acres. It is also the most expensive. The privilege of shooting a brace of driven grouse will cost you £150, so an average day's grouse shooting, bagging 150 brace, is £22,500 split between eight guns.

Grouse command these princely sums because they don't fly like other birds. They rocket along at 60mph, reaching 90mph with a following wind, skimming the hills' contours with the accuracy of a Cruise missile. Aeons of conflict with their major predator, the peregrine falcon, has taught them to stay low, a few feet above the heather, denying the falcon the air space needed for its death-dealing stoop from the clouds.

Hidden in the grouse butts, your head well down, you see the grouse hurtle towards you like a Roger Federer first serve on Centre Court. 'No matter how many times you are lucky enough to shoot driven grouse, your heart is still thumping,' says Lord James Percy. 'The wait is almost too much to bear. Might you get a shot? Will you see the grouse in time? And then it happens. On tilted wings, a pack of maybe 50 grouse scud in front of you, inches from the heather tops, coming towards you at 90mph. In one fluid movement, you raise your gun, fire at the outside bird and watch it crumple into the heather.'

With James Percy, this happens pretty often. Most of the year, he designs Barbour coats. Come autumn, he and his brother, the Duke of Northumberland, form the dreaded Percy Sandwich, which isn't a three-in-a-bed, although lesser grouse shots wish it were. It means you have both Percy brothers either side of your grouse-butt and precious little is going to get past them. Perfect gentlemen, they will never poach the bird heading your way, but will happily (and usually unfailingly) dispatch those you miss.

The Percy brothers are part of a gifted band of top-flight grouse shots that include Hugh van Cutsem, Earl Peel, the Duke of Norfolk and Sir

Edward Dashwood. No matter how tough the birds, they will shoot an average of two grouse for five shots, more when hitting top form. Using two guns, with a man loading, they regularly kill four grouse in front of the butt and a fifth behind.

It is a performance akin to Tiger Woods at the Open or Michael Schumacher at the Monaco Grand Prix. Which can be pretty awe-inspiring when you shoot grouse like me.

Last season, on a hail-lashed day in late October, great packs of birds were being pushed along by a force-eight gale. My neighbour and I were in a dip in the moor, giving a clear horizon of just 30 yards. The drive ended with a handful of birds lying behind us and a Himalayan foothill of empty cartridge cases at our feet. Our ranking as c-list guests was confirmed.

So how do you become a great grouse shot? The simple answer is practice: many of the top guns shoot 100 days a season, on grouse, partridges and pheasants. But you have to have the invitations in the first place.

The short cut is to go to a shooting school. The best ones – the Royal Berkshire, Holland and Holland, West London and E.J. Churchill – have simulated grouse layouts that can ping grouse-like clays at you all day long. The Royal Berkshire has a particularly fiendish one.

'We pride ourselves on replicating tough October grouse, using a mix of different clay targets,' says its director, Dylan Williams. 'You have to get your footwork right and address the bird properly, as you would if you were playing golf or tennis. If you don't and you're trying to shoot an 80mph grouse, you're stuffed.'

Sir Edward Dashwood says: 'Always try to shoot four barrels in front, rather than turn around. That way, you don't have to move your feet and the grouse fly headfirst into the shot, giving an instant kill. But the first shot has to be a very long way in front. Watch Ralph and James Percy shoot. Nearly every bird falls in front of their butts.'

But if your shooting is still more Billie Piper than Billy the Kid, how else do you get on a grouse moor? Being a lucky sperm is the classic route. Most grouse moors are inherited.

Or you can marry one. The story about the keen shooting man asking his daughter to come off the pill the moment she met a grouse-moor heir is only just apocryphal.

Then, of course, there is creeping. In a sporting lodge in Yorkshire, a cushion lies very prominently on the drawing-room sofa. Embroidered on it is the legend: 'I never knew I had so many friends till I bought a grouse moor.'

'Grouse make tarts of us all,' says Sir Max Hastings. Watching big-moor owners enter a room is a revelation: grown-up tycoons go gooier than a pre-teen meeting a boy band.

If that doesn't work, you can always buy your own moor. Jonathan Kennedy, of CKD Kennedy Macpherson, is the world's leading grouse-moor agent. 'When you buy a grouse moor, you're buying into the exclusive rights to the ultimate sport,' he says. 'The purchasers are always self-made individuals who have experienced the thrill of the day on the moor and appreciate the wild nature of their quarry; the fact that there are good years and bad and the interaction with a vibrant, local community, often headed by their gamekeeper. And a top grouse-shooting invitation will attract friends from all over the world and postponement of that "unmissable" board meeting. It's that special.'

It certainly carries a special price tag. Three first-class North Yorkshire moors – Muggleswick, East Allenheads and Wemmergill – reputedly fetched £7 million, £10 million and £6 million respectively when they came on the market in the past couple of years, the last on a 30-year lease.

Having bought the acres, you then have to run them. Costs vary with the size of the moor, but a top moor is going to cost at least £200,000 a year, for an asset that might only produce good sport for two or three years in five.

So why does anyone bother buying one, when they could make better investments and just buy their shooting by the day? 'A good question,' says Simon Bostock, the custodian of an 8,000-acre moor in North Yorkshire and the chairman of the Moorland Association, a group representing owners. 'Taking good years with bad, a moor would do well to return three per cent on annual capital expenditure, assuming all shooting was let on a commercial basis. Which isn't special, but my moor is one of the great loves of my life, my reason to get up in the morning. If you just want to shoot grouse and pay by the day, you would be enormously welcome. Paying guns keep the whole thing ticking.

'But if you want to immerse yourself in the entire ethos of the moor, leasing or buying one allows you to become really involved in the community.'

That involvement, says the shooting lobby, brings real local benefit.

In the north Pennines and North Yorkshire last season, there were very strong populations of grouse, with 10 moors breaking their all-time records.

The Moorland Association surveyed 25 estates in these areas and found 'that they had held 522 shooting days of which 284 were let, pulling in £2,893,534 of revenue to be put back into moorland management – a rare habitat supporting important bird-life. Benefits to the local rural economy included 3,704 bed-nights in hotels, pubs and bed & breakfasts, worth £648,690 to rural-accommodation providers. Just under 18,000 local man-days were bought in, lining local pockets to the tune of £629,979 in the north Pennines and North Yorkshire alone.'

The advantages to wildlife are even more marked. The government recognises this. Last year, Ben Bradshaw, the minister for local environment, marine and animal welfare, visited a grouse moor in Weardale. 'I saw for myself the enormous all-year-round effort that moorland keepers put into managing the habitat for red grouse,' he said. 'This management has huge benefits for a range of important and rare wildlife – for example, merlin, lapwing, curlew and black grouse. It also maintains a globally rare landscape, while boosting the rural economy – particularly in some of England's remotest areas.'

The only body that seems to have a problem with grouse moors is the RSPB. The issue is hen-harriers, a protected species that, if allowed to breed unchecked, eat grouse to the point where grouse moors are no longer viable.

The ongoing debate is an unhelpful distraction for moor owners, who are more worried about the coming season, which is forecast as a disaster. Dr David Baines, the Game Conservancy Trust's director of upland research, and a world authority on red grouse, has just finished counting grouse on two estates. 'I've never seen anything like it,' he says. 'The situation on one moor was abysmal. The other was worse. Grouse were dying from strongylosis in January and they're dying now. With so many moors going down in the same areas at the same time, it will be difficult for some to repopulate.'

The cause was the mild and damp winter, producing 'optimum breeding conditions for the worms' larvae', according to Dr Baines.

But Earl Peel, the owner of Grinton moor, isn't downhearted. 'We've had four or five exceptional years and, if you have these vast numbers of grouse, disease becomes inevitable.'

The red grouse, it seems, faces an uncertain future. So don't hesitate. Buy a day. Marry a millionaire. Become a demon shot. But do it while you can.

14 February 1998
Cost of a Pheasant Day Out
Tom Tickell

Up goes a guinea, bang goes sixpence and down comes a shilling. That still sums up the wacky economics of shooting game birds, just as much as it did before decimalisation when a shotgun cartridge could be purchased for sixpence.

Estates with good shooting certainly do not come cheap but the costs of ensuring pheasants, partridge, quail or grouse are there on cue for the guns in season are also very high. You will need gamekeepers, tied cottages and a host of paraphernalia to have any chance of making things come right.

Buying an estate is bound to leave you facing a seven-figure bill, according to Mark McAndrew who specialises in traditional country properties for estate agents Strutt & Parker. He said: 'Whatever happens, you will need a property with at least 500 acres around it for serious shooting.

'A small estate in the south, say somewhere like Gloucestershire or Wiltshire, with a house, a couple of cottages and perhaps 800 acres, will cost between £2m and £3m. Costs may be marginally lower in Yorkshire, but even in Scotland you will not usually get back much change from £2m. Perhaps you might find an estate in Scotland for as little as £1.5m, but you'd be lucky.' Prices at the other end of the market can be astronomical. One 1,700-acre estate, Newhouse, in Hampshire, has just gone on the market at £9m, and estate agents FPD Savill claim they have no doubt they will get it.

Once you have your estate, new bills arrive. Some are standard, whatever birds you shoot. Almost everyone will employ at least one gamekeeper and perhaps more. Wages, at least in the south, work out at around £20,000 a year and owners normally supply a cottage, rent-free, as part of the package.

Keepers will need a four-wheel vehicle, and even the Toyota trucks cost around £12,000 when they are new. Admittedly, some keepers use Honda Quadbikes, with a feed sprayer attached at the back for pheasants. But usually that supplements your four-wheel drive car, rather than replacing it.

No one buys grouse, for you cannot rear them. Although they live on moorland, people do not put out food for them. Pheasants are very different. People buy them as day-old chicks at around £1 each, though you can get them as six-week-old 'poults' at £2.30 a head.

Shooting dates vary. The grouse season starts on the glorious twelfth – 12 August – and lasts until 10 December. The season for pheasants lasts from 1 October to 31 January, but the number of days shooting is much lower. 'The size of your estate and the number of birds you have will decide how many days shooting you have a year,' said Philip Hope-Cobbold, who owns the Glenham Hall estate in Suffolk and is a keen shot. 'If you have 800 acres, you will probably only shoot six to 10 days a year. Even on a 3,000-acre estate, you won't usually go shooting for more than 30 days a year. Most game birds don't get shot anyway. In practice you shoot a third, let a third survive for breeding stock, and lose a third to predators.'

Figures for each days' bag vary enormously. But you could end up with 200 birds on a 3,000-acre estate, assuming you had eight guns. How much will they be worth? Not a lot at the butchers will often be the answer where, for example, four pheasants could be bought in Highgate, north London, this week for £10. Bear in mind that compares with a cost of £2.30 each when they were just six weeks old.

By far the best hope of gaining a substantial return on capital tied up in the estate is to let it out. Mark Firth, of Roxton Bailey Robinson, specialises in letting shooting rights and reckons everything depends on the type of country. 'If you let out an estate which provides really good terrain for pheasants with deep wooded valleys, you can charge £25 for each bird shot, and your client will pay VAT on top. Figures on less attractive shoots may be only £15 a head,' he said. If the shoot bags 200 pheasants a day on a good estate you can end up with £5,000. But, given very high running costs and a narrow season, few landowners do more than go some way towards cutting their costs. It's certainly no pot of gold.'

Alternatively, if you invite friends to shoot your game birds each guest will normally take away a brace of birds – and owners certainly will not get fat on the proceeds from sale.

Butcher Kennard, the game specialist in the City's Leadenhall market, was selling a brace of pheasant, plucked drawn and ready to eat, at £6 a brace. The price owners selling to the trade receive is even lower.

'This year, people have collected around 60p per bird, or £1.20 a brace,' said Philip Hope-Cobbold. 'Prices overall have been kept down by a flood of game birds coming in from Eastern Europe, but things are beginning to improve. Worries over BSE and pressure for natural foods have made game birds more popular.'

People who are tempted to buy and run shooting estates for profit should remember the City advice for those considering investing in commodity futures: lie down in a darkened room and wait for the feeling to go away. Owning these estates is usually a licence to lose money. But most owners are wealthy enough to ensure that – in this context, if not in their business interests elsewhere – concerns of profit and loss are not high on their agenda.

16 April 1995
Squirrels Fair Game for the Table
Andrew Morgan

It may not have the seasonal symbolism of lamb, or the traditional taste of wild boar or venison. But another animal is joining the butcher's game racks. Squirrel.

In Sussex, grey squirrels are now being sold for meat. They are shot by Graham Woods, a gamekeeper at Petley Farm who was concerned that they were over-running ancient woodland near Battle, attacking thrush nests and eating food intended for the farm's deer herd.

Mr Woods started shooting squirrels three years ago after he came across a thrush's nest being attacked. 'Thrush numbers are low in the area but a grey squirrel was sitting on the edge of the nest eating a chick alive,' he recalls. At first, I thought nature should run its course. But I soon realised that all the nests were being raided and few thrushes were left.'

Grey squirrels are not a protected species, unlike the native red, which they have largely displaced from most of Britain this century. In the first year of culling Mr Woods shot 200, and the quality of the 250-strong deer herd improved with the availability of more nuts. Mr Woods passes the squirrels on to Jim Good, who owns the deer farm and runs its shop.

He started selling them 'oven-ready' after a friend – a US Army major – came back with eight after a foray on the farm. Skinned and cooked, they were presented to Mr Good for tasting.

'I was terrified at first, but after a few drinks I thoroughly enjoyed it,' he says. 'It seemed a good addition to the game menu, particularly in the autumn when they are fat on nuts.'

According to Mr Good, a squirrel makes a meal for two and costs £1.50. The leg resembles that of a pheasant, with the same amount of meat and little fat. Mr Good finds it tender and full of flavour, somewhere between chicken and pheasant.

Meanwhile, squirrel damage to trees has declined at Petley Farm, and the relative abundance of nuts means there are fewer deer fatalities through malnutrition.

'Controlling squirrels is both helping the local environment and providing interesting food,' adds Mr Good. 'It's a balanced exercise all round.' Except, perhaps, for the squirrels.

26 June 1982
Rook Pie Upset for RSPCA

Rook pie on the menu of the Crown Inn, Uploders, Dorset, has upset the RSPCA. The licensees, Mrs and Mrs Robin Upton, pay village lads 20p a time to shoot fledgling rooks with air-guns.

'Shooting small game is quite acceptable by skilled marksmen but shooting by boys whose proficiency might be questionable could result in injured birds dying a lingering death,' said an RSPCA inspector. 'In certain circumstances it might be against the law.'

22 October 2005
The Silent Killers
Jocasta Shakespeare

On a Saturday night, around the fireside at the Hare and Hound pub, a dozen lurchers and eight hunters settle down to pints of Absolution: 8 per cent proof home-brewed ale. At the centre of a circle sits a man

in a leather jerkin with a whetting stone. The scene could be from the
18th century. From dark corners faces glow, intent on the stories passing
around. Field knives are passed up: short blades that catch the firelight.
But these seasoned hunters are no longer allowed to use them on dog-
killed quarry.

A 12lb hare in its white winter coat sits, stuffed, behind the bar:
'Chrissie was walking Jonas when he got that.' With this kind of dog,
bred for speed and intelligence, a little 'walk' can become legend. And
these dog enthusiasts will carry on venturing out regardless of the
hunting ban, which came into force in February. (It is now illegal to
hunt with more than two dogs and to kill fox, hare, mink, mouse and
squirrel with dogs.)

They hardly look like the urban 'antis' idea of hunters: there's
not a pink coat in sight, no classy uniform; just khaki outdoor gear,
heavy boots, jeans and hoods. Outside, there are no four-wheel drive
superwagons; just a few Transit vans and bashed Fords in the car park.
And while police, ahead of the new hunting season, which starts on
1 November, are already worrying about the difficulty of interfering in
illegal foxhunts, these men and their lurchers are likely to slip the net
entirely.

A single lantern marks this pub, on a long dark road to elsewhere,
and it is advisable not to wander in here unaccompanied. A lurcher (not
just any old dog) is the passport to this fireside. With every new entry,
faces swivel, talk is hushed and all eyes check the dog-zone (anything
from 14 to 30 inches above the ground). Comments may then be made
about the capabilities of the animal occupying this space. Here, the
drinkers don't only look like their animals, they are judged according to
their dogs' place in the pack. The landlord's two whippets occupy prime
position at the hearth.

When I take my lurcher, Pixie, to the Hare and Hound, the first
question is: 'Is that a toy or do you work her?' The next question is 'Do
you want to mate her?' Properly trained, lurchers are killing machines.
Properly trained, these dogs are beautiful weapons. Travelling at 30
miles per hour, they can run down a rabbit or a hare so that when the
dog has passed by, the bunny looks as if it's just lain down to sleep:
unbruised, warm, dead. Better perhaps than myxomatosis, which is each
September's curse.

On the walls hang pictures of dogs past and present. A bride
and groom, each holding a leashed lurcher, signifies the ultimate in

romance. Ferrets peep from oversized pockets and a local magazine is open on the page advertising the Blitz 800 metres beam torch used for 'lamping'. One recent visitor to the Hare and Hound was shocked to see air rifles being fired behind the bar. The Weihrauch .22 is a countryman's favourite.

Nor is the poachers' food for the faint-hearted. You may find jugged hare, squirrel or deer's liver on the menu, although tonight it's chicken. 'It's more exciting if it's illegal,' says one client of this 18th-century inn, which has always been a poachers' pub.

Lurchers have been used for centuries to catch illegal quarry. Just 100 years ago, a man could be fined on sight in Derbyshire merely for owning such a dog. Perhaps for this reason, lurchers don't bark. Centuries of illicit night-time hunting have made them silent.

The dogs sit quietly in the pub: sleek, muscled whippets and big, hairy deerhound crosses. They have been worked hard in the fields and are treated as equals, getting scraps and praise. Geoff's whippet is standing on the table, lapping ale from his glass. It's not a party piece. Other drinkers also offer the top of their pints to their dogs. Dog lines are discussed and wild stories told, the canine equivalent of fishing tales: 'My dog killed a cow . . .' It can get very red in tooth and claw.

The end of hare coursing, which is also banned under the new hunting law, is taken personally. 'It's dreadful, isn't it?' says Paul, in the voice he might use for a family death. Brought up a miner, he lived through the strike by running his dogs. 'We lived on rabbit during the strike. It's a good, healthy food. I bred my lurcher bitch and gave away the litter for free. People said they'd pay me when the strike was over. They never did. But we didn't starve.'

Local butchers still pay £1 for a gutted rabbit 'with its jacket on', but they won't buy a bruised rabbit, so the dog must have a 'soft' mouth and be able to kill – or bring the rabbit back alive – without leaving a mark. 'It's a quick death, compared with other ways.'

There are grey areas in the new law, however, which may be exploited. For instance, if a dog kills a hare accidentally, the owner will not be prosecuted. There might be a lot of accidents. 'We used to walk in a line, beat the hares up and slip two dogs on them. Now, we're still allowed to go rabbiting with two dogs, so we'll take along a ferret and two nets, as if we're out catching rabbits. Then if we kill any hares, we can claim they're "accidental".'

Others are less interested in subterfuge. At the Hare and Hound, they like things out in the open. On a Sunday morning, some still meet to run their dogs in the fields, often catching hares.

'Bugger the ban,' says Jack (black beard and a hangover). You don't have to be bloodthirsty to enjoy this sport and the beauty of these dogs in action. A three year-old collie/greyhound/saluki cross is zagging round the field, leaning like a 1000cc Suzuki bike as she takes a corner to zig back again and, without a sound, the hare drops. 'Some dogs just knock the bunny out. Bam! and it's dead.'

Someone suggests an alternative Waterloo Cup with hare coursing and untold pints of Absolution for the winning dog. 'We'll all chip in for the fine.'

16 December 2000

Yob Culture Extends Far into the Countryside

Graham Downing

Having seen one gang of intruders off the Cambridgeshire estate where he works as head gamekeeper, Richard Clarke thought he had overcome the local poaching problem. Then, a few days later, four men pulled up behind him in Newmarket High Street and beat him up. Since then, his fight against poachers has resulted in two more beatings and a war of attrition that has involved violence, theft and criminal damage.

'They drive over the winter corn and look around to see what's available to steal – diesel, farm tools, batteries, workshop equipment,' says Clarke. 'When there's a whole gang of them, they're brave enough to go just wherever they like.'

Clarke's story is not unusual. A survey to be published next week in *Shooting Times & Country Magazine* reveals the scale of poaching and the accompanying problems of theft and criminal damage in the countryside.

Questionnaires completed by 170 gamekeepers, most of them members of the National Gamekeepers' Organisation (NGO), reveal that 90 per cent had suffered from poaching in the past five years, and more than three quarters had suffered from repeated poaching, resulting in losses amounting to thousands of pounds. Their confidence in the police to deal with rural crime is low.

Home Office ministers may vow to cleanse Britain's streets of 'yob culture', but our fields, farms and villages face a growing wave of theft, vandalism and violence.

While poaching occurs throughout Britain, there are distinct regional variations. In Cambridgeshire and Essex, for example, illegal hare coursing is widespread. In parts of the south-west, the biggest problem is deer poaching, which was recorded by 36 per cent of gamekeepers responding to the survey. This is invariably done at night, usually with unsuitable weapons or with coursing dogs, sometimes resulting in horrific cruelty. Severed heads, feet and piles of entrails are left by the roadside, where animals have been butchered.

Though more than half the gamekeepers reported the loss of mature game birds, such as pheasant and partridge, there is a trend towards the theft of young stock and poults from rearing or release pens. As this tends to occur in early autumn, it suggests that stolen birds are being sold on to other shoots willing to turn a blind eye to cheap supplies of poults.

The scale of losses involved varies widely. A third of the game-keepers responding reported losses of less than £250, while half of them sustained losses totalling between £250 and £1,000. These, however, were overshadowed by major thefts such as the £20,000 of forestry equipment plus a brand new vehicle stolen two weeks ago from one Gloucestershire estate.

'Forget the romantic image of the poacher,' says Julian Murray-Evans, editor of *Shooting Times*, joint sponsor of the Rural Crime Survey. 'Today's poacher is an organised criminal. The poacher isn't just after game, he is often also a housebreaker and a vandal. And gamekeepers are the sharp end of their illegal activities. Working alone, in isolated places, keepers and their families routinely suffer broken arms, black eyes, smashed windscreens and worse at the hands of these rural thugs.'

The frustration of gamekeepers facing escalating crime, a dwindling rural police force and lengthening police response times is palpable.

'It may be between 45 minutes and an hour before I see a policeman,' said Eddy Graves, a Gloucestershire gamekeeper. 'I had my windscreen stove in by poachers while I was actually on the phone to the police, and it took them an hour to mobilise. By the time they had sent out the helicopter, a dog handler and five cars, the poachers had gone, and though they did make one arrest later, there was no conviction.'

Richard Clarke tells of a similar incident only last month. Having been punched in the face by a poacher, he followed the assailant's car for 40 minutes into the middle of Cambridge, calling 999 on his mobile phone as he did so. 'I was told there was no way they could help me stop that vehicle, and it took a policeman four days to come and take a statement. He said they couldn't trace the car, and when a farmer phoned me to say he had seen it in a gypsy camp, the police refused to go after it. We're living in a lawless society in the countryside.'

Even when police are present on the scene, they may be unable – or unwilling – to act. When one gamekeeper found a poacher's car bogged down in a field of winter wheat, he thought he had a guaranteed arrest. Yet, with the other exits to the field blocked by estate vehicles, the intruder was able to find a colleague to tow him off, past a waiting police car.' The policeman did nothing and drove off in the opposite direction. We were dumbfounded. Now I've heard that two more local police stations are closing.'

It is no surprise to hear that between 60 per cent and 70 per cent of gamekeepers rate the police response to poaching and associated criminal damage as either poor or useless. Many say they no longer bother to report incidents.

Yet this does not prevent keepers from working alongside the police in crime prevention initiatives. Most are involved in formal neighbourhood watch, poacher watch or farm watch schemes, in addition to their own informal network.

With police officers now so thinly spread across the countryside, rural people are increasingly reporting suspicious-looking strangers or vehicles to the local gamekeeper, and this in turn has helped to foil a whole range of rural crime, from fly-tipping to burglary.

More than ever, gamekeepers are assuming their traditional role as the eyes and ears of the countryside.

8 January 2000
Ground Control
Paula Minchin

'Smell this,' says Simon Lester, as he shoves what looks like a handful of grass under my nose. 'It's spearmint,' he adds, as I breathe in the faintly minty smell.

Simon, who is a gamekeeper on a traditional estate that covers more than 3,000 acres on the edge of the Forest of Dean in Gloucestershire, then reaches into his pocket and retrieves three shiny, dark brown sweet chestnuts, which he prised from their furry cases while feeding his pheasants that morning.

At 43, having worked on several lowland estates across the country, he is one of the most respected headkeepers in Britain and writes weekly about his job in *Shooting Times & Country Magazine*. But, like many others these days, he did not take a conventional route into the profession. In the past, young men followed their fathers and uncles into the job. Now, television engineer and rally driver are just two former occupations of working gamekeepers.

Simon grew up in the Nottinghamshire village of East Bridgford, where his mother encouraged him to press flowers and his grandfathers taught him to shoot and fish. At 21, he was a drummer in a punk band and living in London. However, the lure of the countryside was to prove too strong and within a year he was knocking on the door of gamekeeper Dick Skinner for work on the local estate.

Simon is also proof of the way the job has evolved over the past century – from a man in tweeds with a shotgun over his arm, who supposedly killed everything that moved in order to protect his precious game birds, to a kind of rural policeman, whose work to produce a good day's shooting for his employer benefits the countryside as a whole.

'In the past, less intensive farming and a lack of pollution meant that the habitat was good and game birds thrived in the wild. Gamekeepers were able to spend more time on predator control,' he says. 'Nowadays, we don't have such a good natural habitat, so it has to be created and maintained. We coppice trees, thin out and plant new woodland and maintain hedgerows so that all types of wildlife thrive. We also plant thousands of acres of game-cover crops. These crops, such as sunflower, quinoa and kale, provide food and shelter for game birds but also for many types of songbird.

'We also carry out a programme of predator control that gives more vulnerable species an opportunity to thrive. It's a question of balance.'

Later, while giving me a tour of the estate, with its deer park and herd of fallow deer, Simon points out some pink berries on a small tree. He picks one, then breaks it open to reveal a beautiful, bright orange seed inside. 'This is spindle,' he says. 'It's one of the prettiest wild fruits.' As we wind our way through the steep wooded valley that surrounds his house, it becomes clear that Simon can identify almost every tree, flower and plant on the estate. He indicates the thick carpet of dog's mercury, which is a sign of ancient woodland.

'I like to know that the creatures, plants, trees and flowers are thriving on the ground that I'm looking after,' he says.

Lack of knowledge about the countryside is a matter of increasing concern to Simon. Last year, disappointed by his YTS student's poor grasp of nature, he bought him a book about trees for Christmas. 'I think it's important for all gamekeepers to learn about what's around them.'

As we pass a release pen where hundreds of Simon's new strain of Kansas pheasants mingle under feed hoppers, looking for their next meal, his thoughts turn to the current shooting season. 'My job is to produce a given number of days' shooting for my employer, either on a private or a commercial basis. Towards the end of the pheasant shooting season, which ends on 1 February, we catch the excess hen birds and put them into laying pens. They start laying their eggs in April, the eggs are then incubated and hatched, and the rearing process starts.'

With modern incubators, hatches of more than 70 per cent are achievable. These days, rearing takes place under electric or gas heaters, rather than broody chickens.

The pheasant chicks are fed on a high-protein diet until they are six or seven weeks old. By this time, the heat in the rearing shed has been reduced and they are hardy enough to be released. The poults are transferred into large release sites of several acres, where they become acclimatised to life in the wild.

The main release time is July and although the pheasant shooting season officially starts at the beginning of October, most shoots don't begin until November, when the leaves are off the trees. During this time, the birds have to be fed and watered, protected from foxes and humans, as well as kept on the estate.

The shooting season lasts just four months and most estates shoot 42 per cent of the birds they put down. With hunting under threat, Tony Blair's promise that shooting and fishing are safe while he is in office has done little to convince Simon about the longevity of his profession.

Simon, like the majority of the estimated 3,000 full-time gamekeepers in the country, is a member of the National Gamekeepers' Organisation, which was established two years ago to promote and defend its members' way of life. The organisation shares Simon's concern over the public's lack of understanding about the countryside. It has just established a charitable trust which hopes, among other things, to educate children, not just about shooting but about the countryside as an entity.

'The majority of people expect the countryside to be there, but they don't appreciate the facts of management and the simple truth that nature can be cruel,' Simon says.

'People get emotional about foxes, badgers and birds of prey, but it's secretive creatures such as newts, voles and skylarks that they should be more concerned about.

'The belief that if we left the countryside alone it would have a natural balance is misguided. Mankind has already interfered too much with the natural habitat. We have created the landscape we are accustomed to and we need to look after it.'

6 July 1996
What a Song and Dance

Come, they said, and judge a singing competition. My heart sank. You know what it is with singing – those who can sing won't and those who will sing can't. I could imagine (since this was going to happen in Yorkshire) having to listen to 20 mangled versions of 'On Ilkla Moor Baht' at'.

'It's an inter-hunt competition and you can have a day's mink hunting as well,' said the voice. I perked up a bit and agreed. Hunting songs are different.

Mink hunting is also different. The destruction of mink is a good thing. These nasty little killers should not be in this country. Our revered Ministry of Agriculture, Fisheries and Food licensed their importation for fur farming. The animal rights loonies 'liberated' them and the creatures have since been gobbling up the indigenous wildlife of our ponds, streams and rivers.

Being riparian animals, the hunting of mink is conducted rather as otter hunting used to be. Hounds draw along riverbanks until they get a whiff of mink, then they work up to where the beast is lying (very often in a stick heap or among the tangled roots of a riverside bush) and the hunt is on.

About 100 people, including some rather bewildered looking Hell's Angels, gathered for the meet at the appointed hour – '10.30 for 11 at the Nameless Pub'. As there was no sign of any hounds, we all started trooping into the pub. A rather bleary man appeared behind the bar. 'How the hell did you lot get in?' he growled. This warm, traditional country greeting got the day off to a good start.

At noon there were still no hounds. The hunt secretary was explaining that the master and huntsman was rather 'navigationally challenged'. 'T'booger's still in bed, more like,' said an anonymous voice.

Mink hunting is a leisurely business. When the hounds eventually arrived, they started drawing slowly up the River Rye. These packs tend to be eclectic – some foxhounds, some hairy fox-otterhound crosses and some black-and-tan Dumfriesshire hounds. Nothing seemed to be happening, but it was a lovely day to stroll along a beautiful river in good company.

At last, below Brawby village, there was a great burst of hound voices. A mink was swimming in the muddy waters. Hounds caught that one quickly and there were two more on the go in the same area. These were also caught, to the obvious pleasure of the locals – with one exception. A woman from a newly smartened cottage was not gruntled. 'Incomers,' said a weathered farmer. 'They've probably been feeding the bloody things – they're daft enough.' They pull no punches in Yorkshire.

No more mink were found. The man who said that mink hunting is a bit like 'watching paint dry' was being a little unfair. The description of it as 'glorified rat hunting' might be more accurate, but then hunting rats can be good sport.

To Fadmoor village hall for the singing. Fadmoor is a pretty village on the edge of the North Yorkshire Moors. The hall was packed. There were five teams – Goathland, Sinnington, Old Ampleforth Beagles, Saltersgate (all local packs) and the Mink Hounds. My judge's fee for the evening was never to have an empty whisky glass – I never did.

Hunting and singing have always gone together. Some of the songs are very old, some new (including ones dealing with the political threats to hunting), but most tell of famous hounds, hunts and people.

Each hunt had a team of three singers who sang one song apiece, and there were some truly wonderful voices. The audience listened, then joined in the choruses *con gusto*. There were sad songs ('The Horn of the Hunter'), funny songs ('The Little Brown Dog' – modern, and a new one on me – and 'Joe the Carrier's Lad'), plus hound songs ('Dido, Bendigo'; 'Old Snowball'). You will not hear any of them on karaoke night. These are the songs of the indigenous country people.

This being Yorkshire, there was a 'grand feed' after the stern business of the contest. Then it was best of order again and we all sang and, by heck, come 1am the roof was lifting. It is a grand thing is a good shout – that and a whisky glass on automatic refill.

Oh yes, I almost forgot. The Goathland won.

30 October 2010

Was the Emperor of Exmoor's Death Quite What it Seemed?

Charles Moore

It was Jim Naughtie, on the *Today* programme on Tuesday, who set the nation's moral tone. 'It is an appalling thing,' he said, throwing all BBC impartiality to the wind, 'if you like wild animals.'

Naughtie was reporting the death of the Emperor of Exmoor, a huge stag. The Emperor's reign was brief. He was so named by a photographer, Richard Austin, and introduced to the public in the current rutting season. The picture sold everywhere. Then, three weeks ago, the beast was shot. For some reason, the news took a long time to break. When it did so, we heard a lot from Johnny Kingdom, a sort of Crocodile Dundee of Exmoor, who has a television series on the way. A trophy-hunter 'from abroad, probably Europe', might have paid £10,000 for the head, apparently. The evil deed was quickly denounced across the world.

By Thursday, however, people were beginning to ask questions. Early stories had been full of those phrases we journalists use when we don't know what we are talking about – 'it is claimed', 'rumours have been circulating'. Slightly more rigour now entered the reporting. Would any named person say that he had seen the beast shot? No. You cannot easily cart away a 300lb corpse. If the stalker had left the body and escaped with the head, crows circling the carcass would have identified its presence.

So there is, as yet, no body.

Perhaps there was no death. Is the Emperor, like King Arthur, not dead, but somehow occulted, waiting to return? Some other things have been said that do not quite stand up. The Emperor is 'certain', according to Mr Kingdom, to be the son of Bruno, another famously fine beast from the district, shot 12 years ago. In fact, it is impossible, without DNA testing, to tell who is the father.

The Emperor was also said to be the largest wild mammal in Britain. This is not true. There are bigger stags in Thetford Forest. Nor is it true that His Imperial Majesty, if indeed he was assassinated, was taken much before his time.

Devonian deer managers tell me that, by the look of him, he might have lasted one more season before 'going back'.

And although the Emperor was/is a magnificent specimen, Lord Pearson of Rannoch, one of the nation's red deer experts, assures me that, judging from photographs, the lower 'points' on his antlers are 'fairly weak' and do not have the balanced shape of 'brow, bay and tray' of the perfect specimen.

Nor, by the way, is the Emperor even from Exmoor. He was killed – if he was – near Rackenford, several miles outside the national park. In short, the story is an inverted pyramid of piffle.

Whose interest, then, did it serve, apart from helping sales of Mr Austin's photographs and ratings for Mr Kingdom's programmes? The answer, I suggest, is the desire, deep in the puritan character, to get self-righteously angry about animals.

Let us assume that the Emperor is, indeed, no more. What, exactly, was, as the Rev Dr Naughtie put it, 'appalling' about shooting him? It is not wrong, in general, to kill a deer. They are wild animals with no natural predators in these islands. If they are not shot, they die of natural causes, most commonly of malnutrition. Their welfare is served by killing a percentage of them, because if they grow too numerous, their quality declines and they do too much damage to agriculture, forestry and habitat. If you do not kill a few, there will come a time when you will need to kill a lot, or let them starve.

So you are left with the 'How could you . . . ?' line. 'How could you be so cruel as to kill such a beautiful thing?' As someone who has shot stags quite often, I have sometimes felt sad about it, a feeling which tends to grow as one gets older. But it is not crueller to kill a stag, which is beautiful, than a rat, which isn't. This is a matter of human taste, not of kindness to animals. The person with the fine head on his wall will believe himself to be conferring an honoured immortality on the beast shot. Personally, I am not interested in trophies, but I cannot see that he is morally wrong.

Is it down to money, then? Opinion polls suggest that people agree that 'professionals' should be paid to put down wild animals, but that it is wicked for amateurs to pay to do so. But why is human pleasure in the hunt so frowned on? Men's relationship with wild animals is complex. Throughout history, many of those who have known and liked them the best have enjoyed killing them. This is a fact worth thinking about.

It is particularly illuminated by the case of Exmoor. There, unlike in Scotland, where stalking is part of the rural economy, shooting deer is frowned on. This is because of the hunt, which has long been seen as a 'social compact'. Farmers, often people with very small amounts of land, have consented to have deer managed by hunting with hounds, not by shooting. It is mutual: they let the hunt go on their land; in return, the hunt keeps the deer numbers in balance. Money does not change hands.

Exmoor's – dare I call it – 'Big Society' approach has come under strain with the hunting ban. Under that preposterous law, the hunts can go out with only two hounds. This has reduced their scope. As a result, the social compact has weakened. Farmers have become more likely to take money to shoot the deer (and sell the meat) instead. Such people are known as 'poachers' on Exmoor, even when they are shooting legally, because they are seen as breaking the social compact. The number of the stags in the district is falling (408 this year, compared with 462 in 2003, just before the ban). It is the hunting ban that makes the shooting of beasts like the Emperor more likely.

The most moving novel about the life and death of a wild animal is *The Story of a Red Deer*, by J.W. Fortescue. It is set on Exmoor. In its final scene, the great stag is chased by hounds into the river. The reader longs for him to escape. The stream sings to him, inviting him to its waters:

Nay, raise not your head, come, bury it here;
No friend like the stream to the wild Red-Deer.

He obeys, and drowns nobly.

You might think that Fortescue hated the hunt. No. In his preface, he says he is telling the story 'even as the deer have told it to me in . . . many a stirring chase, and as they have told it to all others that would listen'. Somewhere behind this muddled tale of the Emperor lies something to which more people should, indeed, be listening.

3 July 1994
Killing Fields Along Country Roads
Byron Rogers

The day begins with a soft clunk, and it is a familiar and a horrible sound. One minute the little hare is sitting in the middle of the road in sunlight and I have plenty of time to slow down and pity the frantic darts which take her to the side and the sanctuary of the undergrowth. But then at the last minute she bursts out of this at a right angle. Clunk.

When you move to the country nothing prepares you for the hecatomb which is there each morning in the roads; the flies, by 10 o'clock busy in the eye sockets of a big boar badger. The earth-mover claws have curled as if in sleep but as I put my foot under the body to roll it to the verge I am again struck by the weight. A man with a hangover must somewhere be rehearsing the lies he will tell to his insurance company.

Weekends are the worst, for then you encounter the entire catalogue: foxes, rabbits, pheasants, hedgehogs as flat as dusters. I usually stop, for it is only on television documentaries and in road deaths on the way to Waitrose that most of us in the country see wildlife now. In time, everyone kills something, and the killing is often not complete.

I hit a rabbit and in the driving mirror saw it turn on its shattered stumps, like a child drawing circles in the road. Another car had also stopped so I had to finish the killing watched by a smiling man in a cricket sweater. Please, do not let me make a mess of this . . . I took the rabbit home and skinned it while it was still warm; it felt like putting on a lately worn glove.

'Best time to skin a rabbit,' brooded Colin King, the village butcher in Silverstone. He was watching the cliffs of steel and carbon monoxide hurtling past his window on the A43 to Oxford. His shop is on one side of this, the village on the other; the traffic runs between them like Niagara and you cannot see daylight between the lorries. 'I have to admire anyone who actually makes it to my shop,' he said.

The game I knock down I always pick up, which according to country tradition is against the law. The man who comes along next, he can pick up the rabbit or a pheasant, but not you; otherwise, it was explained to me, we should all go hunting in Sierras. I have just checked with the Northampton police, who assure me that this is indeed the case and that the extraordinary law probably dates back to William the Conqueror. God save us, are there any other of his forest laws still unrepealed?

The disembowelling of game I can just cope with; that and the reminders that this was once a creature with a digestive system, something which has become a huge secret kept from everyone by the neat supermarket trays. It is the feathering I cannot stand, the hour spent crouched in a cold garage over a zinc bucket, listening to Radio 4 and the soft, tearing sounds.

But I hit a pheasant once at 70mph and it was almost oven-ready when I found it, or rather, when I found most of it. I didn't bother to hang it, on account of the dubious way it had met its end, and made a stew the following night. It was like eating dried rubber.

At the time I was going out with a girl whose father subscribed to the whole country-gentleman package: the shooting syndicate, the gun room, the lot. He disliked me intensely, which was why his daughter and I worked out this routine. The father was reading his paper after breakfast. I spoke first.

'Got a pheasant last week.'

'Really, what are you using these days?'

'A Saab.'

The silence behind the *Financial Times* was as huge as a basilica.

I do not shoot, even though I have inherited two guns from my father, one of them a hammered 12-bore so old you can see the brazed mend done by a local blacksmith when someone tried to ram a charge in, thinking it a muzzle-loader. Two generations of my family used it, overlooking the fact that it could have blown apart at any moment in their hands. The guns are over the inglenook, bolted into the stonework at the insistence of the police. I have used them once.

It was breakfast and my daughter, looking out of the window before school, said she had seen something odd in the shrubbery. I got up and there was a rat on its hind legs, stroking its whiskers like a major. The next moment chaos was unleashed as I tried to find a spanner which would release a gun – and which, of course, could not be found. My daughter ran upstairs, sobbing that she had betrayed the rat.

I found the spanner, frantically unscrewed the bolt and put in a cartridge also so old it had a cardboard casing. The rat was still playing with its whiskers. I shot it from the kitchen door, forgetting that in a confined space a 12-bore sounds like a field gun. The rat went to glory, my daughter called me a murderer and I went round to apologise to the neighbours who were puzzled at having heard thunder in a clear sky.

And now I am back from the shops, and the house is in chaos again. I have just asked my daughter to unpack the groceries from the boot of the car, forgetting that the hare is in there as well, a sunburst of entrails and blood. It looks like being a long day in the country.

Down on the Farm

Acres and Acres of Madness

Boris Johnson

At the bottom of the garden we have a paddock, and on evenings like this I can think of no lovelier place on earth. The buds have budded. The trees are in leaf. The lambs are making a racket. The rabbits show a boldness that verges on insolence. Everywhere I look I see nature transpiring at every pore with the green joy of photosynthesis. I see the hawthorn blossom, rolling for miles in great gunsmoke clouds. I see the shade starting to lengthen from the old oak, and the lovely rickety fence, on which I sometimes balance champagne bottles and shoot them off with an airgun, and I lie down on the springy grass and look up at the pale moon in the blue sky and I breathe a sigh of deep and unchallengeable contentment.

Sometimes, you know, I just can't believe my luck. Because it turns out that I am not only the possessor of a magnificent paddock. I am a farmer. Yes, folks, I am a Tibullan agricola. I am Marie Antoinette. I have managed to hitch my wagon to the gravy train of the CAP and clamp my jaws about the hind teat of Defra.

By virtue of possessing 0.3 hectares of grass, excluding the dilapidated outside privy, I am apparently eligible for subsidy! You think I am mad; but read the 98-page booklet provided by the Rural Payments Agency and you will find your lungs tightening and your lips blibbering into a pant-hoot of pure amazement at the insanity of our masters. The government – Brussels – the taxpayer – whoever – is seriously going to pay me 10 euros a year merely for being the owner of this blissful patch of grass and rabbits. I don't have to farm it, in any meaningful sense.

I don't even have to graze a pony, though I could. I can use it for clay pigeons. I can use it for hot-air ballooning, it says here in the pamphlet. I can organise motocross events or nature trails across the paddock. Provided I don't do it for more than 28 days a year, I can even have car-boot sales. I can invite Billy Smart's circus to pitch their big top in the paddock, or I can let it out as a location for television.

Year after year, the cheque will come in from Brussels via Defra, 10 princely euros, as a thank you to me and my family for doing – well, for doing absolutely nothing except luxuriating in the existence of this paddock.

Weeping with laughter, I decide to ring the Rural Payments Agency to find out if I can possibly have read this right. Yes, they say, it sounds like you qualify. Yes, they say, there are plenty of people who have been given subsidy entitlements for having pony paddocks, just like the one you describe. Yes, it is OK to mow it. Yes, it is acceptable to use the land for having barbecues, playing rounders or nude sunbathing. Yes, says the Rural Payments Agency, you can have a pony paddock and attract the subsidy, without going to the trouble of having a pony. Yes, says the agency (now with a tremor of exhaustion in its voice), you are right in thinking that you are getting the money for nothing at all except keeping the land in 'good environmental condition'. Fantastic! I say. Where do I send the form?

And it is only then, of course, that I discover the catch. My paddock qualifies in every respect. This beautiful, if tiny, corner of Oxfordshire is entitled to all the dignity that goes with being a CAP-funded estate – except that, like a complete fool, I missed the deadline, in May 2005, for registering my claim. Through sheer stupidity, I failed to grasp that last year the government changed the basis on which agricultural subsidy is to be paid. Under the reforms of the CAP, farmers are no longer rewarded for growing barley or rearing suckler cows. It is the end of paying Greeks for growing acres of fictitious olives. Under the brilliant new single farm payment, the Greeks and the rest of us are to be rewarded simply for having grown acres of fictitious olives in the past. You no longer need even to pretend to grow the olives; you simply have to show that you have title to the land and that you are keeping it in good nick, olives or no olives; and that is why the pony paddocks of England are now accompanied by EU subsidy.

If I missed the deadline, there were thousands of paddock-owners who were quicker off the mark, who whanged those forms into the Rural Payments Agency – and who caused the monumental chaos with which you will be familiar. Across Britain there are farming families who have been driven deep into debt, and farmers who have contemplated suicide, because of the government's disastrous failure to send out the single farm payments. They were told they could expect the payment in December; then it was February; then March; and when, by mid-March,

Margaret Beckett was forced to come to the Commons and apologise, it was obvious that the system was in meltdown.

And the reason it was in meltdown was at least partly because no one had predicted that the number of subsidy claimants would rise – from 80,000 to 120,000 – as the paddock-owners, the raspberry-growers, the filbert-growers and the possessors of 0.3-hectare marrow patches piled in to register their land.

And, of course, there will be some optimists who point out that the expense can't be overwhelming, not at 10 euros a paddock. But if you look at the Rural Payments Agency booklet, you will see how ever more of our countryside is now being sucked into a bureaucratic vortex of madness. If you claim a subsidy for your orchard (as you may), you have to prove that your trees are 10 metres apart and that the trunks are one metre in circumference; and if you have more than 50 trees a hectare, you've got to prove to the inspector that the bases of the trees have previously been nibbled by sheep.

You can grow cucumbers, cabbages and cauliflowers, but not strawberries or mint! Think of the new legions of bureaucrats being created, who will have to check whether or not you are running your subsidised nudist colony for more than 28 days. Forty thousand new dependants have been created! Untold acres are now under new and pointless subsidy! And they call this reform? No wonder Margaret Beckett was promoted.

26 April 2008
It's Festival Season
Michael Eavis

About 150 years ago, my great-grandfather Joseph drove his cows all the way from Dorset to Park Farm at Pilton, in Somerset. He settled there, marrying Mary from nearby Glastonbury, and raised his family. His eldest son, William, then moved to Worthy Farm, across the valley, and we have been here ever since. Little did these Dorset farmers know what they had set in store for this beautiful village . . .

We went up to record numbers for the Glastonbury Festival last year, and have probably grown as big as we want to. It's virtually a city the size of Oxford that rises up each June. But since the first festival, in

June 1971, we have had nearly 40 years of practice and innovation to make sure it all works smoothly.

Most of our customers (and remember that the majority of them are actually camping in tents) really do believe they are spending a weekend in the countryside.

One of the best experiences of the festival is the fantastic air of excitement and anticipation on the first Wednesday night, before the music even starts. By the evening we're getting on for 90 per cent full, and up in the farmhouse we can hear the buzz and chatter of this huge crowd and know it's going to be a fantastic weekend.

Mendip Council kindly allowed us to increase the numbers, and we were able to expand to the west of the site with some of the finest views in the entire valley. Part of the new land we are using includes the original site of Park Farm.

My youngest daughter, Emily, who is Joseph and Mary's great-great-granddaughter, has started running her own festival area. It's called the Park and incorporates a wealth of ideas and talent that is amazing to experience. Last year she built a huge viewing tower from which you could see the entire spread of the festival. That was a revelation even to me, although I know every inch of the fields and hedgerows round here from ground level.

Many years ago, summers on the farm were very different. I'm old enough to have fond memories of hay-making with horses, and trips on the steam train to the seaside. We have the remains of the old railway line running directly through the middle of the festival site. John Betjeman even passed through here in the 1960s, filming a series for the BBC on railway journeys to the sea; the line went from Shepton Mallet down to Weston-super-Mare.

What has taken the place of haymaking and steam trains is an incredible feast of summer festivals everywhere. I mean popular music festivals, of course, which hit a different note of romanticism. So there's no nostalgia on this farm any more – it's the future we're looking to. English summers have a festival programme that has reached epidemic proportions. You can take your pick from green gatherings, global dance parties, touchy-feely back-to-nature affairs or just simply other shows copying the Glastonbury model.

England must have the highest density of these festivities per square mile in the world. Who knows what number of people collectively participate? It's probably two or three million.

Recently, I had the privilege of presiding over the agricultural show at Shepton Mallet. Every year country people line up their cattle, horses, sheep and pigs with pride. In tents containing chickens, rabbits, cats and dogs dedicated owners tart up their pets for a few days in the hope of winning blue, red or green cards. Or even a rosette, if they're lucky. The traditional English summer has its roots in these things, and they do not change.

It was back in the 1960s when I first saw the Small Faces perform at this self-same Shepton show. It was billed as an attraction for youngsters who obviously weren't going to be cattle or sheep owners. I can remember being so moved by it; the concept of playing pop music in a field to large numbers of people clicked with me.

Was this really the beginning of my adventures in entertainment – a life that took hold of me body and soul for nigh on four decades? I had a farm of dairy cows and an excellent site, I thought, for what could be an extraordinary event. Little did I know then that it would succeed on such a grand scale.

We went through many trials and tribulations over the years, and there were so many times when we almost gave up. I pushed the grace of fate beyond all reason, but somehow I had a deep conviction that if we were doing it right – and for the best of motives – then it would have to succeed.

There were bank loans that put Worthy Farm on the brink of disaster, and New Age travellers hell-bent on free entry and claiming ownership of the land.

There was rain that fell non-stop for days on end and the almost impossible task of producing a suitable infrastructure for such a huge crowd of people. Then licensing, which came into force in 1982, meant we had to convince a majority at the council that what we were doing was good and in some way beneficial to the community.

After failing at that task we had to appeal to the magistrates' court. Fortunately we usually managed to win these cases. It might seem that fate has dealt us a very good hand of cards – but in reality we have worked every inch of the way. We fought hard whenever conflict arose and somehow or other always made it happen. It's true I took chances, but all the time we were gaining in popularity. More and more bands were wanting to play at reasonable fees, and the public were eager to buy tickets. Glastonbury was becoming more than just a name.

It was an idea of how life could be for an idyllic midsummer weekend in the Somerset pasturelands, with music, theatre, dance and poetry as well as 'way out' stalls and eccentricity beyond what you could expect probably anywhere else in the world.

Green politics and fashion have a huge part to play in youth culture today and there will always be something new to be found in these fields in the Vale of Avalon. Beautiful things: challenging art and incredible music.

The festival isn't a full-time job, though there are things that have to be dealt with every day of the year. We're always looking ahead. Fortunately for me I still have my cows and regular milk cheques to keep me nicely grounded. The success of my dairy herd does in part owe its existence to the rent I collect from the festival.

Two-thirds of my neighbours have had to give up milking, but now milk prices have risen enough to produce a real profit from the farm at last. This will have an effect on the quality of farm life and generally add value to the culture of breeding for good-quality cows.

As the warm April sun shines through my drawing-room windows my mind wanders again to all those events that are now being lined up for the summer. It's almost time to make notes of dates and look forward to how wonderful this year could be in England.

Long may the expression of free-thinking people reign over this land.

19 August 2006

All Farmed Out and Nothing to Grow

Adam Edwards

It is a half-hour commute from Waterloo to Guildford and then another 20 minutes to the Surrey–Sussex border. It is a pretty drive, although it is no secret that hidden behind every hedge is a luxury, red-brick bungalow and down every discreet lane is a neat row of commuter-belt homes.

The traffic is heavy but thins south of Godalming as my companion and I motor past the Sir Roger Tichborne pub in Alfold, then turn down a cul-de-sac containing half a dozen neat modern homes. After 200 yards, the road becomes an unmade bridle path that winds through a couple of acres to enter Oakhurst Farm.

'This is the last farm in Surrey,' says Michael Parry-Jones, a property agent for Strutt and Parker, as we step from his 21st-century BMW into the beginning of the past century.

His remark is more pertinent than he imagines. Not only does the farm straddle the county border, but it could also double as the setting for the television series of H.E. Bates's novel *The Darling Buds of May*. More accurately, the farm is of the type that inspired the renowned Victorian artist Helen Allingham, who romanticised Surrey's red-brick, tile-hung rural buildings.

This was once countryside where cranes were bred as delicacies for kings, where hunting and hawking were dominant, and where the pitchfork and haystack were commonplace. Even today, Oakhurst Farm has more in common with *The Hay Wain* than with the suburban Home County it sits in.

'My grandfather bought the farm in 1924 and we have owned and farmed it ever since,' says Nick Ward, who lives in a 16th-century cottage on the edge of the acreage. 'He planted a lot of orchards and started a pig farm. Then my father turned it into a dairy farm in the early 1950s. And after that we had a suckling herd where a single calf stops with its mother until it is 14 months old.'

The farmyard is a last testament to what today sounds like an oxymoron – rustic stockbroker belt. Opposite the ramshackle, red-brick, Georgian farmhouse is a cavernous wooden barn – used for eight decades of wedding anniversaries and birthday parties – with its elderly wooden cider presses intact. Next to it is an ancient, black, clapboard granary adjoining a small millpond. Within welly-throwing distance are stables, cowsheds, chicken sheds, pig pens and a rusting 1950s Massey Ferguson combine harvester.

And now all this – lock, stock and cider barrel, plus 165 working acres – is for sale.

'The farm was losing money in the latter years,' says Nick, whose father was still running it as a working farm until his death earlier this year. 'Nobody can run a small farm profitably around here any more.' He is right. Oakhurst Farm is not merely one of the last traditional working farms around Guildford, it is also one of the few small-acreage, working farmsteads in this corner of England.

'Nobody makes a living from farming a couple of hundred acres,' says Robert Harris, business editor of *Farmers Weekly*. 'The economy of scale and the lack of cheap labour make it uneconomic. The small working farm is agriculturally finished in the south-east.'

Those that are left are rapidly being sold to 'lifestyle buyers' hunting for upmarket secluded country houses, who don't want to see anything nasty in the woodshed. Much like the smart, sophisticated Flora Poste in Stella Gibbons's *Cold Comfort Farm*, who set out to tidy up the untidy lives of her rustic Sussex relations, the modern dweller is gentrifying the pre-war farmhouses and farms faster than it takes to bake a potato in an Aga.

'The dilapidated farm has become an accessory to be done up,' says London-based interior decorator Joanna Wood. 'The new lifestyle buyer doesn't want to live an aggressively rustic life in a tumbledown building with few mod cons. He wants a pretty farmhouse with well-proportioned rooms that is a luxury des res. He wants it to be tidy and clean, and preferably with all the latest gadgetry.'

And so the tumbledown farmhouse of yesteryear and its outbuildings are being transformed into a mini-manor house. Meanwhile, the farmland is of secondary interest.

'Most of the land is used by the lifestyle buyers for horses, rare breeds or organic farming,' says Crispin Holborow, head of Savills' farm agency business. 'Some farms have got a second wind as small businesses, but nowadays there is very little value in the land that comes with a small farm.'

Ultimately, this has led many lifestyle buyers to take EU payments and environmental subsidies and leave the land fallow. 'I can see a day soon when an estate agent will conduct an environmental survey on the farm and use the range of wild species and the rare flora and fauna as a selling incentive,' says Crispin.

Low farm prices, non-existent farm labourers and spiralling house prices have driven the small-acreage working farms to the wall. 'Most small farms now coming to the market have acreages ranging from only 25 to 50 acres,' says Hazel Dalgleish, of the Kent and East Sussex estate agency Freeman Foreman's. 'Many of the farms in the south-east have been split up and land sold off. When a 200-acre farm does come to the market, because of its rarity, there is enormous interest.'

And this month, much of that interest will focus on Oakhurst Farm. But there will be no straw-sucking sons of the soil looking around the property. There will be no inquiries about wheat yields, milk quotas and the nearest cattle markets. The queries will be about the merits of the local Waitrose and how long it takes a 'Chelsea tractor' to get to Guildford at 6am on a weekday morning. For whatever else is true about the future of 'the last farm in Surrey', one thing is certain – it will not house a farmer.

6 August 2007
A Lifetime's Work Demolished
David Sapsted

The Pride family's lifetime in farming lay in ruins last night – consumed by foot-and-mouth.

Their 60-strong herd of beef cattle has been slaughtered, police have sealed their farm and land they rented, and meat in their farm shop has been condemned and destroyed. Every inch of the Prides' Woolfords Farm, at Elstead, Surrey, was being disinfected yesterday while Derrick Pride, 78, and his son, Roger, who now runs the farm, inspected the work going on.

Dressed in a flat cap, wellingtons, a polo shirt and work trousers, Mr Pride Snr could barely speak about the tragedy that has overwhelmed his family since foot-and-mouth was found in livestock grazing on the 30 acres they rent near the village of Normandy, four miles away.

However, he did pay tribute to the support the family had received from the community and denied that they were in any way to blame for the outbreak of the virus.

'The support being given to us locally is giving a lot of comfort,' he said, his eyes red and puffy. 'It is nothing to do with us. It is not our fault. It is something beyond our control.' The Prides are primarily beef farmers, but also let out some farm buildings as stabling.

A friend of Mr Pride said he was distraught over the outbreak. 'The family has been farming for years. They are very traditional farmers who take good care of their animals because they know that provides the best meat. They are genuine, no-fuss sort of people. That this should happen to them is just terrible,' he said.

'The only good news is that they buy fattening stock, so they won't have to build up a herd again from scratch. The question must be, after a disaster like this, though, whether or not they'll have the heart to start all over again. At best, it will take them months to get back up and running.'

Roger Pride arrived at the farm yesterday in a Land Rover. 'I'm afraid that all our comments are going through Defra at the moment,' was his only comment. The only member of the family who would speak was one of Mr Pride Snr's daughters. As she left the farm with her young family, stopping to disinfect their boots, she said: 'Mum and dad are very upset. We are very worried about them because they are quite elderly. We have lost the whole herd.'

Another local farmer said that the Prides ran a 'fantastic' shop selling their own beef. 'This will be terrible for them,' he said. 'They will probably have to close. They are dyed-in-the-wool farming folk and this must be a terrible ordeal for them.'

15 April 2001
Nature Triumphs in Crisis of the Countryside
Adam Lusher

As the foot-and-mouth outbreak drags into the Easter weekend, much of Britain still bears the scars of a countryside in crisis. Many footpaths remain closed, hundreds of farms are out of bounds, and hotels and guesthouses that would normally be full remain deserted.

Yet in the woods and fields, a hidden benefit of the outbreak is quietly emerging.

With more than 50,000 miles of footpaths still closed and many areas declared out of bounds, the declining number of tourists and ramblers has meant that wildlife has been offered an almost unrivalled opportunity to flourish undisturbed.

As a result, conservationists now expect a huge range of birds, wild flowers and mammals to thrive in a way they have not for decades. As Derek Moore, the director of conservation at the Wildlife Trusts, explains: 'In every crisis, there is an opportunity.'

The most obvious beneficiaries are likely to be thousands of ground-nesting birds. With so few dog walkers and ramblers around, they will not be forced to fly from their nests, leaving their eggs exposed to predators. Species likely to benefit include the threatened lapwing and the skylark, whose numbers are thought to have halved in the past 30 years.

The known breeding sites of some of Britain's rarest birds were also being monitored last week. Mr Moore is eagerly awaiting news from Walberswick in Suffolk, where marsh harriers are about to start breeding. 'There is a footpath right through the marsh,' he says, 'and for years we have tried to persuade people to move it because the harriers nest there. It is constant pressure for the birds.'

Already, he says, he is noticing larger animals thriving from the lack of intrusion: 'The bigger, more shy animals are becoming much bolder. Driving around the countryside, I have seen roe deer out in the open in the middle of the day. That would never happen normally.'

Rob Strachan, of the Wildlife Conservation Research Unit at Oxford University, says he is not altogether surprised by what is happening. 'When sites that have previously been heavily used are given a respite, animals generally respond,' he says. 'Irrespective of which species they are, they will be able to utilise areas that were out of bounds before.'

Botanists say plant life will also benefit, particularly if the long-term consequence of foot-and-mouth is an end to overgrazing. In upland areas, plants such as the mountain pansy and field gentian could flourish. Cowslips, too, once a familiar sight in the countryside, could make a comeback.

'It would be a silver lining,' says Dr Simon Thornton-Wood, the head of botany at the Royal Horticultural Society Garden, Wisley, Surrey. 'Cowslips declined horrendously between the 1950s and 1980s. Everyone used to know what a cowslip looked like. Not any more.'

In spite of the benefits to wildlife, however, many conservationists are adamant that the real silver lining will come with Tony Blair's promised 'long, cool look' at farming. Foot-and-mouth, they hope, will finally drive home the need to look after the traditional livestock farmer.

Already they are pressing the government to recognise the value of the farming families that have helped create the landscape which attracts so many tourists.

They claim that 60 per cent of England's Sites of Special Scientific Interest rely on grazing by sheep and cattle. Many of Britain's rarest butterflies, such as the Adonis Blue, would not be able to survive without the livestock and farmers threatened by the foot-and-mouth crisis.

'The best conservationists in Britain are the family farmers,' Mr Moore says. 'If we fail to recognise that, we will never make progress.

'Some extremists just want to leave the land entirely alone, but what makes Britain so wonderful for wildlife are the different farming practices that produce this mosaic of habitats.

'In every crisis, there is an opportunity. I hope that, once this is all over, we will be able to recognise the true value of farmers to the British countryside. We need to keep farmers farming. The future of wildlife in this country depends on them.'

5 August 2003
Letter to the Editor
Does British Farming Have a Future?

SIR – The biggest danger of high earners buying farms deep in the country is that they may suddenly develop the urge to show the locals how farming should be done, investing large amounts of money in equipment and mopping up local land and labour at highly exaggerated prices and creating a highly unstable local economy. Then, when reality sets in, they disappear like the morning dew, leaving the locals to suffer the financial consequences. This has happened before – in the 1950s, when business people were given tax breaks to invest in agriculture.

Tom Sharp
Sandbach
Cheshire

6 September 2008
Follow That Camel
Jasper Gerard

Camel trekking; foraging for leaves to supply gastropubs; hosting swinging parties. Ah, just a few of the charming rustic crafts providing employment for horny-handed men of soil in the modern countryside.

Long gone are the days when your village could boast a butcher, baker and candlestick maker. *Country Life* articles seem to be forever introducing us to Wiltshire's last thatcher, Dorset's last coppicer or Lincolnshire's last dry-stone waller. The theme? That traditional crafts are dying as typical country dwellers earn their living less from hedgerows than from hedge funds. Even where there is demand for stonemasons or ironmongers, cobblers or farriers, you will be lucky to find a practitioner with much more zest than Young Mr Grace.

There is some truth to the thesis. Certainly in the Home Counties, it's hard for anyone employed on the land to live in the houses once allotted to them. Along my lane in a still rural stretch of Kent, Keeper's Cottage is the smart residence of an interior designer, the Old Post Office is owned by a surveyor and the home farm of the local estate is presided over by a City trader – and all he seems to grow is rich. Where you do come across a rustic handle, it is often slightly contrived, belonging to some urbanite playing briefly at being Hugh Fearnley-Whittingstall. The other day, I was introduced to a shepherd. Far from being a gnarled old boy with a crook, she turned out to be a well-spoken, attractive young lady who was off to study industrial design.

But is this tale of rural decline the whole picture? While we are losing craftsmen – often more due to the reluctance of a younger generation to learn the skills than to any lack of demand – the countryside is also gaining a new class of rural worker.

Some are simply folk who a generation ago would have toiled in the Smoke and have moved out for some country air. My village numbers a man who designs book covers, a documentary-maker, a violinist, a bodyguard to a rock star, a psychiatrist, an importer of port, an Egyptologist, a chef and enough City types to fill a trading floor. Take out the odd farmer, and the villagers could be interchangeable with residents in one of the better streets of Chiswick.

But there are also practitioners of new trades that rely, in their different ways, on the countryside. Take foragers. As the *Daily Telegraph* restaurant critic, I find foraged leaves on menus as regularly as my seventies predecessors must have found Black Forest gâteau. Numerous folk are now employed in this field, which is reflected in the emergence of classes in foraging, such as at Cornwall's Wild Food School. This produces graduates who trawl for culinary curios that include pennywort, alexanders, sea purslane and bulrushes. They supply (for at least £15 a kilo) the growing number of sophisticated rural restaurants that in turn provide employment for chefs, front-of-house managers, organic farmers, interior designers, traditional furniture-makers, website designers, florists and even restaurant critics.

Myriad other thriving quirky country industries suggest that Arcadia can adapt to forge a prosperous future.

The Country Land & Business Association has compiled an 'Alternative Enterprise' directory of new rural businesses to provide money-making ideas to members. It is as long as a phone book and bewildering, as this tiny selection suggests: adopt-a-tree, agricultural chaplain, badger-watching tours, balloon service, bay tree production, bell-ringing weekends, bison breeding, cashmere goats, cyber-pub, etiquette courses, granny activity holidays, guanaco (llama) breeder, leaves to curd (tofu making), life swap, massages, medieval banquets, moonlight walks, mystic weekends, opera house, ostriches, paintballing, pet headstones, pudding service, singles parties, water buffalo, wild boar and willow sculpting.

As you see, you can hardly accuse countrysiders of burying their heads in the sand – and that includes the ostrich breeder.

Take Chris Oates of Cornish Camels. He is a farmer with a herd of seven camels who takes tourists trekking on the Goonhilly Downs to supplement his earnings from producing organic meat from rare-breed Welsh Black cattle and Gloucester Old Spot pigs.

'I was coming in from the cows one evening,' he says, 'and I told my son: "I'd like to see a line of camel across that heathland." It can look very brown, almost like a desert. Next thing my son was on the internet and said: "I've found the camels. They're in a circus in Bulgaria."'

They set off immediately to buy the camels. After much bureaucracy and quarantine, they were brought 'home' to Cornwall and Oates fell in love. 'We had three baby camels born this year,' he smiles. 'It supplements farm earnings, but has also become a passion.'

Bruce Wright had a similar idea, except with llamas. They are used as pack animals to carry swish picnics for day trippers in Nottinghamshire. They are also hired out as novelties. They were the star turn at a recent society wedding at a castle, where they led the bride and groom into the marquee. Not that it has been entirely plain chomping: 'When we bought them, they were meant to be trained, but there is no way they were,' says Wright. 'I remember them bolting when I blew my nose. They did the same the first time we took them on the road and they heard a car in the distance going through a puddle.'

Five years ago, Richard Gill took over his parents' Peak District farm outside Chesterfield. At agricultural college, he had grown painfully aware he would have to diversify: 'Lecturers were saying you will have to try caravan parks, go-carting, anything.' On graduating, he discovered that the dairy business 'was getting a kicking from supermarkets' and so he gambled on putting into action a proposal he had devised for a university exercise: buffalo farming.

'I bought a huge quantity of buffalo meat first, and flogged it at a farmers' market. It sold out in a couple of hours. People were attracted to the idea of meat with half the cholesterol and fat of beef. Now we have 300 buffalo – we bought all the surplus stock in the UK.'

On the Isle of Wight, the Abbott brothers run a successful lavender farm. Despite having poor soil, they have transformed the business in a decade. They have a national lavender collection and sell lavender oil in bottles and to perfumers. They also sell lavender by mail order and the farm has become a tourist attraction with a tearoom. The Abbotts work hard, but climbing mountains in Spain searching for wild lavender doesn't sound like a bad job. Next, the Abbotts are diversifying into roses. And if that sounds adventurous, consider that one of their neighbours lets his land for a pop festival.

Not all countryside entrepreneurs are major landowners. One firm has made a mint producing bras for women with fuller figures. Others seem to be built on a quirky idea, such as moonlit walks or mystic weekends. As for the cyber-pub, does it leave you with only a virtual-reality hangover?

And so to swinging. To the horror of neighbours, farmer Roger Stanbury turned from milking cows to hosting swingers' parties in his converted barn near Barnstable, Devon. Club Vanilla accommodates pole-dancers and a whirlpool bath. Oh, and double beds for customers in need of a lie-down. When asked if he fears villagers might object, Stanbury replies that country folk are pretty liberal these days.

A small family farm that once employed a veritable gang of agricultural workers is now more than likely to be a hobby farm without staff. But that doesn't mean the farmhouse no longer provides employment. The owners probably have a gardener and cleaner around regularly, as well as fencers, stable hands, swimming-pool repairmen, tennis coaches and baby-sitters. A booming industry in my village is gardening – and we are no longer talking about a few old boys who'll take payment in kind of a few turnips. Now they are 'landscape gardeners' and charge up to £100,000 to redesign gardens for the wealthy.

The difference is that far from being derived from the land, wealth is mainly now spent on the land. Money is earned, at least initially, in the city and spent in the countryside and a lot of secondary rural businessmen are cashing in. As one local craftsman slyly tells me: 'There's a lot of City money around here. And I intend to get my hands on some of it.'

While many of these country jobs might not be as bucolic as trusty farm workers hoeing in smocks between hearty gulps of cider, the countryside still sustains a large workforce – much of it supported by that endangered specimen, the City bonus. But as long as that quaint old craft of hedge-fund management survives, the berries in the by-ways of rural Britain will continue to provide rich pickings.

4 September 2011
Just Say Cheese
Anne Cuthbertson

Within seconds of arriving at Alex James's farm I am whisked into the kitchen, past a hoard of lightsabre-wielding children, and fed cheese. He is chuckling away at reaction in the press to his new range of supermarket cheeses, which include toast-shaped Cheddar and tomato ketchup 'blankets' and – the one that left the food critics choking on their crackers – a 'Cheddar tikka masala'.

'It's fantastic,' he says. 'The gastro equivalent of punk rock.'

His three-year-old daughter Sable joins me for a potato and Spudsworth melting cheese cubes. It's much like the Swiss raclette Alex first tried as a teenager and which he found so thrilling it kept him awake all night. As for the cumin-flavoured tikka cheese, though not exactly to my taste, it's not the food crime it's been made out to be. 'It's fun, it's just a bit of bloody fun!' he says.

If there was a face of British cheese, Alex James would like to be it. He has won an award for his goats' milk Little Wallop, and made a blue cheese called Blue Monday. Good Queen Maude, a sheep's cheese, is next.

The cheese nerve centre is Churchill Heath Farm, his rambling rural home in Kingham. And yes, that's near Chipping Norton.

'Oh God, don't write about Chipping Norton,' he says, holding his head in his hands. 'This year Chipping Norton has become the evil of darkness.'

The gilded Cotswold triangle is home to a number of political and media figures linked to the phone-hacking scandal, from Rebekah Brooks to the Camerons, Elisabeth Murdoch and Jeremy Clarkson. Alex, too, has been dubbed a member of 'the Chipping Norton set'. He shrugs. 'While all this was going on, I was in my "foodio" just trying to make cheese melt.'

Alex wants me to try his cheese on toast and leads me to a specialist grilling machine in a converted outbuilding. We leave the kitchen, with its huge picture window looking out onto a trampoline, bouncy castle and wooden pirate ship with slide. We pass through a warren of rooms, where cubbyholes are crammed with the small shoes of his five children under the age of seven. There's a playroom, a laundry where three washing machines and two tumble dryers are always on the go, and Alex's music room where a drum kit, double bass, cello, violins and guitars remind you that this country cheese-maker was in one of Britain's biggest bands of the nineties.

Alex James was the bass player in Blur, the band which dominated the charts and whose single 'Country House' beat Oasis's 'Roll With It' to the number one slot in 1995, making the *Ten O'Clock News*. He lived out of a suitcase on tour, was inebriated on champagne at the Groucho, picked up Brit awards and cavorted in hotel rooms around the world, as is expected of a rock star. Then, just as Blur was disintegrating, he met Claire Neate, a video producer.

'We fell in love in Little Barrington,' he says. He and Claire got married in 2003 and on their honeymoon, Alex surprised everyone by selling his bachelor pad in Covent Garden and buying a run-down 200-acre farm in Oxfordshire.

The farm is still a work in progress. Built of golden Cotswold stone, it dates back to the late 1700s. Foot-and-mouth and BSE had left the previous owner, an intensive beef farmer, 'on his knees' and the property was derelict. Only after peeling away wallpaper and plaster did they discover some beams were rotting and it needed gutting. 'But all the decent builders and plumbers in the area had remortgaged their own houses and were doing them up, so we could only get three village bong-heads who spent months out here. That's how you learn,' says Alex.

He found himself getting stuck in, bulldozing up an enormous concrete silage clamp and loving it. 'I'm the world's greatest jumper-inner,' he says. He tackled ditches, the well and spring water supply, fields and drains, trees and ancient woodland, and livestock (he now has sheep and, no longer a vegetarian, just finished eating the last of the pigs). He learns from local farmers, land agents and wise old boys. 'Expertise is the cheapest thing you can spend your money on,' he nods.

Today, a low stone wall is being built by a chap called Neil, and there are piles of slates, tiles, wooden pallets and rubble everywhere. Alex points to a digger in the front garden. 'Look at that – far more exciting than a Range Rover.' The pond is sludgy. It's not done up or magazine-shoot perfect, and I get the impression Farmer James likes it that way. 'Running a farm is like running a small country. Something's always escaping, broken down, falling apart or leaking.'

When we eventually get to the 'foodio', unfortunately the Wallace and Gromit-style cheese-grilling machine blows a fuse, trips the lights and triggers an outburst of swearing from its cheese-mad creator. Disappointed, Alex steers me past the offices of other artisan cheese-makers who operate from his farm (Crudges and British Cheese Awards creator Juliet Harbutt) and towards the living larder that is his fruit and vegetable garden. He pulls up little carrots, rinses them under an outdoor tap and hands me one. 'I don't peel veg any more,' he says, and who can blame him.

The maze of raised beds are stuffed with asparagus, celeriac, leeks ('good with cheese'), onions, lettuces and cabbage. We eat plums and Russet apples (also 'good with cheese') straight off the branches in the orchard, where Alex is adding to the tree collection each year. He's excited by his medlars ('you have to leave them to rot', he explains) and thrilled his fig survived the harsh winter. Next, he would love a nuttery.

We end up in amongst a forest of triffid-sized heritage tomatoes in a glass house attached to one of his barns. 'I've gone crazy on tomatoes,' he says. I nod. 'The Victorians built orangeries; I have a tomato shed, a "tomatory".'

We sit in the tomatory on a scruffy sofa and chairs and munch cherry tomatoes – 'One in three tastes of white truffles,' he says.

Alex is hosting his own festival next weekend, a food and music extravaganza. 'It's the perfect reflection of my life,' he says. Some 10,000 people are expected at Harvest, where food stars Hugh Fearnley-Whittingstall, Monty Don and Mark Hix 'headline' alongside bands such as Athlete and The Feeling.

Alex loves country life, gobbles it up hungrily. He has an eagerness to try new things, combined with a respect for tradition. I notice a ragged Union flag hangs from a pole outside. 'I've felt better about things since that went up,' he smiles.

28 September 2002
Watch the Birdie
Peter Marren

Chris Knights is a farmer who photographs birds. His piece of England, 9,000 acres in the flat, sandy Breckland region of Norfolk, takes full advantage of modern machinery and know-how to produce carrots, parsnips and lettuces for the nation's supermarkets.

And yet, unlike so many big, profitable farms, Knights' land still teems with wildlife. His headlands form feeding grounds for old English grey partridges. His fields are visited by skylarks, lapwings and the rare stone curlew. He has even managed to hang on to that recently red-listed bird, the house sparrow. How does he do it?

The reason is made clear in the first paragraph of his hope-filled book, *The Feather and the Furrow*. Knights likes birds. If he sees a plover's nest when harrowing his parsnips in the spring, he either steers round it, or stops, gets out of the tractor, moves the nest, and then moves it back again. Most farmers, in my experience, would not see the nest.

He has also maintained margins bright with poppies and mayweeds in summer, and doesn't give his hedges an annual thrashing with the flailer. Nor has he ploughed up the ancient drove roads that have criss-crossed this open country since farmers first began growing crops here, far back in prehistory.

No one who doesn't love birds could have taken the stunning, often memorable colour pictures that fill this book. Some are the product of patient waiting for the right moment, others have snatched a fleeting chance, like the geese passing the full moon at dawn, or the trio of puffins posing like fashion models against a colourful backcloth of thrift and lichen.

One of Knights' most celebrated shots is of a stone curlew braving up to a curious lamb. He captures the instant when the two make eye contact, the furious bird outstretched like a heraldic eagle, the lamb caught in a moment of ruminative bemusement. One longs to know what happened next. The skill of the photographer shows in the relaxed nature of most of his subjects. A grebe gently offers a feather to the zebra-striped grebelet riding on its back.

The two fighting cock pheasants are too intent on knocking one another to pieces to notice. One seems about to jump into the other's arms, like Queen Elizabeth and Essex dancing a galliard.

The clear message is that farming and wildlife can go together, with a bit of give and take. Why then have farm birds suffered such devastating losses over the past 25 years? The grey partridge, for example, has declined by 82 per cent and, except in Norfolk, is no longer a familiar bird (everyday partridges are now the dimwitted, but widely bred, French partridge).

The implication, surely, is that four-fifths of farmers don't care much about English partridges. This might be the problem. Farmers should not be blamed for the mistakes of agricultural policy, which are the fault of purblind politicians, union fat cats and uncaring civil servants. But too many farmers have had the instinctive love of countryside and wildlife knocked out of them at agricultural college.

Fortunately, Knights doesn't bang on about that. He aims some entertaining side-swipes at conservationists who learn everything from their own pamphlets, at twitchers for ticking instead of watching birds, and ramblers who march straight through fields rather than following the more interesting way around them.

Mostly, he writes simply and affectionately (but not sentimentally) about the birds and other animals he knows, around the farm in summer and winter, on the nearby washes and mudflats, and further afield in the pine forests of the Cairngorms.

In a postscript on new arrivals, Knights predicts that the gorgeously coloured bee-eater will take advantage of the warming climate and start to nest here. So they did this year.

The Feather and the Furrow is a vivid record of wild birds made by someone who knows them intimately. It suggests we don't have to create desolation to live. There's an alternative — and it isn't more red tape. Just more farmers who like birds.

26 July 2003

Ploughs are 'Ripping Up Our History'

Charles Clover

Thousands of archaeological sites face being destroyed by modern farming methods, English Heritage said yesterday.

Intensive ploughing has arguably done more damage in six decades than traditional agriculture had done in the preceding six centuries, said Simon Thurley, the chief executive.

'We are, quite literally, ripping up our history,' he said. 'In doing so we are also doing irreparable damage to the character and fascination of our much-loved countryside.'

He added: 'We cannot blame farmers for what has been happening. They have only been doing what society has asked and agricultural policy has dictated.'

English Heritage called for changes in the law and to the system of farm subsidies.

In a report entitled *Ripping Up History*, the government's conservation advisers said the June reform of farm subsidies and the government's review of heritage protection created an opportunity to solve a crisis that has been growing for more than a century.

Dr Thurley said that despite 120 years of increasingly sophisticated ancient monuments legislation, 3,000 nationally important ancient monuments were still being ploughed. English Heritage has no powers to monitor the damage or compel farmers to manage them better.

Dr Thurley gave the example of Dyke Hills in Oxfordshire, an Iron Age site of considerable importance, where work began in 1870 to level the defensive walls to turn pastureland into arable, prompting protests that led to the first Ancient Monuments Act in 1882. It was 'saddening', he said, that Dyke Hills was still being ploughed.

Damage to a Roman mosaic at Pillerton Priors in Warwickshire was caused by a single episode of ploughing in wetter than normal weather.

'A monument that may have taken decades to construct, or may have been revered as sacred for many centuries, can be swept away in a matter of hours,' said Dr Thurley.

Farm tractors were up to 10 times more powerful than tractors in the

1940s, he added. The point of a ploughshare pulled by such machines exerted pressures no site could withstand.

At the Roman cemetery at Owmby in Lincolnshire a plough had wrenched off half the lid of a limestone coffin, scarring the surviving half. Skeletons in shallow graves, unprotected by coffins, were being obliterated.

Dr Thurley, formerly the director of the Museum of London, added: 'One can only imagine the outcry if the artefacts so carefully exhibited in our museums were to be damaged in this way. But why should we be more complacent because equally important, or perhaps even more important, artefacts are being destroyed simply because they are archived in the open-air museum of the wider landscape?'

Some 94 per cent of medieval 'ridge and furrow' in the Midlands had now been destroyed, according to a recent survey. For example, ploughing at Arbury Banks, Northants, had destroyed half the protective covering of ridge and furrow, and was damaging the underlying rare Iron Age fortifications.

A 1998 survey showed that one monument a year, including long barrows that date back 6,000 years and are the oldest man-made things in the landscape, had been destroyed since 1945.

English Heritage is calling for the overhaul of laws on scheduled ancient monuments, which were framed in the 1970s, to remove the blanket permission to plough in all cases and to allow English Heritage to monitor and manage sites, if necessary paying compensation to the farmer.

It is calling for no additional important and well-preserved sites to be turned over to the plough and for greater emphasis on protecting archaeology in the new generation of agricultural schemes, which will reward farmers who look after the landscape and environment.

12 September 1998
A Lonely Furrow
Rory Knight Bruce

In my father's house there may not be many mansions, but there is plenty of farm machinery. Since his death last year it has been my unlikely responsibility to manage his 143 Devon acres and to come to terms with something from which the idyll of a country upbringing had heretofore protected me: paying the bills.

Rural bereavement still mesmerises creditors into temporary decorum, but after nine months they were getting restive, despite reassurances they would be paid on the Grant of Probate. One machinery supplier sent in an interest bill of more than £300 on a debt of barely £3,000.

It became tricky to walk in the High Street of Crediton, our local town (despite being largely unknown there), because of small creditors pursuing me like Dickensian duns. To avoid a pitchfork revolution, the rule is that everyone must be paid at the same time.

But this unseemly pressure was not the reason I decided to let the land and sell the Suffolk flock and machinery. It is more simple than this, as Paul Wiseman, a partner with the land agent Michelmore Hughes, which has looked after our land for most of this century, explained to me: 'If you carry on like this, you will soon be insolvent.'

Carrying on 'like this' was to employ one man, Ken Woodgates, and supplement the losses that all small farms now incur. During my father's lifetime he had the income from estate rents to supplement these losses, something I do not have as it goes to my elder brother. In recent years, those losses have been between £10,000 and £14,000 a year.

Paul Wiseman, whose office in Totnes covers much of the West Country, believes mine is the last farm to have been run in this way. 'Farming is now large agribusiness,' he says. 'Today, you need 500 acres to be viable.' For other small farmers, who work the land themselves, he believes the prospects are grim. 'Farming cannot live on subsidies.'

His wisdom is borne out not just by nearby small farms, which are heavily in debt, but warnings in the *Farmers Weekly*. 'Incomes set to fall as pound soars' read one headline this year. 'Farmers quit and take early retirement in response to Budget' ran another.

This is all in stark contrast to the traditional, conservationist way in which my father farmed and of which I am immensely proud. He refused pesticides and declined certain grants in the belief he would be taking money from the more needy. It was typical and rightful paternalism at its most gentle, as befits a landlord who (war-time excepted) lived and died on his well-tended acres.

The modern age is less considerate to such Hardyesque notions. Yet, if my father was Michael Henchard, the Mayor of Casterbridge, he would recoil from any parallel with Donald Farfrae, the penny-pinching and unscrupulous pillager of lives and land. Yet round and about, stories persisted.

In the local pub, the Beer Engine in the hamlet of Newton St Cyres, locals would sidle up to me. 'So it's true you're selling all the land?' one would say, looking darkly into his pint of Rail ale. Theories reported back to me by lifelong friends were more colourful. 'It's to fund his hunting,' was one (something I have always done out of my own pocket, never having asked for, or been given, a serious shilling from home).

'Doesn't he go gambling in Monte Carlo?' was another theory. This may well relate to four days I spent in Monte Carlo two years ago, when I slept in a converted garage. The nearest I got to the casino was when hitching a lift in a car which was going that way and it crashed.

There was some comic relief. A local grandee asked if he could squeeze some of his machinery into my sale anonymously as he didn't wish to appear disloyal to farming.

Preparing the date of the sale with the auctioneer, Husseys of Exeter, was more difficult. They had so many sales on, it was difficult to fit me in. As Alan Webber, the auctioneer, said: 'There is no light at the end of the tunnel. Lifelong farmers are making the decision to get out now.'

Of course it is good business for auctioneers in the short term, but where will it leave their bread-and-butter jobs of market day and grass lets?

Eventually, we set a date. Ken Woodgates (who has been friend and tutor to me for the 37 years he has worked at home) spent three weeks getting the lambs with their ewes, which is how they are sold. He also laid out in meticulous rows the machinery we had used all our working lives, though he declined to witness the sale, staying with the sheep instead.

But it is testimony to his reputation, and that of my father, that more than 200 farmers turned up for the sale. The wet weather, I was told, also helped, as farmers don't feel guilty about leaving their land.

The first lot was an old binder, now worn with neglect, which we used to use in my childhood to make stooks for thatch. It went for £10.

Starting at 11 a.m., Alan Webber moved quickly on, a shoal of bargain hunters gathering around him and the implements. To his bidding price, they would raise their heads, as grazing cattle would to a passing fox.

Sheep-netting, hammers, old drinking troughs, implements you see dolled up in pubs were all there. Men such as Frank Hookway, now retired, who helped seasonally on the farm (and played football with me after work), came to pay their respects, as much to their own lives as my father's.

I wanted it to be festive, the celebration of a bygone age, once more caring and innocent. My brother came and touched the roguing forks of his youth, before letting them go for a song. Robin Grant-Sturgis, my father's greatest friend, beseeched me jokingly to withdraw a water bowser for him. But he didn't have the heart for it, either. We knew, silently, that to conserve you must change.

I talked to the Ayres family, who have taken the land let, and with whom I went to the local school. Our late fathers rode together at point-to-points. They will be good custodians of the land for the next five years. Although the income will not be large, there will be no more bills to pay.

2 August 2009
The Land Girls
Jessica Fellowes

On a chilly April night in Suffolk, Karen White was tucked up in bed, trying to get some rest before another day at the office. But she was soon shaken awake: a cow was calving and having difficulties – could she come down and help? It may have been cold, dark and half- past midnight but Karen soon had half her arm inside a cow, trying to work out which way round the calf was. 'It was too hard in the end. We couldn't save it, even with the vet's help,' she says. Within hours, though, Karen was back in her suit and off to work. Because Karen has two jobs: her nine-to-five position tackling coastal erosion for the Environment Agency and the one that swallows up the rest of her time – farmer's wife.

'Being a farmer's wife is a tough but vital role,' says Emma Penny, the editor of the weekly paper *Farmers Guardian*. 'They might have a job off the farm, but they'll still be active and involved – they'll be the housekeeper, bookkeeper and IT specialist. As a support for their husband they are crucial.'

Emma Harrison would certainly agree. In a bright kitchen with the flotsam of a farming family life scattered about – high chairs, splashy paintings tacked to the fridge, wellies by the back door – Emma, 31, dishes out mincemeat curry for lunch, 'made from our cows, of course'.

She and her husband Rob, 32, rent two farms near Chipping Campden in the Cotswolds – one from her parents, which is arable, and, 15 miles away, the dairy farm belonging to his parents, home to a 200-strong herd. 'My job is to make Rob's life easier,' says Emma, mother to Ned, nine months, and Wilf, two and a half, 'whether it's putting food on the table, answering the phone or ringing around to get quotes for fencing.'

She is the fifth generation to work on her family farm and, like all the wives I met, sees her role almost as a vocation. 'It's in my blood. It's hard to explain but you've either got it or you haven't,' she says. 'In some ways I feel I've gone back to my gran's way of life. Me looking after the boys full time is better for us because I can really be a part of what Rob does. His job isn't nine to five: it's everything.'

Rob and Emma first met at swimming club when they were 10 years old, although they know this only because Emma's mother recognised Rob when he came to pick up Emma some 15 years later. 'For ages, mutual friends kept telling me I should meet Rob,' she says. 'And people said the same to him about me. But over the years we had other relationships or were just too busy. We both went to agricultural college in different parts of the country. We each had a very close-knit social scene going on: everyone mixes well because you tend to have similar backgrounds. We would party hard during term time, then work hard in the holidays, when you get jobs on farms. I didn't want to marry a farmer; I never thought I'd marry anyone. Then I met Rob in the local pub. His lifestyle suits me – outdoors in the fresh air, working with animals and the land.

'We kept bumping into each other, which I think he was planning. Finally, we arranged to go to a ball. It wasn't meant to be a date – a group of us were going – but one by one everyone else dropped out and I gradually realised it was a date. The rest is history.'

After college Emma worked on a dairy farm in Zimbabwe (from which she had a hair-raising departure in the middle of the night when supporters of Robert Mugabe threatened to attack), then as a strawberry marketer, a salad technologist and, until very recently, as a food-chain adviser for the National Farmers' Union. Even so, Emma didn't realise quite what she would take on as a farmer's wife. 'We got married in November 2005 – that was the only month Rob could get away for a honeymoon. He booked three weeks in New Zealand because he wanted to see all the dairy farms. On one day of my honeymoon we went round eight farms.'

There's no question a dairy farm is hard work. British dairy farmers are unable to set the price for their produce or even have contracts with their buyers. 'The sale price of milk is 23p per litre and to produce it costs, on average, 27p per litre. We manage to produce it for less but we have nothing left over to re-invest. Rob works long hours during the week, and even on his days off he's working for a few hours. He tries to have at least one meal a day with the boys and it's set in stone that he's there for their bedtime. But there isn't much flexibility in our lives.'

Still, Emma is very contented. 'It's an amazing life. I have a husband who is so happy in his job and children who are in fresh air, seeing animals every day.' Emma and Rob are keen for the boys to get involved in the future – Wilf might be just a toddler but already he sits in on farm meetings. 'Rob's parents did that for him, too. We think it's important that he understands how it all works.'

The couple are unusually young to be farmers. It is an expensive business to get into. Many farmers have to inherit a going concern in order to get into the business, but that in itself can be a source of tension. If a farmer and his wife have worked all their lives on a farm they may be unwilling to hand over the reins when they reach retirement age.

It's a scenario that's familiar to Karen White, 36, and her husband, also called Rob, 39. They live on Peakhill Farm, which is owned by Rob's father. Rob has worked there since he was 16 and now manages the wholly organic farm and its shop, in Saxmundham, Suffolk. Alongside her day job, Karen talks to the shop staff about supplies, bags up the salad at the weekends and drives it to outlets, runs educational days on the farm with schools and is, as she says, 'the general dogsbody – but a small farm can't run without a woman behind it'. Nevertheless, it isn't technically their farm: Rob's parents live in the farmhouse and Karen and Rob live in a cottage a mile down the road. 'Most young farming couples can't live on the farm,' says Karen. 'You can't move the parents off the farm because you haven't got the capital. We could swap houses but they love it where they are. So we're not pressurising them to move.'

As Karen shows me round the picture-perfect farm with its herd of 40 South Devon cattle it's clear that she feels a real connection to it – 'you can't work on the land and not be attached to it' – but she refers frequently to the battle she has for her husband's time. 'The farm is your husband's mistress. He's preoccupied with her all day, and then comes home and talks about her all night,' she says.

Most farmers have huge overdrafts, which is not surprising when you consider that a new tractor can cost about £75,000 and a combine harvester £200,000. 'The only reason we can survive now is because our house doesn't have a mortgage and we don't have any loans – we're unusual in that way,' says Karen. 'Also, the money I get pays for extra things like new shelves or freezers for the shop.' But nor do they have much in the way of holidays – a week every two years seems to be their average. Yet Rob's passion for farming has rubbed off on Karen. 'Last year we took a weekend off for my sister's wedding, and when we got back I discovered that the seedlings I'd spent 10 days sowing were all victims of a fungal rot. I just cried. I won't go away during such a crucial time again!'

Life is equally busy for Debbie Keeble and her husband, Andrew, both 43, who run the third biggest sausage company in the country. Debbie was raised on her parents' 800-acre pig farm, Berryhills, in North Yorkshire, and still lives there now, renting it from her father. Like Emma and Rob, the couple grew up just 15 miles apart, but didn't meet until they were 19, 'and that was pretty much it – we got married at 23'. For the next 10 years they were pig farmers, working for her father for a combined wage of £12,000 a year. There were no holidays or weekends off, and the work was relentless.

'It was and still is a massive juggle,' says Debbie. 'In the early days we had extra jobs to keep everything afloat. I can remember being heavily pregnant and exhausted from mucking-out pigs. Knowing I'd have to go out in the mud again soon, rather than mess up the bed I fell asleep under the kitchen table.'

Eventually, Debbie cracked and spent three months' wages on a computer. She went on several courses then wrote a business plan – against the odds. Not only did her mother, a traditional farmer's wife, not understand Debbie bringing in an au pair to look after her four children, but life was so hectic, 'we had to do business planning in the bathroom, the only quiet time'.

They had made their own bacon and sausages for years and decided sausages were the way ahead: 'They've got the wow factor. We started with a couple of pigs a week and now we're using 5,000.' They no longer use their own farm to supply the meat but are strict about using small abattoirs where they can trace the supply. 'Good pig farming is all about the husbandry,' explains Debbie.

Debbie and Andrew now enjoy their success – even managing a holiday to Brazil in 2002 – and the children work with them as they travel the length of the country going to food shows to promote the brand, Debbie & Andrew's. Debbie is grateful to farming for another reason: her son Roddy, 15, is severely dyslexic, 'but luckily he is on a farm, so instead of school he does a mechanic's course and looks after 30 sheep'. The threat of swine flu looms but has so far not affected business: 'The forecast for the world is bad, prices will go down because of it, but we haven't noticed a shift in sales yet.' Meanwhile, Debbie is in demand as a speaker. She recently gave a presentation at the Women in Rural Enterprise conference and last year won the prestigious Women in Farming award.

'I used to be so shy I couldn't even talk on the phone to the supermarkets. I can't believe how pathetic I was,' she says, laughing. Now it's a different story. 'Andrew tells me his dreams and I work out how we're going to do it.' A typical farmer's wife, in other words.

30 September 2006
'Wow, I've Not Felt a Sheep Before'
Christopher Middleton

Everyone's always telling us townies how little we appreciate the countryside and how terrible it is that urban children think potatoes grow on shelves. Well, here's an opportunity for us city folk to have an on-farm experience that will open our eyes to the facts of agricultural life.

It's called the Feather Down Farm Stay Experience, and it's a concept that has been brought to Britain by the man who brought us Center Parcs, one Luite Moraal.

The idea is that you stay on a bona fide working farm, run by farmers who are 'passionate guardians of the countryside', and that you share their daily routine by doing things such as fetching eggs from the hen coop and spending the day out in the fresh air, without 'the clamouring radio and droning TV'.

Also, instead of sleeping in a tiny tent, or a chintzy spare room in the farmhouse, you get to stay in up-market canvas homes the size of a large caravan. Rather than spending the night in a static-charged nylon cocoon on top of rock-hard ground, you stretch out in a nice, soft bed with cotton sheets. Plus there's a flushing indoor loo.

Initially, my family and I aren't certain what to think. There are five of these super-tent structures on the farm we visit (near Alton), and, from the outside, they have a rather military, brown rectangular look. Three of them command sweeping views of the surrounding countryside, while the other two look out on to a grassy, little play area, complete with hen house and cuddly-animal pens.

If the tent exteriors give off a very Baden Powell kind of message, their interiors are altogether more Ikea.

Opening the flap of our tent is rather like the curtain going up at the start of a play, with stage directions reading: 'Act One: kitchen of the woodcutter's cottage, just outside Stockholm; a stove and dining table stand atop rustic floorboards, while an old suitcase has been placed on top of the cupboards for effect.'

Without a moment's hesitation, our son Charles and his friend Ollie (both 11) gravitate to the bedstee, a traditional (so we discover) Dutch sleeping area, built into the wall like an elevated airing cupboard. They then spend the rest of the weekend either shut tight inside this little, wooden world, playing imaginary war games, or else in the fields playing real-life war games, with hard, green walnut-like fruits (they collect them in wheelbarrows to use as ammunition).

For some reason we can never quite fathom, the (wood-burning) stove warms the tent like nobody's business, and turns baked beans molten in seconds; but when it comes to heating up water for the tagliatelle, it seems to take 45 minutes to go from nought to boiling, and even then we can't be sure if the agitation on the water isn't just us walking across the floorboards.

So plenty of opportunity to watch water boil, but as for tuning in to the rhythms of farm life, there isn't nearly as much scope for this as we had hoped (or the brochure had promised).

Rather than dogging our welly-booted hosts' footsteps at milking and threshing time, we find ourselves wondering where it is all happening. Not only are we (and our neighbours) repeatedly beaten to the egg-collecting, but we also miss the llama-feeding (it turns out there are three of these creatures in an upper field). And although we hear the sound of farm machinery, we can never quite identify where it is coming from.

'I think perhaps I should put up a blackboard saying what's happening each day and when,' suggests our affable host farmer, Will Brock, and we all agree.

Other suggestions from grass-roots level include giving out a map of the farm showing nice walks, plus some blurb about its history (Brocks have farmed here for 100 years and several are buried in the lovely little 13th-century church next door).

'We only opened in August, so we're still getting a feel for what people want,' says Will, who as well as looking after all the guests, and cooking pizza in the bread oven come sundown, has to farm his 650-acre estate with the help of just one other human being, his father, Thomas.

Farmer Will and his chef-wife, Anna (ready-made organic meals in the freezer), are the first couple in the UK to have signed up for the Feather Down franchise. The tents are delivered on the back of a Dutch lorry (and put up within a couple of days), and so is the seemingly ancient and immovable outdoor bread oven.

And although still distinctly deficient on the farm-education side, there's no doubt that the overall set-up is a genuine godsend for families with small children, offering a mixture of adventure and security: parents can sit out and read their papers, while being run up to every now and then and told, 'Mummy, I've touched a chicken!', or 'Wow, I've never felt a sheep before!'

Does a stay at Feather Down push your face into the muddy reality of rural living? No, but it does achieve that most elusive ingredient in a family break: balance.

You're half indoors, half outdoors, in accommodation that is part-house, part-tent. You've got running water, but no electricity, you're both a paying holidaymaker and a guest on someone else's land. And you're learning a little about the countryside without having your nose rubbed in it.

6 May 2006

The Birdman of Deeping Fen
Robin Page

Do not phone farmer Nicholas Watts at 4.30am during the months of May and June. Although he will be up, he'll already be out on his farm. He won't be lambing, checking calves or even doing office work, however, but walking along a hedge or a dyke checking the progress of the nesting birds. Although virtually every conservation body in the land condemns the pastime, Watts has continued his childhood interest

out of a genuine desire to know when and where birds are nesting on
his farm.

If he had a research grant and a PhD, what he does would be regarded
as 'science', but because he reverts to being a more orthodox farmer
during the day, he is merely regarded, by some, as mildly eccentric.

Watts lives on the Lincolnshire Fens, in the aptly named Deeping St
Nicholas, where he farms 2,000 acres. Like his grandfather, father and
three daughters, Watts, 62, was born in the farmhouse of Vine House
Farm. He started looking for birds' nests at the age of four, when his
ambition was to become a gamekeeper or an engine driver. His father
had other ideas, however, and set him to work on the land.

Today, all these years later, his earlier ambitions have not been
entirely forgotten; he acts as gamekeeper/wildlife warden on the farm
and has also restored a piece of Fenland railway. In days past, when
fields were long and thin and far from the nearest road, many local farms
had small-gauge railway tracks running across them, along which horses
could drag trucks of potatoes from the fields to the major roads. Watts
has restored a length of this miniature railway as part of his museum of
farming bygones and antiquities.

Since 1982, he has also kept detailed records of the birds who nest
on his farmland. After a decade of detailed observation, he had a clear
picture of what was happening – and it was disastrous. Bird numbers
were in free-fall. The skylark population had dropped by 60 per cent
over the 10 years and corn buntings by a staggering 90 per cent – and
this on the land of a farmer who had tried to encourage them to nest.

It was also the year that 'set-aside' started. 'I hoped there would be
an opportunity to do something for the wildlife,' says Watts, 'but there
wasn't. So I grew a little wheat and other crops on set-aside as wild-bird
cover. They loved it. I also gave wheat to the Wildfowl Trust at Welney
to feed their swans.'

At the same time, he worked with Emorsgate Seeds of King's Lynn
to create not the 'grass margins' and 'beetle banks' of conventional
conservation farming but great wild-flower strips 20 metres wide across
some of his larger fields. In addition, he left 'weed margins' to encourage
seed-producing plants such as fat-hen, chickweed and knotgrass. These
additions have provided a habitat for owls, kestrels, whitethroats, linnets,
reed buntings and finches. In addition, the wild pheasant population has
soared – allowing him to have a few shoots a year, providing birds for
the kitchen.

Birds of all species are flocking back to the farm: barn owls, for example, have been aided by a number of brick nesting towers. Watts has also been elected on to one of the local drainage boards and has reduced the practice of cutting the dyke banks from twice to once every year. 'Drainage has not been compromised, and we have created a wildlife corridor,' he says. 'Now there's a pair of reed warblers nesting every 50 yards, and this year seven of the nests had a cuckoo's egg in them, too.'

Watts has advised the RSPB (Royal Society for the Protection of Birds) and the BTO (British Trust for Ornithology) how rape should be harvested to help nesting birds. He also believes that hedge-cutting should not be allowed before September, in order to protect the linnets that often nest late and on the very edge of a hedge. To help the birds on his farm, Watts controls the number of foxes and members of the crow family. 'Too many predators survive unnaturally during the winter by eating road kills,' he says.

Where Watts has 50 pairs of common terns breeding, he controls the numbers of egg-eating moorhens. As a result, they successfully reared 75 young last year, compared with other local colonies that had a very bad year.

Watts also believes that having a variety of crops spread over the farm – not grown in large blocks – encourages birds to nest. He now grows a total of 19 different crops (compared to the average prairie farmer's three), including organic vegetables for Marks & Spencer and Waitrose, which he regards as the only supermarkets that really consider the farmer.

Two 'crops' that he insists are vital for international conservation are golden linseed, which produces similar oils to our depleted fish stocks, and electricity – he is shortly to get three wind-turbines on his farm. 'We really have got to stop raping the planet,' he says.

Watts's birdseed has been such a success that he now grows it commercially, including 150 acres of sunflowers, as well as canary seed, white millet, red millet and even Niger, which is normally grown in India and Ethiopia. His complex bagging and mixing barn is in complete contrast to his farm museum. 'My birdseed business is now just as important as the mainstream crops on the farm and at busy times it employs up to 30 people,' he says.

From his hard work and vision, Watts has created something governments have failed to do for many years – a living and a working countryside.

I took a bag of Watts's black sunflower seeds home with me, and my garden greenfinches, chaffinches and house sparrows have gone mad. I just hope they don't get too fat to fly.

19 March 1984
Letter to the Editor
Infernal Machines of Countryside

SIR – Is there any torment to equal that inflicted upon country dwellers by the noise, persistent and relentless, from those infernal machines known as bird scarers.

If a prisoner were forced to listen daily to heavy explosions for months on end, seven days a week at two-minute intervals from early daylight to nightfall, the voice of the civil rights campaigners would be heard, loud and clear, in condemnation of such inhumanity.

Surely in these days of high technology it cannot be beyond the wit of man to devise an effective machine which would be quieter than the present type which pollutes the environment for miles around.

H.M. Williams

13 August 1994
Faith in a Gamble That's Paying Off
Robin Page

It is just over a year since the launch of the Countryside Restoration Trust. It has been a momentous 12 months; the response has been startling and every aim has been reached.

The trust has purchased its first 22 acres of land; its second block of 18 acres is being bought on Michaelmas Day – 29 September; nearly 900 'Friends of the Countryside' have signed up and in the past few days the amount of money raised has topped £100,000, largely due to the generosity of *Daily Telegraph* readers.

Twelve months ago it was a very different story. Being deeply concerned at the decline in the appearance and wildlife wealth of the general countryside, I had wanted to launch the Countryside Restoration Trust. The aim was to buy intensively farmed land and restore it – not to tell farmers what they should be doing but to show them that profitable farming can co-exist with wildlife and attractive landscapes. It is a message that is urgently needed in great swathes of Britain, particularly in eastern England.

A landowner had promised us 40 acres of land, if we could raise the money, alongside a small tributary of the Cam, but prospects were not good. Indeed, a professional fundraiser suggested that if we launched we would raise only £2,000.

The return of otters to the brook forced our hand. We wanted to keep their habitat safe and improve it – we had to go ahead and buy it. After consulting with my fellow trustees, including Sir Laurens van der Post, Elspeth Huxley, Jane Wallace, Gordon Beningfield, Jonathon Porritt and Jill Barklem, we launched.

I was full of trepidation – so much so that I went cap in hand to friends, relations and trustees trying to secure interest-free loans in case the advice of the professional had been correct. Feeling awkward and embarrassed, I begged promises of £20,000.

I need not have worried; after my first article in *Weekend* in July 1993, letters and money flooded in and we bought the first 22 crucial acres, naming it Telegraph Field. The money for the remaining 18 acres – Holt Field – is now ready and waiting.

Sadly, the otter holt on the second field no longer appears to be in use. The otters are still very active, leaving regular footprints and droppings, but badgers appear to have found their wood-pile holt and disturbed them. As a result, the otters are now using other resting places in the area, mainly bramble tangles and old willows.

In just 12 months the rest of Telegraph Field has been transformed from arable monoculture to a rich diversity of habitat. The new hedge, nearly 500 yards of it, again planted in the main by *Telegraph* readers in the cold and wet, has been a great success.

The list of trees and shrubs is impressive: hawthorn, blackthorn, wild privet, field maple, dogwood, wild crab-apple, oak, ash, hazel, wild rose, spindle, wild pear and sweet chestnut. We intend to add holly, for the Holly Blue butterfly, and buckthorn, the food plant of the caterpillar of the Brimstone butterfly.

On one side of the hedge we have planted eight-and-a-half acres of Miriam Rothschild's hay meadow mixture. Again, because of the cold, wet spring it had a dreadful start, but when warmer rain came it grew quickly and, despite the recent drought, it appears to be doing well. It will take several years to settle down to suppress the arable weeds, but already clover, bird's-foot trefoil and many small grasses are showing that a good start has been made.

When Dr Dick Potts, director-general of the Game Conservancy, visited the site, he was impressed. In the headlands he found insects and plants vital to the survival of young birds and he saw English (grey) partridges too: 'You know you have a rare bird here,' he enthused. In fact, in half an hour he saw more English partridges on the trust's few acres than he sometimes sees on 10,000-acre estates in a whole day.

Any effort at restoration needs help. The National Rivers Authority has been very co-operative, digging out an old meander, filled in during 1971 – the height of drainage mania. They have tried to raise the water level with two flint riffles containing many tons of flint.

With the recent drought they have not been entirely successful as the low flow has allowed the water to flow through the flint, instead of being stopped by it. Perhaps a winter's silt will block the holes; failing this we'll consider a plug of clay.

Around the meander we have planted purple loosestrife, marsh marigold, water avens, yellow iris, ragged robin, monkey flower, hemp, agrimony, water mint and water forget-me-not. At the moment, the loosestrife – the 'long purples' of John Clare – look a picture.

All the hard work of watering, weeding and topping is now delivering its rewards. Already wildlife is returning; the first breeding birds at the meander were a pair of wild mandarin ducks, while one evening I stood and watched a hobby for 20 minutes as it hunted spectacularly over the barley. The most recent and surprising arrivals were spotted only last week by Robert Goodden, the butterfly expert, who instantly saw several attractive Brown Argus butterflies feeding on the flowers of bird's-foot trefoil. Last week the site was also visited by Sir Laurens van der Post; he, too, was impressed.

Now, with a secretary just employed and a director about to be appointed, thanks to generous financial help from the Countryside Commission and the Ernest Cook Trust, we are ready to take our next step – or jump in the dark. We now want to raise more than £1 million to buy and restore a complete English farm.

We want barn owls and bee orchids thriving between the crops of cereals, and we want livestock grazing in sensibly sized fields, fringed with trees. We want the general countryside to return to being a place of beauty, rich in wildlife, while at the same time producing good food and keeping jobs on the land.

We have already seen that it can be done. In a year a small dream has become reality; now we want to extend our vision.

24 July 1976

From Tenpenny Close to Hungry Hill

J.H.B. Peel

One of my small fields is called Harepie, which I take to mean 'a pie made of hares'. In other words, the place was a poacher's paradise. Philology, however, may deceive the uninitiate. In theory, for example – though never in practice – a gazetteer of place-names might translate Harepie as: 'Hare, from Old English *haer* or stony ground.' Pie is probably a variant of *Puy*, a local chief (cf. Weston Puy in the same county).'

Nevertheless, I continue to believe that Harepie means what it appears to say, though why it should say so puzzles me because the field covers scarcely one-third of an acre, and is, in fact, no more than a triangular paddock. Was it formerly included in a much larger field where hares really did enjoy a living space? We shall never know, because we shall never discover when the property was divided by dry-stone walls.

Field-names often trace the extent to which husbandry has either advanced or remained static. Thus, the word 'Devil' commonly connotes sour or infertile soil as in Devil's Patch, Devil's Dingle, Devil's Furlong, Devil's Churchyard, Devil's Acre. Even when the land has been reclaimed, the old names abide, as in Devil's Own, Devil's Land, Devil's Bank, Devil's Tail.

At the other extreme you will find a litany of grateful paeans, as in Mount Prosperous, Mount Pleasant, God's Garden, High Heaven, Paradise, Providence, Fillpockets, Bountiful, Promised Land, Canaan, Milk-and-Honey, Pound of Butter. Once again, however, a non-philologist may misinterpret the true meaning of a field-name and also of a regional name. Herefordshire's Golden Valley acquired its soubriquet when the Normans misread the name of the local river, writing Our as D'or or 'Gold.' The valley therefore became 'golden' and the river became D'Or, ultimately Dore.

What are we to make of Egypt and Gibraltar in England's green and pleasant land? Were the fields so-named by immigrants from those distant places? Were they named by Englishmen who had travelled thither? Probably not, for such fields are commonly to be found on the perimeter of farms, and their names are synonyms for remoteness, as in Moscow, Mount Sinai, Nineveh, No Man's Land, Furthest, Beyond, Land's End, World's End, Utter End, Distant, Hem, Skirts. Sometimes the name dates the baptism, as in New York, North Carolina, Isle of Elba, Spioncop. Nineteenth-century farmers were fond of naming their fields after a famous battle: Trafalgar, Waterloo, Balaclava, Inkerman.

Many fields recall a rural benefactor, as when the rent or produce of Holybread was bequeathed to provide part of the Sacrament. Lamplands likewise provided 'a light to lighten the Gentiles' in church. Other specific benefactors were described by fields called Quire, Vestry, Chancel, Bellrope, Vicar, Priest, Glebe.

In the years when parish boundaries were imprinted on young minds via young backsides ('beating the bounds'), certain fields marked a halting place at which the parson either said a prayer or recited a passage from the Bible. The fields then acquired such names at Paternoster, Gospel, Amen Corner, Prayer Plot, Allelujah, Boundary Piece, Parish Pride. Other fields utter an ominous echo, like the one near East Stoke in Nottinghamshire, which is still called Dead Man's Field because it marks the site where Lambert Simnel and his rebels were defeated by the King's Army.

Field-names pose many questions, not all of which are linguistic. Did Greedy Guts consume vast amounts of fertiliser, or did it yield large quantities of crops? Did Cuckold's Haven receive its extra-marital name because of one man's disillusion, or because it was a communal Lover's Lane? Which of two bad neighbours owned Quarrelsome? How much clay went to the naming of Treacle? Who were the weary tillers of Labour-in-Vain, Mount Misery, Mount Famine, Cheat All, Starve Mouse, Hunger Hill, Cold Comfort, Old Misery, Break Back, Empty Furrow? Who were the happy husbandmen of Beans-and-Bacon, Long Gains, New Delight, All's Well, Largesse, Lucky, Plenty Patch, Feastfield, Ripeness, Riches?

Our forefathers had a flair for attaching poetical names to prosaic facts.

Muddy Patch neatly evokes the place where three field-gates allow cattle to churn a wintry surface. Marl, too, describes itself neatly; as also do the squelching Squob, Slob, and Quob. Equally precise, though now confused by changes in the language, is Brickfield, the *brec* or plot of land broken-up for cultivation. Five Days Math is a meadow whose *math* or mowing lasted from Monday till Friday. Twelve Days Work is a field that could be ploughed in a dozen days. Pastures near a road were apt to announce their charges to drovers seeking overnight enclosure for livestock: Halfpenny Piece, Threepenny Patch, Tenpenny Close.

The same practical poetry was used to define the shape of a field: Brandy Bottle, Cocked Hat, Leg of Mutton, Halfmoon, Sugar Loaf. Small fields received appropriate names, such as Thimble, Mousehole, Handkerchief Piece, Little Bit, Tiny, Pinpoint, Child's Yard. At other times such fields suffered a classical and facetious overstatement: Hundred Acres, Thousand Furlongs, Million Roods.

By uprooting their hedges and demolishing their walls, some farmers have provided material for a new generation of field-namers. A topographer in the year 2076 may find himself descanting on the aptness of Windworn, Hedgeless, Six Months Math and Ten Mile Meadow.

12 November 1978
How Green is Their Valley?
Byron Rogers

'At your baag?' It was a lazy Cotswold voice. The bag, a small airline satchel, lay on the ground. A three-legged greyhound was hopping worriedly around it. I nodded. The satchel contained a radio (it was the last day of the Test), some tobacco, two pipes, a pair of sunglasses and a bottle of Ambre Solaire: it was, I thought, the complete agricultural labourer's kit for 1978,

'Better move 'im. Old dog pisses on baags.'

I picked the bag up. The first day at the farm had aroused feelings I had not known since my first day at school: above all else I wanted something to mark me out. A three-legged dog supplementing the sun-tan oil would have fixed me forever in the folklore of these men. They would have remembered that summer. I had begun to regret the Ambre Solaire.

It was just before eight o'clock in the morning. A watery August sun was hardening like a poached egg in the sky. In the yard they were tinkering with the engine of their flagship, the new £23,000 combine harvester. Two tractors and a caterpillar-tracked vehicle stood nearby, awaiting oil and diesel.

It was like that scene you get in American films about Pearl Harbour, the parked planes being checked before take-off. That was the first shock.

Go back far enough in any ancestry, past the towns, past the castles, and you come to the land, to a man breaking the earth, one eye on the clouds. The ruthless left early. Most had to wait until the Industrial Revolution breathed discontent into their ears. But five of my ten uncles had been farm labourers in their youth. I was just two generations away from the land, and I was nervous.

I had had the fantasy for years that I could go back, to pick up the realities of wind and rain that the 1944 Education Act had twitched away.

If you come from the rural working class it can be a source of smugness at a dinner party, imagining yourself there like an astronaut amid the loud, uneasy voices. But I had never gone back before.

It had not been difficult getting the job. The small ads of the *Farmers Weekly* reverberate with cries for harvest help from the shires. Reading them you step back into a quite different world. There is an innocence to it. 'Female agricultural student . . . will turn hand to anything.' 'Christian parents of sceptical 16-year-old . . . seek sympathetic farmer.' 'Strong 15-year-old girl seeks two weeks' unpaid work on a farm . . .' Only occasionally does the absurd jargon of Wilsonian Britain intrude. 'Assistant stockperson wanted . . . Herdsperson . . . Pig Herd Person . . .'

In the end I got a job as a labourer on an arable farm in Warwickshire. Driving licence? Yes. Tractor experience? None. But there were, I intimated gently, generations of farm labourers stretching back to the brown crosses on birth certificates, which was how on my first morning I found myself on an immaculately tidy yard being given a driving lesson on the Crawler, the caterpillar tractor, by William, an excavator driver helping out with the harvest. I had never seen a farm like this. I had never seen anything like the Crawler either.

With its tracks it looked like a tank, and moved so slowly it should have been beyond the most ambitious Luddite to wreck. But it pulled a set of disc harrows to break up the land after the rape harvest: turn too sharply right and you could shatter these. The discs, I was told repeatedly, cost £1,600.

I was given one piece of equipment, a set of ear-muffs. Without these, said William, I would sink into pure sound and vibration, leaving the day and the sun and everything behind me. The vibration, he went on, would even then get into my dreams.

He talked about the old days. His father, said William with wonder, had thought nothing of stacking hay bales with a pitchfork all day, building great walls of it. Now a tractor did this work. On our farm there was just one pitchfork: it looked like a piece of industrial archaeology.

He talked of the old tractors with their starting handles. 'When oi was a small boy oi thought oi'd have a swing on the old booger. Blow me, if old booger didn't staart up an' swing me.' He had a laconic turn of phrase.

Like most countrymen he was very curious. Any cover I might have intended for my reasons for working there was worn away by the steady gentle barrage of William's questions. Behind them there was the unvoiced feeling that I was some kind of intruder while he, as naturally as a stone or tree, belonged. He genuinely loved the land, especially the sensation of being alone in a field, going about his work.

You get used to loneliness as a writer, but the loneliness of harrowing a 36-acre field is a peculiar thing. So little happens even in the country beyond, over the railway embankment, that it is like being adrift at sea in a small boat. You lose your sense of time. When a train passes it is reassuring, reminding you that somewhere else in the world there are people. You are increasingly aware of the old lies told by nature poets: that in all that summer land if suddenly a gate slammed anywhere, if any human being of any kind appeared, it would be the most wonderful and exciting event of the day.

The field was so large that it took half an hour to harrow its perimeter. It was as big as some of the smallholdings my uncles had farmed. Hedges had been ripped out to make it this size, but that, said one of the brothers, was about as big as a field should ever be. Any larger and a man would find it too depressing to work.

Not being able to turn right, I had to execute a series of leftward arabesques at each corner, scoring long loops into the soil. My first circuit was frightening. There seemed to be so many things to remember: the steep slopes, the telegraph pole in the field, the coppices. In the churned wake seagulls and lapwings swooped to gobble the uncovered shoots. It really was like a ship at sea.

After a few circuits the field began to assume a personality. One coppice, butting out into the circuit I was making, I hated because it upset the pattern. The slope out of sight of the big house I loved. Every third circuit I would stop there briefly to listen to the Test. But the last time I did this the Crawler stalled and I was unable to re-start it for a long time. In my guilt I dropped the earmuffs and failed to find them. The rest of the day on the Crawler passed in a daze. I drove back to my lodgings in my Morris Traveller marvelling at the peace of the evening: I could not hear the engine at all.

But there is one strange feature about the land which you come on very quickly. It brings you closer to the etymology of words you may have used all your life. Harrow a field for a day, and you feel you have journeyed back to the beginnings of language: the word *harrowing* came out of this.

The next day I worked in the barn, helping the youngest of the brothers with the drier. This was an enormous machine, fixed deep in the foundations, to dry off the harvest grains. They had gathered in close on 100 tons of rape. At around £150 a ton it was a considerable crop. The rape plant is that beautiful yellow growth people see in fields and mistake for mustard. It has recently become popular with farmers as it is much in demand for vegetable oil. But when the brothers' father had planted it first after the war his neighbours had thought he was growing weed. Dried, the seed looks like lead shot.

In the barn was a large storage drum, about 40 feet in diameter, 4 feet deep in rape. You moved in there like a man in a snowdrift. There was an auger in the centre which emptied it and fed the drier. The rape got everywhere – into your shoes, your trousers, even the body orifices. And all the time the auger, which let out a low contented purr when filling, sharpened to a grating whine when you were not shovelling fast enough. I had misheard the farmer: I had thought he had said ogre. It did seem quite possible, as the sweat ran down, that there could be some insatiable old man down there bellowing for rape. There must be other ways of putting that.

It was like one of those impossible jobs in mythology, counting out grains of sand on a foreshore. Nothing seemed to lower the level. The youngest brother joined and we worked like men on a chain gang. We stopped once, sinking into the rape. It felt very cool against the body. My companion confided that it was an extraordinary thing to make love on. An active bachelor, his nocturnal forays had been described by William. 'He gets everywhere.'

On the third day the new combine was used for the first time. The eldest brother stood proudly on it, as though leading a Roman triumph. They had only bought the thing, whispered one of his brothers, to keep him happy. It was tradition that he alone drove the combines. Blond-bearded, a small Viking who has missed the last longship, he passed dreamily down the lane.

But given the present rate of inflation it is worth their while trading in their combines after only a few years' service. The total value of machinery on the farm came to over £70,000. The price of land in the area worked out at £1,000 an acre: invested as a capital sum the farm would bring them more in income than as a working unit. It is part of the present unreality of farming. It was still a way of life, the brothers' father had said, but there was something in his voice which hinted that it was not only you he was trying to convince.

Even 20 years ago six men would have been required in the wheat field. Now it is just two, one driving the combine, the other driving a tractor and trailer alongside to receive the grain. The old social life of the farm, the gathering at harvest, has gone for ever, and the loneliness will get worse.

That was why, said the youngest brother brightly, farmers tended to run a bit wild in company. They were making up for the days in the long fields.

He enjoyed one afternoon. Under the drier there was what they called The Hole, a very narrow shaft about 30 feet. Grains fell in there, and they had to be swept up else there was a danger that they might take root among the foundations. At any rate, that was what he said when he asked me to sweep it out. It was very dark there and so cramped you had to crouch. There were cobwebs and strange noises, and odd wet things scurrying over your hand. People would have written pamphlets about this in the dawn of the Industrial Revolution. Once I saw a grinning face in the opening of the shaft: he had, said one of his brothers, been mad to get me down The Hole.

I was so eager not to do anything wrong that I must have been fair game. Once, when it rained, I drove on and on in the Crawler, thinking this was expected of me. I was matted with rain. I only stopped when William, snug and grand in his tractor cabin, drove up to tell me not to be such a silly booger.

The strangest incident was the last day, when the photographer came. It was strange because it was embarrassing. My mentors stood round grinning as he photographed me on the Crawler. I felt like a boy at school whose parents have turned up.

I don't think I did too badly in the end. The eldest brother, over a few pints, said graciously that I had been shaping up well. He then spoilt it all by saying that, of course, it wasn't brute enthusiasm they wanted any more but brains. But a man gets a bit light-headed after a day on the combine, passing in triumph through the sheaves of wheat.

Certain things I shall not forget. The first is that it is very hard work, though the old sunrise to sunset servitude is gone. A farm labourer works a 40-hour week for £47.30. Anything beyond that is overtime, at £1.50 an hour. On other farms some of the old perks, like free eggs and milk, must persist, but on a modern mechanised farm with no hens and no cows, they are as much part of the past as feudal tenure. There were no tied cottages. I went to bed each night like a piece of walking masonry, usually at half-past nine.

The second thing I shall not forget was the excitement I felt, going into Stratford to buy tobacco and seeing a crowd of people. It was like a pit pony being let out. One of my local predecessors as a farm labourer, a man who had possibly worked the same acres, summed it up best. In later life he had turned playwright, and as Miranda in *The Tempest* says with wonder, 'O brave new world, that has such people in't.' Shakespeare must have been on the land to know that feeling.

Even now, I find myself looking at the sky in the morning. A week on the farm brings the weather into your life. If it is too dry they will not be able to work the land. If it is too wet they will not be able to work. It was like that 2,000 years ago, said the eldest brother, and it will be like that in 2,000 years' time.